The Healthy PC: Preventive Care, Home Remedies, and Green Computing

Second Edition

Guy Hart-Davis

Mc Graw Hill

New York Chicago San Francisco Lisbon
London Madrid Mexico City Milan New Delhi
San Juan Seoul Singapore Sydney Toronto

The McGraw-Hill Companies

Library of Congress Cataloging-in-Publication Data

Hart-Davis, Guy.
The healthy PC : preventive care, home remedies, and green computing /
Guy Hart-Davis.—2nd ed.
p. cm.
Rev. ed. of: The healthy PC / Carey Holzman. 2003.
ISBN 978-0-07-175291-6 (pbk.)
1. Microcomputers—Maintenance and repair. I. Holzman, Carey. Healthy PC. II. Title.
TK7887.H65 2011
004.16—dc23 2011040789

McGraw-Hill books are available at special quantity discounts to use as premiums and sales promotions, or for use in corporate training programs. To contact a representative, please e-mail us at bulksales@mcgraw-hill.com.

The Healthy PC: Preventive Care, Home Remedies, and Green Computing, Second Edition

1234567890 DOC DOC 10987654321

ISBN 978-0-07-175291-6
MHID 0-07-175291-9

Sponsoring Editor
Roger Stewart

Editorial Supervisor
Patty Mon

Project Manager
Anupriya Tyagi,
Cenveo Publisher Services

Acquisitions Coordinator
Joya Anthony

Technical Editor
James Kelley

Copy Editor
Bart Reed

Proofreader
Lisa McCoy

Indexer
Rebecca Plunkett

Production Supervisor
James Kussow

Composition
Cenveo Publisher Services

Illustration
Cenveo Publisher Services

Art Director, Cover
Jeff Weeks

Cover Designer
Mary McKeon

This book is dedicated to Teddy.

About the Author

Guy Hart-Davis is the author of more than 70 computer books, including *iPad and iPhone Administrator's Guide, Integrating Macs into Windows Networks, Mac OS X System Administration,* and *How to Do Everything: iPhone, iPod, and iTunes, Fifth Edition.*

About the Technical Editor

James Floyd Kelly is a freelance author from Atlanta, Georgia. He has degrees in both English and industrial engineering and has written on a variety of subjects that include building CNC machines and 3D printers, LEGO robotics, open-source software, and the Samsung Galaxy Tab and Motorola Xoom tablets.

Contents

PART III Upgrade Your Hardware and Operating System

Acknowledgments

I'd like to thank the following people for their help with this book:

- Roger Stewart for asking me to write this revised edition of the book
- Carey Holzman for writing the first edition of the book
- Joya Anthony for handling the acquisitions end of the book
- James Floyd Kelly for reviewing the manuscript for technical accuracy and contributing many helpful suggestions
- Bart Reed for editing the manuscript with a light touch and good humor
- Anupriya Tyagi for keeping the schedule and production of the book within industry-approved norms
- Cenveo Publisher Services for laying out the pages
- Rebecca Plunkett for creating the index

Introduction

Is your PC vital to you?
Would you like it to run faster?
Does it ever crash?
Do you need to keep yourself and your family safe online?

If you answered "yes" to any of these questions—or to all of them—then congratulations. You've picked up the right book.

This book shows you how to keep your PC healthy—running well, free from viruses and other malware, and safe for you and your family to use.

Is This Book for Me?

Are you a normal person—not a PC expert?

Do you want to keep your PC running well, or maybe get it running a bit better—but not spend fistfuls of dollars and half your waking hours turning it into a speed demon?

Do you want to solve problems with Windows... but not pore over technical details and fiddle with arcane settings?

Then, yes, this book is for you.

Which Versions of Windows Does This Book Cover?

This book covers Windows XP and Windows 7. These are the versions of Windows that most people are using at this writing. But most of the content applies to Windows Vista as well.

What Will I Learn from This Book?

In Part I of this book, you learn to tune up, optimize, and protect your PC:

- Chapter 1 walks you through getting your PC to run faster. You learn what's slowing your PC down and then take action to fix the problems. You disable unnecessary startup items, sort out Windows' services, give your PC extra virtual memory, and defragment the hard drive.

- Chapter 2 explains how to free up space on your PC's hard drive. Drives tend to fill up over time, and the lack of space can cripple your PC. To fix the problem, you run Disk Cleanup, slim down the Recycle Bin, and reclaim space from the System Restore feature. If necessary, you take a bite out of the paging file, remove any programs you no longer need, and archive your old files.
- Chapter 3 shows you how to protect your PC against attacks, viruses, and malware with three quick moves. First, you install vital patches and fixes to squash bugs and close off paths of attack. Second, you install the best free software to keep your PC safe. And third, you turn on Windows Firewall to slam the door shut on network and Internet threats.

In Part II, you learn to use networks and the Internet safely:

- Chapter 4 tells you how to connect your PC safely to a network. You learn how to connect to both wired and wireless networks, how to choose TCP/IP settings manually if needed, and how to clamp down on the items Windows is sharing. You also learn how to keep intruders out of your own wireless network.
- Chapter 5 takes you through how to connect to the Internet safely. We identify the threats, choose the right type of Internet connection for your needs, armor up your network router, and check your security using an online probe.
- Chapter 6 shows you how to surf the Internet safely. You learn how to deal with the threats of malicious web pages and viruses, how to protect your PC from attackers, and how to keep your private data to yourself.
- Chapter 7 explains how to enjoy e-mail, instant messaging, and social networking safely. We talk about the benefits of each of these online technologies and then look at the different threats you face and discuss the best ways to deal with them.
- Chapter 8 tells you how to keep your children safe online by using Windows' Parental Control features. You can limit the websites your children visit, allow them to communicate only with approved people, and restrict the types of games they play.

In Part III, you learn how to upgrade your PC's hardware and operating system:

- Chapter 9 shows you how to add memory to your PC and either replace the hard drive or add an extra hard drive. You learn how to find out how much memory your PC can hold, where to get the right memory, and how to install it. Similarly, you check how many hard drives your PC can hold, decide whether to replace the drive or add a drive, and then perform the operation.
- Chapter 10 takes you through the process of upgrading from Windows XP to Windows 7. Microsoft has made this upgrade awkward, but this chapter tells you what you need to know to get your settings, data, and programs successfully transferred to Windows 7.
- The Green Computing Appendix provides information on how to reduce your PC's energy use, keep toxins out of landfills, and generally avoid wrecking the planet.

What Are Those Boxes and Bars For?

To make its meaning clear without using far more words than necessary, this book uses a number of conventions, four of which are worth mentioning here:

- Note, Tip, and Caution paragraphs highlight information to draw it to your notice.
- Sidebars provide extra information. Read them to deepen your understanding of essential topics.
- The pipe character or vertical bar denotes choosing an item from a menu. For example, "choose File | Open" means that you should click the File menu and select the Open item on it. Use the keyboard, mouse, or a combination of the two as you wish.
- For setting options, Windows uses many check boxes—boxes that have two states: *selected* (with a check mark in them) and *cleared* (without a check mark in them). This book tells you to *select* a check box or *clear* a check box rather than "click to place a check mark in the box" or "click to remove the check mark from the box." Often, you'll be verifying the state of the check box, so it may already have the required setting—in which case, you don't need to click at all.

Where Is This Book's Companion Website?

Throughout this book's chapters, you'll see references to materials on the book's companion website.

To go to this book's companion website, follow these steps:

1. Open your web browser.
2. Click in the address box or press ALT-D to select the current entry.
3. Type www.healthypcandmac.com.
4. Press ENTER.

PART I Tune Up, Optimize, and Protect Your PC

1 Make Your PC Run Faster

When you bought your PC, it ran like a champion, or at least at a good clip. But over the months and years it has slowed down to the point where you can barely use it. Even turning the PC on and logging into Windows takes several minutes of grinding—a far cry from the snappy way it ran at first.

In this chapter, we'll look at ten changes you can make quickly and easily to get your PC running faster. These changes range from disabling unnecessary startup items and sorting out Windows' services to giving your PC more virtual memory and defragmenting the hard drive. These changes will greatly improve the speed at which your PC runs—but we'll improve things further with other speed-ups later in the book. (We can't pack everything into the first chapter without upsetting the publisher.)

Before we start fixing the problems, we'll take a look at what has changed to slow your PC down so much.

Find Out What's Slowing Your PC Down

As we humans age, we naturally slow down. But your PC is a machine, and machines scorn the concept of aging—don't they?

Sooner or later, all machines wear out—but if you maintain them carefully, they can keep going for many years. So if you're prepared to put in some time and effort maintaining your PC, you can keep it running well for five, seven, or even ten years. You can certainly keep it running long beyond the two or three years after which computer manufacturers imply you should really be buying a new PC.

So—assuming your PC isn't from the twentieth century—what has slowed it down?

Most likely a variety of causes, but these seven are usually the main culprits:

- Too many programs loading automatically at startup.
- Too many Windows services running. (A *service* is an automated system process.)
- Too many hardware devices connected to the PC.
- Bad or buggy drivers. (A *driver* is a piece of software that enables Windows to identify and work with a particular piece of hardware. For example, a printer driver enables Windows to identify your printer and print documents on it.)
- Too many visual effects, or "eye candy."
- Too little memory (RAM) or virtual memory (fake RAM) available.
- Too little hard drive space available.

You can tackle all these causes. And you can make your PC run faster again. In this chapter, we'll tackle all these problems, except for adding RAM, which we'll cover in Chapter 9.

Note Antivirus software can also slow your PC down. We'll talk about choosing antivirus software and keeping it under control in Chapter 3.

Disable Unnecessary Startup Items

If your PC takes forever to start up, or it takes ages to get Windows to a usable state after you log in, chances are it's loading too many startup items. You may have set some of these items to start up, but more likely various programs you've installed have set their helper programs or utilities to start up automatically, because the developers simply know you'll find the programs indispensable.

As you'd imagine, the solution is to disable any startup items you don't actually need to run. To do that, you need to see which items Windows is running, and then work out what each does and whether you need it.

Caution Tread carefully when disabling startup items. As you'll see shortly, some of the items are extras that you can disable without problems—but others are essential to keeping your computer's systems running. For example, if you disable a graphics startup item, you may prevent your PC from loading Windows successfully.

Open System Configuration Utility and Examine Your Startup Items

To see which items are running at startup, you use a tool called System Configuration Utility on Windows XP and System Configuration on Windows 7. I'll refer to it as "System Configuration Utility" for simplicity. System Configuration Utility works in the same way in Windows XP and Windows 7, so we'll look at both operating systems together. We'll use Windows XP for the examples.

Open System Configuration Utility

To open System Configuration Utility, follow these steps:

1. Run the msconfig.exe program in one of these ways to launch System Configuration Utility:
   - **Windows XP** Choose Start | Run to display the Run dialog box (shown here). Then type **msconfig** and press ENTER or click the OK button.

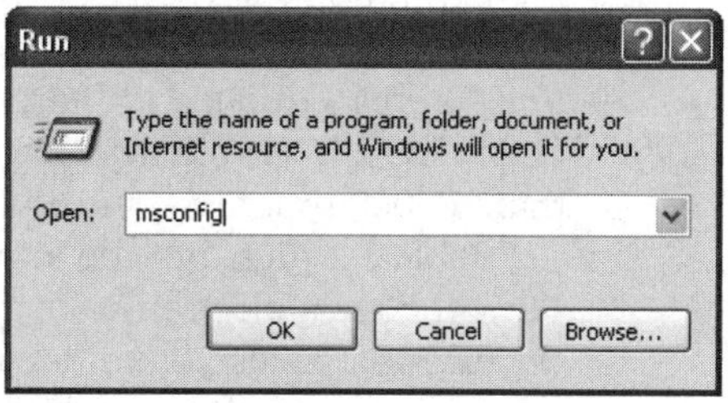

   - **Windows 7** Click the Start button to display the Start menu, and then type **msconfig** and press ENTER.
2. Click the Startup tab to display its contents (see Figure 1-1).

Here you can see all the programs Windows is loading automatically at startup. On the sample PC, there are about 30 programs. No wonder startup takes ages.

What you need to do now is work out which of these programs you actually need to run and which you can dispense with.

Find Out What the Startup Items Are and What They Do

Some of the programs have straightforward names from which you can easily identify them. For example, Adobe Reader Speed Launch is a program that runs automatically at startup to enable the Adobe Reader program to launch more quickly. Similarly, the HotSync Manager program in the Palm folder is for managing synchronization of Palm devices.

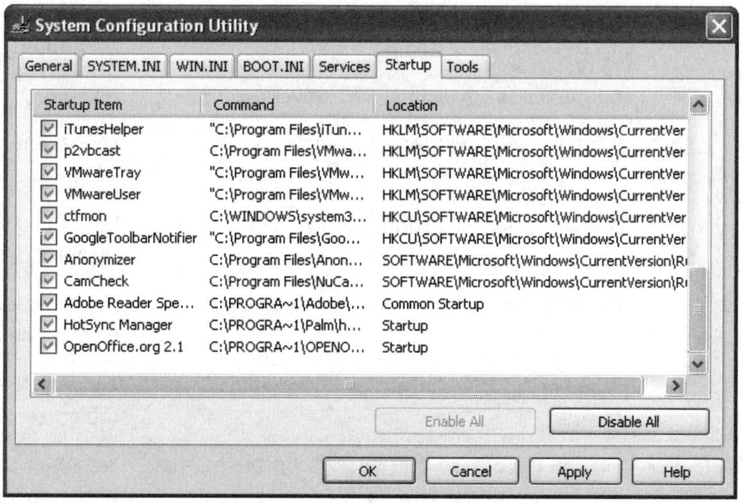

FIGURE 1-1 Use the Startup tab of System Configuration Utility to disable any startup programs you don't need.

Other programs have cryptic names such as SM1BG. To find out what such a program is, look up the name on the Internet. A general search, such as putting the name into the Google search engine or the Bing search engine, will give lots of results, along with conflicting advice about whether the program is your best friend or deserves a quick and merciful release from its toils. For more focused advice, try Uniblue's ProcessLibrary (www.processlibrary.com), which has the lowdown on more than 50,000 programs and 140,000 system processes.

Table 1-1 digs into the startup items on the sample computer I'm using here. Your PC will have a different selection of startup items, but some may be the same—and the example gives you an idea of how to approach the process of whittling down a slew of startup items to only those you need.

TABLE 1-1 Startup Items on a Typical Computer and What They Do

Startup Item Name	What It Is	OK to Disable?
igfxtray	Intel Graphics configuration and diagnostics program	No.
hkcmd	Intel multimedia device tool	No.
PROMon	Intel network card monitor	No.
Smtray	SoundMAX tray icon for sound cards with ADI chipsets	Yes—you can access the important controls in other ways.
mobsync	A process for synchronizing offline files in Internet Explorer	Yes, if you don't need offline files.
hpztsb07	A utility for monitoring HP printers	Yes, if you don't need to monitor HP printers.
SM1BG	A program for managing USB drives	No.
StatusClient	A program for monitoring HP printers	Yes, if you don't need to monitor HP printers.
hpbpsttp	A program for monitoring HP LaserJet printers	Yes, if you don't need to monitor LaserJet printers.
MemCheck	A part of Trend Micro antivirus software	No (unless you uninstall or disable the antivirus software).
atwtusb	A helper program for Aiptek USB graphics tablet drivers	Yes, if you don't use a graphics tablet.
GoogleQuickSearchBox	The Google button that appears on the taskbar, which you can click to open a Search window	Yes—you can search easily with a web browser.
AppleSyncNotifier	A program for synchronizing iPods, iPads, and iPhones	Yes, if you don't need to sync an iPod, iPad, or iPhone.

TABLE 1-1 Startup Items on a Typical Computer and What They Do (*continued*)

Startup Item Name	What It Is	OK to Disable?
jusched	A program for checking for updates to Sun Microsystems' Java suite	Yes, if you don't mind checking for updates manually.
qttask	A program for opening Apple's QuickTime media player	Yes.
iTunesHelper	A program for speeding up iTunes startup and for monitoring for when you connect an iPod, iPad, or iPhone	Yes—but only if you no longer use the iPod, iPad, or iPhone.
ctfmon	A program for monitoring alternative input to Microsoft Office programs	No.
GoogleToolbarNotifier	A program that checks that Google is your default search engine	Yes, but you may need to uninstall it.
CamCheck	A program for detecting when you plug in a webcam	Yes, but you may need to initialize the webcam manually.
Adobe Reader Speed Launch	A program for speeding up the launch of Adobe Reader	Yes.
HotSync Manager	A program for managing the connection of Palm devices	Yes, unless you synchronize a Palm device.
OpenOffice.org 2.1	A program for making the OpenOffice.org program launch more quickly	Yes, unless you use OpenOffice.org frequently.

Just scan the table—there's no test at the end of the class—and you'll see that the startup items fall into three main groups:

- **Essential items** Some startup items are needed to make your PC's vital components—the graphics card, network card, or audio chipset—work. Disabling these startup items brings grief.
- **Helpful items—if you're using the hardware** When you install the software for a hardware device, you often get helper programs that run at startup. For example, installing the software for an iPhone adds startup items, including Apple Sync Notifier and iTunesHelper. You'll want to run these startup items as long as you're using the iPhone. If you switch to a different device, you no longer need these items, so you can stop them from running.
- **Largely useless items** When you install the Google Toolbar (which helps you search both the Internet and your PC for whatever tickles your fancy), Google wedges the GoogleToolbarNotifier in among your startup items. This ugly little program simply checks that you're using Google as your search engine. Startup items like this, you can safely stop.

Stop a Startup Item from Running

When you've decided you don't need a particular startup item, clear its check box on the Startup tab in System Configuration Utility.

Clearing the check box is easier than shooting fish in a barrel, but you need to make sure that the startup item isn't more vital than you thought. To do so, clear just the one check box and then click the Close button.

System Configuration Utility then displays the System Configuration dialog box (shown here). Click the Restart button to restart your PC.

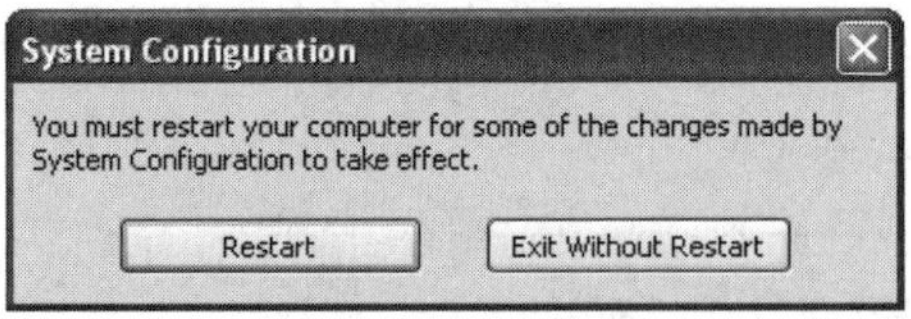

When your PC restarts, log on as usual. System Configuration Utility then runs automatically and displays the System Configuration Utility dialog box shown here.

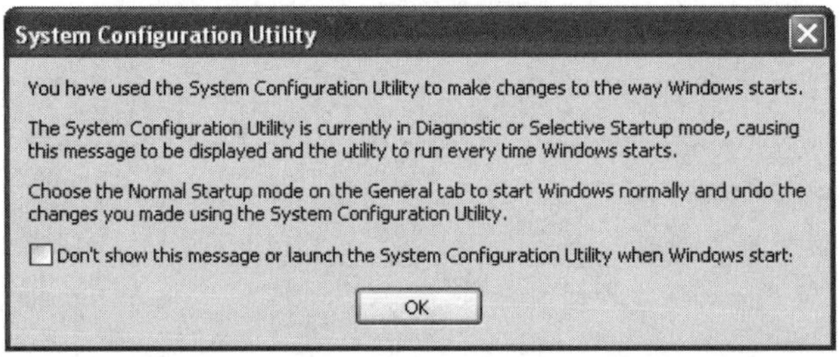

Normally, you'll just want to click the OK button to launch System Configuration Utility so that you can continue turning off unnecessary startup items. Leave System Configuration Utility open for a while, and use your PC as normal to make sure the startup item you've turned off hasn't lost any functionality you need.

If you find you *have* lost functionality, select the startup item's check box again in System Configuration Utility, click the Close button, and then restart your PC again. If you find your PC won't start, see the nearby sidebar for instructions on using Safe Mode to recover.

Assuming your PC runs normally, you can try turning off the next startup item you don't think you need. Again, restart your PC and check that all is well before proceeding.

When you finish turning off startup items you don't need, you can leave System Configuration Utility running so that you can continue with the next section (which covers turning off Windows services you don't need).

If pruning the startup items has sped your PC up enough for now, select the Don't Show This Message Or Launch The System Configuration Utility When Windows Starts check box in the System Configuration Utility dialog box that opens after restart. The next time you start Windows after that, System Configuration Utility doesn't run automatically; when you need it again, launch it by running **msconfig**, as described earlier in this chapter.

Sort Out Windows Services

After stopping any startup items you don't need, sort out the services that Windows is running. A *service* is a system process that Windows runs for you. Most services run automatically, which is usually the best way, as it means you don't need to mess with them. But if Windows is set to run too many services, they can slow your PC down.

Recover from Turning Off a Vital Startup Item

If you turn off a startup item that Windows considers vital, your PC won't be able to load Windows properly. To recover, use Safe Mode like this:

1. Restart your PC:
   - If Windows has managed to load, restart it from the Start menu as usual.
   - If Windows has stopped loading partway, press your PC's restart button to restart it. Or press the power button (you may need to hold it down for several seconds) to turn off the PC, and then restart it.
2. When Windows prompts you to press F8 for advanced options, press F8 to display the Windows Advanced Options menu screen in Windows XP or the Advanced Boot Options screen in Windows 7. If Windows has failed to load, it often displays this screen automatically; other times, you need to load it manually. The next illustration shows the Windows Advanced Options menu for Windows XP.

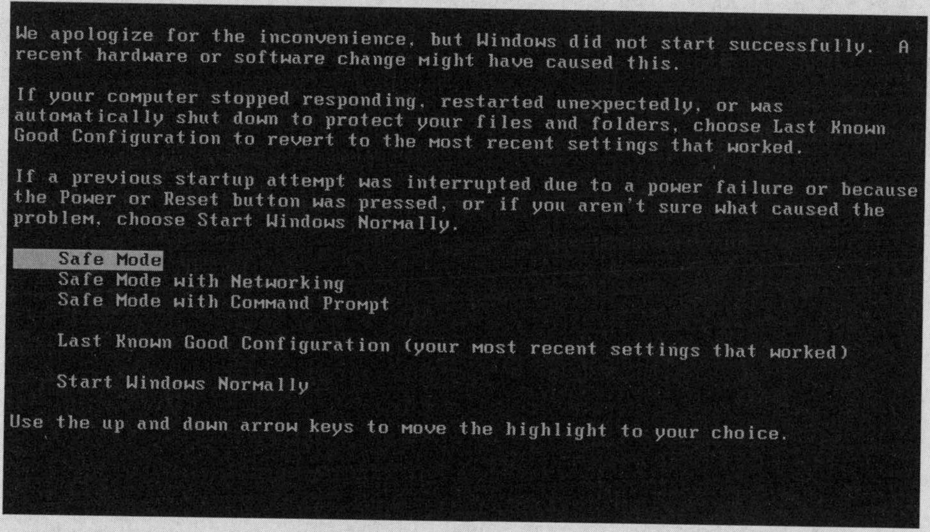
We apologize for the inconvenience, but Windows did not start successfully. A recent hardware or software change might have caused this.
If your computer stopped responding, restarted unexpectedly, or was automatically shut down to protect your files and folders, choose Last Known Good Configuration to revert to the most recent settings that worked.
If a previous startup attempt was interrupted due to a power failure or because the Power or Reset button was pressed, or if you aren't sure what caused the problem, choose Start Windows Normally.
Safe Mode
Safe Mode with Networking
Safe Mode with Command Prompt
Last Known Good Configuration (your most recent settings that worked)
Start Windows Normally
Use the up and down arrow keys to move the highlight to your choice.

3. Press UP ARROW to select the Safe Mode item and then press ENTER. Windows starts in Safe Mode, which uses a limited set of hardware and a low screen resolution to work around problems.

(continued)

4. If the Desktop dialog box opens, as shown in the next illustration, click the Yes button.

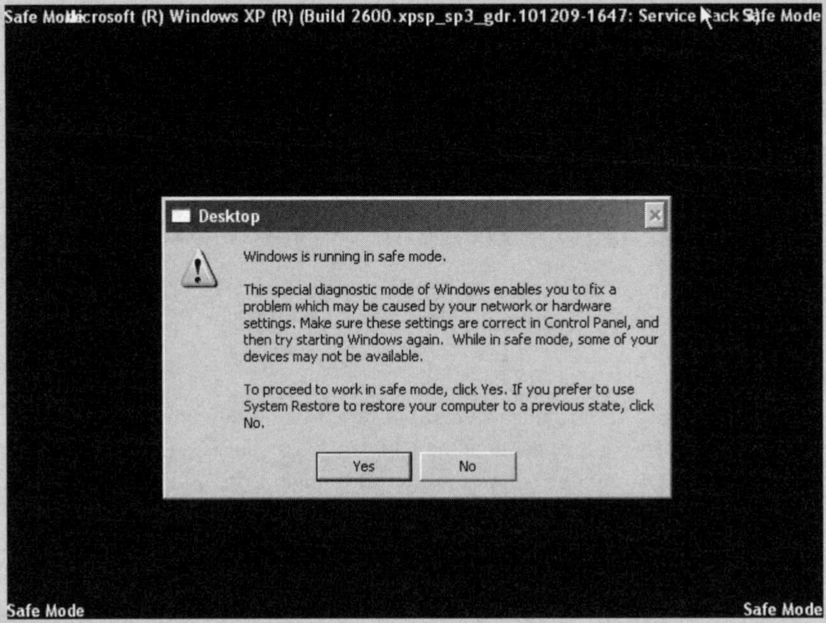

5. Now start System Configuration Utility as usual:
   - **Windows XP** Choose Start | Run to display the Run dialog box. Then type **msconfig** and press ENTER or click the OK button.
   - **Windows 7** Click the Start button to display the Start menu, then type **msconfig** and press ENTER.
6. Click the Startup tab to display its contents.
7. Select the check box for the startup item you last disabled.
8. Click the Close button.
9. Restart Windows.

See Which Services Windows Is Running Automatically

To see which services Windows is running automatically, launch System Configuration Utility and display the Services tab.

1. Run the msconfig.exe program in one of these ways to launch System Configuration Utility:
   - **Windows XP** Choose Start | Run to display the Run dialog box. Then type **msconfig** and press ENTER or click the OK button.
   - **Windows 7** Click the Start button to display the Start menu, then type **msconfig** and press ENTER.
2. Click the Services tab to display its contents. Figure 1-2 shows the Services tab for a PC running Windows 7.

As with the startup items, you need to turn off only the services that Windows doesn't require. Turning off vital services can stop Windows from running properly, so you must proceed carefully. Make sure you know what a service does and turn it off only if it's nonessential. Also, check that your PC runs happily without that service before turning off any others.

As you can see in Figure 1-2, there's a long list of services—in fact, the typical PC has between 100 and 200 services. Some services run automatically at startup, whereas others run only when they're needed. For example, the Power service runs automatically to manage your PC's power policy, whereas the Windows Installer service runs only when you're installing software.

Because this is a short book, we don't have space for full lists of services, so we'll look at some quick examples to give you the feel of what services do and which you can eliminate. Visit this book's companion website to see lists of the services that Windows XP and Windows 7 will typically be running. To identify other services, put the service's name into your favorite search engine on the Internet; you'll get plenty of results.

On a typical PC, most of the services are ones Microsoft has created and provided. Although you can definitely turn off some of these services, as you'll see shortly, you may want to start with the non-Microsoft services, which tend to be less essential.

To narrow down the list of services to only the non-Microsoft ones, select the Hide All Microsoft Services check box in the lower-left corner of the System Configuration Utility window. The upper screen in Figure 1-3 shows the resulting list for the sample Windows 7 PC, whereas the lower screen in Figure 1-3 shows a longer list of non-Microsoft services running on the sample Windows XP PC.

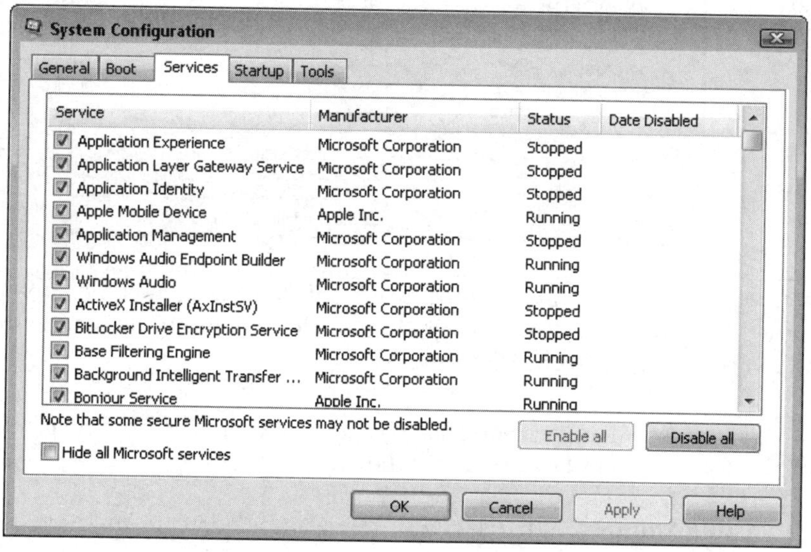

FIGURE 1-2 On the Services tab of System Configuration Utility, you can turn off any services you do not need to run.

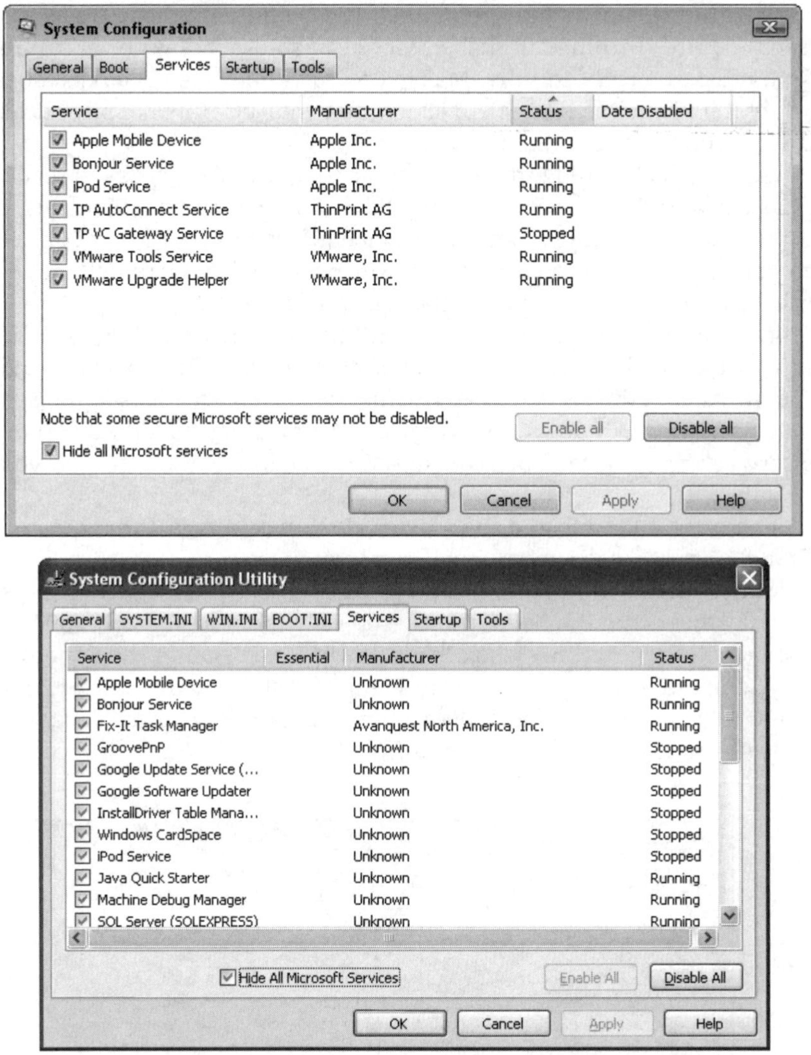

FIGURE 1-3 **Select the Hide All Microsoft Services check box if you want to see only third-party services running on your PC. The upper screen is from Windows 7; the lower screen is from Windows XP.**

You can see that both Services tabs list three services from Apple, Inc. (the Windows XP PC lists the manufacturer as Unknown):

- **Apple Mobile Device service** This service detects any iPod, iPad, or iPhone you plug in.
- **Bonjour Service** This service enables hardware and software devices to communicate across the network using Apple's protocol called Bonjour.

For example, your PC can share its iTunes library with iTunes running on another PC or Mac on the network, while your PC can print on printers that Macs are sharing.

- **iPod Service** This service is for managing the iPods, iPads, or iPhones you connect to your PC.

Once you know this, you can easily decide whether to disable these services:

- If you've stopped using your iPod, iPad, or iPhone with your PC, disable the Apple Mobile Device service and the iPod Service.
- If you don't use iTunes' sharing capabilities, or other Bonjour-based sharing (such as that of printers or digital cameras), disable the Bonjour Service.

For other services your PC is running, use either the list of common services on this book's companion website or an Internet search to identify what the service does. You can then decide whether or not to disable it.

Remove or Disable Hardware You No Longer Use

One of the things that can really gunk up your PC is unnecessary hardware. Windows has to manage every device you connect to your PC, so extra hardware not only draws more power but also takes more processor cycles.

Because of its physical presence, unnecessary hardware tends to be easier to see than startup items and services—you won't suddenly find a dozen printers attached to your PC that you didn't know about, whereas you won't see even twice that number of unwanted startup items. But even if you rarely add hardware, it can still add up over the years, so it's a good idea to have a clear-out now and then—especially of desktop PCs, which tend to accumulate more clutter than laptop PCs.

So take a look first at the devices you've attached to your PC. If you have connected external drives, printers, scanners, audio interfaces, or TV tuners you no longer need, disconnect them. If you're removing several devices, it's best to shut down the PC first; if you're removing only a device that you can stop by using the Safely Remove Hardware icon in the system tray, stop it there first and then remove it.

If the extra devices are ones you've installed in your PC, you will definitely need to power it off before you remove them. But you can also temporarily disable a device you don't need, without actually removing it from your PC. This is useful when you don't need the device now but you may need it in the future and you don't want to keep opening up your PC and performing minor surgery on it.

To disable a hardware device, you use Device Manager. Follow these steps:

1. Open Device Manager. The following bulleted paragraphs show the easiest way. The nearby sidebar explains another way you might like to know.
   - **Windows XP** Choose Start | Run to display the Run dialog box. Then type **devmgmt.msc** and press ENTER or click the OK button.
   - **Windows 7** Click the Start button to display the Start menu, then type **devmgmt.msc** and press ENTER.

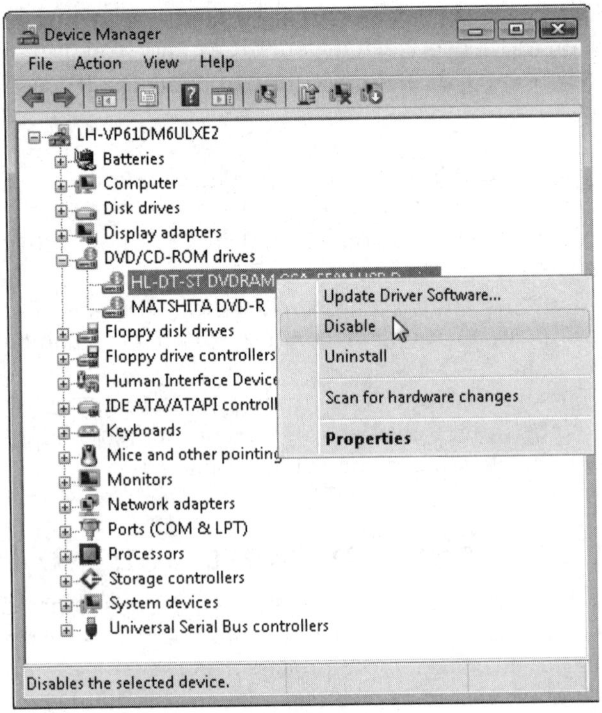

FIGURE 1-4 You can quickly disable a device by using Device Manager.

2. Click the + sign to expand the device category that contains the device. For example, click the + sign next to DVD/CD-ROM Drives to expand the category (see Figure 1-4).
3. Right-click the device you want to disable and then click Disable on the context menu. Windows displays a confirmation dialog box, warning you that disabling the device will make it stop working, as shown here.

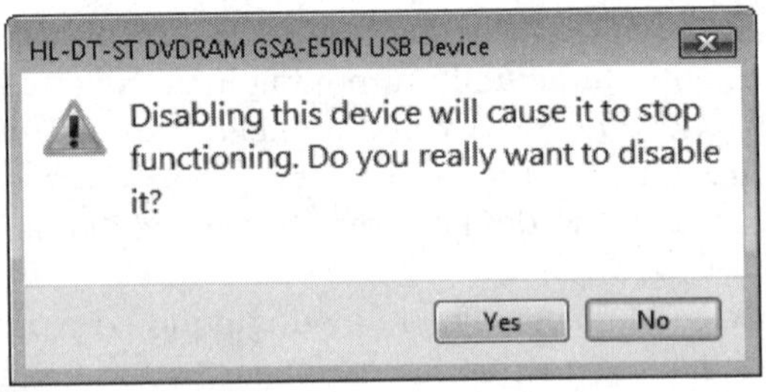

4. Click the Yes button. Device Manager disables the device.
5. If you need to resolve driver issues, leave Device Manager open. Otherwise, click the Close button (the × button) or choose File | Exit to close it.

Open Device Manager in Other Ways

In the main text, you open Device Manager the easy way—by typing the name of its program file (**devmgmt.msc**) in the Run dialog box in Windows XP or the Search box on the Start menu in Windows 7.

You can also open Device Manager by going through the user interface—but it takes longer, and the details are different on Windows XP than on Windows 7. Still, you'd probably want to know, so this sidebar provides the easiest way to do it.

To open Device Manager on Windows XP, follow these steps:

1. Click the Start button to open the Start menu.
2. Right-click the My Computer item to display the context menu.
3. Click the Properties item to display the System Properties dialog box.
4. Click the Hardware tab to display its contents.
5. Click the Device Manager button to open Device Manager.

To open Device Manager on Windows 7, follow these steps:

1. Click the Start button to open the Start menu.
2. Right-click the Computer item to display the context menu.
3. Click the Properties item to display the System window in Control Panel.
4. In the left column, click the Device Manager link to open Device Manager.

Identify and Remove Bad Drivers

Bad drivers are a real menace on the road, where they can cause wrecks and bring traffic to a grinding halt. But they can be just as much of a menace on your PC, because they can cripple it entirely.

As you know, a *driver* is a piece of software that enables Windows to identify a particular hardware device and work with it. For example, when you drop a month's lunch money on a new printer and plug it in, Windows needs the driver to tell it that what's at the other end of the USB cable is a printer rather than a wireless network adapter, a TV tuner, or a flash drive. And if you don't have the right driver, you might as well not have connected the device, because it won't work.

To sort out problems with drivers, you use Device Manager, which you met in the previous section. So start by opening Device Manager if it's not currently open:

- **Windows XP** Choose Start | Run to display the Run dialog box. Then type **devmgmt.msc** and press ENTER or click the OK button.
- **Windows 7** Click the Start button to display the Start menu, then type **devmgmt.msc** and press ENTER.

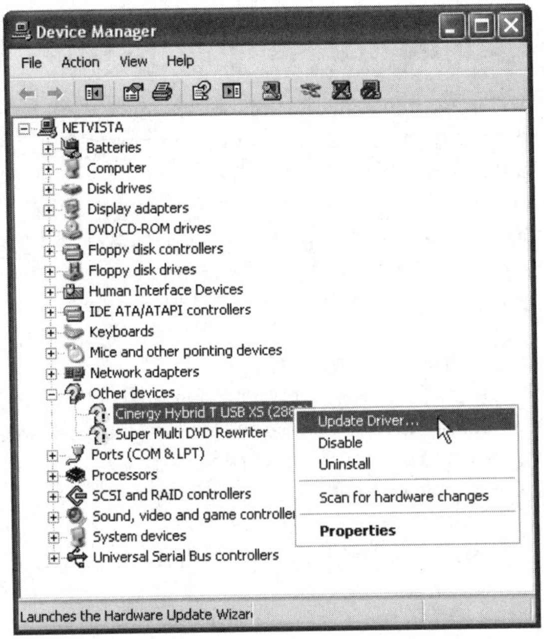

FIGURE 1-5 To resolve problems with a device, try updating its driver.

Once you open Device Manager, you'll see a question mark with a superimposed exclamation point next to any device that Device Manager isn't happy with. Figure 1-5 shows two examples in the Other Devices category in Device Manager in Windows XP.

Right-click a device and then click Update Driver or Update Driver Software on the context menu. A wizard opens to walk you through updating the software. Follow the wizard's steps to locate a suitable driver and install it.

Tip When you're resolving driver problems, it's usually best to allow Windows to download the latest available driver from the Internet rather than using a driver you have on a CD. All other things being equal, the newest driver will contain fixes for problems with the device.

Turn Off the Indexing Service

To help you find the files you need, Windows automatically scans through your files and builds an index of their contents. This is great if you need to search often, but it means that the Indexing service may be making your PC run more slowly. If you don't search often, you may want to turn off the Indexing service to see if performance improves.

To turn off the Indexing service, follow these steps:

1. Click the Start menu and then click My Computer on Windows XP to open a My Computer window or click Computer on Windows 7 to open a Computer window.

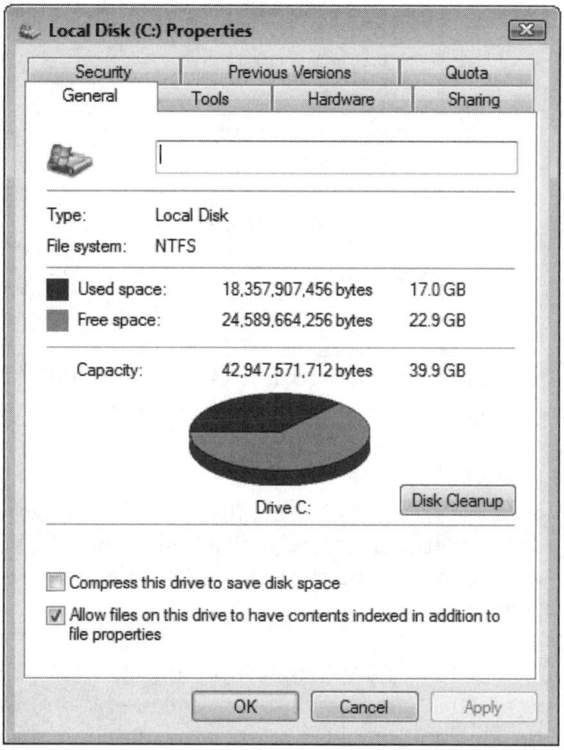

FIGURE 1-6 Clear the Index This Drive For Faster Searching check box on the General tab of the Properties dialog box for your PC's hard drive. The check box's name varies depending on the version of Windows.

2. Right-click the hard drive for which you want to turn off indexing. If your PC has only one hard drive, right-click that drive.
3. On the context menu, click Properties to display the Properties dialog box for the hard drive. The General tab appears at the front, as in Figure 1-6 (which shows Windows 7).
4. Clear the check box that controls indexing. Microsoft keeps experimenting with different names:
   - **Windows XP** Allow Indexing Service To Index This Disk For Fast File Searching
   - **Windows 7** Allow Files On This Drive To Have Contents Indexed In Addition To File Properties
5. Click the OK button. Windows displays the Confirm Attribute Change dialog box (Figure 1-7 shows the Windows 7 version of this dialog box).
6. Select the Apply Changes To Drive, Subfolders And Files option button.
7. Click the OK button. Windows starts changing the Index attribute of the files and folders on the hard drive.

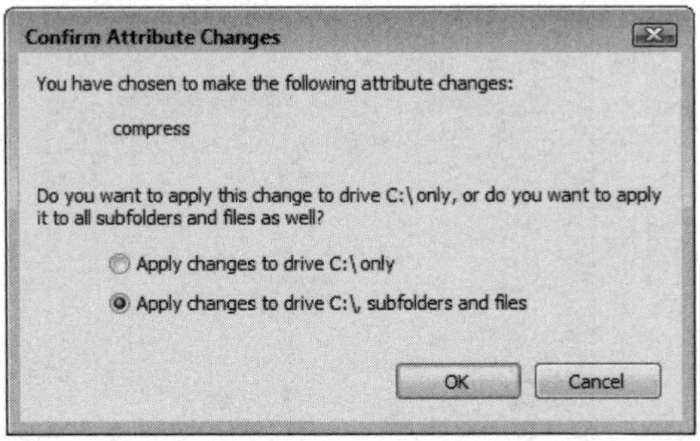

FIGURE 1-7 In the Confirm Attribute Changes dialog box, choose the lower option button to apply the changes to the drive, its subfolders, and their files.

Note If Windows 7 displays the Access Denied dialog box when you click the OK button in the Confirm Attribute Change dialog box, click the Continue button. Go through User Account Control and provide the Administrator credentials required to make the change.

8. If Windows displays the Error Applying Attributes dialog box, click the Ignore All button. This dialog box appears because Windows cannot turn off indexing on all the files on your PC's startup drive—so you need to let it skip over those files.

Note Changing the attributes of files and folders to turn off indexing can take several minutes, depending on how fast your PC is and how many files and folders you've stuffed onto it.

Give Your PC More Virtual Memory

As well as the physical memory (RAM) that your PC contains, Windows uses space on the hard drive as virtual memory for storing data temporarily. You can adjust the amount of virtual memory available to Windows.

Note Normally, you'll want to make sure Windows has plenty of virtual memory available, but when you're squeezed for space on your hard drive, you may need to *reduce* the amount of space Windows is using for virtual memory.

Note You may also be able to give your PC more physical memory by adding RAM. We'll look at how to do this in the section "Add Memory to Your PC" in Chapter 9, which discusses hardware upgrades you can easily perform.

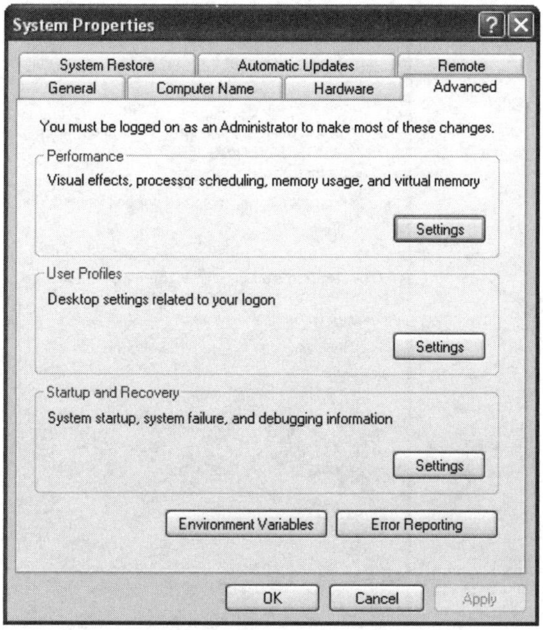

FIGURE 1-8 On the Advanced tab of the System Properties dialog box, click the Settings button in the Performance box to display the Performance Options dialog box.

To see how much virtual memory Windows is using, and to change the amount if necessary, follow these steps:

1. Open the System Properties dialog box:
   - **Windows XP** Press WINDOWS KEY–BREAK.
   - **Windows 7** Press WINDOWS KEY–BREAK to display the System window in Control Panel. Then click the Advanced System Settings link in the Tasks list on the left to display the System Properties dialog box.
2. Click the Advanced tab to display its contents (see Figure 1-8).
3. Click the Settings button in the Performance box to display the Performance Options dialog box.
4. Click the Advanced tab to display its contents (see Figure 1-9).
5. While you're here, make sure the Programs option button is selected in the Processor Scheduling box. In Windows XP, make sure the Programs option button is selected in the Memory Usage box as well.
6. Click the Change button in the Virtual Memory box at the bottom to display the Virtual Memory dialog box. Figure 1-10 shows the Virtual Memory dialog box for Windows XP on the left and the Virtual Memory dialog box for Windows 7 on the right.

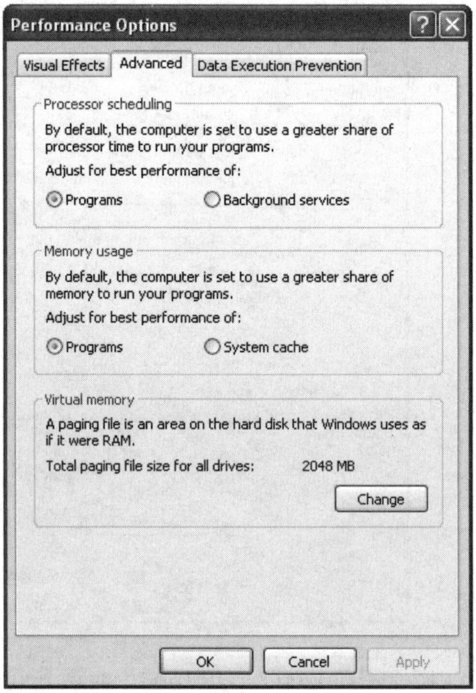

FIGURE 1-9 On the Advanced tab of the Performance Options dialog box, make sure both of the Programs option buttons are selected. Then click the Change button in the Virtual Memory box.

Note In Windows 7, clear the Automatically Manage Paging File Size For All Drives check box at the top of the Virtual Memory dialog box if you want to change the virtual memory settings.

7. If your PC has multiple hard drives, click the hard drive you want to affect.

Note Microsoft recommends using a paging file 1.5 times the amount of RAM in your PC—for example, a paging file of 1.5GB if your PC has 1GB of RAM, or a paging size of 3GB if your PC has 2GB of RAM. You can try going up to 2 times the amount of RAM to improve performance.

8. To have Windows manage the size of the paging file, select the System Managed Size option button. To use a custom size, select the Custom Size option button; then type the starting size in the Initial Size text box and the maximum size in the Maximum Size text box.

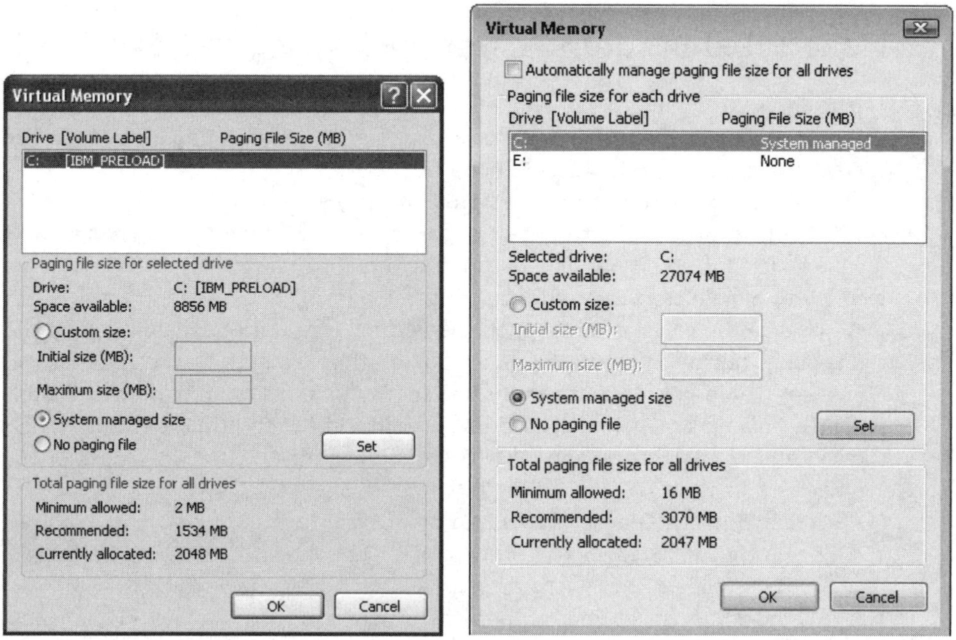

FIGURE 1-10 In the Virtual Memory dialog box, choose how much virtual memory to give Windows and which drive to place it on. The Virtual Memory dialog box on the left is for Windows XP; the Virtual Memory dialog box on the right is for Windows 7.

Tip To prevent Windows from changing the size of the paging file, enter your maximum value in both the Initial Size text box and the Maximum Size text box.

9. Click the Set button to apply your choice.

Note You can turn off the paging file for a drive by selecting the No Paging File option button. If your PC has two hard drives, turn off the paging file for the system drive (the drive that contains Windows) and put the paging file on the other drive to improve performance. If your PC has just one drive, don't turn off the paging file on it—Windows does need virtual memory.

10. When you've made your choices, click the OK button to close the Virtual Memory dialog box.
11. If you want to change the visual effects that Windows is using, work as described in the nearby sidebar. Otherwise, click the OK button to close the Performance Options dialog box and then click the OK button to close the System Properties dialog box.

Make Windows Run Faster by Turning Off Eye Candy

If your PC is struggling to run Windows at a good speed, part of the problem may be that Windows is trying to use too many visual effects. By turning off some of this eye candy, you may be able to make Windows run faster.

You're most likely to run into this problem with Windows XP, because XP will run on PCs with very modest amounts of graphics memory. Windows 7 demands far more graphics memory, so if your PC can run Windows 7, it most likely has enough graphics memory to handle the visual effects.

To change the visual effects, open the Performance Options dialog box by clicking the Settings button in the Performance box on the Advanced tab of the System Properties dialog box. (See the main text for instructions on opening the System Properties dialog box.) Then click the Visual Effects tab to bring it to the front, as shown here, and select the appropriate option button:

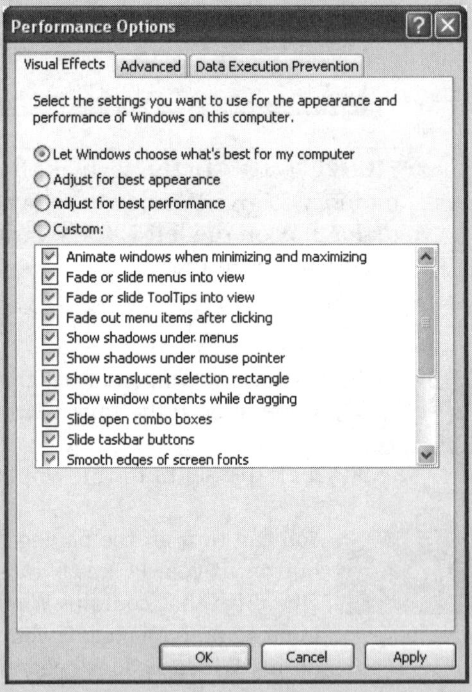

- **Let Windows Choose What's Best For My Computer** Select this option button to let Windows choose settings. This is the default setting. In the list box, Windows selects the check box for each visual effect it considers a good idea for your PC.
- **Adjust For Best Appearance** Select this option button if you want to turn on every visual effect Windows has. Don't do this if your PC is running slowly. When you select this option button, Windows selects all the check boxes in the list box.
- **Adjust For Best Performance** Select this option button to speed up your PC as much as possible. This is what you'll likely want to do first. Windows clears all the check boxes in the list box.
- **Custom** Select this option button if you want to pick and mix the visual effects. Normally, it's best to select the Adjust For Best Performance option button—which makes Windows clear all the check boxes in the list box—and then select the check box for any visual effect you can't do without.

Click the Apply button to apply your choice, and you'll see how Windows looks with your selection of visual effects applied. The following illustration shows how Windows XP looks with all the effects turned off—just like Windows 2000 Professional, if you ever met it.

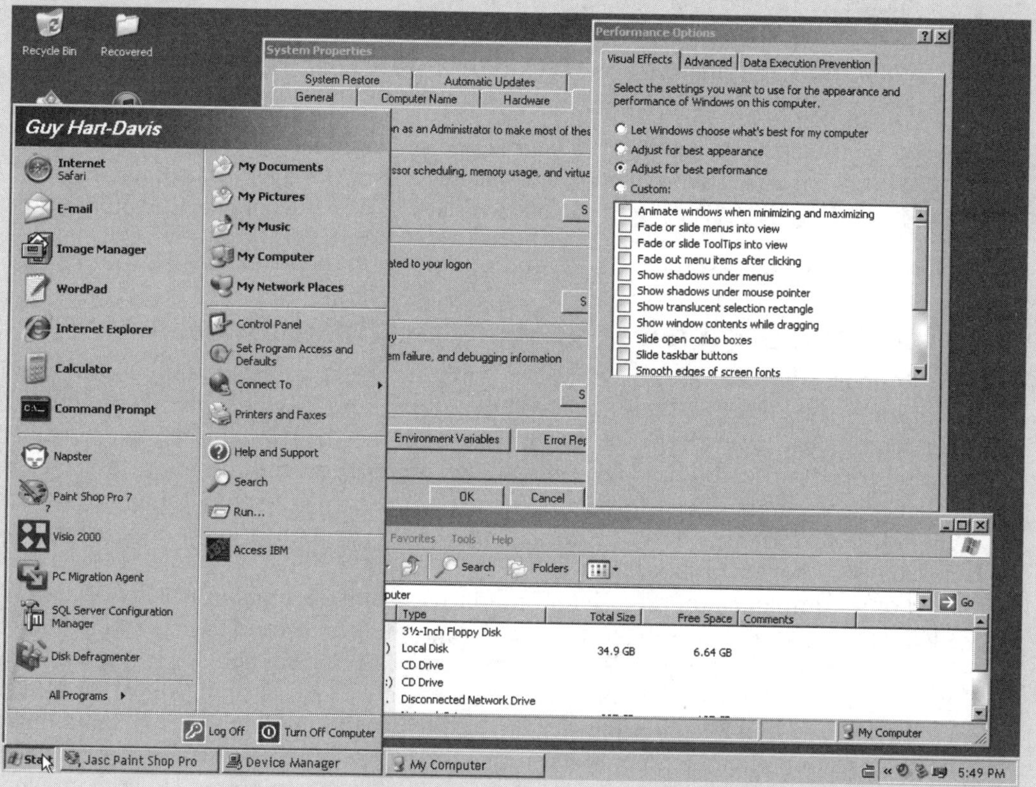

Give Windows 7 a Kick with ReadyBoost

The next way you can speed up Windows 7 is by using ReadyBoost. ReadyBoost allows you to plug a USB memory stick or similar memory device into your PC and assign it for use as extra memory. Windows stores small chunks of frequently needed data on the ReadyBoost device, from which Windows can retrieve the data more quickly than if the data were stored on the hard disk.

Note You can use only one memory device for ReadyBoost at a time.

Understand When ReadyBoost Can Be Helpful

Look to use ReadyBoost in any of the following situations:

- You've already installed the maximum amount of RAM that your PC can have, and performance is still disappointing.
- Your PC doesn't have its maximum amount of RAM, but to increase the RAM, you would need to replace some or all of the existing memory modules.
- Your PC requires a doctorate in mechanical engineering to access the RAM.

Note If you can easily add RAM to your PC, do so before trying ReadyBoost. RAM will give you a far greater performance improvement. However, ReadyBoost is well worth trying, especially if you already have a spare memory device you can use.

- You've borrowed someone's PC and find performance lacking.

Find Memory That Will Work for ReadyBoost

ReadyBoost requires memory that can store and return data quickly enough to supplement RAM effectively. Many USB 2.0 memory devices *are* fast enough to use for ReadyBoost, but others are not, including some that claim to be very fast. The problem is that ReadyBoost requires all the memory in the memory device to be consistently fast, whereas some devices use a special high-speed memory gateway to get better performance out of a larger bank of slower memory. Such an arrangement doesn't work for ReadyBoost.

Some companies market memory devices as being suitable for ReadyBoost. With such devices, you're on safe ground—although the prices tend to be higher than for regular memory devices. If a device isn't marked as being suitable for ReadyBoost, make sure all its memory can provide at least 1.75 megabytes per second (Mbps) for 512KB random writes, and 2.5 Mbps for 4KB random reads. Finding out this information usually involves reading the manufacturer's specification sheet.

If you already have a USB 2.0 memory stick, it'll cost you nothing to find out whether it works for ReadyBoost.

Note At this writing, USB 3.0 is available but is not yet widespread. In theory, USB 3.0 memory sticks should work fine with ReadyBoost, if you can afford them.

Configure ReadyBoost on Your PC

Once you've chosen your device, configure ReadyBoost on your PC. Follow these steps:

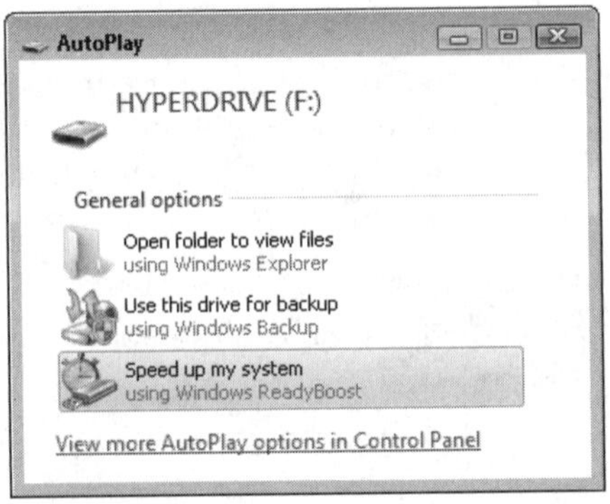

1. Plug the drive into a USB port on your PC. (You can also use a USB hub, but plugging it directly into a port usually gives more consistent results.) Windows displays the AutoPlay dialog box for the drive.

Note If Windows doesn't display the AutoPlay dialog box for the drive, choose Start | Computer to open a Computer window. Right-click the icon for the USB drive and choose Properties. Windows displays the Removable Disk Properties dialog box. Click the ReadyBoost tab.

2. Click the Speed Up My System Using Windows ReadyBoost link. Windows displays the ReadyBoost tab of the Removable Disk Properties dialog box (see Figure 1-11).

Note If the ReadyBoost tab of the Removable Disk Properties dialog box shows the message "This device does not have the required performance characteristics for use in speeding up your system," click the Test Again button once or twice. (The Test Again button appears only when the device fails the ReadyBoost hurdle.) Windows seems to find some USB devices marginally too slow on the first or second read, but passes them on a retest. If Windows gives you this message persistently, try a different device.

3. Select the appropriate option button:
   - **Dedicate This Device To ReadyBoost** Select this option button if you want to use the device only for ReadyBoost. If the device's capacity is 4GB or less, this is usually the best choice. If the device's capacity is greater, select the Use This Device option button and specify how much space to give ReadyBoost.

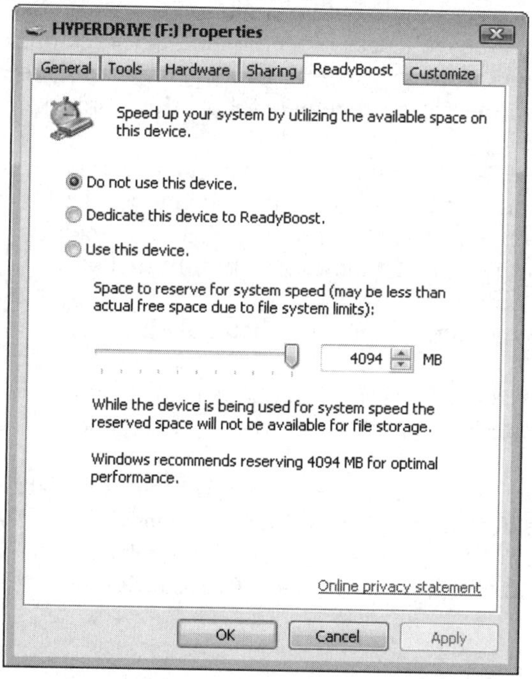

FIGURE 1-11 On the ReadyBoost tab of the Removable Disk Properties dialog box, set up the device for use as ReadyBoost memory.

- **Use This Device** Select this option button if you want to decide how much space to give ReadyBoost. Either drag the slider to the appropriate position, or adjust the value in the box either by clicking the spin buttons or by typing. Microsoft recommends setting ReadyBoost to a value between 1 × and 2.5 × the amount of RAM in your PC—the higher the value, the more performance boost you should get. For example, if your PC has 1GB RAM, you might set anywhere from 1,024MB to 2,536MB of ReadyBoost memory.

Note The biggest ReadyBoost value you can set is 4,096MB (4GB), assuming your USB memory device is capacious enough. The smallest is 256MB. You'll normally get the greatest performance improvement by using the largest recommended amount.

4. Click the OK button. Windows closes the Removable Disk Properties dialog box and starts using the drive for ReadyBoost.

You should now see a performance improvement, especially during long computing sessions or when you have many applications and documents open. However, the difference may not be dramatic.

Remove a ReadyBoost Device

For best effect, you should leave the memory device attached all the time you use your PC. This is easy to do with a desktop PC, where you can plug in a USB memory stick and simply leave it, but having a memory stick protruding from a laptop PC tends to be awkward—so you'll probably want to remove it.

To remove the memory device, follow these steps:

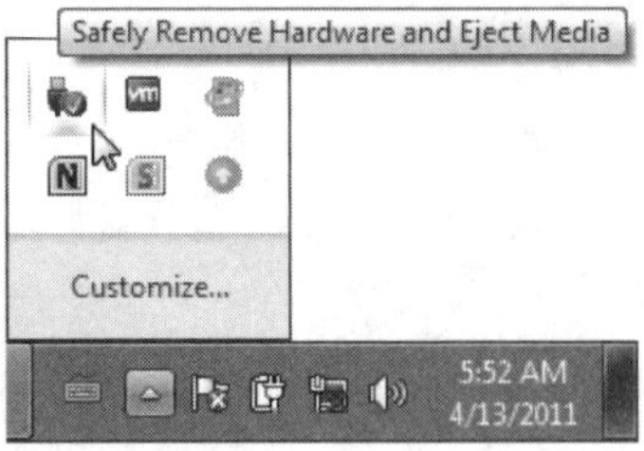

1. Click the Safely Remove Hardware icon in the notification area (the icon with the green circle containing a white check mark). You may need to click the Show Hidden Icons button first, as shown here.
2. On the menu that appears, click the entry for the drive.
3. When Windows displays the Safe To Remove Hardware pop-up message, unplug the device.

Note Windows *mirrors* (stores a copy of) all the data that's stored on the ReadyBoost device in a file on your hard disk, so removing your ReadyBoost device doesn't have any bad effects—Windows simply retrieves the data it needs from the hard disk rather than from the ReadyBoost device.

Defragment the Hard Drive

As you use your PC, it writes files to the hard drive all the time—not just the documents and other files you create and tell it to save, but also hundreds or thousands of files that it uses to store information temporarily, track what's going on, and generally keep Windows running.

Without getting too technical, each hard drive is divided up into tiny areas called *blocks*. When your PC saves a file, the file takes up one or more blocks. For example, if the block size is 4K, and you save a file that's 3K, it takes up one block. A 5K file takes up two blocks, a 9K file takes up three blocks, and so on.

The blocks can be more or less anywhere on the disk. Ideally, the blocks that store a file are next to each other. That way, the hard drive's read head can read them quickly all at once. If the blocks are spread out all over the hard drive, the hard drive head has to travel farther to round them up. So opening the file takes longer.

Note This discussion of defragmentation applies only to hard disk drives that contain spinning platters. If your PC has a solid state device (SSD) instead of a hard disk drive, you do not need to defragment it. This is for two reasons. First, an SSD is designed so that it can access data in any of its blocks quickly, so there's no benefit to arranging each file's data in contiguous blocks. Second, because SSDs eventually wear out, defragmentation can cause them to wear out sooner—so it's a bad idea.

What's the Difference Between a Hard Disk and a Hard Drive?

There's no difference—they're both shorter terms for what's formally called a hard disk drive, a drive that contains a hard disk as opposed to another kind of disk, such as a floppy disk. This book uses the term "hard drive," as it's perhaps the more widely used of the two terms.

That was easy—but these days there's a wrinkle: Instead of regular hard disks, some PCs have solid state drives. These are drives that consist of memory chips rather than thin platters spinning at speeds that would put your car's engine in the red zone. Solid state drives, or SSDs as they're known for short, are great because they give much better performance than hard drives, take up less space, and are far more resistant to shock.

The disadvantage is that SSDs are not only far more expensive than hard disk drives but also much lower in capacity. Prices are coming down, but at this writing (summer 2011), you can get a 2TB (terabyte) hard drive for less than $100, whereas a 512GB SSD—a quarter of the size—costs more than $1,000.

In this book, I'll use the term "hard drive" to refer to your PC's primary storage device. Where we run into considerations that are specific to SSDs, I'll mention them. Otherwise, everything about hard drives applies to SSDs too.

When the blocks of your files are spread out across the drive, the drive is said to be *fragmented*. You can speed things up by *defragmenting* (or *defragging*) the drive. The defragmenter moves the blocks around so that as many files as possible have all their blocks close to each other.

Defragmenting a drive can take several hours, so you'll probably want to set it going when you're about to leave your PC—for example, when you head off to work, or last thing at night.

Defragment Your PC's Hard Drive on Windows XP

To defragment your PC's hard drive on Windows XP, follow these steps:

1. Choose Start | All Programs | Accessories | System Tools | Disk Defragmenter to launch Disk Defragmenter (see Figure 1-12).
2. In the list of drives, click the drive you want to defrag. If your PC has just the one hard drive, Disk Defragmenter will have selected it already.
3. Click the Analyze button. Disk Defragmenter examines the disk and then displays a dialog box, as shown here.

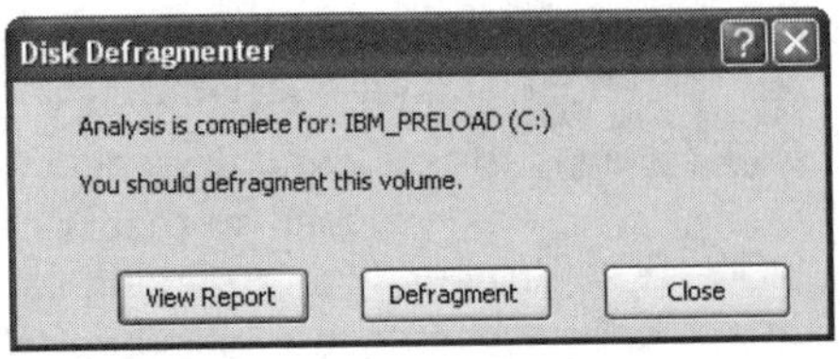

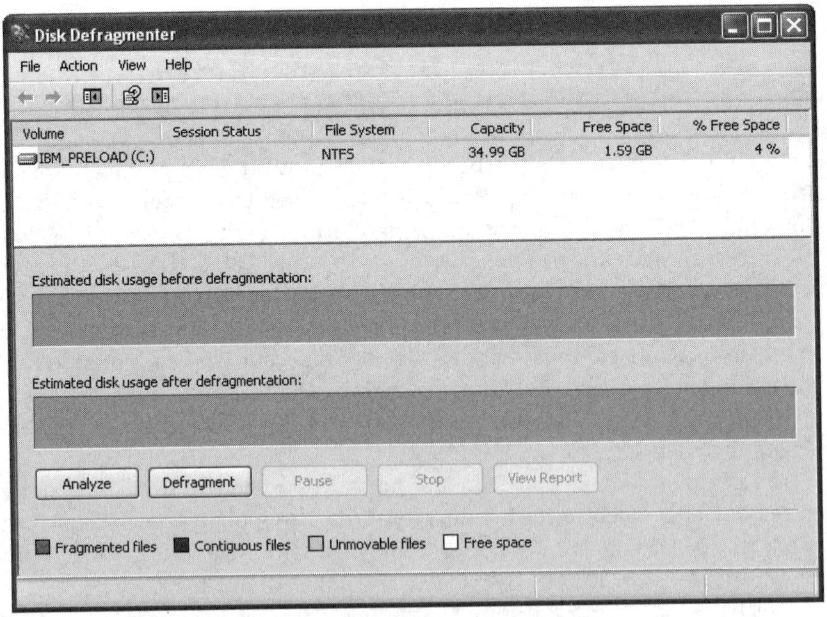

FIGURE 1-12 Disk Defragmenter rearranges the blocks on a hard disk so that the disk head can read files more quickly.

4. If the dialog box says you should defragment this volume, you can go ahead and click the Defragment button. But what you may want to do first is click the View Report button to display the Analysis Report dialog box (see Figure 1-13). This gives you a battery of statistics about how big the drive is, how much free space it has, and how fragmented it is. Scroll the Volume Information box down a little so that you can see the Volume Fragmentation readout and then note the Total Fragmentation figure so that you can compare it with the drive after you defragment it.

Note You can also print the analysis report by clicking the Print button or save it to a file by clicking the Save As button.

5. Click the Defragment button to start defragmentation running. Disk Defragmenter displays a colored representation of the disk usage before defragmentation and after defragmentation in the middle of the window—it may be hard to see much difference between the two—and a progress readout at the bottom.

Note If Disk Defragmenter warns you that it needs more free space before it can defragment the drive effectively, close Disk Defragmenter and free up some space as discussed in the section "Regain Drive Space with Disk Cleanup" in Chapter 2.

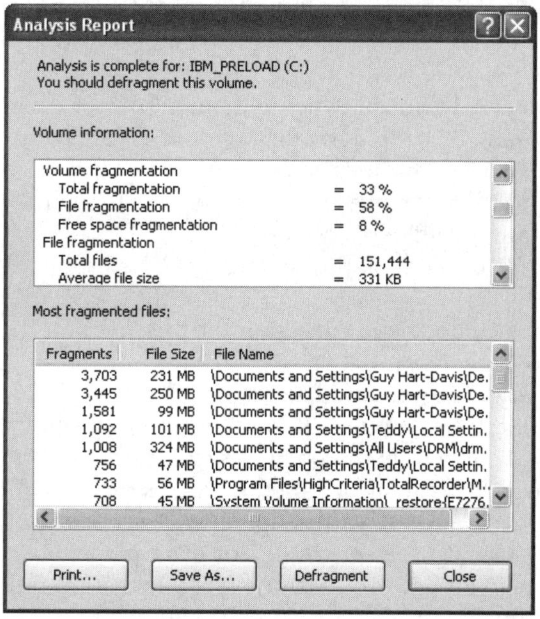

FIGURE 1-13 Open the Analysis Report dialog box to see the details of the drive's fragmentation levels.

6. For best results, leave Disk Defragmenter to finish defragmentation. You can work on the PC if necessary, but defragmentation runs fastest if it has the processor's full attention.
7. When defragmentation finishes, Disk Defragmenter displays a dialog box as shown here.

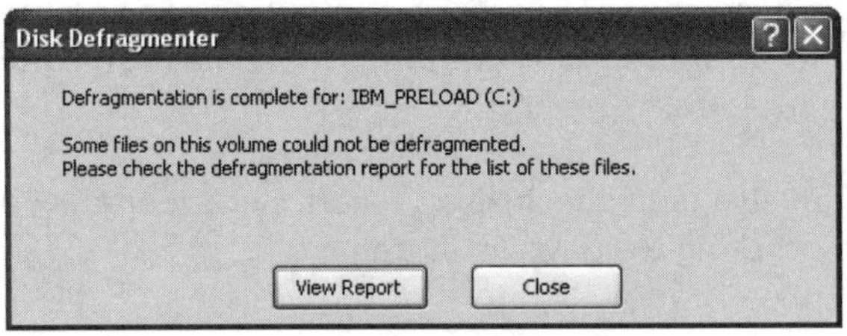

8. Click the View Report button to display the Defragmentation Report dialog box. This is similar to the Analysis Report dialog box that you met earlier in this section.
9. Examine the report; click the Print button if you want to print it, or click the Save As button if you want to save it. Then click the Close button to close the Defragmentation Report dialog box.
10. Click the Close button (the × button) or choose File | Exit to close Disk Defragmenter.

Defragment Your PC's Hard Drive on Windows 7

To defragment your PC's hard drive on Windows 7, follow these steps:

1. Choose Start | Control Panel to open a Control Panel window.
2. In the View By drop-down list, choose either Large Icons or Small Icons (whichever you prefer).
3. Click the Performance Information And Tools link to display the Performance Information And Tools window.
4. In the left pane, click the Advanced Tools link to display the Advanced Tools window.
5. Click the Open Disk Defragmenter link to open the Disk Defragmenter window (see Figure 1-14).
6. Set up a defragmentation schedule like this:
   a. Click the Configure Schedule button to display the Disk Defragmenter: Modify Schedule dialog box (see Figure 1-15).
   b. Select the Run On A Schedule check box.
   c. Use the Frequency drop-down list, Day drop-down list, and Time drop-down list to set up the schedule. For example, choose Weekly in the Frequency drop-down list, Wednesday in the Day drop-down list, and 12:00 A.M. (Midnight) in the Time drop-down list.
   d. If your PC has multiple drives that can be defragmented, as my victim PC does here, click the Select Disks button to display the Disk Defragmenter: Select Disks For Schedule dialog box (see Figure 1-16). In the Disks To Include

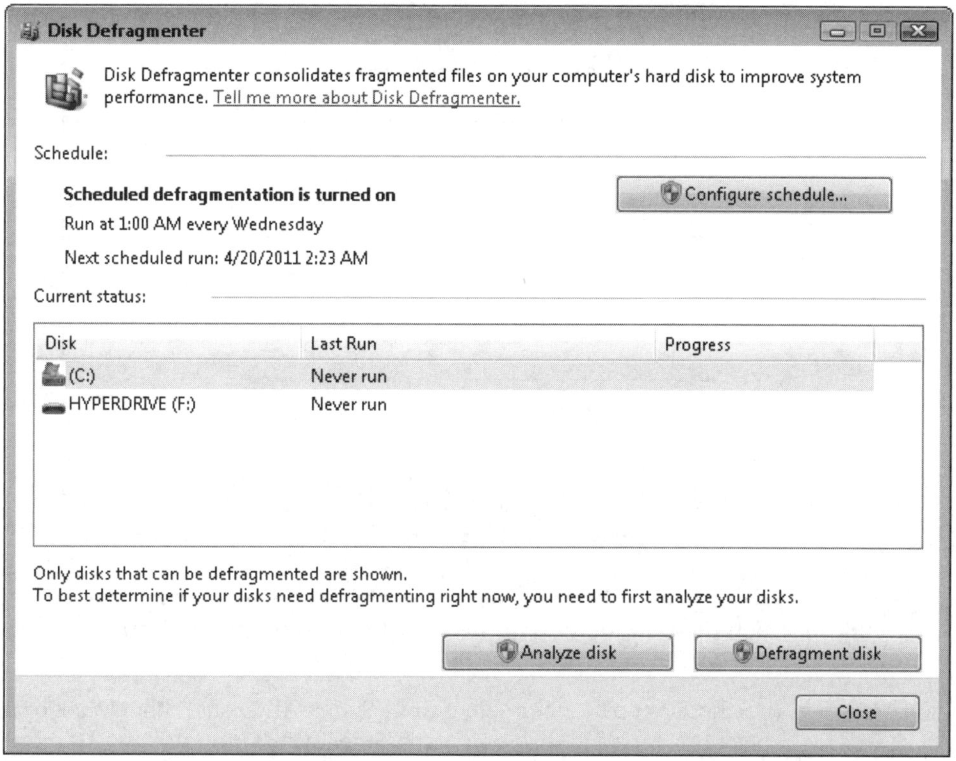

FIGURE 1-14 In Windows 7, you can either run Disk Defragmenter automatically on a schedule or run it manually when you want.

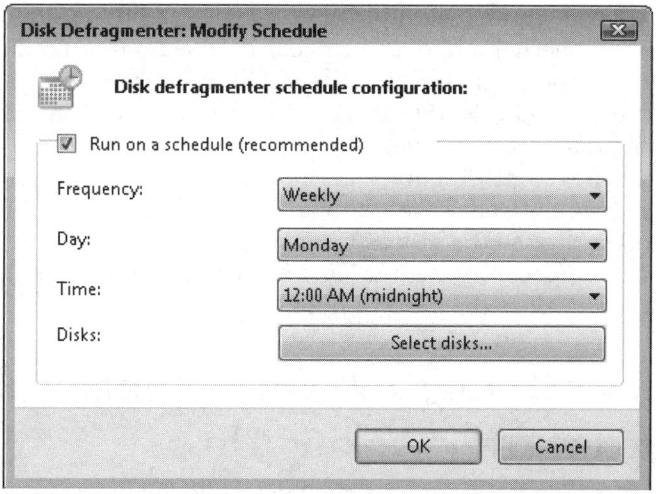

FIGURE 1-15 Use the Disk Defragmenter: Modify Schedule dialog box to set up a defragmentation schedule for the hard drives in your Windows 7 PC.

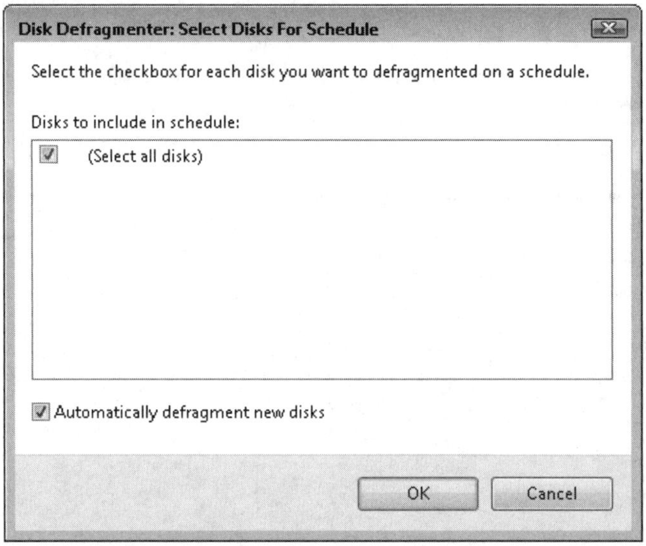

FIGURE 1-16 In the Disk Defragmenter: Select Disks For Schedule dialog box, choose which disks to include in the scheduled defragmentations.

In Schedule box, either select the "(Select All Disks)" check box or select the check box for each disk you want. Select the Automatically Defragment New Disks check box if you want Windows to include new disks you add. Then click the OK button to close the Disk Defragmenter: Select Disks For Schedule dialog box.

e. Click the OK button to close the Disk Defragmenter: Modify Schedule dialog box and return to the Disk Defragmenter window.

7. To see whether a hard drive needs defragmenting now, click the drive in the list box and then click the Analyze Disk button. Disk Defragmenter analyzes the drive and then displays a readout next to its item in the list box giving the fragmentation percentage.
8. If the fragmentation percentage is above 10 percent and you want to defragment the drive now, click the Defragment Disk button. Disk Defragmenter displays a readout next to the disk as it works.
9. When Disk Defragmenter has finished defragmenting the drive, click the Close button to close the Disk Defragmenter dialog box.

Set Windows to Log You On Automatically on Startup or After Waking Up

If your PC is taking ages to start up and a while to log you on to Windows, you may want to set the PC to log you on automatically so that you can start the machine, get a cup of coffee, and come back to find it fully up and running. Even when your PC is running well, you may want it to log you on automatically, simply to save you a little time and effort.

Caution Setting your PC to log you on automatically is handy, but it removes your main defense against someone else accessing your PC against your will—your password. Set up automatic logon only if you're confident nobody else will be able to access your PC when you leave it unattended. (You'll know if this is a reasonable expectation.)

Similarly, you may want your PC to log you on automatically when you resume after you have locked Windows or it has gone to sleep. You can do this too—at the same cost to your security.

Set Windows to Log You On Automatically on Startup

To set Windows to log you on automatically, follow these steps:

1. Open the User Accounts dialog box (Figure 1-17 shows the Windows XP version) in one of these ways:
   - **Windows XP** Choose Start | Run to display the Run dialog box. Then type **control userpasswords2** and press ENTER or click the OK button.
   - **Windows 7** Click the Start button to display the Start menu, and then type **netplwiz** and press ENTER.

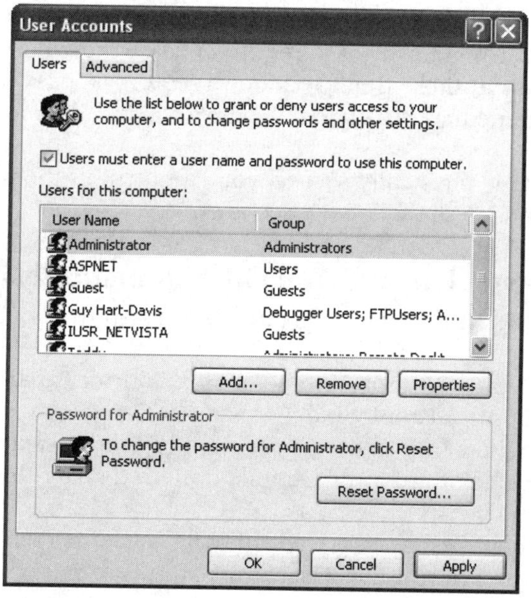

FIGURE 1-17 To set up automatic logon, clear the User Must Enter A User Name And Password To Use This Computer check box in the User Accounts dialog box.

2. Clear the User Must Enter A User Name And Password To Use This Computer check box.
3. Click the Apply button. Windows displays the Automatically Log On dialog box (shown here).

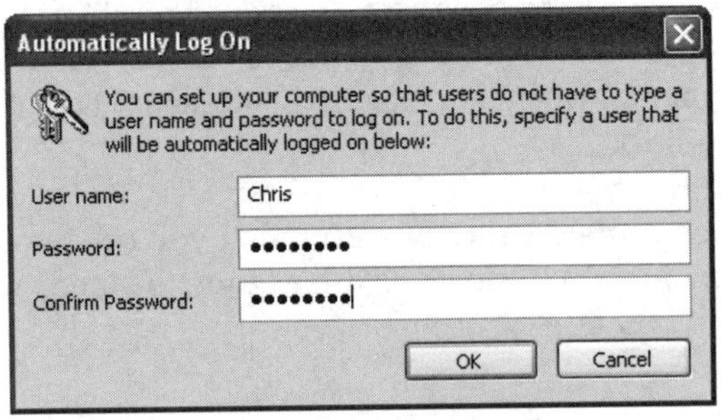

4. Type your user name in the User Name text box.
5. Type your password in the Password text box and the Confirm Password text box.
6. Click the OK button. The Automatically Log On dialog box closes.
7. Click the OK button. The User Accounts dialog box closes.

You can now restart Windows to check that it logs you in automatically.

Set Windows to Log You On Automatically on Wakeup

If you set Windows to log you on automatically when you fire up your PC, you may also want to set Windows not to require a password when you wake it from standby or hibernation. At these times, Windows requires a password to make sure it's you, rather than someone unauthorized, who's waking Sleeping Beauty from her digital slumbers.

If your PC is physically secure, you can turn off the password requirement using the instructions in the following sections.

Set Windows XP to Log You On Automatically on Wakeup

To set Windows XP to log you on automatically on wakeup, follow these steps:

1. Chose Start | Control Panel to open a Control Panel window.
2. If the Control Panel window opens in Category view, click the Switch To Classic View link in the upper-right corner to switch to Classic view.
3. Double-click the Power Options item to display the Power Options Properties dialog box.
4. Click the Advanced tab to display its contents (see Figure 1-18).
5. Clear the Prompt For Password When Computer Resumes From Standby check box.
6. Click the OK button to close the Power Options Properties dialog box.

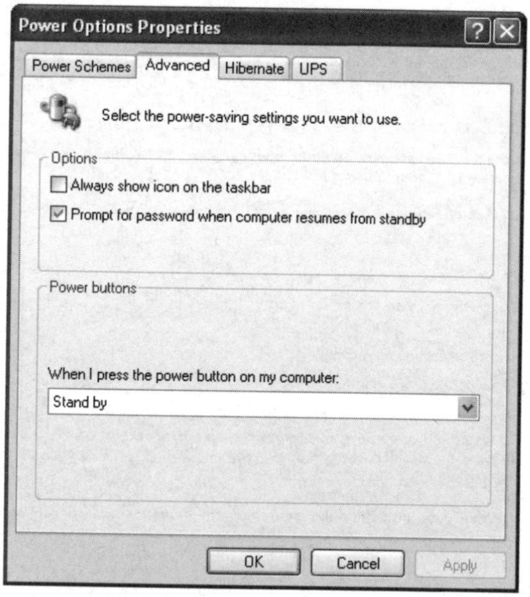

FIGURE 1-18 On the Advanced tab of the Power Options Properties dialog box for Windows XP, clear the Prompt For Password When Computer Resumes From Standby check box if you want to resume your computing session without typing your password.

Set Windows 7 to Log You On Automatically on Wakeup

To set Windows 7 to log you on automatically on wakeup, follow these steps:

1. Choose Start | Control Panel to open a Control Panel window.
2. In the View By drop-down list, choose Large Icons or Small Icons (again, your choice).
3. Click the Power Options item to display the Power Options window.
4. In the left panel, click the Require A Password On Wakeup item to display the Define Power Buttons And Turn On Password Protection window (see Figure 1-19).
5. Click the Change Settings That Are Currently Unavailable link to make the settings at the bottom of the window available.
6. Select the Don't Require A Password option button.
7. Click the Save Changes button. You can then click the Close button (the × button) to close the Control Panel window.

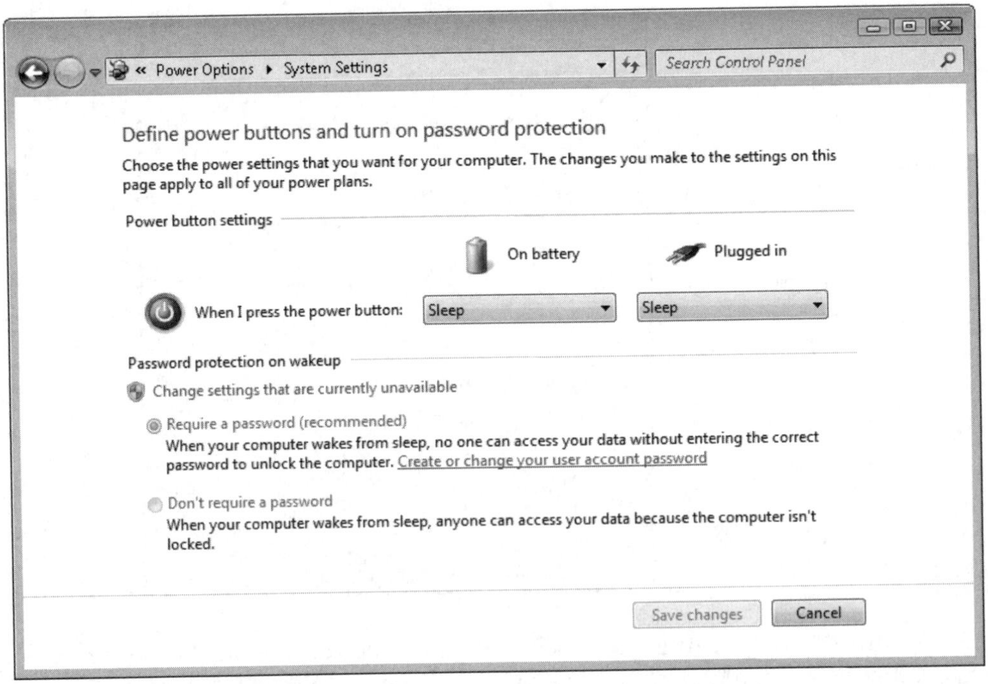

FIGURE 1-19 From the Power Options | System Settings window, you can turn off the password normally required when you wake your PC from its slumbers.

2 Free Up Space on Your PC's Hard Drive

If you work, you probably know Parkinson's Law of Work: "Work expands so as to fill the time available for its completion." And if you have a PC, you'll have run into its corollary: "Data expands to fill the space available for storage."

In other words, however big your PC's hard drive seemed when you got the PC, the drive is probably stuffed with files now.

Running out of space on the hard drive like this can completely hamstring your PC. Not only do you then have no space for storing your files, which is a problem in itself, but Windows struggles to manage its files and to use virtual memory efficiently.

In this chapter, we'll look at how you can free up space on your PC's hard drive. We'll start by getting rid of useless files using Windows' Disk Cleanup feature. This is the sort of cleanup you'll probably want to run regularly—perhaps every few months—just to get rid of files neither you nor your PC needs anymore.

We'll also look at several other moves you can make to reclaim hard drive space. These moves range from reclaiming space from the Recycle Bin, System Restore, and the paging file to removing any programs you don't need and archiving your old files. All these tasks help you get more drive space for your uses, but some of them are more specialized than others, and you'll want to use them only when you're really pushed for space. For example, you can turn off hibernation to reclaim the disk space the hibernation file needs, but you'll want to do this only if you don't need to use hibernation.

At the end of the chapter, we'll look at how to get more hard drive space by adding an external hard drive to your PC. This is quick, easy, and effective—but it does have some disadvantages you should be aware of.

Why Does Your PC's Hard Drive Need Free Space—and How Much?

When you're stuffing clothes into a travel case before heading to the airport, you're probably more concerned with fitting everything in than making things easy to access. As long as you avoid the charge for extra baggage, you're fine—unless the TSA chooses to unpack the whole case.

Your PC's hard drive is good at packing files into available space, but if you fill it too full, performance drops off dramatically. When the drive is full, not only must it save files in blocks located in different parts of the drive rather than arranging all the blocks neatly where the drive head can read them quickly, but Disk Defragmenter can't rearrange the files efficiently to improve the situation. (See Chapter 1 for instructions on setting up and using Disk Defragmenter).

So how much free space should you keep on your PC's hard drive? There's no fixed answer, but you should try to keep at least 15 percent of the hard drive free. This is the level below which Disk Defragmenter can't run. As usual, more free space is better.

So if your PC's hard drive is only 40GB, you'd want to keep at least 6GB free. That may seem a painful amount to sacrifice, but the performance benefits are worth it—and if you're short of space now, you can use some of the moves described later in this chapter to gain the extra gigabytes you need. Similarly, if the hard drive is a terabyte, keeping 150GB free will give Windows plenty of space to write files to disk efficiently.

Regain Drive Space with Disk Cleanup

The best way to start regaining drive space is to run Windows' Disk Cleanup program, which walks you through several straightforward moves for freeing up space.

It's easy to lose track of disk space until you find you're running out, so what you'll probably want to do first is see how much drive space is occupied and how much is free. We'll start there and then run Disk Cleanup.

Find Out How Much Drive Space Is Occupied and How Much Is Free

The easiest way to find out how much drive space is occupied and how much is free is to use Windows Explorer. Follow these steps:

1. Open a My Computer window or a Computer window:
   - **Windows XP** Choose Start | My Computer to open a My Computer window.
   - **Windows 7** Choose Start | Computer to open a Computer window.
2. Right-click the hard drive and then click Properties on the context menu to display the Properties dialog box for the drive. The General tab shows a Used Space readout and a Free Space readout, together with a graphic showing how much of the drive is used and how much is free. Figure 2-1 shows an example from Windows XP. As you can see, more than 95 percent of the 34.9GB drive is full—so we need to do something about it.

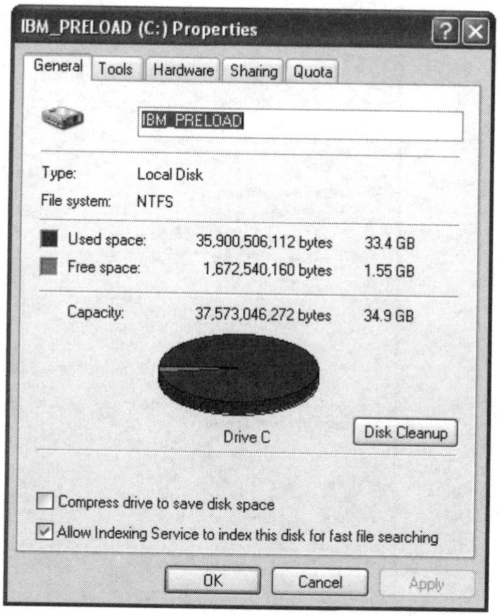

FIGURE 2-1 The General tab of the Properties dialog box for a drive shows how much space is used and how much is free. This drive is stuffed with data.

Run Disk Cleanup

To start freeing up disk space, click the Disk Cleanup button on the General tab of the Properties dialog box for the drive. This example uses Windows XP, but the procedure for Windows 7 is almost the same. I've noted the few differences.

Note In Windows XP, you can also run Disk Cleanup by choosing Start | All Programs | Accessories | System Tools | Disk Cleanup. In Windows 7, choose Start | Control Panel | Performance Information And Tools | Open Disk Cleanup.

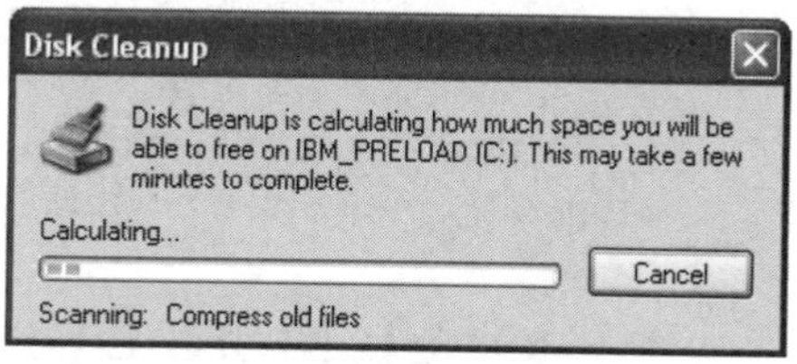

After you click the Disk Cleanup button, you see the Disk Cleanup dialog box, shown here, for a few minutes while Disk Cleanup works out which files it can get rid of, which it can compress, and what your other options are.

Disk Cleanup then displays the Disk Cleanup dialog box shown in Figure 2-2, with the Disk Cleanup tab at the front. This tab contains the first wave of cleanup moves you can perform.

Table 2-1 explains the items Disk Cleanup offers to remove and any disadvantages to removing them.

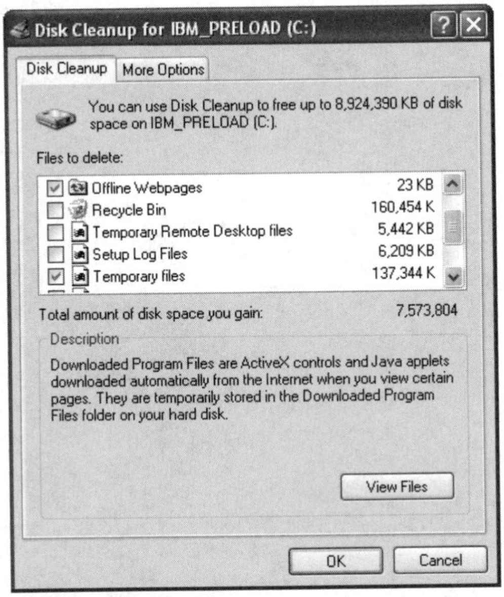

FIGURE 2-2 On the Disk Cleanup tab of this Disk Cleanup dialog box, select the check box for each category of items you want to remove.

Select the check box for each item you want to remove. To decide which items to remove, look at their sizes on the right of the Files To Delete list box. Deleting the temporary Internet files, emptying the Recycle Bin, and deleting temporary files will usually get you the most space. On Windows XP, you can compress old files as well.

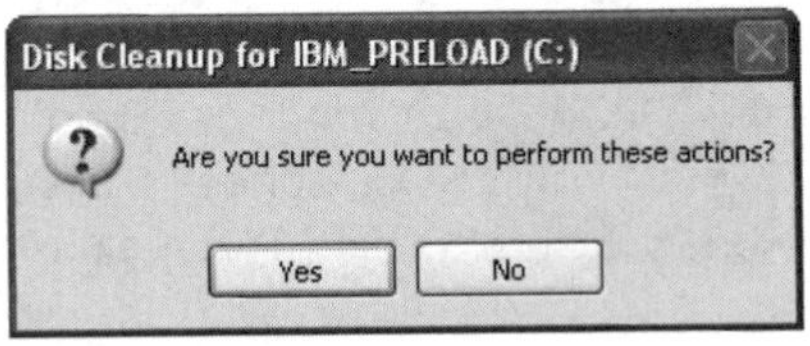

When you've made your choices, click the OK button. Disk Cleanup displays a confirmation dialog box like the one shown here.

Click the Yes button to proceed. Disk Cleanup then removes the items you specified. If you chose to compress old files on Windows XP, the Disk Cleanup operation may take a while to complete.

Free Up More Disk Space

After Disk Cleanup has cleaned up the first wave of victims, decide whether you need to clear more space on your PC's hard drive. You can do so by using the options on the More Options tab of the Disk Cleanup dialog box. The left screen in Figure 2-3 shows the More Options tab for Windows XP, and the right screen shows the More Options tab for Windows 7.

TABLE 2-1 Items Disk Cleanup Can Remove

Disk Cleanup Item	Explanation	Disadvantages to Removing the Item
Downloaded Program Files	ActiveX controls and Java applets Internet Explorer has downloaded	Internet Explorer may need to download these controls and applets again.
Temporary Internet Files	Cached content elements to speed up the display of web pages	Removing these files may slow down web browsing.
Microsoft Office Temporary Files	Log files and temporary data files created by the Office programs	You won't be able to use the log files to troubleshoot issues.
Offline Web Pages	The files used for storing offline favorites	You won't be able to access offline favorites without synchronizing them again.
Recycle Bin	Files and folders you've put in the Recycle Bin	You won't be able to restore any of the files or folders.
Setup Log Files	Log files in which Windows records setup information	You lose troubleshooting information you might need.
Temporary Remote Desktop Files	Picture files used to speed up Remote Desktop Connection sessions	Remote Desktop Connection sessions to computers you've accessed before may be slower.
Temporary Files	Orphaned temporary files created as a workspace by applications	None—these files should have been deleted already.
WebClient/Publisher Temporary Files	Temporary storage for the WebClient/Publisher service	WebClient/Publisher performance may be slower.
Compress Old Files	Compresses files you haven't used for a specified number of days (change the number if necessary)	(Compressed files aren't removed—just compressed.) Compressed files may be slower to access. Compressing the files takes Disk Cleanup a few minutes. This option is only in Windows XP.
Catalog Files for the Content Indexer	Redundant old catalog files from indexing	None.
Thumbnails	Small pictures of your picture, video, and document files used for displaying thumbnail views in Windows Explorer windows	Displaying thumbnails in Windows Explorer windows will be slower, as Windows will need to create the files again.
Windows Error Reporting Files	Text file containing information for reporting errors and checking for solutions	You lose some potentially useful information and gain very little space.

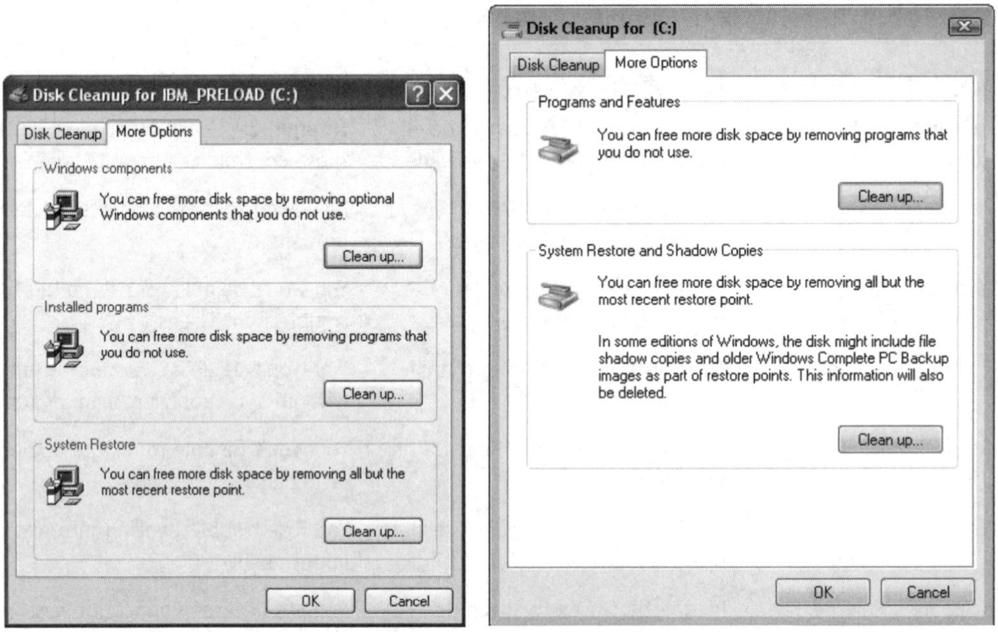

FIGURE 2-3 From the More Options tab of the Disk Cleanup dialog box, you can dig into further areas of Windows where you can save space. The left screen is from Windows XP; the right screen is from Windows 7.

As you can see in the figure, these different versions of the More Options tab offer more or less the same thing, but arranged differently. Windows XP gives you three items to clean up:

- **Windows Components** These are optional Windows features that you can remove if you don't need them. For example, if your PC has the dreadful MSN Explorer program installed, you can reclaim a few megabytes by removing it. We'll look at how to do this in just a moment.
- **Installed Programs** These are the programs installed on your PC. Any you no longer need, you can remove. This is something you'll likely want to do both

Finding the More Options Tab of Disk Cleanup in Windows 7

At first, Windows 7 hides the More Options tab of the Disk Cleanup dialog box. To display the More Options tab, click the Clean Up System Files button. If User Account Control demands your credentials, provide them. The More Options tab then appears in the Disk Cleanup dialog box; click the tab to display its contents.

separately from Disk Cleanup as well as during Disk Cleanup, so we'll look at it in the section "Remove Programs You Don't Need," later in this chapter.

- **System Restore** System Restore automatically stores snapshots of your PC's state so that you can restore your PC to how it was before you, Windows, or malware did something horrible to it. These snapshots are called *restore points.* The Clean Up button here gives you a quick way of disposing of all the restore points except the most recent one.

Windows 7 gives you two items to clean up:

- **Programs and Features** Clicking this Clean Up button opens the Programs And Features screen in Control Panel. You can then remove any programs you no longer need. We'll look at how to do this in the section "Remove Programs You Don't Need," later in this chapter.
- **System Restore and Shadow Copies** As in Windows XP, System Restore automatically stores restore points containing a picture of your PC's state so that you can restore it to an earlier state after a mishap. You can click this Clean Up button to get rid of all the restore points except the most recent one, plus any *shadow copies*—that is, backup copies of essential system files that Windows 7 automatically keeps as insurance against disaster.

We'll go through these moves over the course of the rest of this chapter, starting with removing Windows components.

Remove Windows XP Components You Don't Need

One of the moves you can make from the More Options tab of the Disk Cleanup dialog box in Windows XP is to remove Windows components you don't need. Removing these components is only just worth doing for reclaiming space—you can get rid of only a few handfuls of components, and they don't take up a huge amount of space. But you may want to have a clear-out of the components you don't need on the general principles of streamlining Windows and making sure you're not running services you don't need.

Note You can't remove Windows components in this way on Windows 7.

To remove unneeded Windows components on Windows XP, follow these steps:

1. Click the Clean Up button in the Windows Components box on the More Options tab of the Disk Cleanup dialog box to display the Windows Components Wizard (see Figure 2-4).

Note If you don't have the Disk Cleanup dialog box open, you can launch the Windows Components Wizard from the Start menu. Choose Start | Run to display the Run dialog box, type **appwiz.cpl**, and then press ENTER or click the OK button. In the Add Or Remove Programs window that opens, click the Add/Remove Windows Components button in the left pane to open the Windows Components Wizard.

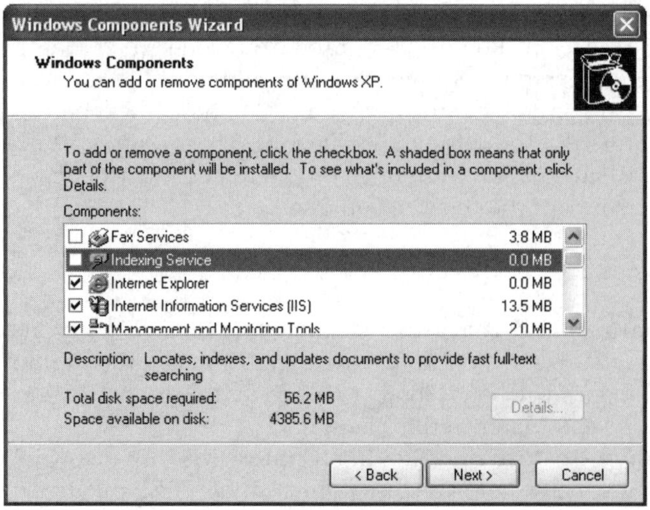

FIGURE 2-4 In the Windows Components Wizard, clear the check box of any component you want to remove from Windows XP.

2. Clear the check box for each component you want to remove. See Table 2-2 for details on the components and their subcomponents. Depending on the version of Windows XP you have, only some of these items may be available.
3. Click the Next button. You'll see a progress screen as the Windows Components Wizard removes the components.
4. When the Completing The Windows Components Wizard screen appears, click the Finish button to close the Windows Components Wizard.

Tip If you're really short of space, you can also remove Windows Messenger, the Accessibility Wizard, Pinball, and WordPad. See this book's website for instructions.

Throttle Back System Restore's Voracious Appetite

The next item on your hit list is System Restore. As you'll remember from earlier in this chapter, System Restore saves snapshots of your PC's state so that you can revert to them if things go wrong. These snapshots are called *restore points.* System Restore creates a restore point automatically every 24 hours as well as when you take actions that may foul up your PC, such as installing programs or drivers. You can also create a restore point manually whenever you think it is a good idea.

By default, Windows devotes 10–15 percent of your PC's hard drive to System Restore. System Restore is a great feature and can save your bacon, so it's important to keep it creating restore points. But if you're short of hard drive space, you'll probably decide that this tithing is excessive.

You can reclaim hard drive space from System Restore by deleting all the restore points except the most recent one. In Windows XP, you can also change the amount of hard drive space set aside for System Restore.

TABLE 2-2 Components and Subcomponents the Windows Components Wizard Can Remove

Component	Subcomponents
Accessories and Utilities	*Accessories:* Calculator, Character Map, Clipboard Viewer, Desktop Wallpaper, Document Templates, Mouse Pointers, Paint *Games:* Freecell, Hearts, Internet Games, Minesweeper, Solitaire, Spider Solitaire
Fax Services	None
Indexing Service	None
Internet Explorer	None
Internet Information Services	Common Files, Documentation, File Transfer Protocol Service, FrontPage 2000 Server Extensions, Internet Information Services Snap-In, SMTP Service, World Wide Web Service (Printers Virtual Directory, Remote Desktop Web Connection, Scripts Virtual Directory, World Wide Web Service)
Management and Monitoring Tools	Simple Network Management Protocol, WMI SNMP Provider
Message Queuing	Active Directory Integration, Common (Core Functionality, Local Storage), MSMQ HTTP Support, Triggers
MSN Explorer	None
Networking Services	RIP Listener, Simple TCP/IP Services, Universal Plug and Play
Other Network File and Print Services	Print Services for Unix
Update Root Certificates	None

Delete All Restore Points Except the Most Recent

To delete all restore points except the most recent, click the Clean Up button in the System Restore box on the More Options tab of the Disk Cleanup dialog box. Disk Cleanup displays a confirmation dialog box. Figure 2-5 shows the Windows XP version of this dialog box on the top and the Windows 7 version on the bottom.

Click the Yes button on Windows XP or the Delete button on Windows 7 to purge the old restore points.

Teach System Restore to Be Less Greedy in the Future

In Windows XP and Windows 7, you can change the amount of space System Restore devours. Normally, you'll want to decrease the space rather than increase it.

FIGURE 2-5 You can delete all the restore points except the most recent in Windows XP (above) or Windows 7 (below).

Change the Amount of Space System Restore Takes on Windows XP

To change the amount of space System Restore takes up on Windows XP, follow these steps:

1. Press WINDOWS KEY–BREAK to display the System Properties dialog box.
2. Click the System Restore tab to display its contents (see Figure 2-6).

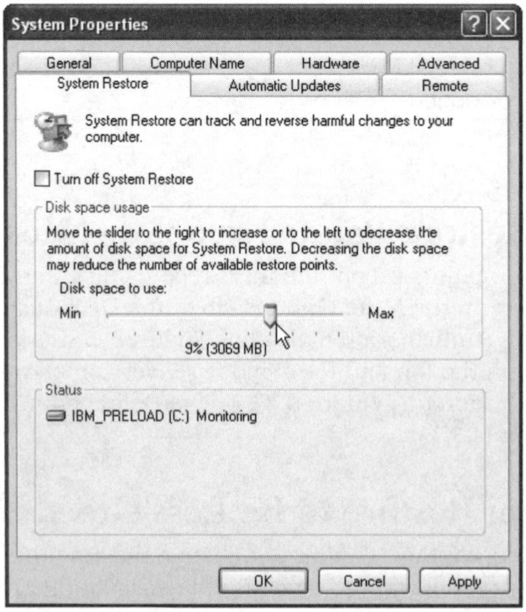

FIGURE 2-6 In Windows XP, drag the Disk Space To Use slider to set the amount of space System Restore can take up on your PC's hard drive.

3. In the Disk Space Usage box, drag the Disk Space To Use slider to the percentage you want to give System Restore. The readout after the percentage shows how many megabytes this is.

Note 200MB is the absolute minimum space you can give System Restore. With less than 200MB, System Restore cannot run. Unless you're desperate for hard drive space, it's best to give System Restore at least 300MB; 500MB is a better bet.

4. Click the OK button to close the System Properties dialog box.

Caution You can turn off System Restore entirely by selecting the Turn Off System Restore check box on the System Restore tab of the System Properties dialog box. This isn't a good idea, because you may not be able to recover after trouble occurs.

Change the Amount of Space System Restore Takes on Windows 7

To change the amount of space System Restore uses on Windows 7, follow these steps:

1. Press WINDOWS KEY–BREAK to display the System window.
2. Click the System Protection link in the left pane to display the System Protection tab of the System Properties dialog box (shown on the left in Figure 2-7).

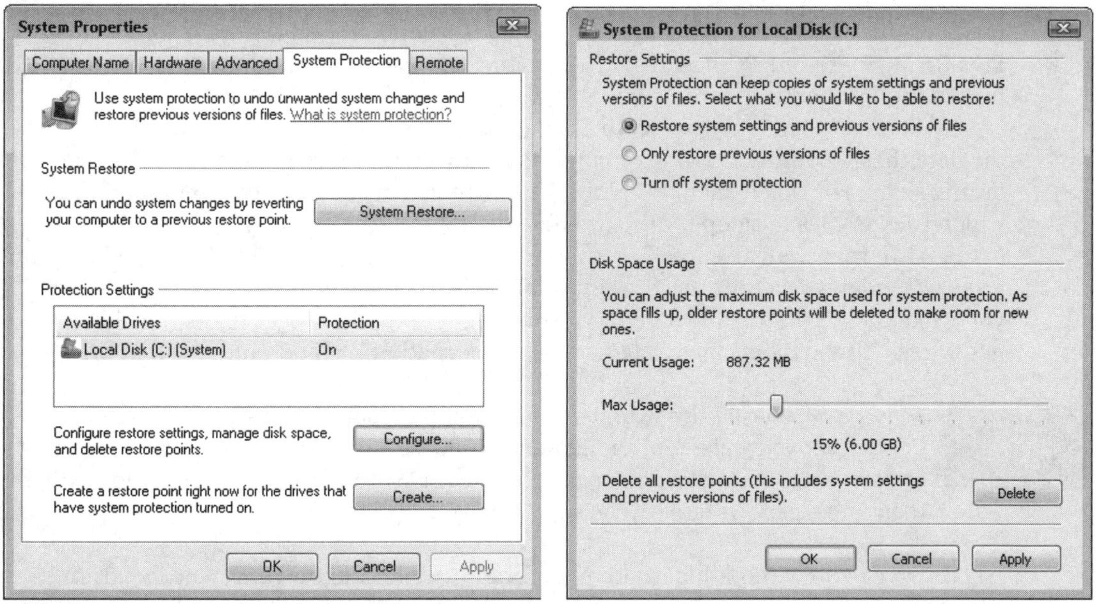

FIGURE 2-7 Click the Configure button on the System Protection tab of the System Properties dialog box (left) to display the System Protection dialog box (right). You can then drag the Max Usage slider to change the amount of space System Restore takes up on Windows 7.

3. If your PC has multiple drives, click a drive in the Available Drives list. If your PC has a single drive, it will be selected already.
4. Click the Configure button to display the System Protection dialog box for the drive (shown on the right in Figure 2-7).
5. In the Restore Settings area, make sure the Restore System Settings And Previous Versions Of Files option button is selected.

Note You can turn off System Restore for the drive by selecting the Turn Off System Protection option button in the Restore Settings box in the System Protection dialog box for the drive. But normally you'll want to use System Restore to protect your system settings and previous versions of files.

6. In the Disk Space Usage area, drag the Max Usage slider to set the maximum amount of space you want System Restore to be able to take.
7. Click the OK button to close the System Protection dialog box.
8. If your PC has multiple drives, repeat steps 3 through 7 for each drive for which you want to configure System Protection.
9. Click the OK button to close the System Properties dialog box.

Turn Off Hibernation

Just as bears wisely crawl into caves for the winter and sleep until spring has brought an abundant supply of foods, so too can your PC hibernate when energy is scarce (either for you or your PC) and then wake up when you or the PC is full of energy.

When your PC hibernates, it writes all the data that's currently in RAM to a file on the hard drive. This file, which is called the *hibernation file,* is the same size as your PC's RAM. So if your PC has 4GB of RAM and you use hibernation, there will be a 4GB hibernation file on the hard drive.

By contrast, when you put your PC to sleep, it keeps all the data in RAM. Holding the data there requires a trickle of power, so your PC's battery gradually gets used up during sleep. For this reason, Windows 7 uses a form of sleep called *hybrid sleep,* in which the PC goes to sleep for the first few hours, then automatically writes the data to the hard drive and goes into hibernation to stop using power. This is why, when you wake a Windows 7 PC after a short interval of sleep, it wakes up in a flash; but when you wake the PC after several hours of slumber, it takes far longer to resume, because it has to read all the hibernated data from the hibernation file and put it back in the RAM.

Note Windows XP doesn't use hybrid sleep. If you put your PC to sleep, it stays asleep until either you wake it or the power runs out. So if you're planning for your PC to have a nap for a day or longer, it's a good idea to put it into hibernation rather than into sleep. (Alternatively, shut it down altogether.)

If you can do without hibernation, you can turn it off to prevent Windows from taking this chunk of space. You can turn off hibernation on any version of Windows, but you're most likely to need to turn it off on Windows XP, simply because PCs running Windows XP are typically older and so have smaller hard drives than PCs running Windows 7.

Turn Off Hibernation in Windows XP

Windows XP lets you turn off hibernation through the user interface. To do so, follow these steps:

1. Choose Start | Control Panel to open a Control Panel window.
2. If Control Panel opens in Category view, with Pick A Category at the top, click the Switch To Classic View link in the Control Panel box in the upper-left corner to switch to Classic view.
3. Double-click the Power Options icon to display the Power Options Properties dialog box.
4. Click the Hibernate tab to display its contents (see Figure 2-8).
5. Clear the Enable Hibernation check box.

Note Look at the Disk Space For Hibernation box to see how much disk space is free and how much the hibernation file is taking up.

6. Click the OK button to close the Power Options Properties dialog box.
7. Click the Close button (the × button) to close the Control Panel window.

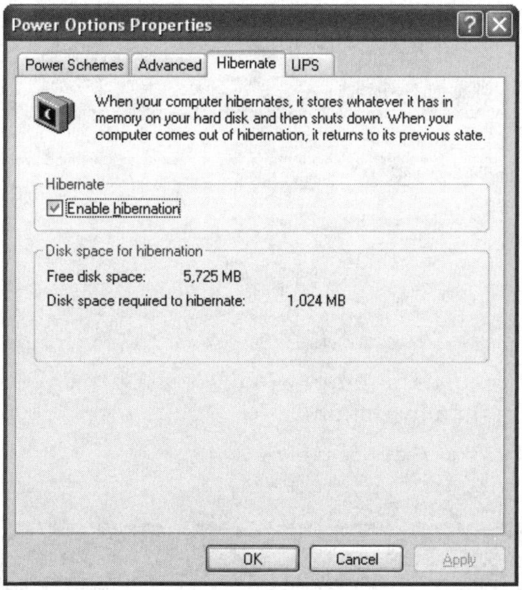

FIGURE 2-8 To turn off hibernation on Windows XP, clear the Enable Hibernation check box on the Hibernate tab of the Power Options Properties dialog box. The Disk Space For Hibernation box shows the amount of free disk space and how big the hibernation file is.

Turn Off Hibernation in Windows 7

Windows 7 doesn't provide a user interface control for turning off hibernation, so you have to use Command Prompt. Follow these steps:

1. Click the Start button to open the Start menu.
2. Type **cmd** in the Search box. You'll see the cmd item appear in the Programs list.
3. Right-click the cmd item to display the context menu, and then click Run As Administrator, as shown here. You do this to open what's called an *elevated command prompt*—a Command Prompt window that's running with Administrator privileges.
4. In the User Account Control dialog box that appears, as shown here, checking that you want to run the Windows Command Processor program, click the Yes button.

5. In the Command Prompt window that opens, type the following command, as shown in the illustration.

```
powercfg.exe /hibernate off
```

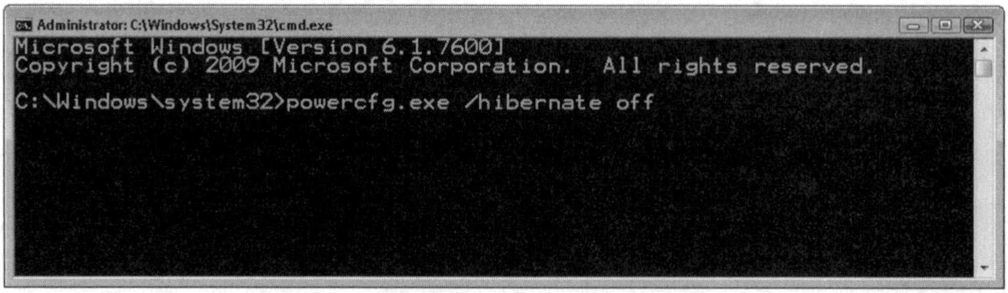

6. Press ENTER to run the command. The prompt appears again in the Command Prompt window, but that's the full extent of Windows' reaction.
7. Click the Close button (the × button) to close the Command Prompt window. (If you prefer, you can type the exit command and press ENTER instead.)

Note When you want to turn hibernation back on, repeat these steps but use the command **powercfg.exe /hibernate on** instead.

Reclaim Disk Space from the Recycle Bin

Another feature that Windows automatically gives part of your PC's hard drive to is the Recycle Bin. When you delete a file, Windows puts it into the Recycle Bin, and you can recover it until either you empty the Recycle Bin or the Bin overflows and Windows gets rid of its older contents automatically.

To give you this flexibility about recovering files, Windows XP automatically devotes 10 percent of the space on your hard drive to the Recycle Bin. You can reclaim some or all of this space easily. Windows 7 sets the Recycle Bin to a fixed size that is usually much less than 10 percent of the hard drive—but you may want to get back some of this space too.

Note The only disadvantage to reducing the size of the Recycle Bin is that fewer files will fit in it. Unless you tend to keep many files in the Recycle Bin and fish out items you threw away months ago, this is not usually a problem.

To reclaim disk space from the Recycle Bin, follow these steps:

1. Right-click the Recycle Bin icon on your Desktop, and then click Properties to display the Recycle Bin Properties dialog box. The left screen in Figure 2-9 shows the Recycle Bin Properties dialog box for Windows XP; the right screen in Figure 2-9 shows the Recycle Bin Properties dialog box for Windows 7.

Note If the Recycle Bin icon doesn't appear on your Desktop, you can access the Recycle Bin through Windows Explorer. In Windows XP, choose Start | My Computer, and then click the Up button on the toolbar of the My Computer window to display the Desktop folder. In Windows 7, choose Start | Computer to open a Computer window. In the Address box, click the right arrow to the left of Computer, and then click Desktop on the drop-down list. You can then right-click the Recycle Bin icon and click Properties on the context menu.

2. Change the Recycle Bin's maximum size:
   - **Windows XP** Select the Use One Setting For All Drives option button. Then drag the slider to set the percentage of the hard drive you want to give the Recycle Bin—for example, 5%.

Caution Unless your PC's hard drive is 10GB or less, give the Recycle Bin at least 1GB of space.

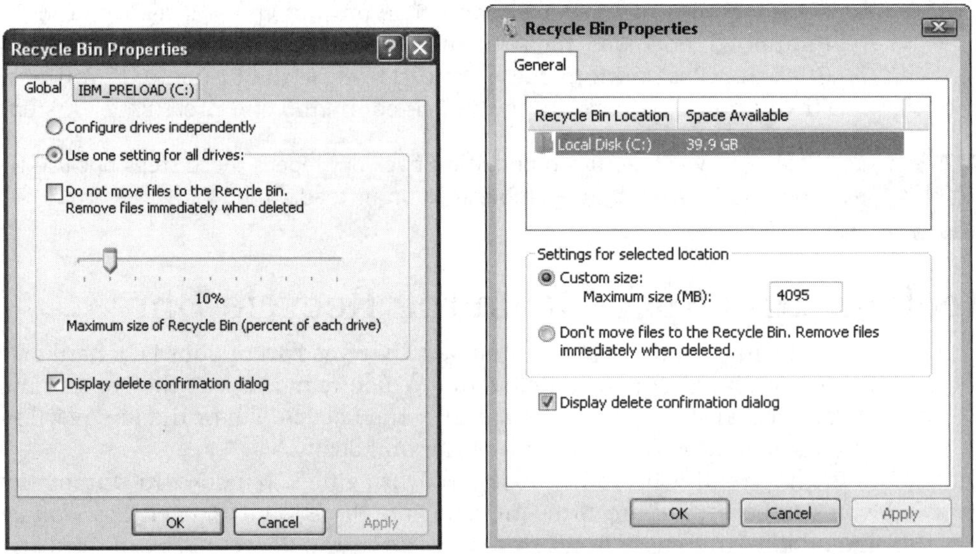

FIGURE 2-9 Use the Recycle Bin Properties dialog box to reduce the amount of space the Recycle Bin can consume on your PC's hard drive. The left screen shows the Recycle Bin Properties dialog box in Windows XP; the right screen shows the Recycle Bin Properties dialog box in Windows 7.

- **Windows 7** Make sure the Custom Size option button is selected. Then enter the number of megabytes in the Maximum Size text box. For example, enter **2048** if you want to give the Recycle Bin 2GB of space.

3. If you want to prevent Windows from confirming each deletion, clear the Display Delete Confirmation Dialog check box. Otherwise, leave this check box selected, as it is by default. The following illustration shows the Windows 7 version of the confirmation dialog box.

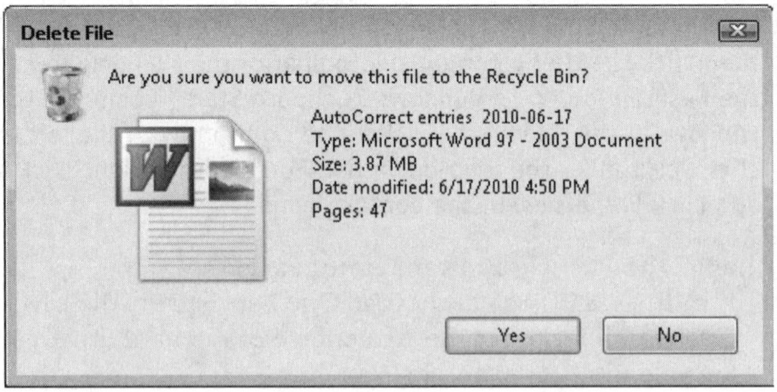

4. Click the OK button to close the Recycle Bin Properties dialog box.

Note If you want to stop using the Recycle Bin altogether, select the "Do Not Move Files To The Recycle Bin. Remove Files Immediately When Deleted" option button in the Recycle Bin Properties dialog box. With this option on, Windows deletes files immediately when you give the Delete command. Some people like this setting as a definite way of getting rid of files they no longer need, but it gives you no margin for error.

Reclaim Space from the Paging File

As you saw in Chapter 1, Windows uses a chunk of the hard drive for virtual memory—an area that it uses to supplement the RAM, the actual physical memory in your PC. Windows reserves this chunk of hard drive space, so it's not available to you, and puts the paging file on it.

As we discussed in Chapter 1, Windows requires virtual memory in order to run properly, and normally it's a good idea to give Windows as much virtual memory as it needs—between 1.5× and 2× the amount of RAM in the PC. But if you're strapped for hard drive space, you may want to reduce the amount of virtual memory available so that more space is available to you.

Caution Reclaim hard drive space from the paging file only as a short-term measure—for example, in order to keep enough free space to allow your PC's hard drive to run acceptably until you replace it with a larger drive. In the long term, you'll get better performance from giving Windows plenty of virtual memory as long as the hard drive can afford it.

To reclaim space from the paging file, set it to the same size as your PC's RAM. Follow these steps:

1. Follow the instructions in the section "Give Your PC More Virtual Memory" in Chapter 1 to open the Virtual Memory dialog box.
2. Select the Custom Size option button.
3. Enter the size equivalent to your PC's RAM in the Initial Size (MB) box and the Maximum Size (MB) box. For example, if your PC has 1GB of RAM, enter **1024** in each of these boxes.
4. Click the Set button to apply the size.
5. Click the OK button to close each of the dialog boxes in turn.

Remove Programs You Don't Need

One of the great things about PCs is the sheer number of programs you can install and run on them—anything from productivity tools such as office suites and graphics editors to time-sinks such as first-person-shooter games and instant-messaging programs.

One of the worst things about PCs is that most PCs, as a result, end up with many programs installed on them that the owner doesn't use. These useless programs not only take up hard disk space but can also make Windows unstable.

To streamline your PC and keep it running well, set aside an hour or two to strip out all the programs you don't use. When you're ready, proceed as described in the following sections. The first section covers Windows XP; the second section covers Windows 7.

Remove Programs on Windows XP

To remove programs from your PC on Windows XP, follow these steps:

1. Choose Start | Control Panel to open a Control Panel window.
2. If Control Panel opens in Category view, with Pick A Category at the top, click the Switch To Classic View link in the Control Panel box in the upper-left corner to switch to Classic view.
3. Double-click the Add Or Remove Programs icon to display the Add Or Remove Programs window. At first, the Change Or Remove Programs tab on the left is selected, as shown in Figure 2-10.

Note If your PC has many programs installed, it may take a minute or two to display the list in the Add Or Remove Programs window.

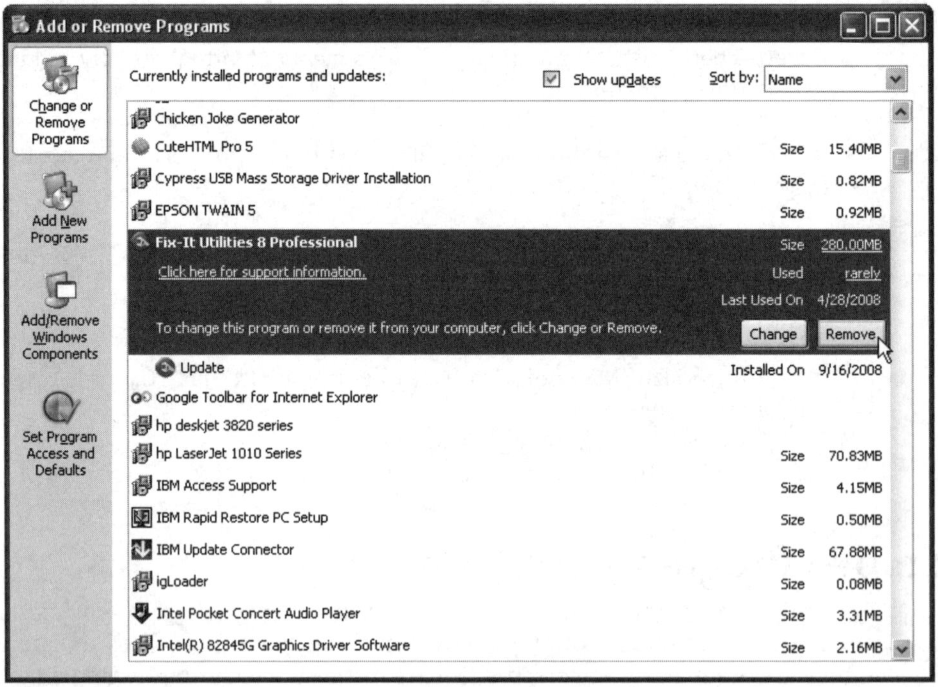

FIGURE 2-10 Use the Add Or Remove Programs window to remove programs you don't use from your Windows XP PC.

4. In the Currently Installed Programs And Updates list, click the program you want to remove.

Tip To see which programs you haven't used frequently, open the Sort By drop-down list and then click Date Last Used. The Sort By drop-down list also lets you sort by Name, by Size, and by Frequency Of Use.

5. Look at the Used readout to see how frequently you've used the program (for example, Rarely). Look also at the Last Used On readout to see when you last used it.
6. If you're sure you want to remove the program, click the Remove button. The Add Or Remove Programs dialog box (shown here) opens to confirm the removal.

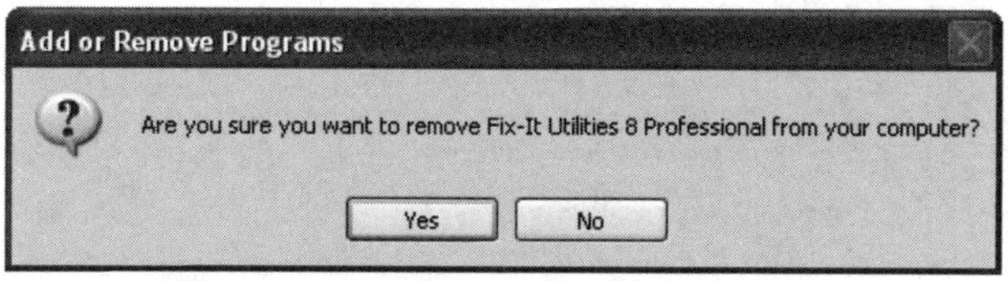

7. Click the Yes button. The uninstall routine begins. Normally, you'll see a progress readout, as in the example shown here.

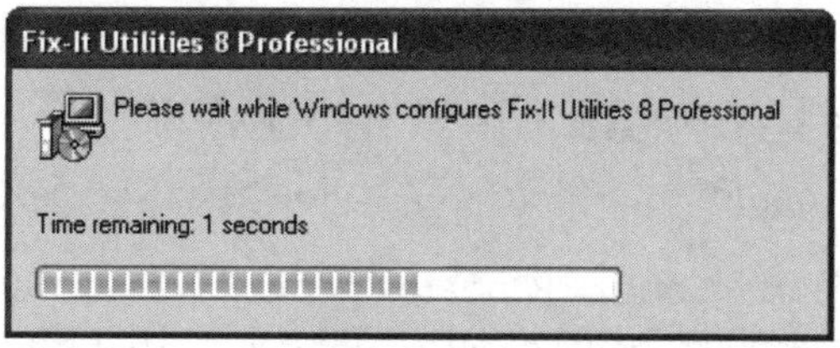

Note Some uninstall routines involve extra steps in addition to those shown here. This depends on the program's features and how its programmers designed it to uninstall.

8. If the uninstall routine prompts you to restart your PC, as shown here, click the Yes button.

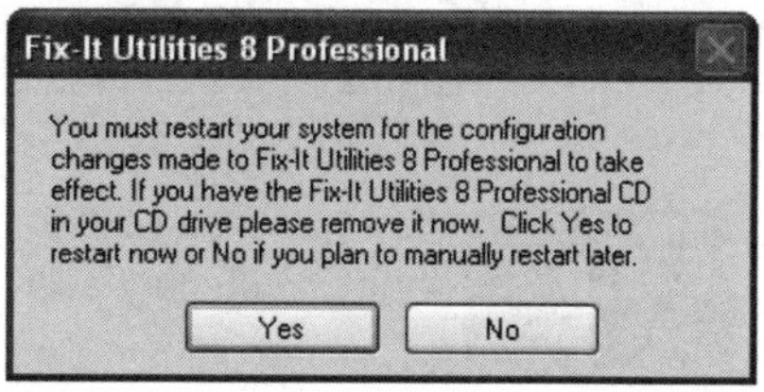

Note When you're removing multiple programs, you can click the No button to refuse a restart for the time being, remove other programs, and then restart Windows. But if you have the patience, it's better to restart after each removal that demands a restart. Restarting each time ensures that all the program's detritus has been dealt with successfully and that removing the program hasn't made Windows unstable.

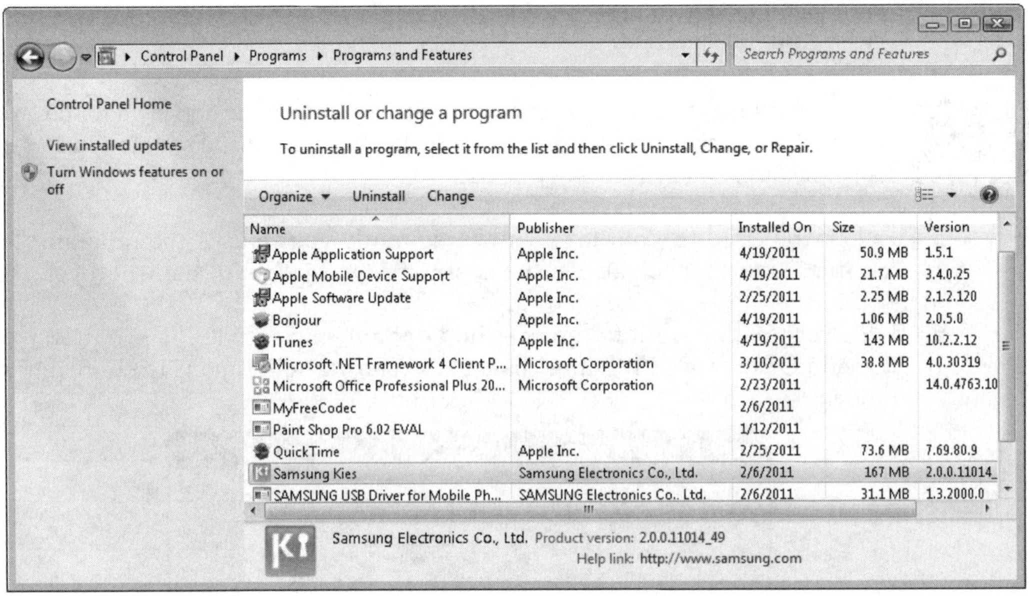

FIGURE 2-11 Use the Uninstall Or Change A Program screen in the Programs And Features window to remove a program from your Windows 7 PC.

Remove a Program on Windows 7

To remove a program on Windows 7, follow these steps:

1. Choose Start | Control Panel to open a Control Panel window.
2. Change the view if necessary. Make sure that Category is selected in the View By drop-down list in the upper-right corner of the Control Panel window.
3. Under the Programs heading, click the Uninstall A Program link to display the Programs And Features window with the Uninstall Or Change A Program screen displayed. Figure 2-11 shows the Uninstall Or Change A Program screen for Windows 7.

Tip You may need to drag the right border of the Programs And Features window to the right to display all the information you want to see about the programs.

4. Click the program you want to remove.
5. Click the Uninstall button to launch the uninstall routine. Usually, you'll see a confirmation dialog box such as the one shown here.

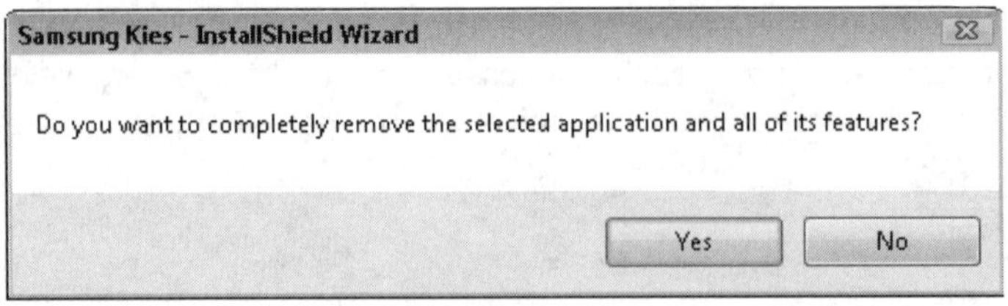

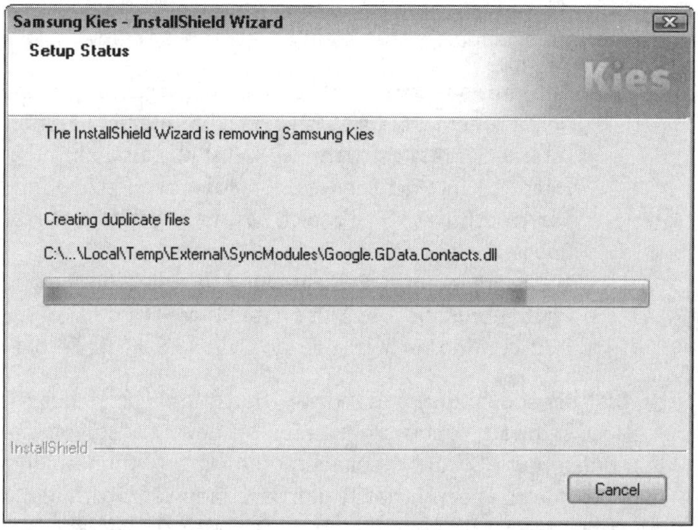

FIGURE 2-12 Most uninstall routines keep you informed about their progress.

Note Some programs have an Uninstall/Change button rather than a plain Uninstall button. Click this button to remove the program.

6. Normally, you'll see a progress readout, such as that shown in Figure 2-12, as the uninstall routine removes the program.
7. If the uninstall routine prompts you to restart your PC, click the Yes button or the Restart button.

Note When you're removing multiple programs, you can refuse a restart for the time being, remove other programs, and then restart Windows. But if you have the patience, it's better to restart after each removal that demands a restart. Restarting each time ensures that all the program's files and associations have been disposed of successfully and that removing the program hasn't made Windows unstable.

Identify and Remove Crapware from Your PC

Many new PCs come with many unwanted programs preinstalled. Some of these programs are free. Others are trial versions designed to get you to pay for the full version. All of them take up space on your PC and slow it down. People call these programs many names, but the most widely used name is *crapware*.

All crapware programs *can* be useful—but each program is likely to be useful to only a few of the people the PC manufacturer inflicts it on. The PC manufacturers claim they install crapware to provide useful software, but the real reason is that the software companies pay them to include it.

(Continued)

Here are examples of the main categories of crapware programs you'll meet:

- **Antivirus software** Trial versions of programs such as McAfee Antivirus, Norton Internet Security, and PC-cillin Internet Security
- **Internet-access software** AOL Install, Earthlink Setup files, Get High Speed Internet!, Internet Service Offers Launcher, NetZero Internet Access Installer
- **Search utilities** Dell Search Assistant, Dell URL Assistant, Google Desktop, Google Toolbar, Yahoo! Toolbar for Internet Explorer
- **Music programs** HP Rhapsody, MusicMatch Jukebox, Yahoo! Music Jukebox
- **Photo programs** MS Plus Photo Story, Picasa
- **DVD-burning software** Roxio MyDVD LE, Sonic RecordNow

That list should give you a taste—but it only scratches the surface of crapware.

Most crapware comes preinstalled on new PCs, so you can hardly avoid it. If you order your PC from the manufacturer rather than buying it from a store, you may be able to specify that it not have crapware installed. You will usually need to pay extra for this privilege, but it's worth the money.

Other crapware installs by default with software you've downloaded. So each time you install new software, clear the check boxes for any optional components you don't need.

You can use the regular techniques described in this chapter to remove crapware programs from your PC. But if your PC has a whole slew of crapware, you may be able to save time by using a dedicated crapware-removal tool. This is a good move, especially if you've just got a new PC and found it slow as a dog to boot.

One of the best crapware-removal tools is PC Decrapifier, shown here. You can download it for free from the PC Decrapifier website (www.pcdecrapifier .com/download). You don't even need to install it on your PC, as it runs from the distribution file.

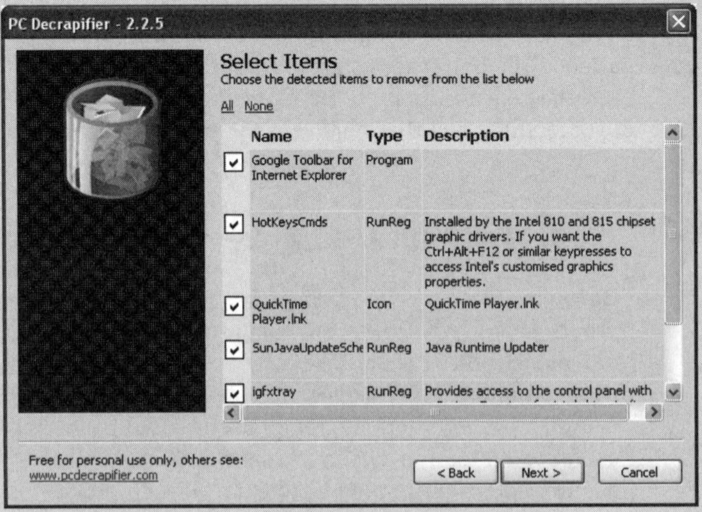

Archive Your Old Files

An obvious but highly effective means of clearing space on your PC's hard drive is to remove from it the files that you still need to keep but that you don't need to access frequently. For example, perhaps you have the last seven years of tax information on your PC but look at it only when April 15th is looming. If so, you could archive most of those years to an external drive or recordable disc and reclaim the space they're taking up.

Note You'll notice I'm doing you the courtesy of assuming that you've already deleted files you actually don't need at all. But if you haven't done that, now might be the time to have a good clear-out of your virtual closets.

The most straightforward way to archive your old files is to buy an external drive and simply move all your old files onto it using Windows Explorer. This is simple and effective, and you can use Windows' search features to find particular files when you find you need them.

But if you have a lot of files, you'll probably want to take a more nuanced approach, separating your files into different types (documents, photos, music, videos, and so on) by folder and keeping offsite copies of any mission-critical files—for example, on an online storage site.

Note Chapter 9 shows you the most effective way to back up files from your PC—and restore them to a different PC if necessary.

Add an External Hard Drive

When you need more space quickly, you can add an external hard drive to your PC.

Note Chapter 9 shows you how to replace your PC's internal hard drive.

Connect an External Drive

To connect an external drive, plug in the power supply if the drive has one. Then connect one end of the USB cable to the drive and the other to a USB port on your PC.

When you connect the drive, Windows detects it and loads the drivers for it. You'll see a sequence of pop-ups announcing what's happening. Figure 2-13 shows a typical sequence of pop-ups for Windows XP.

You can then choose Start | My Computer (on Windows XP) or Start | Computer (on Windows 7), and you'll see the external drive in the My Computer window or Computer window.

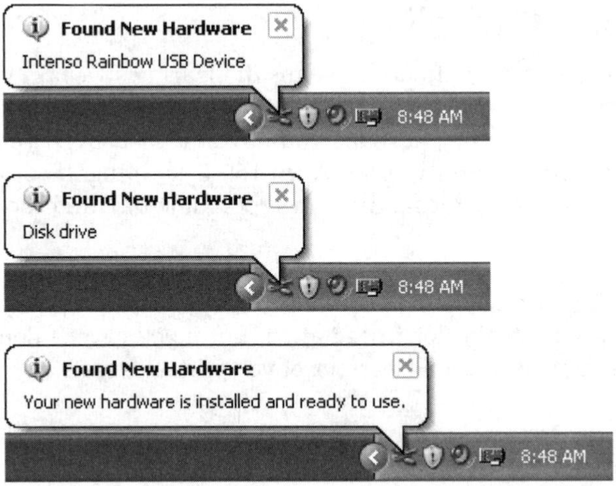

FIGURE 2-13 Windows detects a USB drive and automatically loads drivers for it. When you see the message that your new hardware is ready to use, you can begin using it.

Understand the Pros and Cons of External Hard Drives

Like most any technology, external hard drives have pros and cons you'll want to understand before you buy one.

These are the main advantages of external hard drives:

- **Easy to connect** Gone are the days when you had to choose between SCSI (pronounced "skuzzy"), FireWire, and other standards for external drives—and perhaps add an extra connector card for it. USB won the standards battle. These days, most external hard drives connect via USB, which has been built into all standard PCs for the last ten years. By contrast, internal hard drives use various different connection types—and they have different physical sizes.
- **Minimal installation required** Windows includes drivers for most USB drives. So when you connect a drive, Windows automatically loads the drivers required, and you can start using the drive without fuss.
- **Wide range of choices** So many USB drives are available that the problem is not finding a suitable drive but choosing from the plethora of drives.
- **Capacious** USB drives come in all sizes, up to 8TB (terabytes), giving you enough space to store a significant chunk of the Library of Congress.
- **Affordable** You can buy a 1TB drive for $50 or so, so you can easily add a huge amount of drive space to your PC.
- **Portable** You can easily move an external hard drive to another computer. This is great for transferring files or for changing from one PC to another.

(Continued)

All these advantages are great. But you'll want to be clear on the disadvantages of external hard drives too:

- **Noise** External drives tend to be much noisier than internal drives, especially if they have cooling fans. Look for a drive designed with a cooling case that includes radiator-style fins to dissipate the heat the drive creates.
- **Power supply** Many drives require their own power supply, which means finding room for another "wall-wart" power pack on a socket strip. Compact USB drives can run from USB ports (some drives use a single port, but others need two ports to deliver enough power), but these drives tend to have lower performance than drives that use a power supply.
- **Response time** Even though the USB system, or *bus,* is pretty fast, it's much slower than the bus inside your PC. So even the fastest USB drive transfers data much more slowly than your PC's internal hard drive. The USB external drive is also sharing the USB system with all the other USB devices you've plugged in, which can further slow down transfers.
- **Spin-up time** Most USB drives go to sleep automatically after a period of inactivity to save both electricity and wear to the drive. When you try to use the drive again, it takes a second or two to *spin up,* or start going again. You'll often hear a "whee-click" noise accompanying spin-up.

Format the Drive with NTFS if Necessary

Most external drives come formatted with the FAT32 file system, which Windows can use just fine, so you don't need to format them. But if you want to get the best performance, you can format the drive with the NT File System, or NTFS for short.

To reformat the external drive, take the following steps. The screen shows Windows XP, but the process is the same in Windows 7, with the one tiny exception noted.

1. Choose Start | My Computer on Windows XP to open a My Computer window, or choose Start | Computer on Windows 7 to open a Computer window.

Format Your External Drive with NTFS if You Use Large Files

If you work with large files, format your external drive with NTFS rather than FAT32. The maximum file size for FAT32 is 4GB—less than the size of a large movie file. By contrast, NTFS files can go up to the full size of the drive, minus a little overhead.

NTFS has other advantages over FAT32, including efficiency, performance, and tracking changes to files. You can also enable compression on the drive, which lets you store greater amounts of uncompressed files on the drive. But being able to store huge files tends to be the killer benefit.

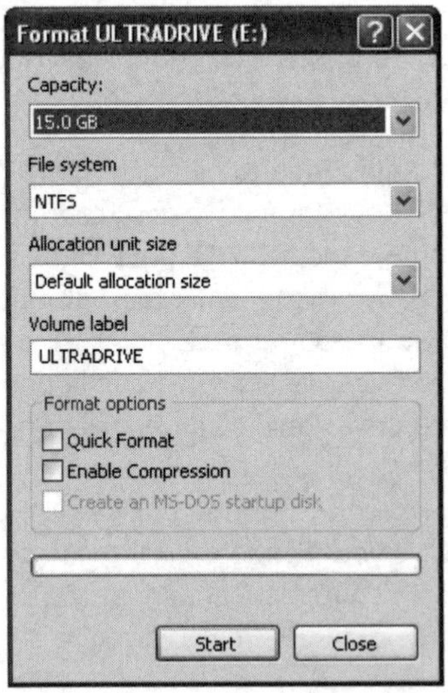

FIGURE 2-14 Use the Format dialog box to format an external drive with the NT File System (NTFS) if you need to put very large files on the drive.

2. Right-click the drive and choose Format from the context menu to display the Format dialog box. Figure 2-14 shows the Windows XP version of the Format dialog box with settings already chosen.
3. Make sure the Capacity drop-down list shows the correct capacity for the drive. Normally, Windows gets the capacity right and doesn't allow you to change it.
4. Open the File System drop-down list and choose NTFS.
5. In the Allocation Unit Size drop-down list, choose Default Allocation Size. This setting is normally selected by default. You can choose a specific block size here, but usually it's best to let Windows choose.
6. If you want to change the drive's name, type the new name over the current name in the Volume Label box.
7. In the Format Options box, make sure the Quick Format check box is cleared. A quick format doesn't fully erase all the data on the drive, so it's better to do a full format, even though it takes much longer.
8. On Windows XP, select the Enable Compression check box if you want to compress the data on the drive. Compressing the data enables you to pack in more uncompressed files, but it makes the drive perform more slowly—so choose your evil here.
9. Click the Start button to start the format. Windows displays the Format dialog box shown here to make sure you're prepared to erase all the data from the drive.
10. Click the OK button. Windows formats the drive and then displays the Formatting: Format Complete dialog box shown here.
11. Click the OK button to close the Formatting: Format Complete dialog box.
12. Click the Close button to close the Format dialog box. (The Close button replaces the Cancel button when the format finishes.)

3 Protect Your PC Against Attacks, Viruses, and Malware

To keep your PC healthy, you need to protect it against attacks, viruses, and other malware. In this chapter, I'll show you three moves you must make to keep your PC protected.

Your first move is to install all the latest patches and fixes that Windows needs to eliminate bugs and close off paths of attack. You can either set Windows to take care of these updates for you or handle them yourself.

Your second move is to install software that protects your PC against viruses, against other malicious software, and against attacks. There are many different types of protection software—some good, some bad, and some downright ugly. In this chapter, I'll show you the best free program for protecting a Windows PC. We'll get it, install it, configure it, and then use it to evict some malware.

Your third move is to turn on Windows Firewall, the protective barrier that helps keep network and Internet threats out of your PC. I'll show you how to turn on Windows Firewall and how to make sure that particular programs you need can get through the firewall.

Note In this chapter, I'm assuming that your PC has an Internet connection, because most people do these days. But because we can't discuss everything at once, we'll leave the details of Internet attacks on your PC to Part II of this book.

Let's get started.

Keep Windows Updated with the Latest Patches and Fixes

To keep your PC both in good shape and protected against attacks, malware, and viruses, you need to keep Windows updated with the latest patches and fixes that Microsoft provides. To help you do this, Windows includes a tool that not only can check automatically for updates but also install them automatically. This tool is called Automatic Updates on Windows XP and Windows Update on Windows 7. We'll start by making sure this tool is set up the way you want it.

Downloading and installing updates automatically is great for many people, but you may need to control when your downloads happen. Or you may prefer to decide exactly which updates you apply and which you duck. So I'll also show you how to check for Windows Updates manually and choose which ones to install.

You may also need to update Windows with a service pack, a big bundle of fixes. We'll look at how to do that in this section as well.

Set Windows Update to Download and Install the Latest Fixes

Your first move toward keeping your PC protected is to make sure Windows Update is set to download and to install the latest security fixes Microsoft releases.

Set Windows XP to Download and Install Updates

To set Windows XP to download and install updates, follow these steps:

1. Choose Start | Control Panel to open a Control Panel window.
2. If Control Panel opens in Category view, with Pick A Category at the top, click the Switch To Classic View link in the Control Panel box in the upper-left corner to switch to Classic view.
3. Double-click the Automatic Updates icon to display the Automatic Updates dialog box (see Figure 3-1).
4. Select the Automatic option button.

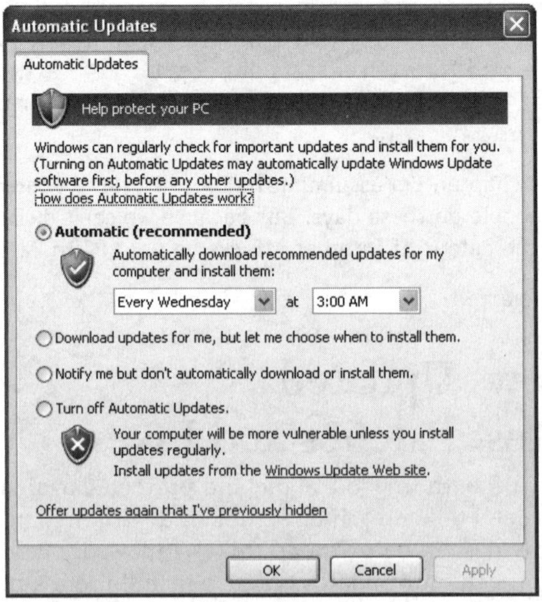

FIGURE 3-1 In the Automatic Updates dialog box, select the Automatic option button and then choose a schedule that suits you.

Why You Should Pick Wednesday Morning to Check for Updates

Security fixes fall into two broad categories: the few that are screamingly urgent, and all the rest.

When Microsoft fixes a high-priority problem, it releases the update as soon as it's available. You'll often read about these lights-and-siren updates online or in the newspapers, because the problems they're fixing are serious and affect many people.

For standard-priority and lower-priority updates, Microsoft groups them together and releases them on the second Tuesday of each month. Updates that fix problems are also called patches, so people call this day "Patch Tuesday."

To keep your PC protected, it's a good idea to download and install all relevant updates as soon as possible. So if you check for updates once a week, make it early on Wednesday morning. That way, you'll get the Patch Tuesday updates a few hours after Microsoft makes them available.

Choose Whether to Download and Install Updates Automatically

The Automatic Updates feature on Windows XP and the Windows Update feature on Windows 7 let you download updates automatically and install them automatically.

Normally, downloading the updates automatically is a good idea. When it's downloading updates, Windows uses a technology called *bandwidth throttling* to make sure it's not preventing other programs from using the Internet connection. Bandwidth throttling means that when Windows detects other programs using the Internet connection, it reduces its download speed so that it's not using the whole connection. When the connection is otherwise inactive, it lets rip, so that it gets the updates as soon as possible.

The main exception is if you need to run your downloads at a particular time rather than when Windows discovers updates are available. For example, if you have a slow connection at home but can get a fast connection at the local coffee shop, you may prefer to get your updates with your latte.

Installing the updates automatically is often a good idea—but with greater reservations than about downloading them. The problem is that, after some updates, Windows must restart to get everything working again. So if you allow Windows to install updates, you must save all your open documents before leaving your PC on nights when Windows will check for updates. If you set Windows to check for updates every day, this is easy enough to remember. But if you opt for weekly checking, it's easy to forget. You may find it easier to install updates manually at a time that suits you.

After Windows installs updates, it displays a pop-up balloon in the notification area to let you know. The example shown here is from Windows 7. Otherwise, the process can be so seamless that you hardly notice.

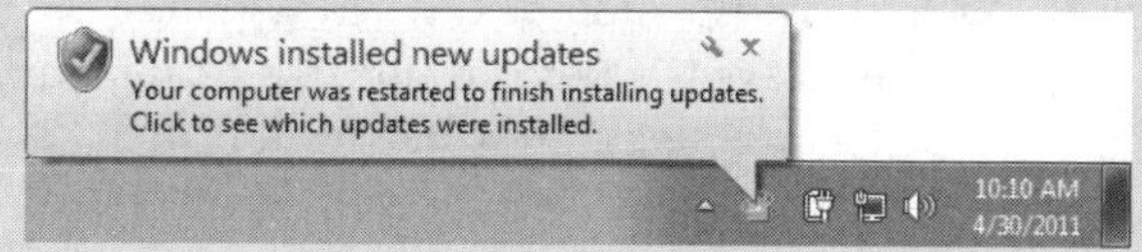

5. Use the two drop-down lists to choose how often and when Windows checks for updates:
   - **First drop-down list** Choose Every Day if you want to check every day. If you prefer to check once a week, choose Every Sunday, Every Monday, Every Tuesday, Every Wednesday, Every Thursday, Every Friday, or Every Saturday. As mentioned in the nearby sidebar, Every Wednesday is the best choice for getting updates quickly.
   - **Second drop-down list** Choose the hour—for example, 3:00 A.M.

Note Windows Update can wake your PC from sleep to get updates, so you can set a time in the dead hours of the morning as the time to check for updates even if you put your PC to sleep at night. But if you turn your PC off at night, Windows can't get the updates.

6. Click the OK button to close the Automatic Updates dialog box.

Set Windows 7 to Download and Install Updates

To set Windows 7 to download and install updates, follow these steps:

1. Choose Start | Control Panel to open a Control Panel window.
2. If the Control Panel window opens in Category view, open the View By drop-down list and click Small Icons.
3. Click the Windows Update link to display the Windows Update window in Control Panel (see Figure 3-2).

Note If the Windows Update window shows a red shield with a cross on it and a message telling you to turn on automatic updating, click the Turn On Automatic Updates button. Windows Update then checks for updates.

4. In the left column, click the Change Settings link to display the Change Settings screen (see Figure 3-3).
5. Open the Important Updates drop-down list and choose the Install Updates Automatically item.

How to Get to Windows Updates You've Hidden on Windows XP

If you've chosen to hide any of Windows XP's updates rather than install them, you can get them back. To do so, click the Offer Updates Again That I've Previously Hidden link in the Automatic Updates dialog box. When Windows displays the Restore Updates dialog box (shown here), click the Yes button.

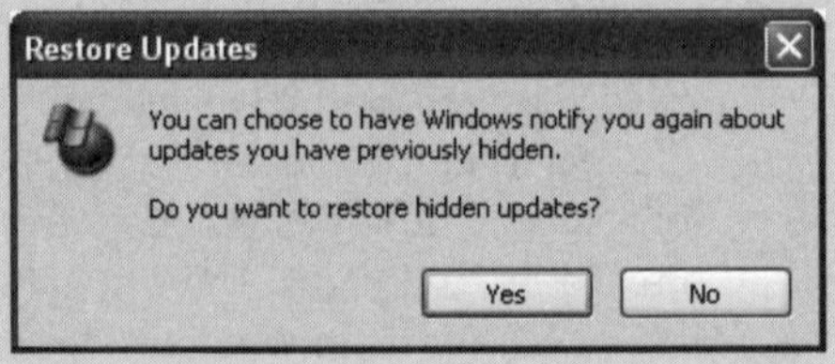

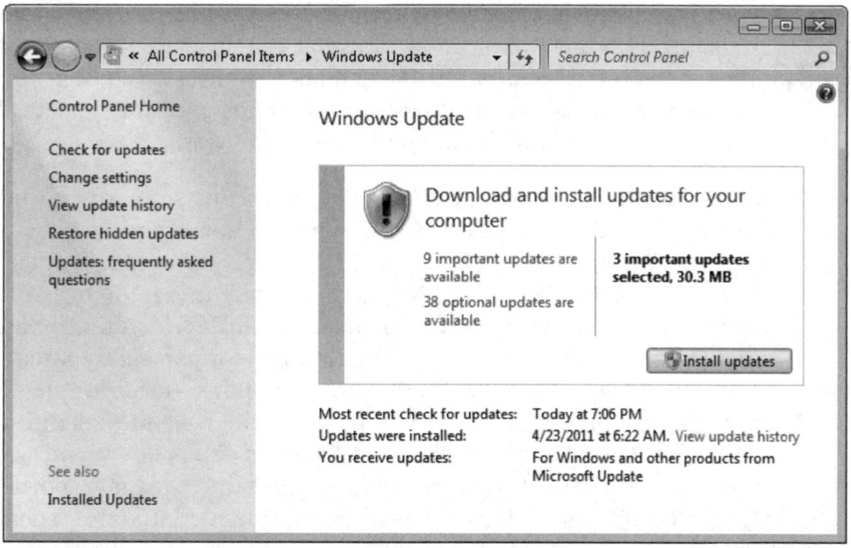

FIGURE 3-2 In the Windows Update window, click the Change Settings link in the left column to display the Change Settings screen.

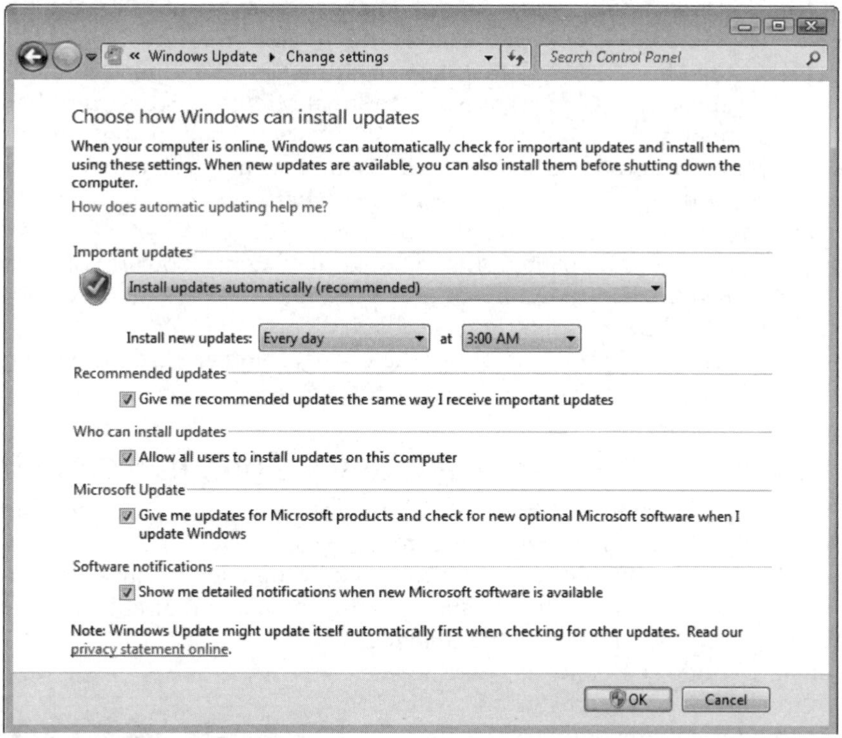

FIGURE 3-3 On the Change Settings screen, choose how Windows Update should run on Windows 7.

Note If you want Windows Update to download updates but let you decide which to install, click the Download Updates But Let Me Choose Whether To Install Them item in the Important Updates drop-down list. If you want to control the downloading as well as the installation, click the Check For Updates But Let Me Choose Whether To Download And Install Them item.

6. If you selected the Install Updates Automatically item, open the Install New Updates drop-down list and choose when to install the updates. Choose Every Day if you want to check every day. If you prefer to check once a week, choose Every Sunday, Every Monday, Every Tuesday, Every Wednesday, Every Thursday, Every Friday, or Every Saturday. As mentioned in the nearby sidebar, Every Wednesday is the best choice for getting updates quickly.
7. Open the At drop-down list and choose the hour—for example, 2:00 A.M.
8. In the Recommended Updates area, select the Give Me Recommended Updates The Same Way I Receive Important Updates check box if you want Windows Update to treat recommended updates the same way as important updates. Generally, it's a good idea to install recommended updates, so you'll probably want to select this check box.
9. In the Who Can Install Updates area, select the Allow All Users To Install Updates On This Computer check box if you want all users to be able to run Windows Update and install the updates. If you're in favor of getting Windows Updates quickly, select this check box. If you want to vet each available update yourself to decide whether to install it, clear this check box.
10. In the Microsoft Update area, select the Give Me Updates For Microsoft Products And Check For New Optional Microsoft Software When I Update Windows check box if you want Windows Update to check for updates to Microsoft products. These updates are less necessary than Windows updates, but your PC's software is likely to run better if you get them.
11. In the Software Notifications area, select the Show Me Detailed Notifications When New Microsoft Software Is Available check box if you want Windows Update to display details of new versions of Microsoft software. This may be helpful, but it's not strictly necessary.
12. Click the OK button to apply the changes you've made to Windows Update. The Windows Update screen appears again.

Check for and Install Windows Updates Manually

If you choose not to let Windows install updates automatically, you can install them manually as described in this section.

If you've set Windows Update to check for updates, it will alert you automatically when updates are available, as shown here. You can either click the message balloon to jump right into installing the updates or start Windows Update as described in the following sections when you're ready to install the updates.

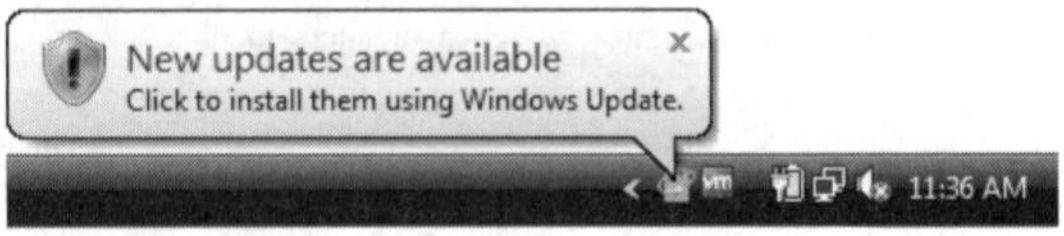

Check for and Install Windows Updates Manually on Windows XP

To check for and install Windows updates manually on Windows XP, follow these steps:

1. Choose Start | Control Panel to open a Control Panel window.
2. If Control Panel opens in Category view, with Pick A Category at the top, click the Switch To Classic View link in the Control Panel box in the upper-left corner to switch to Classic view.
3. Double-click the Automatic Updates icon to display the Automatic Updates dialog box (shown in Figure 3-1, earlier in this chapter).
4. Click the Windows Update Web Site link near the bottom of the dialog box. Windows launches your web browser (for example, Internet Explorer) and displays the Welcome page on the Microsoft Update website (see Figure 3-4).
5. Click the Express button to get the Express Results list, which shows high-priority updates your PC needs (see Figure 3-5).
6. Read through the list to see what you're installing. Click the + sign to the left of an item to expand the detail for an item.
7. Click the Install Updates button to install the updates.
8. If the Installing Updates dialog box tells you that you must restart your computer to make the updates take effect (see Figure 3-6), click the Restart Now button.

After Windows restarts and you log in, you can resume work (or play) as normal.

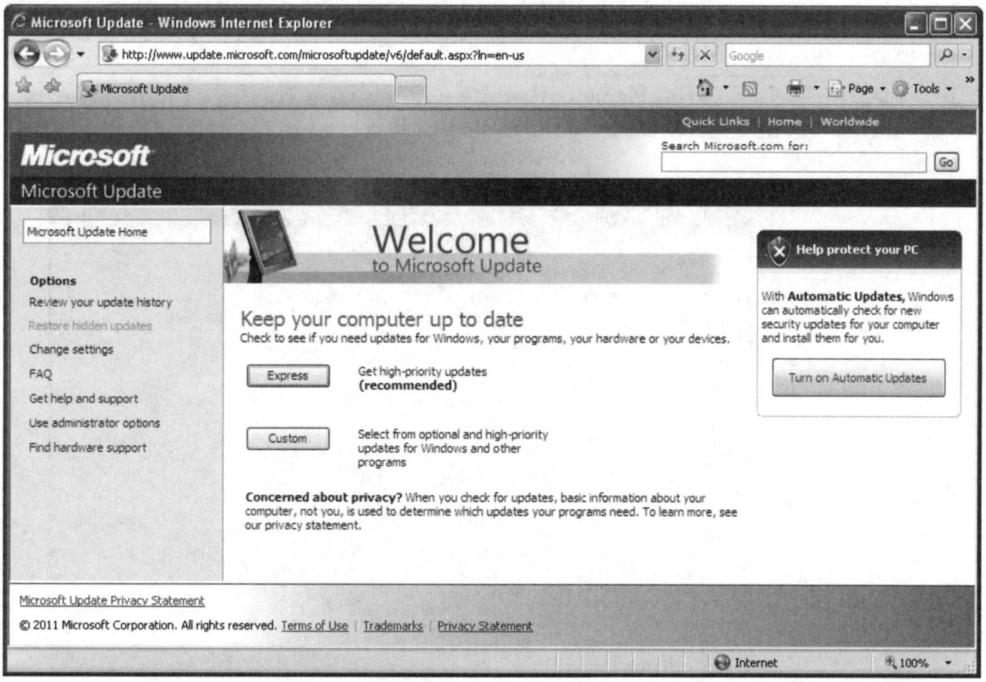

FIGURE 3-4 On the Welcome page of the Microsoft Update website, click the Express button to quickly install high-priority updates.

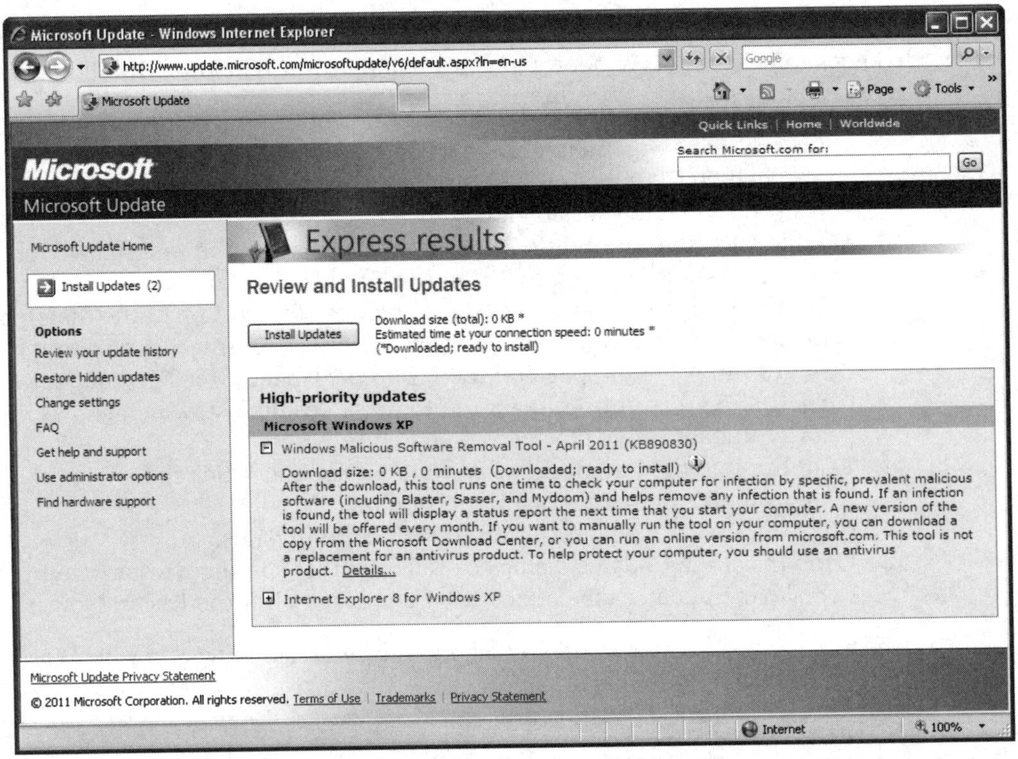

FIGURE 3-5 On the Express Results page, review the list of high-priority updates and then click the Install Updates button if you want to install them.

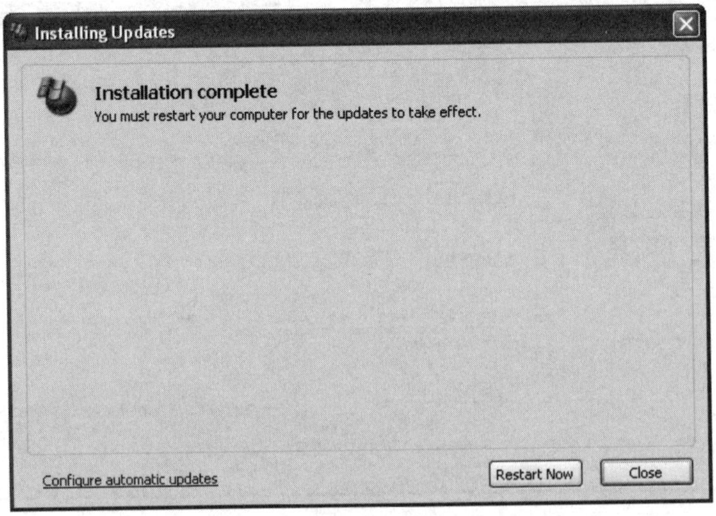

FIGURE 3-6 After installing updates to Windows, you may need to restart your PC.

Check for and Install Windows Updates Manually on Windows 7

To check for and install Windows updates manually on Windows 7, follow these steps:

1. Choose Start | Control Panel to open a Control Panel window.
2. Switch to viewing icons by opening the View By drop-down list and clicking either Large Icons or Small Icons.
3. Click the Windows Update link to display the Windows Update screen in Control Panel.
4. Click the Check For Updates link in the left column to get the very latest updates (see Figure 3-7).
5. Windows Update displays a summary of the updates it has found (see Figure 3-8).
6. Click the Install Updates button to start installing the updates. If you want to install only some updates, see the sidebar titled "Choose Which Updates to Install."
7. If Windows Update displays a Software License dialog box (Figure 3-9 shows an example), read the terms and then select the I Accept The License Terms option button if you want to install the update. Then click the Finish button.

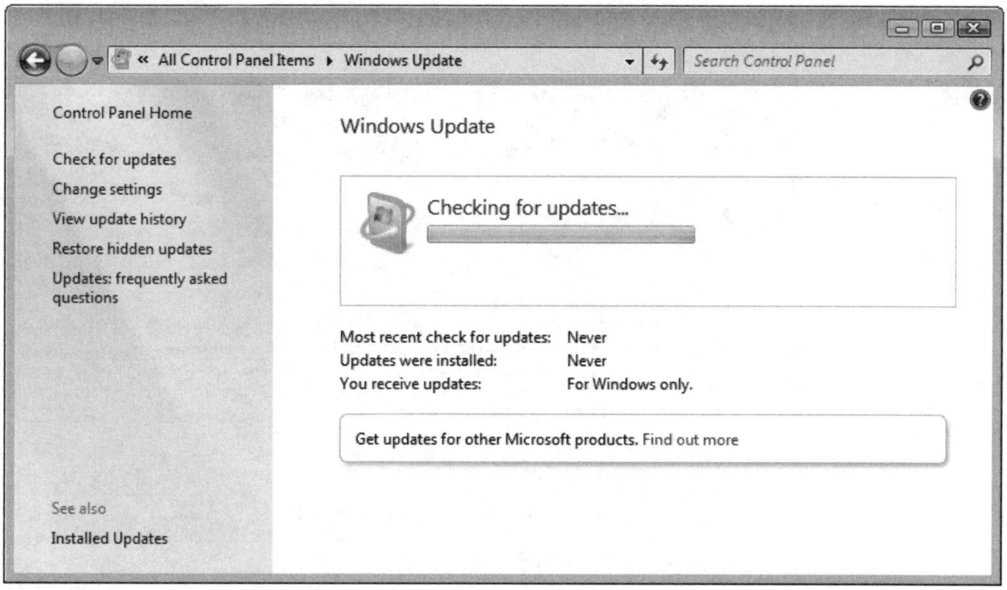

FIGURE 3-7 Even if Windows is set to download updates automatically for you, it's worth checking for the latest updates before installing updates manually to make sure you update your PC as fully as possible.

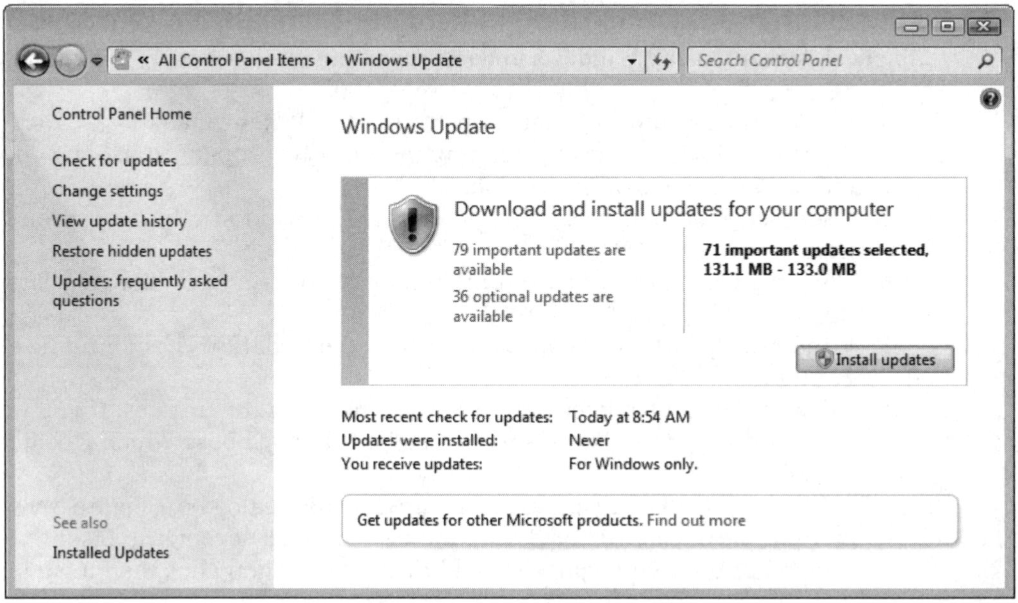

FIGURE 3-8 After Windows Update finds updates, you can either install them all by clicking the Install Updates button or choose which updates to install by clicking the Important Updates link or the Optional Updates link.

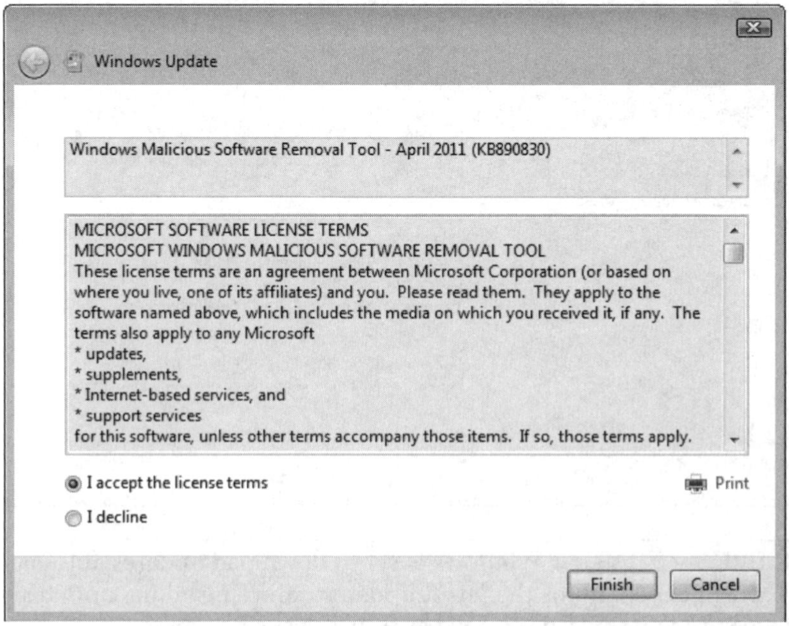

FIGURE 3-9 For some updates, you need to accept the Software License.

FIGURE 3-10 The Windows Update window shows you how the updates are progressing.

8. Windows Update shows you its progress as it installs the updates (see Figure 3-10).
9. If Windows Update prompts you to restart your computer, as shown here, click the Restart Now button as soon as is convenient. If you need to finish up your work before restarting, choose 10 Minutes, 1 Hour, or 4 Hours in the Remind Me In drop-down list, and then click the Postpone button.

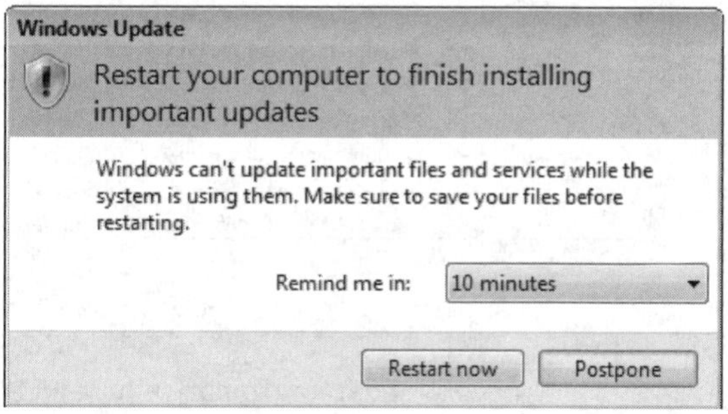

Update Windows to the Latest Service Pack

The fixes and patches you get via Windows Update are great, but if you've been coasting along without updating your PC, you may need to apply an entire service pack to get it up to date.

A *service pack* is simply a giant bundle containing a whole slew of recent updates for an operating system. At this writing (Summer 2011), the versions of Windows this book covers have reached the following service packs:

- **Windows XP** Service Pack 3
- **Windows 7** Service Pack 1

Choose Which Updates to Install

Usually, it's best to install all the updates Windows marks as important. The easiest way to do this is to click the Install Updates button in the Windows Update window.

If you want to choose which updates to install, click the Important Updates link. Windows Update displays the Select Updates To Install window with the Important tab at the front, as shown here.

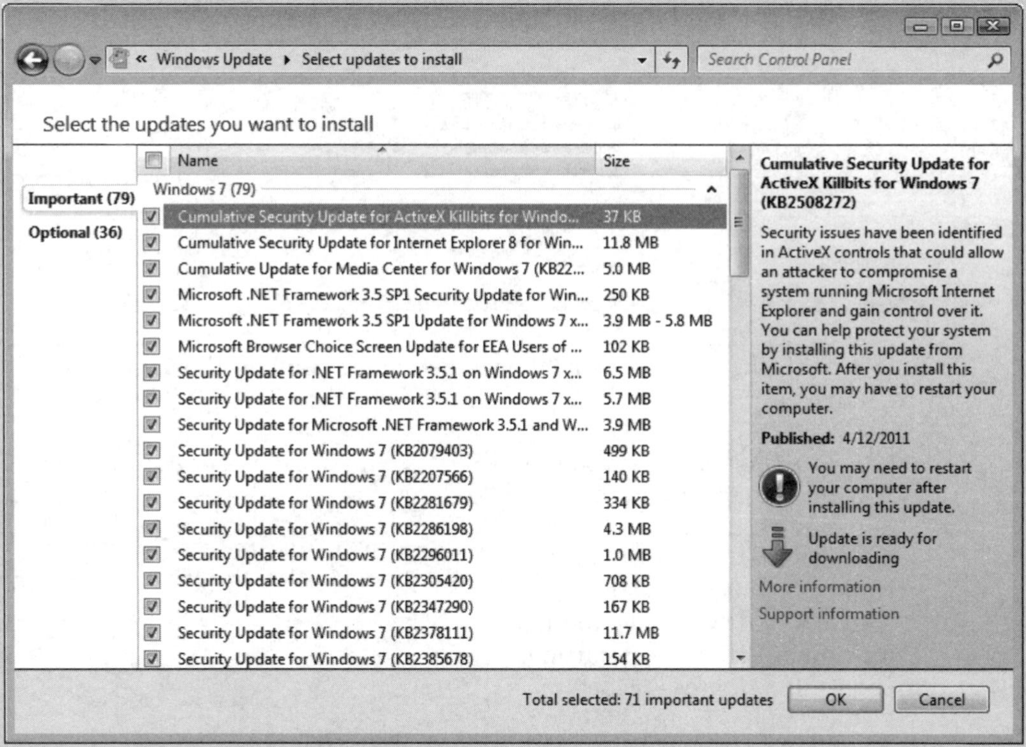

Windows Update automatically selects the check box for each update on the Important tab. Clear the check box for any update you don't want to install. To see what an update involves, click the update and then look at the right pane.

If you want to look at the list of optional updates to see if any look helpful to you, click the Optional tab. Windows Update leaves these check boxes cleared, so you need to select the check box for any update you want to install.

Many of the optional updates are language packs—Arabic Language Pack, Bulgarian Language Pack, Croatian Language Pack, and so on. You don't need to install these unless you (or other people) use these languages on your PC.

When you've selected the updates to install, click the OK button to return to the Windows Update window. Then click the Install Updates button to install the updates you chose.

Windows Update can download service packs for you, but because the service packs are typically several hundred megabytes apiece, you may find it more convenient to download them separately. Or, if someone you know has downloaded the service pack you need, you can get them to put a copy on a CD or a USB thumb drive and spare you the download.

This section walks you through the process of installing Service Pack 3 on Windows XP. The process of installing service packs on Windows 7 is similar, but the details vary.

After you get the service pack, set aside an hour or so to install it. Close all the programs you're running and then double-click the distribution file.

Note If Windows Update downloads the service pack for you, it may launch the installation as well. If so, that's fine—there's just so much less for you to do.

First, you'll see the service pack extract its files, as shown in the next illustration. Then, when the installation wizard opens, click the Next button to start the installation. Figure 3-11 shows the Software Update Installation Wizard, which is the wizard for installing service packs on Windows XP.

Next, you'll see the License Agreement, to which you must agree if you want to install the service pack. After you clear this hurdle, the Software Update Installation Wizard displays the Select Options screen (see Figure 3-12).

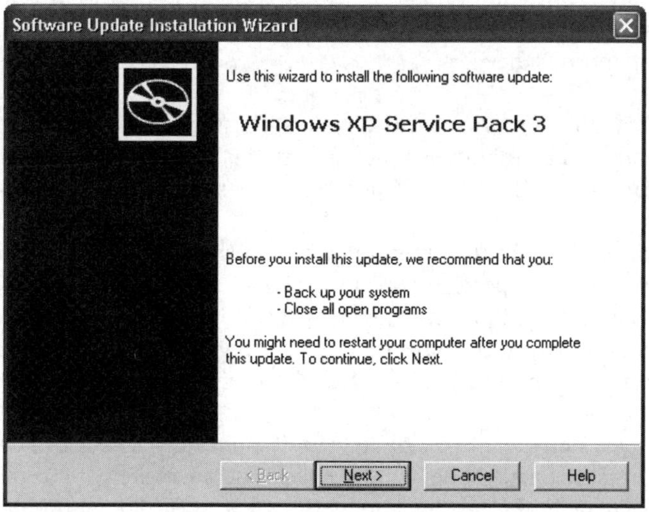

FIGURE 3-11 In the Software Update Installation Wizard, click the Next button to start the installation.

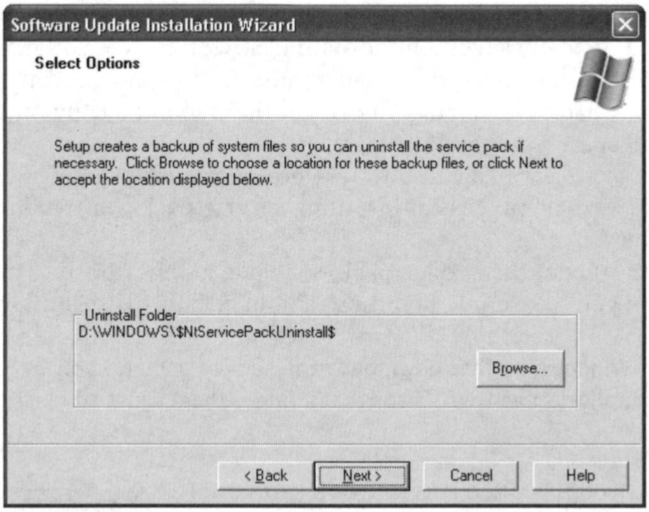

FIGURE 3-12 On the Select Options screen of the Software Update Installation Wizard, you can change the folder in which the wizard creates a backup of system files in case you need to uninstall the service pack.

On the Select Options screen, you can choose the folder in which the wizard stores backup copies of system files so that it can restore them if you uninstall the service pack. The default location, a folder with a name such as $NtServicePackUninstall$ in your PC's Windows folder, is fine unless your PC's main hard drive has less than 1GB free. If so, click the Browse button and use the Browse For Folder dialog box to pick a folder on another drive.

Caution Installing a service pack can consume as much as 1GB of space on your hard drive. Part of the problem is that the installer backs up the files it replaces so that you can restore them later if necessary. These files can take 500MB or more.

Click the Next button when you've chosen the folder, and the update runs—or walks, or crawls, depending on how frisky your PC is feeling. Don't work on your PC while it's updating; just give the wizard time to do its work.

When the wizard displays the Completing The Windows XP Service Pack Installation Wizard screen (see Figure 3-13), click the Finish button. Your PC then restarts.

Note If you don't want to restart your PC right now, select the Do Not Restart Now check box and then click the Finish button. When you've taken care of whatever is delaying the restart, choose Start | Turn Off Computer and then click Restart to restart your PC.

FIGURE 3-13 Click the Finish button to close the Software Update Installation Wizard when it finishes installing the service pack.

Protect Your PC with Microsoft Security Essentials

To keep your PC protected against viruses, spyware, and other malware, you must install security software.

As you'll know if you've watched TV or read a newspaper anytime in the last five years, you can get a vast number of different security programs. Some are free; others are short-term trial versions designed to open your wallet for a full version; and others cost top dollar straight out of the box and wrap Windows up so tightly in various security mechanisms that your PC can hardly breathe, let alone run.

If you're looking to protect your PC without paying through the nose, you have several options. At this writing, your best bet is Microsoft Security Essentials, a security program from Microsoft. Not only is Microsoft Security Essentials free, but (as you're aware) Microsoft knows Windows inside out, has painfully intimate knowledge of the threats Windows faces, and has a strong interest in keeping malicious software out of Windows.

Note If your PC already has other antivirus software installed and running, and you are happy with it, you don't need to install Microsoft Security Essentials. If you do want to install Microsoft Security Essentials, you must disable your current antivirus software.

Get and Install Microsoft Security Essentials

To get and install Microsoft Security Essentials, follow these steps. This example shows Windows XP, but the steps on Windows 7 are the same, apart from the details of the user interface.

1. Open your web browser.
2. Go to www.microsoft.com/security_essentials.
3. Click the download link to display the Download Microsoft Security Essentials window (shown here).

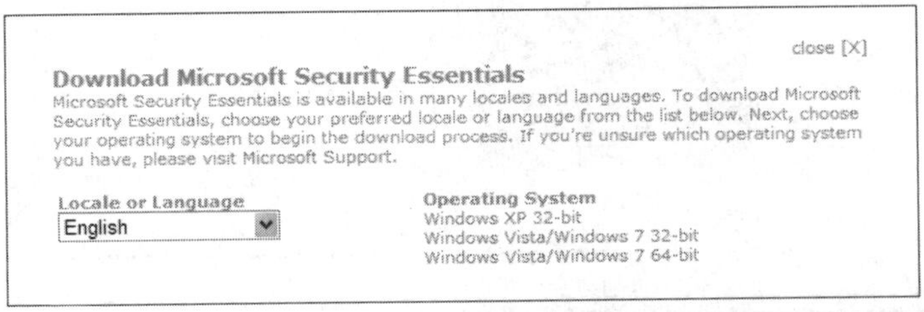

4. In the Locale Or Language drop-down list, choose your locale or language—for example, English.
5. In the Operating System area, click the link for the operating system you're using. In this example, I clicked the Windows XP 32-Bit link. The File Download – Security Warning dialog box appears, as shown here.

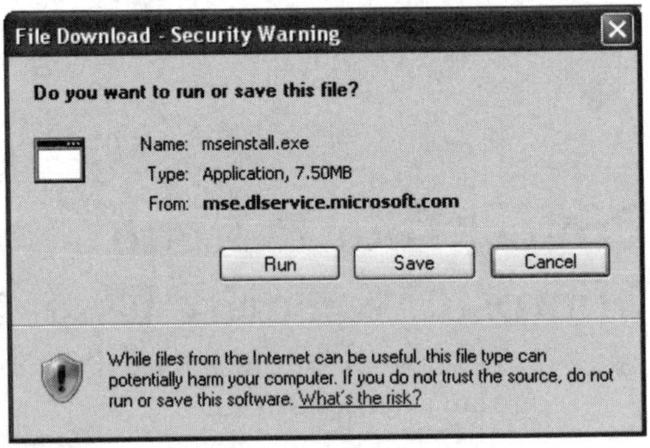

6. Click the Run button to run the installer from the download file. You'll then see the Download dialog box as the browser completes the download.
7. When the download finishes, Internet Explorer displays the Internet Explorer – Security Warning dialog box, shown here.

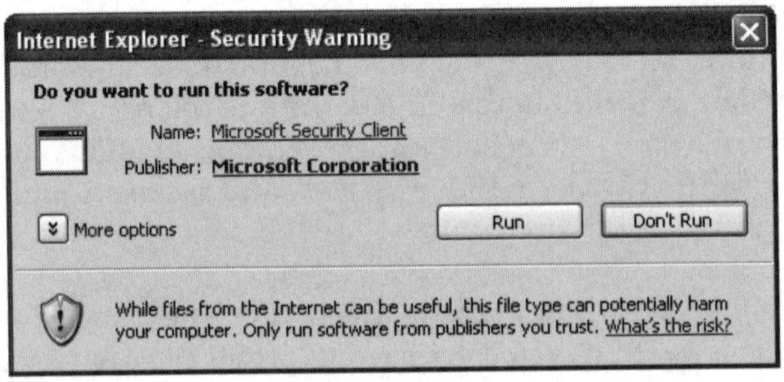

8. Make sure the Name says Microsoft Security Client and the Publisher appears as Microsoft Corporation.
9. Click the Run button. The installer displays the Welcome To The Microsoft Security Essentials Installation Wizard screen (see Figure 3-14).
10. Click the Next button to display the Microsoft Security Essentials Software License Terms screen.
11. Read the terms (or click the Print button to print them if you'd prefer a hard copy), and then click the I Accept button if you want to proceed.
12. On the Join The Customer Experience Improvement Program screen, select the Join The Customer Experience Improvement Program option button or the I Do Not Want To Join The Program At This Time option button, as appropriate.
13. Click the Next button to display the Optimize Security screen (see Figure 3-15).
14. Select the If No Firewall Is Turned On, Turn On Windows Firewall check box.
15. Click the Next button. The wizard displays the Ready To Install Microsoft Security Essentials screen.
16. Click the Install button. The installation runs, and the Completing The Microsoft Security Essentials screen then appears (see Figure 3-16).
17. Make sure the Scan My Computer For Potential Threats After Getting The Latest Updates check box is selected.
18. Click the Finish button. The wizard closes.

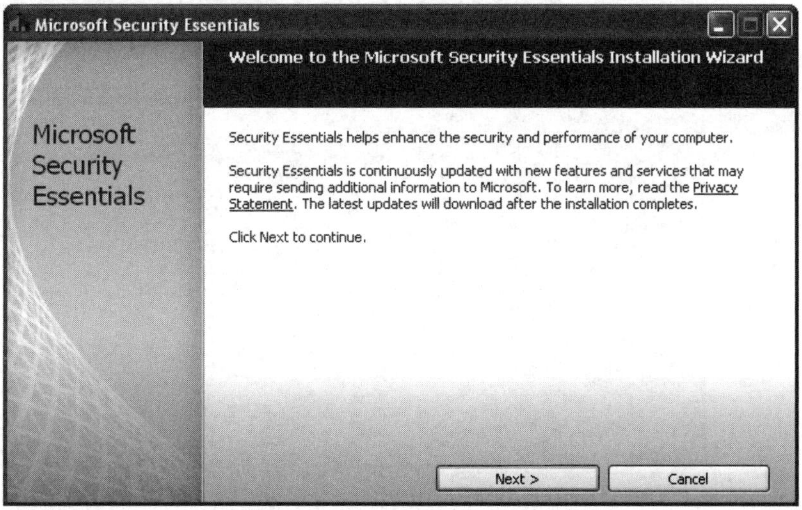

FIGURE 3-14 Follow through the steps of the Microsoft Security Essentials Installation Wizard to install Microsoft Security Essentials.

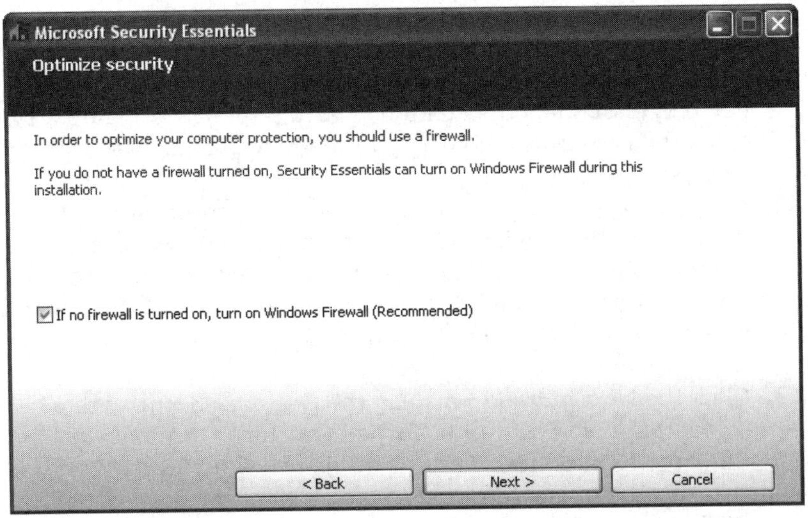

FIGURE 3-15 On the Optimize Security screen of the Microsoft Security Essentials Installation Wizard, select the If No Firewall Is Turned On, Turn On Windows Firewall check box.

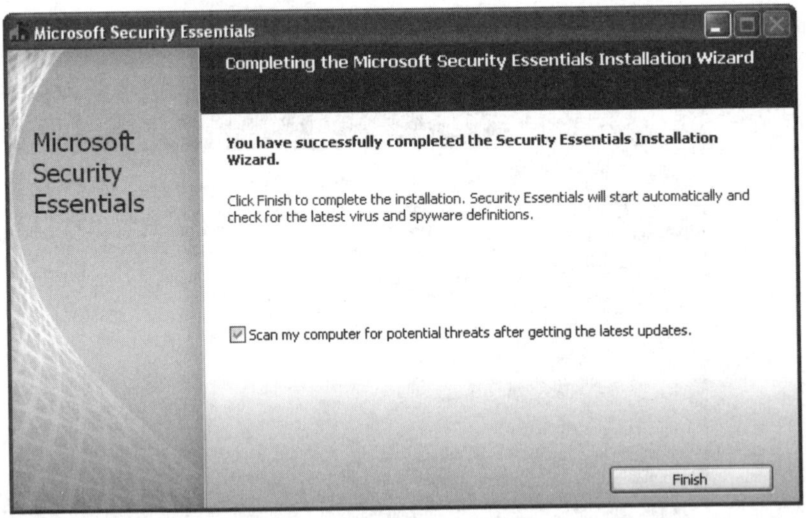

FIGURE 3-16 On the Completing The Microsoft Security Essentials Installation Wizard screen, select the Scan My Computer For Potential Threats After Getting The Latest Updates check box and then click the Finish button.

Keep Microsoft Security Essentials Updated with the Latest Virus Information

After the Microsoft Security Essentials Installation Wizard closes, Microsoft Security Essentials starts downloading any available updates (see Figure 3-17). The updates include information that enables Microsoft Security Essentials to identify the latest viruses and malware.

Note You can update Microsoft Security Essentials at any point by displaying the Update tab and then clicking the Update button on it.

After the update finishes, Microsoft Security Essentials starts scanning your PC, as described in the next section.

Scan Your PC for Threats

After updating itself, Microsoft Security Essentials automatically scans your PC for threats. You'll see a progress indicator while the scan runs (see Figure 3-18).

If Microsoft Security Essentials finds something it doesn't like, it displays a yellow icon with an exclamation point at the bottom of the window. We'll look at how to review and eliminate threats in the next section.

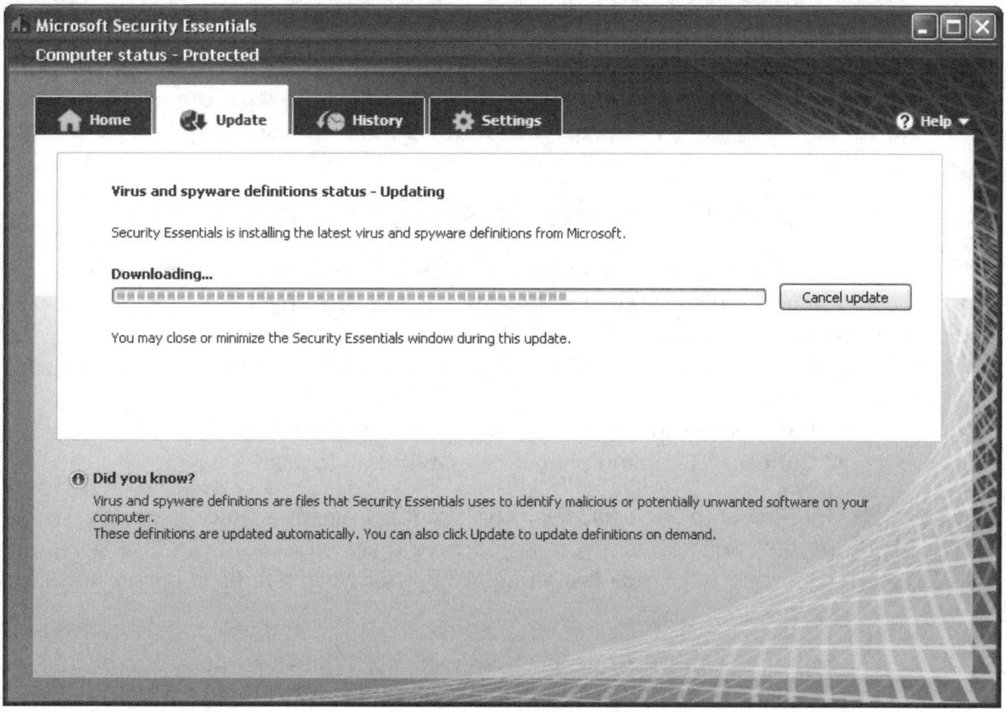

FIGURE 3-17 Microsoft Security Essentials downloads the latest security updates.

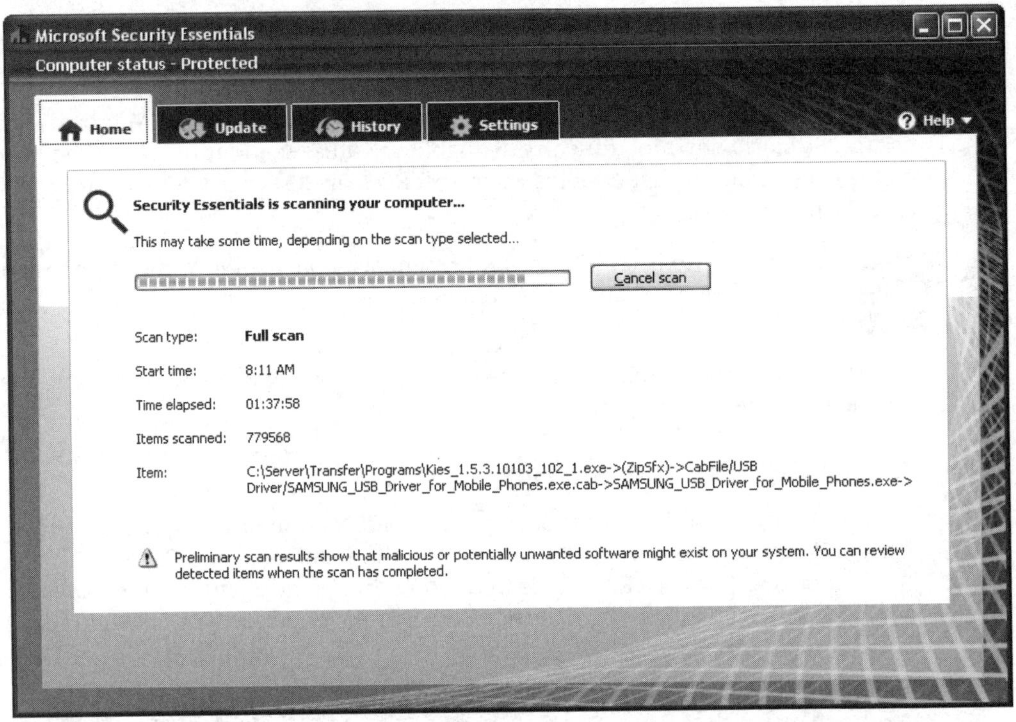

FIGURE 3-18 The Home tab shows Microsoft Security Essentials' progress as it scans your PC for threats. The yellow triangle icon with the exclamation point indicates that Microsoft Security Essentials has found something potentially vicious.

You can also scan your PC at any time by following these steps:

1. Click the Home tab to display it. Figure 3-19 shows the Home tab as it appears when Microsoft Security Essentials is not running a scan.
2. Select the option button for the scan type you want:
   - **Quick** Scans the folders that are most likely to be infected by viruses and malware
   - **Full** Scans all the folders on your computer
   - **Custom** Lets you choose which folders to scan

Tip The first scan Microsoft Security Essentials runs is a Quick scan. It's a good idea to run a Full scan as soon as you have time. A Full scan can take several hours, so setting it running last thing at night or when you head out to work is the best bet.

3. Click the Scan Now button. If you selected the Custom option button, the Microsoft Security Essentials dialog box shown in Figure 3-20 opens. Select the check box for each drive or folder you want to scan and then click the OK button.
4. The scan runs.

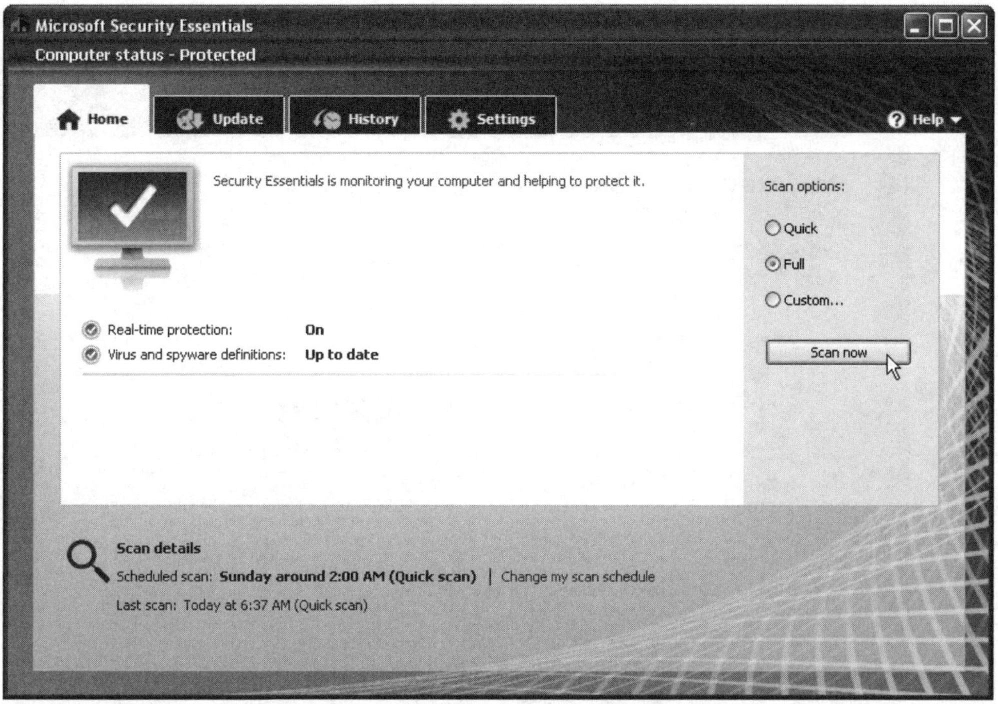

FIGURE 3-19 To scan your PC for threats, select the Quick option button, the Full option button, or the Custom option button on the Home tab of Microsoft Security Essentials and then click the Scan Now button.

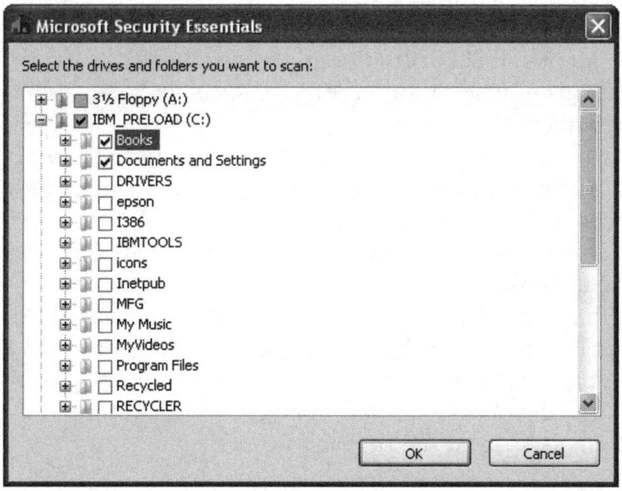

FIGURE 3-20 When running a Custom scan, select the check box for each drive or folder you want to scan. Click a + sign to expand a drive or folder; click a – sign to collapse a drive or folder.

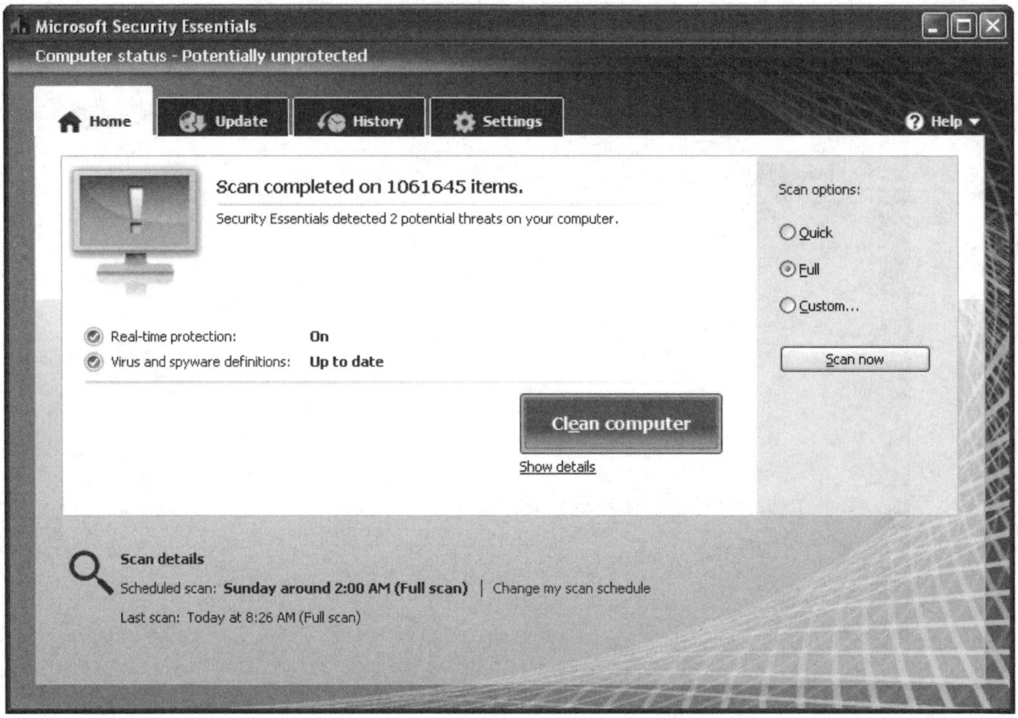

FIGURE 3-21 At the end of the scan, the Home tab shows you whether Microsoft Security Essentials has found anything potentially dangerous.

When Microsoft Security Essentials completes the scan, it displays the Home tab with details of what it found. Figure 3-21 shows the Home tab with two potential threats identified.

At this point, you can simply click the Clean Computer button to get rid of the problems. But if you want to see what Microsoft Security Essentials has found, click the Show Details link under the Clean Computer button. Microsoft Security Essentials displays the Microsoft Security Essentials Alert dialog box (see Figure 3-22), which contains a list of the problems.

Click the item you want to examine and then click the Show Details button to display the Details pane at the bottom of the dialog box (see Figure 3-23). You can then see what category the problem has (for example, Adware or Remote Control Software), the description of the problem, the recommended action (for example, to get rid of the item), and the files involved.

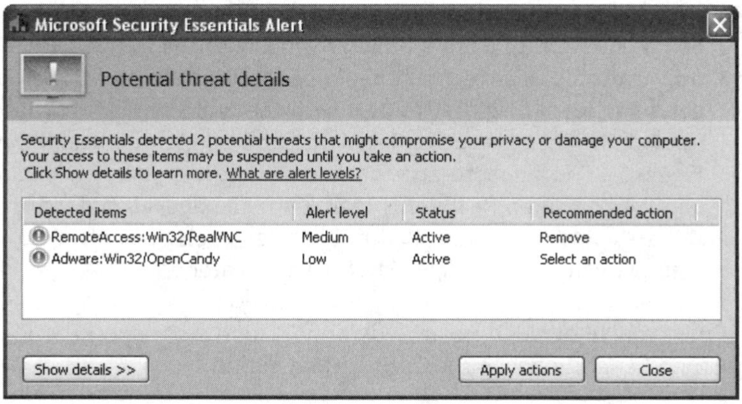

FIGURE 3-22 Open the Microsoft Security Essentials Alert dialog box to see the details of the problems Microsoft Security Essentials has found and to decide how to handle them.

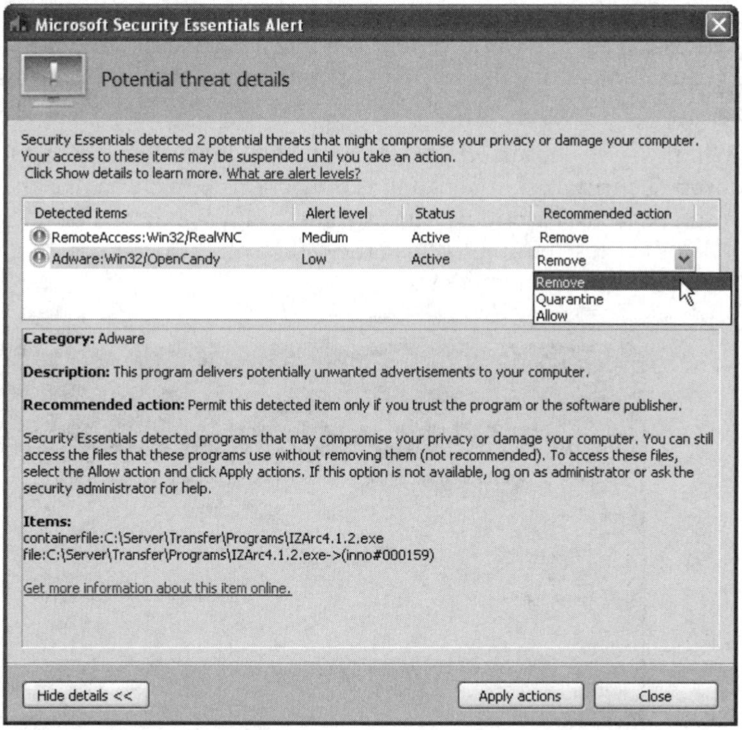

FIGURE 3-23 View the details of the problem to decide how you want to deal with it.

Note Click the Get More Information About This Problem Online link in the Alert dialog box if you want to open a browser window to the Malware Protection Center on Microsoft's website. You'll see a page with details of the problem. Read the details to learn how best to deal with the problem. For many programs, you'll need to make an executive decision. For example, the RealVNC item that stars in Figure 3-25 is a remote-access program that lets you view or control your PC from another computer. RealVNC is legitimate and aboveboard, so you'll want to keep it—assuming you've installed it. If someone else has installed it surreptitiously on your PC, you'll want to get rid of it immediately.

When you've decided what to do about the threat, open the Recommended Action drop-down list and choose the appropriate action:

- **Remove** Removes the offending file.
- **Quarantine** Moves the offending file to a safe location and prevents it from running. If you find you miss functionality the file provided, you can move it back out of quarantine and start using it again. Alternatively, you can remove it.
- **Allow** Leaves the file in place and tells Microsoft Security Essentials that it's okay.

Tip Remove any file you're certain is a threat. Quarantine any file you're not sure is a threat. Allow any file you're positive is on the side of the angels.

When you've chosen what to do with each item, click the Apply Actions button. Microsoft Security Essentials applies the actions you chose and then updates the Microsoft Security Essentials Alert window with the details (see Figure 3-24).

Click the Close button to close the Microsoft Security Essentials Alert dialog box and return to the main window.

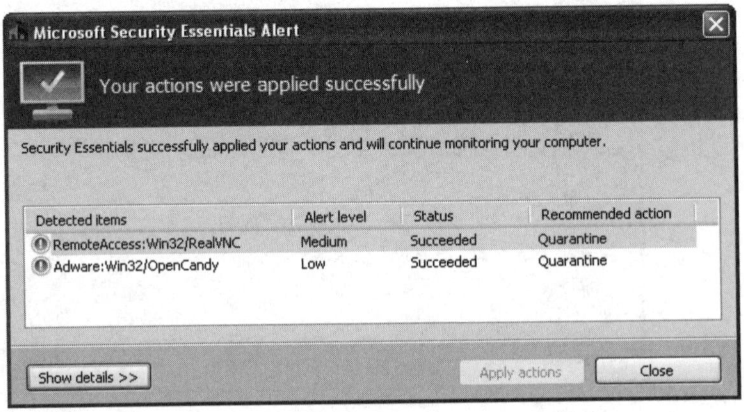

FIGURE 3-24 The Microsoft Security Essentials Alert dialog box confirms that it has taken the actions you chose. Click the Close button to return to the main window.

Move a File Out of Quarantine

After putting a file in quarantine, you can take as long as you want to decide whether to remove it or allow it. When you decide, follow these steps:

1. Click the History tab to display its contents.
2. Select the Quarantined Items Only option button to narrow down the list to the items in quarantine.
3. Select the check box of each item you want to affect, as shown here.

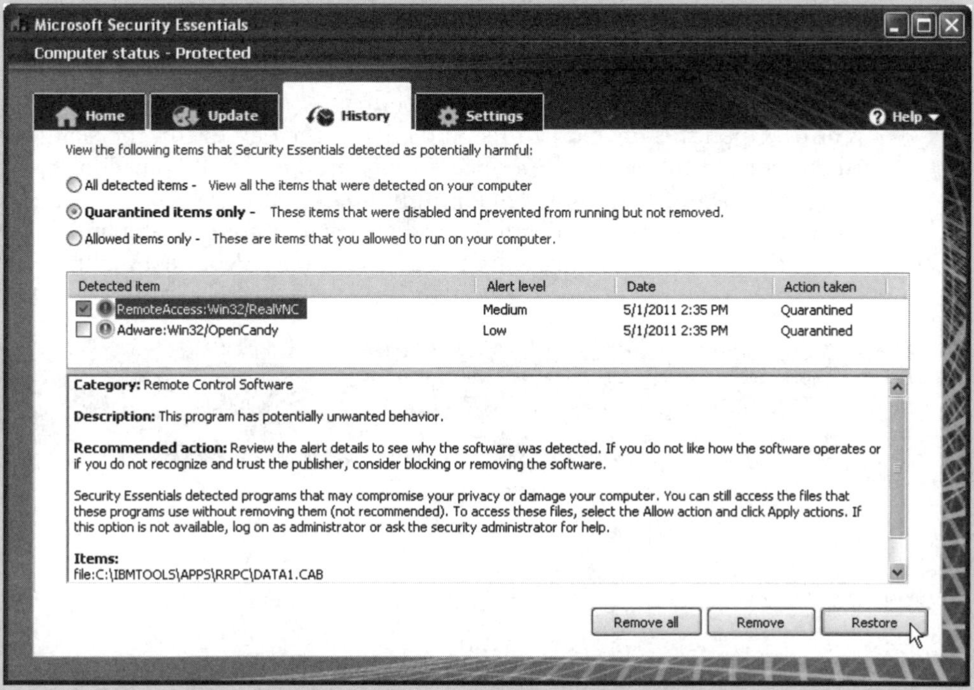

4. Click the Remove button or the Restore button, as needed. If you want to get rid of all the quarantined items, click the Remove All button.
5. When you restore an item, Microsoft Security Essentials confirms that you understand the item may pose a threat, as shown here. Click the Yes button if you're sure you want to proceed.

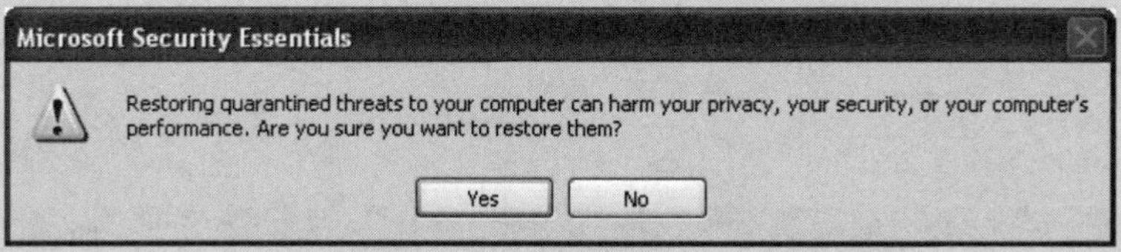

6. When you finish dealing with your quarantined files, click the Home tab to display its contents again.

Configure Microsoft Security Essentials to Run Your Way

When you install Microsoft Security Essentials, the program uses default settings that work well for many people. But you can protect your PC even better if you spend a few minutes configuring Microsoft Security Essentials as discussed in this section.

Choose Scheduled Scan Settings

To start configuring Microsoft Security Essentials, click the Settings tab. The Scheduled Scan category of settings appears at first, as shown in Figure 3-25.

Now choose settings as follows:

- **Run A Scheduled Scan On My Computer** Select this check box.
- **Scan Type** Open this drop-down list and choose Full Scan. The default is Quick Scan, but a Full Scan protects your PC better.
- **When** Open this drop-down list and choose the day to run the scan on. I recommend running the scan once a week on the day of your choice, but you can choose Daily if you want maximum protection.
- **Around** Open this drop-down list and choose the hour at which to run the scan. The dark watches of the night are usually best unless you're a night owl.

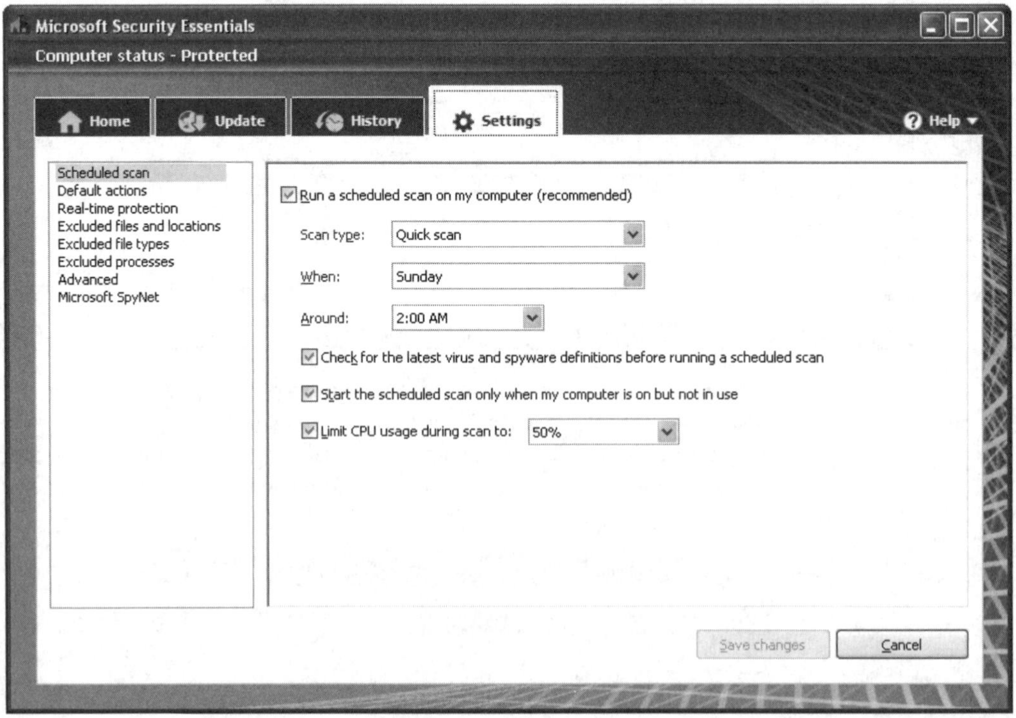

FIGURE 3-25 You can beef up your PC's protection by choosing custom settings for Microsoft Security Essentials. Start by scheduling a full scan of your PC once a week.

- **Check For The Latest Virus And Spyware Definition Before Running A Scheduled Scan** Make sure this check box is selected.
- **Start The Scheduled Scan Only When My Computer Is On But Not In Use** Select this check box if you may be using your PC at the time you set for the scan to run.
- **Limit CPU Usage During Scan To** If you want to avoid Microsoft Security Essentials hogging all the processor cycles, select this check box and then choose the percentage in the drop-down list. Choosing 50% should leave your PC responsive enough for light use.

Tip If you're pretty sure you won't be using your PC when Microsoft Security Essentials is scanning, you can clear the Limit CPU Usage During Scan To check box. Alternatively, select this check box but use the drop-down list to set a high limit, such as 80%. Giving Microsoft Security Essentials free access to the processor will get your scans finished faster.

Choose Default Actions Settings

Next, click the Default Actions item in the left pane to display the Default Actions category of settings (see Figure 3-26). You can then choose these settings:

- **Severe Alert Level** Choose the action to take for the highest-rated threats. Your choices are Recommended Action (see the nearby Note), Remove, and Quarantine. Quarantine is usually the best choice here.

Note In each of the drop-down lists in the Default Actions category, you can choose Recommended Action to have Microsoft Security Essentials follow Microsoft's recommendation for handling this specific threat. The recommended action for most severe threats is Remove, but Microsoft Security Essentials allows other potentially serious threats to continue to run. In most cases, this is because the potential threat comes from software you may have installed deliberately.

- **High Alert Level** Choose the action to take for threats rated high. Your choices are Recommended Action, Remove, and Quarantine. Quarantine is usually the best choice.
- **Medium Alert Level** Choose the action to take for threats with a medium rating. Your choices are Recommended Action, Remove, Quarantine, and Allow. Quarantine is usually the best choice.
- **Low Alert Level** Choose the action to take for threats rated low. Your choices are Recommended Action, Remove, Quarantine, and Allow. Allow is usually the best choice, because these threat alerts may be triggered by programs you've installed deliberately.
- **Apply Recommended Actions** If you've selected Recommended Action in any of the drop-down lists, select this check box to allow Microsoft Security Essentials to take the recommended actions.

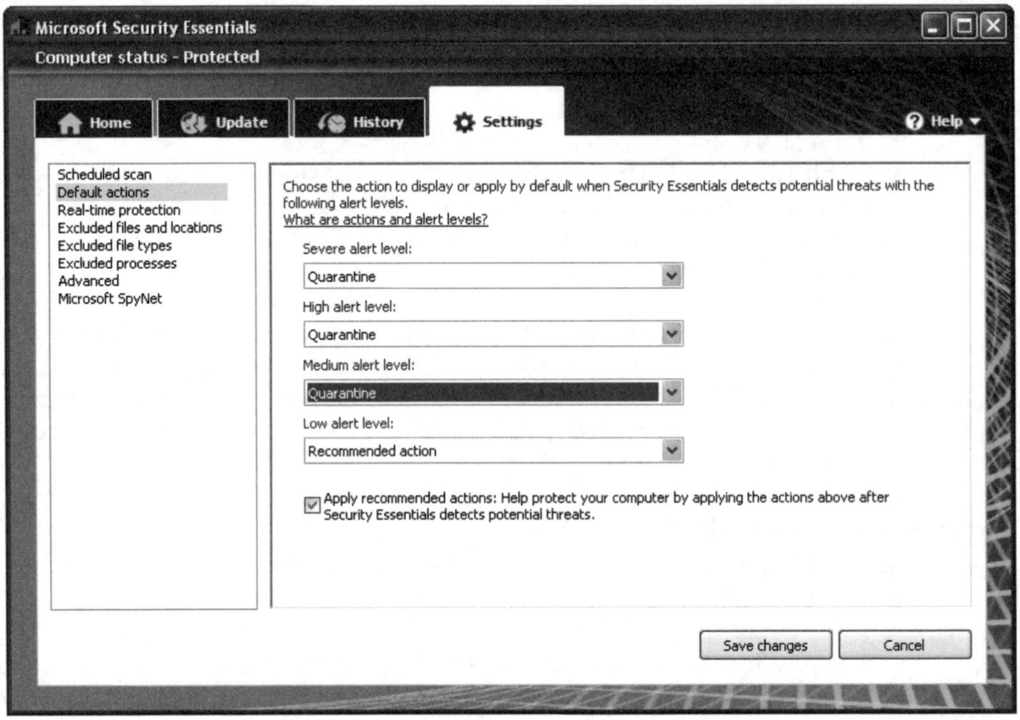

FIGURE 3-26 In the Default Actions category of settings, choose how to handle different levels of threats.

Choose Real-Time Protection Settings

Next, click the Real-Time Protection item in the left pane to display the Real-Time Protection category of settings (see Figure 3-27). You can then choose these settings:

- **Turn On Real-Time Protection** Select this check box to turn on the protection features that run in real time. You'll almost always want to keep these features running, because they can protect your PC from many virus and malware attacks.
- **Scan All Downloads** Select this check box to have Microsoft Security Essentials scan files you download from the Internet and files you receive attached to e-mail messages or instant messages.
- **Monitor File And Program Activity On Your Computer** Select this check box to have Microsoft Security Essentials monitor programs and files for suspicious activity. In the drop-down list, choose Monitor All Files. The other settings in the drop-down list are Monitor Only Incoming Files and Monitor Only Outgoing Files, but it's better to monitor all files.

Caution Turn off real-time protection only if your PC is not powerful enough to run the features.

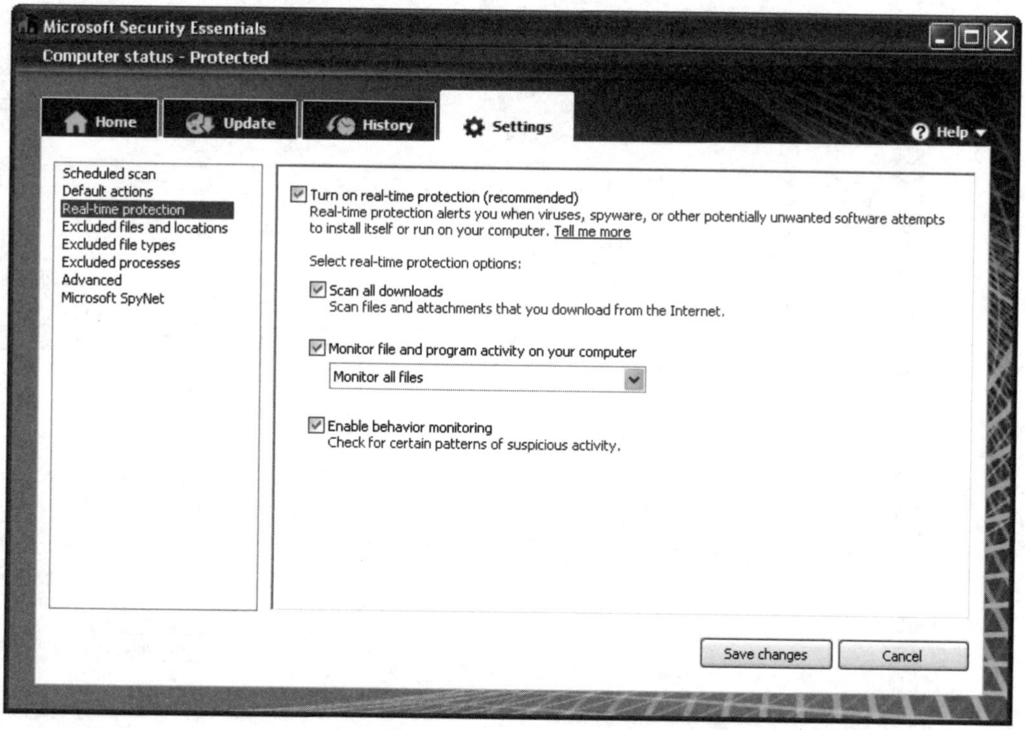

FIGURE 3-27 In the Real-Time Protection category of settings, make sure real-time protection is on and that Microsoft Security Essentials is monitoring downloads, file and program activity, and potentially suspicious behavior.

- **Enable Behavior Monitoring** Select this check box to have Microsoft Security Essentials monitor your PC for suspicious activity that might indicate a malware attack.
- **Enable Network Inspection System** Select this check box to have Microsoft Security Essentials monitor your network connection for suspicious activity. This monitoring helps protect against "zero-day exploits," attacks that use newly discovered vulnerabilities that Microsoft hasn't yet fixed. This setting appears only for Windows 7, not for Windows XP.

Choose Excluded Files And Locations Settings

Now click the Excluded Files And Locations item in the left pane to display the Excluded Files And Locations category of settings (see Figure 3-28). Here, you can build a list of files or folders you want to exclude from Microsoft Security Essentials' scans.

To add a file or folder to the list, click the Browse button, choose the item in the Microsoft Security Essentials dialog box that opens, and then click the OK button.

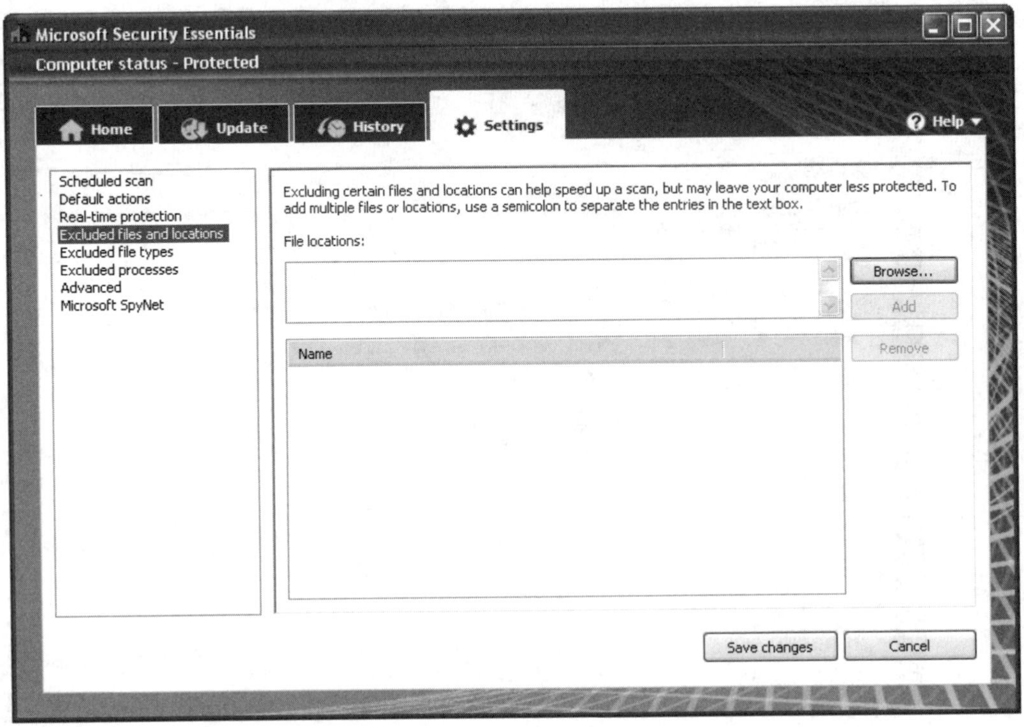

FIGURE 3-28 In the Excluded Files And Locations category of settings, you can specify files and folders you want to exclude from scans.

Note Exclude files or folders only if you have a good reason to. Otherwise, it's much better to scan all the files on your PC for threats.

Choose Excluded File Types Settings

Next, click the Excluded File Types item in the left pane to display the Excluded File Types category of settings (see Figure 3-29). This category lets you exclude particular file types from scans by specifying their file extensions.

For example, if you want to exclude your Excel workbook files from scans, you can specify the .xlsx file extension. Just type **xlsx** in the File Extensions box and then click the Add button to add the file extension to the list.

Caution Don't exclude any file types from scans unless Microsoft Security Essentials is consistently flagging a particular file type as a threat and you are certain that the file type is harmless. This is seldom the case. The figure shows one file type already excluded and another about to be excluded so that you can see the controls better; this isn't a recommendation.

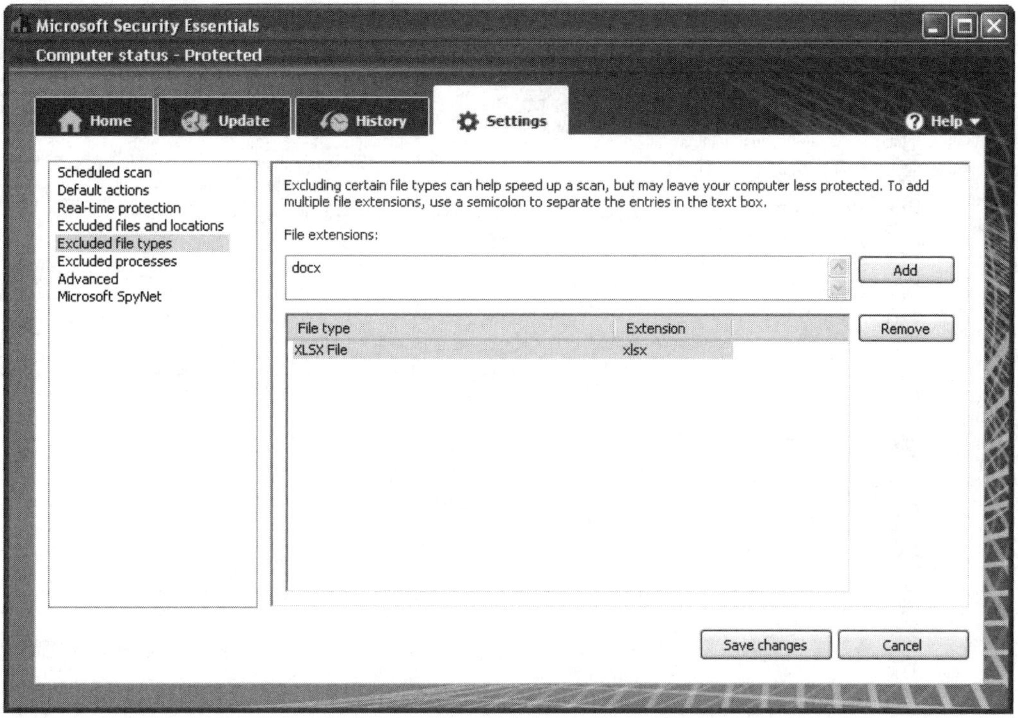

FIGURE 3-29 In the Excluded File Types category of settings, you can exclude particular file types from your scans, but doing so is not usually a good idea.

Choose Excluded Processes Settings

Next, click the Excluded Processes item in the left pane to display the Excluded Processes category of settings (see Figure 3-30). This category lets you exclude specific processes from scans by specifying their names.

For example, if you want to exclude Windows Explorer from scans, you can type **explorer.exe** in the Process Names box and then click the Add button to add the program to the list. (This is an example, not a recommendation.)

Caution Don't exclude any processes from scans unless an expert you trust has advised you to do so.

Choose Advanced Settings

Now click the Advanced item in the left pane to display the Advanced category of settings (see Figure 3-31). You can then choose the following settings:

- **Scan Archive Files** Select this check box to scan Zip files and other archive files for threats. This is a good idea.

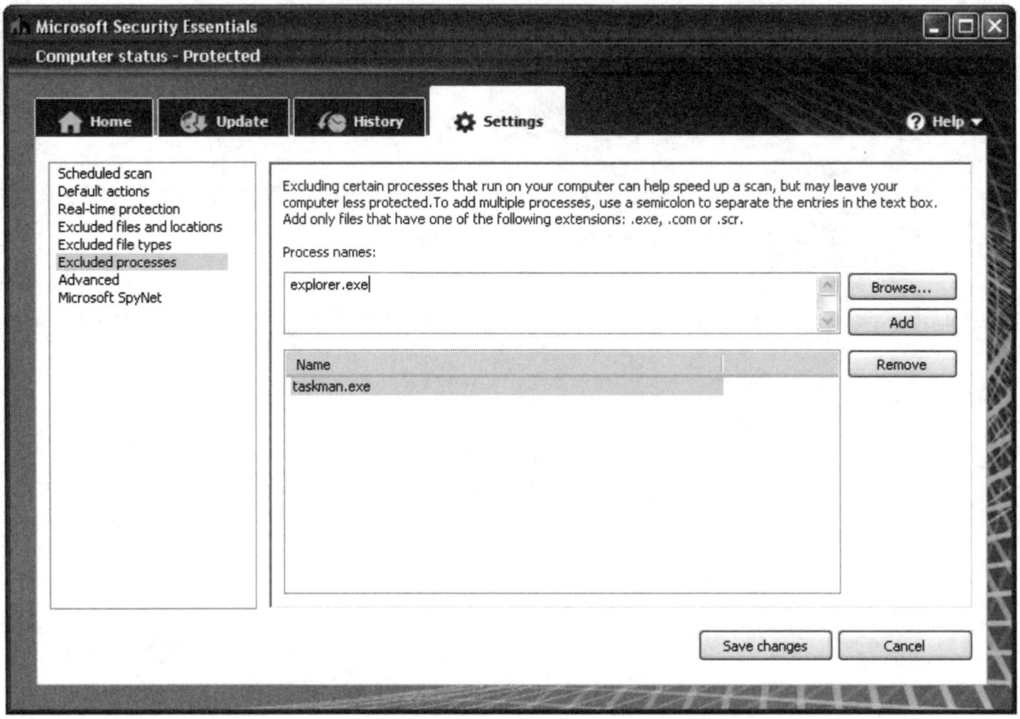

FIGURE 3-30 In the Excluded Processes category of settings, you can exclude specific programs from scans. This is not usually a good idea.

- **Scan Removable Drives** Select this check box to scan removable drives, such as USB thumb drives, when scanning your PC. Removable drives are a prime vector of malware, so scanning them is helpful.
- **Create A System Restore Point** Select this check box to have Microsoft Security Essentials create a restore point in System Restore before taking action against a potential threat. Creating a restore point makes it easier for you to restore your PC to how it was before if Microsoft Security Essentials removes a program that was helpful rather than a threat.

Note The downside to creating a restore point is that the restore point takes up more space on your PC's hard drive. This isn't usually a concern unless the hard drive is running low on free space.

- **Allow All Users To View The Full History Results** Select this check box only if you want any user of the PC to be able to see all the threats on the History tab.

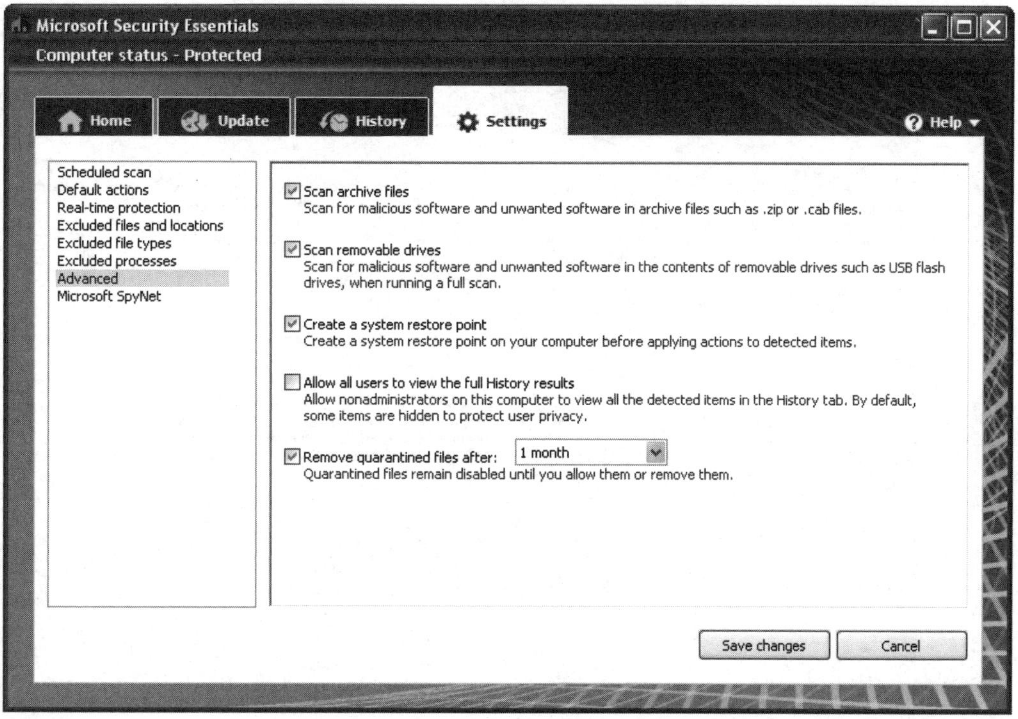

FIGURE 3-31 In the Advanced category of settings, your choices include scanning removable drives, creating a system restore point before taking actions, and removing quarantined files automatically when they reach the end of their shelf life.

Some threats can compromise user privacy, so normally you'll want to keep this check box cleared. With it cleared, only administrators can see the full list of threats.

- **Remove Quarantined Files After** If you want to remove quarantined files automatically after a specific length of time, select this check box and then choose the length of time in the drop-down list: 1 Day, 2 Days, 3 Days, 4 Days, 1 Week, 2 Weeks, 1 Month, or 3 Months.

Tip Removing quarantined files automatically helps keep down the number of files lurking in quarantine while you decide what to do about them. But in most cases you'll get better results from visiting the quarantined files every now and then and deciding which to remove and which to restore.

Choose Microsoft SpyNet Settings

Finally, click the Microsoft SpyNet item in the left pane to display the Microsoft SpyNet category of settings (see Figure 3-32). Then select the level of involvement

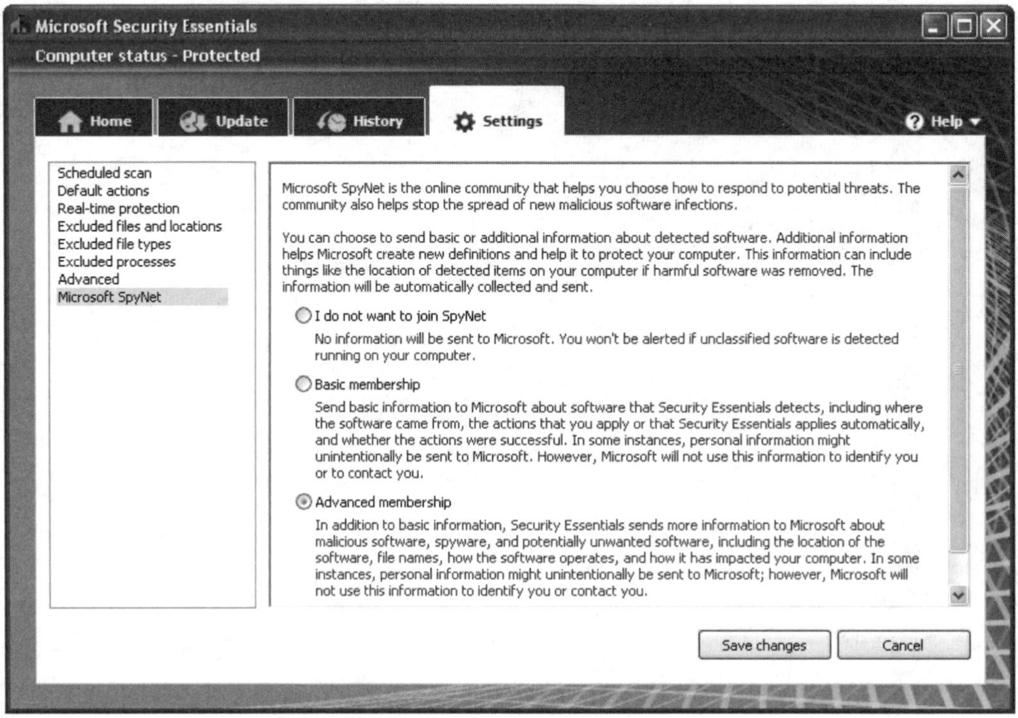

FIGURE 3-32 In the Microsoft SpyNet category of settings, choose among the I Do Not Want To Join SpyNet option button, the Basic Membership option button, and the Advanced Membership option button. Then click the Save Changes button to save your changes.

you want in Microsoft SpyNet, the support community for fighting malicious software infections:

- **I Do Not Want To Join SpyNet** Select this option button to avoid sending any malware information to Microsoft.
- **Basic Membership** Select this option button to send the minimum amount of detail to Microsoft about any malware that turns up on your PC, the effect it has, and how well Microsoft Security Essentials deals with it.
- **Advanced Membership** Select this option button to send full details to Microsoft about any malware that turns up on your PC.

Note By becoming a member of SpyNet, you help make Microsoft Security Essentials more effective both for yourself and for other people. Given what a bane viruses and malware are, supporting Microsoft Security Essentials like this is a good move. The downside is that Microsoft might receive some of your personal information along with the details of the malware. But as Microsoft promises not to use such information to identify you or contact you, this risk seems worth the reward.

Save Your Microsoft Security Essentials Settings

When you finish choosing settings for Microsoft Security Essentials, click the Save Changes button to save the changes.

You can then click the Home tab to display its contents, make sure that it's not waving any distress flags in your general direction, and then click the Close button (the × button) to close the Microsoft Security Essentials window. Microsoft Security Essentials continues running in the background, and you can access it at any point by clicking the Microsoft Security Essentials icon (the icon with the check mark) in the notification area (shown here).

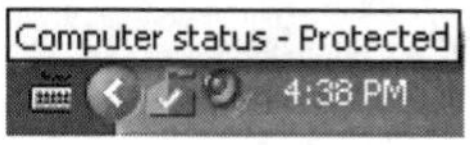

Turn On Windows Firewall and Decide Which Traffic to Let Through It

Next, you need to make sure that Windows Firewall is turned on. Windows Firewall is a protective feature that prevents unauthorized communications from the Internet from coming into your PC. Briefly, a firewall has a list of types of data that are allowed to pass into the PC. Anything that's not permitted, it blocks.

Note If you have installed and configured Microsoft Security Essentials, it may have turned on Windows Firewall for you. Still, it's a good idea to check that Windows Firewall is on and that it has suitable settings.

Turn On and Configure Windows Firewall on Windows XP

In this section, we'll look at how to turn on Windows Firewall in Windows XP and how to choose which traffic the firewall allows to pass.

Turn On Windows Firewall in Windows XP

To turn on Windows Firewall on Windows XP, follow these steps:

1. Choose Start | Control Panel to open a Control Panel window.
2. If Control Panel opens in Category view, with Pick A Category at the top, click the Switch To Classic View link in the Control Panel box in the upper-left corner to switch to Classic view.

Do I Need to Turn On Windows Firewall If My Internet Router Has a Firewall?

Yes. Even if your Internet router has a firewall—and you've turned it on—you should turn on Windows Firewall as well. Windows Firewall will help to protect your PC from threats on other PCs that share your network.

Turning on Windows Firewall is especially important if your PC is a laptop that you connect to other networks—for example, Wi-Fi networks at airports or other public places.

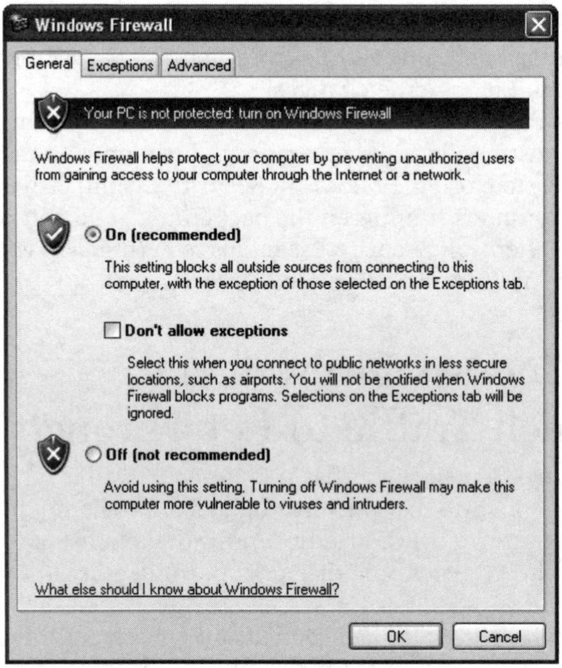

FIGURE 3-33 Select the On option button on the General tab of the Windows Firewall dialog box to turn on the Windows Firewall in Windows XP.

3. Double-click the Windows Firewall icon to display the Windows Firewall dialog box. The General tab appears at the front at first (see Figure 3-33).
4. Select the On option button to turn Windows Firewall on.

Tip If you need to use your PC on a public network such as the Wi-Fi network in a coffee shop, select the Don't Allow Exceptions check box on the General tab of the Windows Firewall dialog box to temporarily turn off the exceptions.

You can now choose which traffic to allow to pass through the firewall, as discussed in the next section.

Choose Which Traffic Can Pass Through the Firewall on Windows XP

To choose which traffic can pass through Windows Firewall on Windows XP, follow these steps:

1. In the Windows Firewall dialog box, click the Exceptions tab to display its controls (see Figure 3-34).

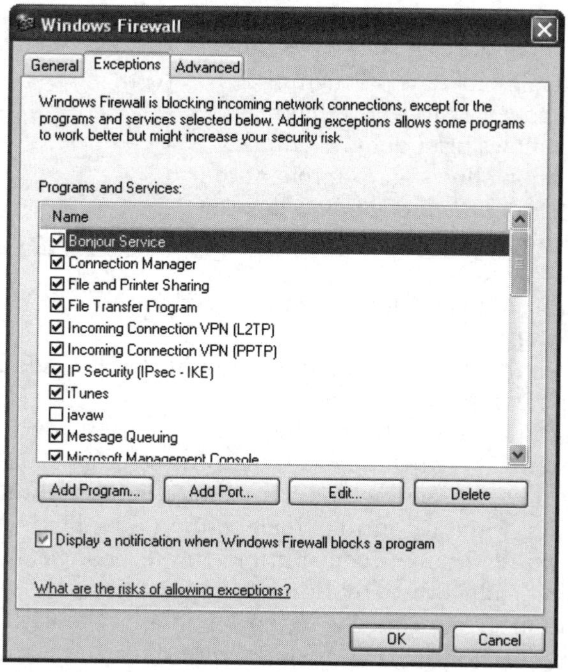

FIGURE 3-34 On the Exceptions tab of the Windows Firewall dialog box for Windows XP, select the check box for each program or service you want to allow through the firewall.

2. Look at the Programs And Services list box. This list shows the programs and services currently set up to go through the firewall. A check mark shows that the exception is turned on; if there's no check mark, the exception is inactive for now, but you can turn it back on if you need to.

Note In Windows, a *service* is a program that Windows runs automatically to get things done. For example, the File And Printer Sharing service you see in Figure 3-34 runs automatically to enable Windows to share files and printers on the network. If you prevent this service from getting through Windows Firewall, Windows can't share files and printers. (Sometimes, not being able to share files and printers is helpful and desirable.)

3. In the Programs And Services list box, clear the check box for any program or service you don't want to let through the firewall. See the nearby sidebar for advice.

4. If you want to see what a particular program or service is, double-click it to display its Edit A Program dialog box or Edit A Port dialog box, which shows brief details. The next illustration shows an example of the Edit A Program dialog box. Click the OK button when you're ready to close the dialog box.

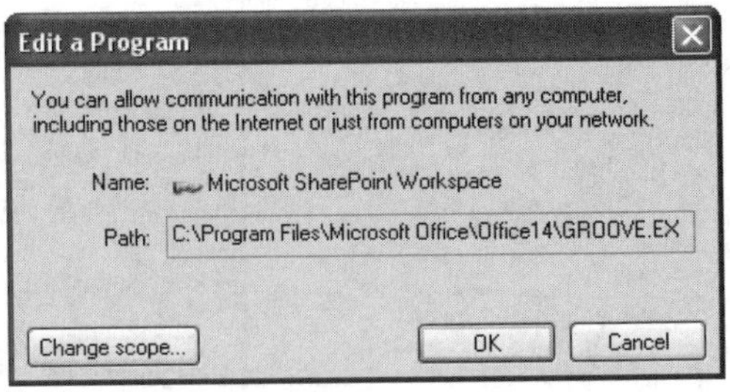

5. If you need to add a program that can go through Windows Firewall, follow these steps:
   a. Click the Add Program button to display the Add A Program dialog box (see Figure 3-35).
   b. In the Programs list box, click the program you want to add. If the program doesn't appear there, click the Browse button, use the Browse dialog box to locate the program, and then click the Open button.
   c. If you want to control which computers this firewall exception applies to, click the Change Scope button. In the Change Scope dialog box (shown here), select the Any Computer (Including Those On The Internet) option button if you want the exception to apply to the Internet. Select the My Network (Subnet) Only option button if you want the exception to apply only to computers on your immediate network; this is usually the best choice. Then click the OK button.

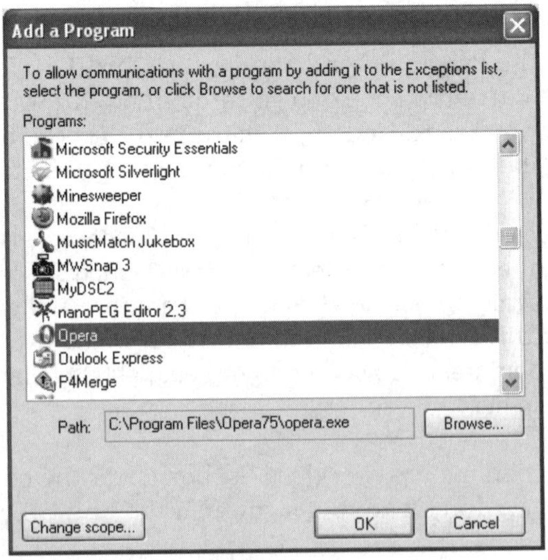

FIGURE 3-35 Use the Add A Program dialog box to add a program to the list of allowed programs for Windows Firewall.

Note In the Change Scope dialog box, you can also select the Custom List box and then type a list of IP addresses in the text box. Normally, this option is best left to network administrators.

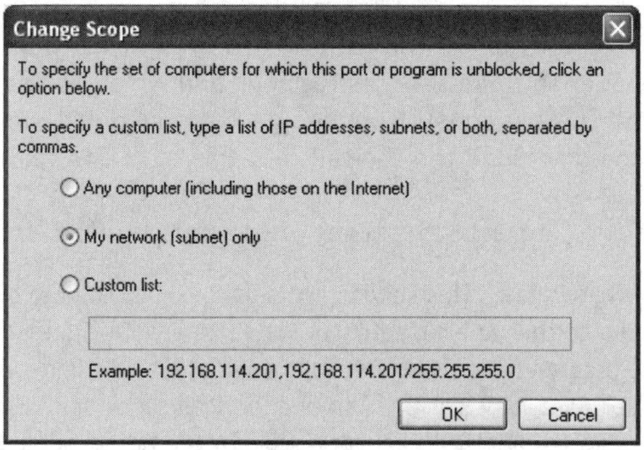

d. Click the OK button to close the Add A Program dialog box. The program you specified appears in the Programs And Services list on the Exceptions tab.

6. Select the Display A Notification When Windows Firewall Blocks A Program check box if you want to see an alert when Windows Firewall blocks a program from communicating. Seeing this alert is usually helpful, as it prompts you to decide whether to create an exception for the program.
7. Click the OK button to close the Windows Firewall Settings dialog box. You can then click the Close button (the × button) to close the Control Panel window.

Turn On and Configure Windows Firewall on Windows 7

In this section, we'll look at how to turn on Windows Firewall in Windows 7 and how to choose which traffic the firewall allows to pass.

Turn On Windows Firewall in Windows 7

To make sure Windows Firewall is turned on in Windows 7, follow these steps:

1. Choose Start | Control Panel to open a Control Panel window.
2. In the View By drop-down list, choose either Large Icons or Small Icons (whichever you prefer).
3. Click the Windows Firewall button to display the Windows Firewall window. Figure 3-36 shows this window with Windows Firewall turned off, which is strictly not recommended. As a result, the window is lit up like a Christmas tree with warnings.

Note If Windows Firewall is turned off, you can click the Use Recommended Settings button in the Update Your Firewall Settings box to turn on Windows Firewall with default settings.

How to Decide Which Programs and Services to Allow Through Windows Firewall

When you look at the list of programs and services in the Programs And Services list box on the Exceptions tab of the Windows Firewall dialog box, you may find it hard to decide which programs and services to block and which to allow.

Don't worry. This is normal. Most people not only don't know which programs and services are going through the firewall, but they also don't know what Windows calls them.

Here are two examples of the types of services you may want to block:

- **Bonjour Service** This service, which appears at the top of the list in the nearby figure, is a service that Apple's products install to enable iTunes, iPhones, iPads, and other Apple programs and devices to find each other on the network. If you don't use these features, you can clear the Bonjour Services check box.
- **Incoming Connection VPN services** In the figure, you'll see that the Incoming Connection VPN (L2TP) check box and the Incoming Connection VPN (PPTP) check box are selected. These exceptions allow other computers on the network or the Internet to connect to my PC via virtual private networking (VPN) via either the Layer 2 Tunneling Protocol (L2TP) or the Peer-to-Peer Tunneling Protocol (PPTP). I'm not using these connections at the moment, so I can clear their check boxes to increase my computer's security. (You most likely won't need to run these services either.)

To stop one of the programs or services from going through the firewall, clear its check box. You can select it again later if necessary.

To remove an exception altogether, click the item and then click the Delete button. When Windows displays the Delete A Port dialog box (shown here) or the Delete An Application dialog box, click the Yes button. You can set up the exception again later if necessary, but doing so is more work than simply selecting the check box for an existing exception.

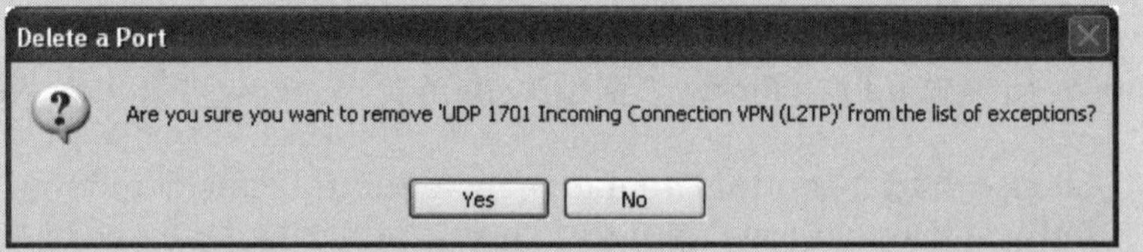

If you end up blocking something vital, it's not the end of the world—you can turn it back on easily enough. What'll happen is either you'll find you can't perform some move you take for granted, such as accessing someone else's music library using iTunes, or Windows will display a dialog box telling you that it has blocked a program or service from communicating through the firewall. When you see this dialog box, you can click the Allow button to create an exception for the program or service. Normal service then resumes.

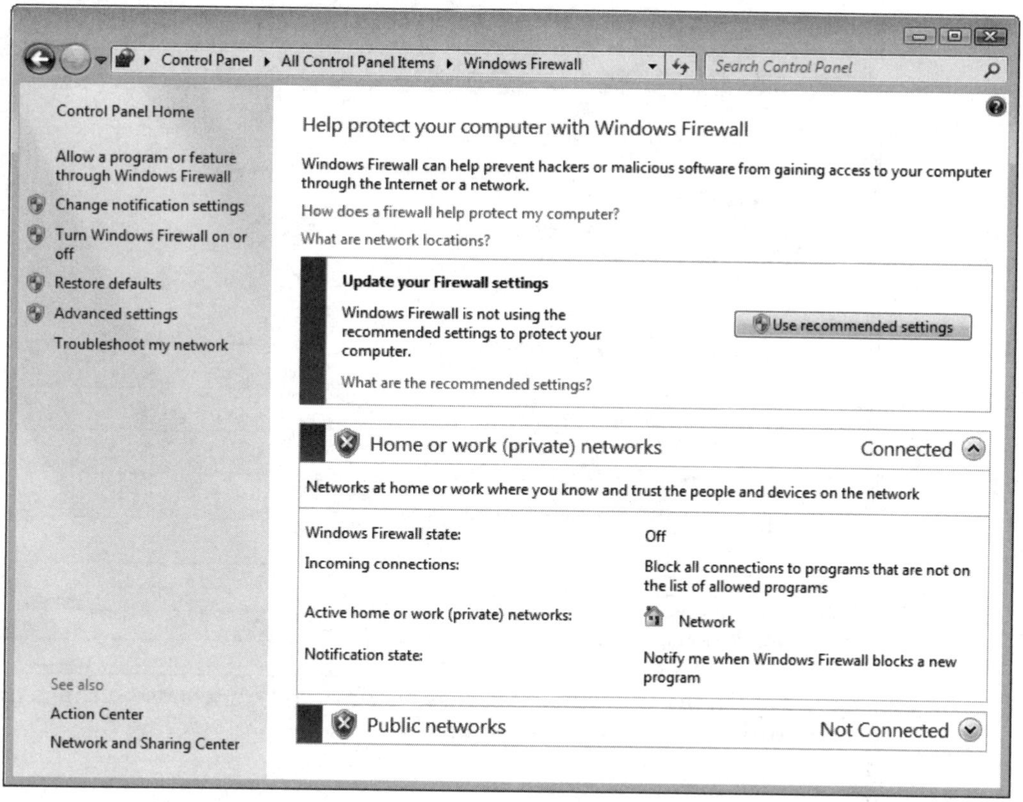

FIGURE 3-36 If Windows Firewall is turned off in Windows 7, the Windows Firewall window provides a Use Recommended Settings button that you can use to apply protection quickly.

4. To configure Windows Firewall, click the Turn Windows Firewall On Or Off link. The Customize Settings window appears (see Figure 3-37).
5. In the Home Or Work (Private) Network Location Settings area, choose these settings:
   - Select the Turn On Windows Firewall option button.
   - Clear the Block All Incoming Connections, Including Those In The List Of Allowed Programs check box.
   - Select the Notify Me When Windows Firewall Blocks A New Program check box.
6. In the Public Network Location Settings area, choose these settings:
   - Select the Turn On Windows Firewall option button.
   - Select the Block All Incoming Connections, Including Those In The List Of Allowed Programs check box.
   - Select the Notify Me When Windows Firewall Blocks A New Program check box.

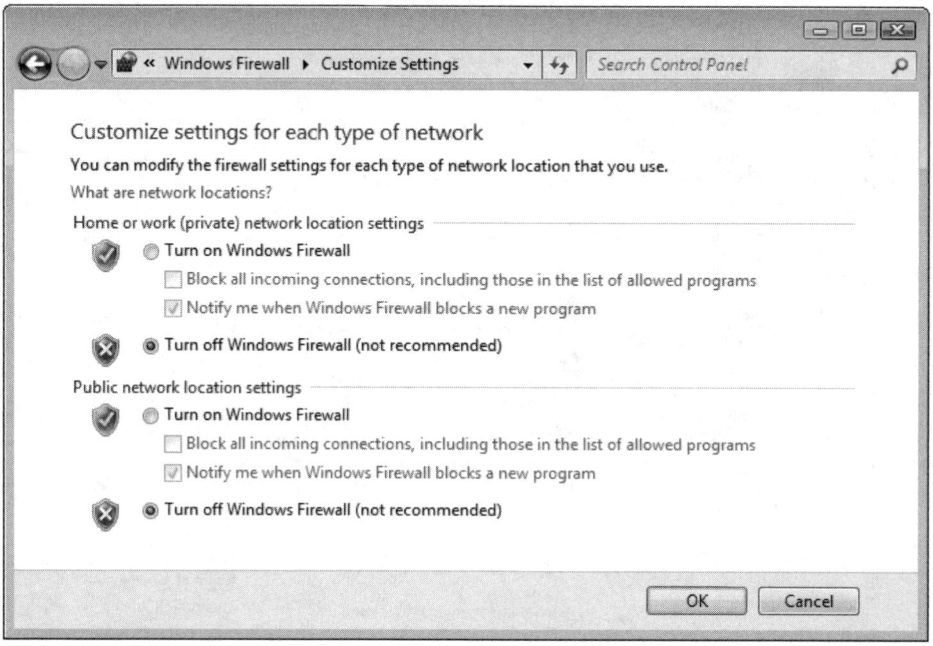

FIGURE 3-37 In the Customize Settings window, you can choose settings for home and work networks and for public networks.

7. Click the OK button to apply your choices. You'll then see the Windows Firewall window again, but Windows Firewall is now on, so the warning messages have gone, as in Figure 3-38.

Leave the Windows Firewall window open so that you can set up any exceptions you need, as discussed in the next section.

Choose Which Traffic Can Pass Through the Firewall on Windows 7

To choose which traffic can pass through Windows Firewall on Windows 7, follow these steps:

1. Open the Windows Firewall window as discussed in steps 1–3 of the list in the previous section.
2. In the left pane, click the Allow A Program Or Feature Through Windows Firewall link. The Allowed Programs window opens.
3. To allow a program or feature through Windows Firewall, select the check box in the Name column. Windows selects the corresponding check box in the Home/Work (Private) column automatically.

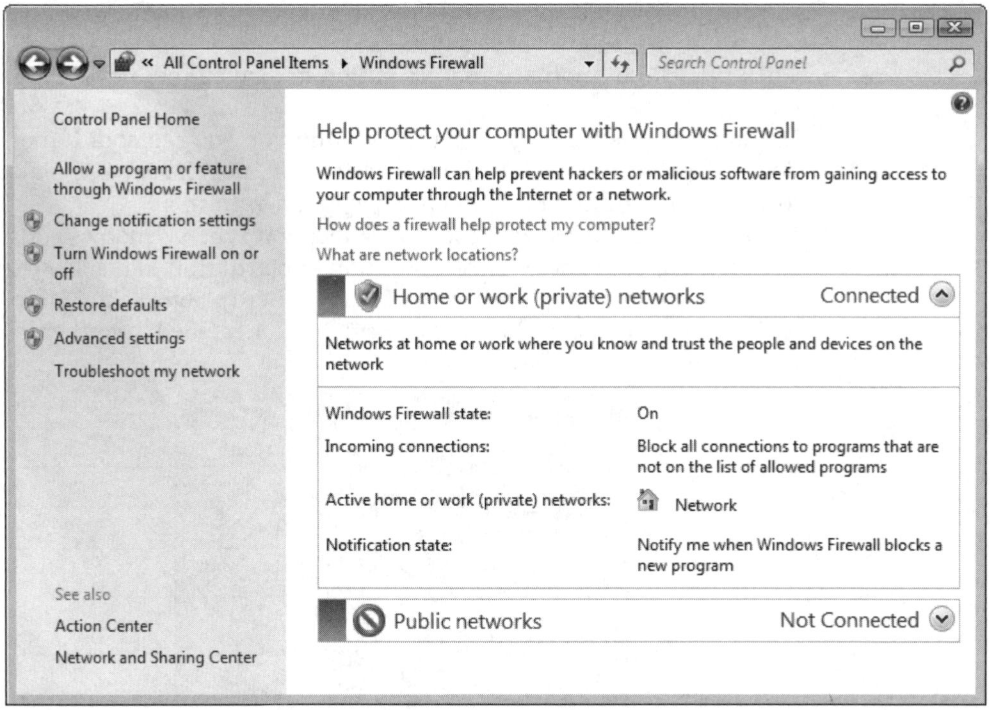

FIGURE 3-38 After you turn on Windows Firewall, the warnings vanish from the Windows Firewall screen.

4. If you need the program or feature to go through the firewall when you're using public connections as well, select the check box in the Public column.
5. If you want to see what a program or feature does, click it and then click the Details button to display the Properties dialog box for the connection. The next illustration shows the Properties dialog box for the Remote Assistance feature. Click the OK button when you're ready to close the Properties dialog box.

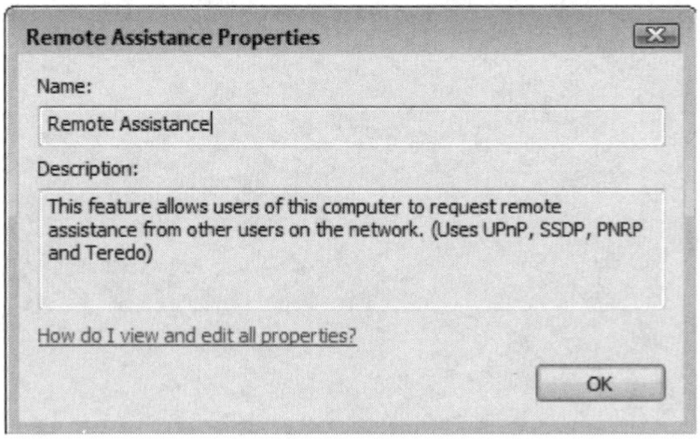

6. If the program or feature you want doesn't appear in the Allowed Programs And Features list, follow these substeps:
   a. Click the Allow Another Program button to display the Add A Program dialog box.
   b. In the Programs list box, click the program you want to add. If the program doesn't appear there, click the Browse button, use the Browse dialog box to locate the program, and then click the Open button.
   c. If you want to control which network location types Windows adds this program for, click the Network Location Types button to display the Choose Network Location Types dialog box (shown here). Select the Home/Work (Private) check box or the Public check box, as needed, and then click the OK button.

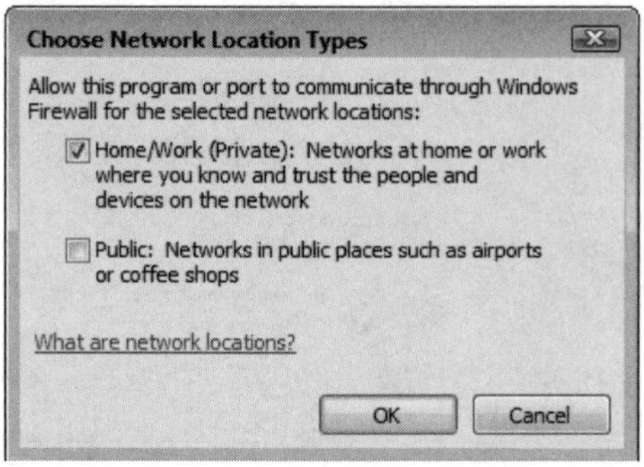

   d. Click the Add button. Windows adds the program to the list and selects the Home/Work (Private) check box or the Public check box, depending on your choice.
7. Click the OK button to close the Allowed Programs window. The Windows Firewall window appears again, and you can click the Close button (the × button) when you're ready to close it.

PART II Use Networks and the Internet Safely

4 Connect Your PC Safely to a Network

To get just about anything done on your PC these days, you need to connect it to other computers via either a local area network or the Internet.

In this chapter, I'll show you how to connect your PC to a network without compromising its safety—or your own. In the next chapter, we'll look at how to connect safely to the Internet.

First, we'll go over connecting to a wired network and securing that connection. Second, we'll cover establishing a connection to a wireless network and making that connection secure. Third, I'll show you how to choose TCP/IP settings for a network connection manually if you need to; usually, Windows sets them automatically for you. Fourth, we'll make sure your PC is sharing only those items you want to share. Fifth and last, we'll go through what you need to do to protect your own wireless network.

Connect Safely to a Wired Network

A wired network tends to be much more secure than a wireless network. This is simply because the cables that make up the network tend to be confined within the building, and any intruder tapping into the network is easy to detect. For example, an attacker can connect a PC or device to the network switch, but to do so, he needs to have physical access to the switch, and usually needs to leave whatever device he connects somewhere that you can discover it.

(If you feel the previous paragraph states the obvious—you're right, it does. But you'll perhaps appreciate the differences when we consider the vulnerabilities in wireless networks later in this chapter.)

Note In case you're wondering, intelligence agencies have various crafty tools that enable them to tap into wired networks. For example, hi-tech "sniffer" tools can read the signals going through an Ethernet cable without actually tapping into it. Similarly, scanners not only can detect the signals going to a CRT monitor but can also display what they show, giving an attacker a picture of what you're seeing onscreen. But if you're facing attackers armed with tools this sophisticated, you need advice from heavyweight lawyers rather than from this lightweight book.

How a Wired Network Works

As you'll know if you have one, an Ethernet network looks something like Figure 4-1. Each computer or device connects via a network cable to a central switch box that passes the signals back and forth.

These days, the central switch box is usually a *network switch,* a device that builds an internal map of the computers on the network and passes along data only to the destination computer, where the computer grabs it. Older networks used *network hubs*—devices that simply send the data they receive along all the wires so that the destination computer (wherever it is) can grab the data. A switch gives better performance than a hub because it manages the network's capacity more smartly—there's much less data crashing about the network looking for its destination.

If you're putting together a small network with a broadband Internet connection, you'll probably use a DSL router or cable router that includes a switch for a wired network, a wireless access point for a wireless network, or both.

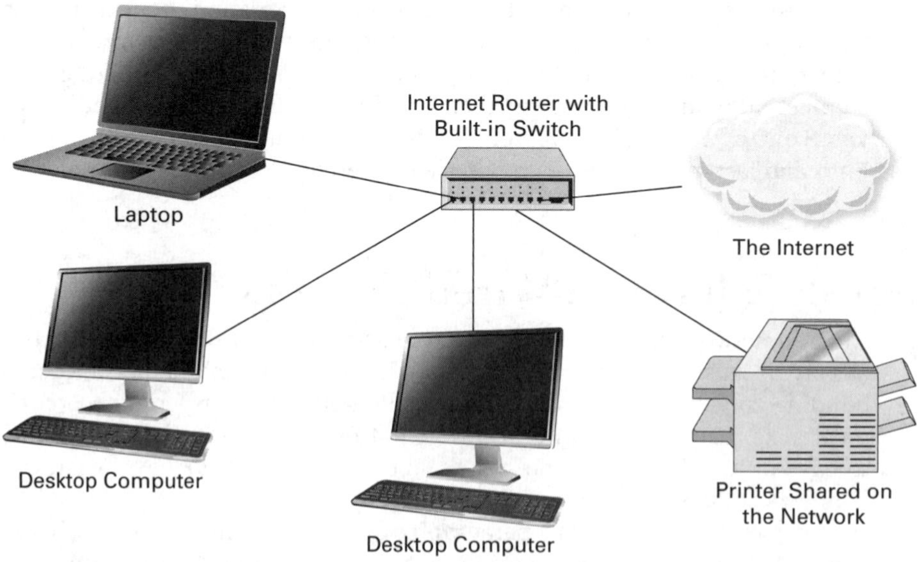

FIGURE 4-1 A wired network is based around a central switch box that directs the data to the PCs and other devices.

Understand Wired Network Technologies and Choose the Right One

Almost all wired networks use one of the three main Ethernet standards:

- **Ethernet** Regular Ethernet, also called 10BaseT, has a maximum speed of 10 megabits per second, or 10 Mbps. A megabit is a million bits of data. Each byte consists of eight bits. So a 10 Mbps connection can transfer at most 1.25 megabytes (MB) per second.
- **Fast Ethernet** Fast Ethernet, also called 100BaseT, has a maximum speed of 100 Mbps. So it can transfer at most 12.5MB per second.
- **Gigabit Ethernet** Gigabit Ethernet, also called 1000BaseT, has a maximum speed of 1000 Mbps. So it can transfer at most 125MB per second.

If you need to set up a wired network for just a few computers, and you don't yet have an Internet router, your best bet is to get a router with a built-in switch. Many Internet routers include a four-port switch, which is enough for a small network. Others include both wired and wireless switches, which enable you to build a bigger network using both technologies.

If you need a larger network than a built-in switch in a router can provide, or if you already have an Internet router, buy a switch and connect it to the router or the built-in switch.

If you're buying a new switch, Gigabit Ethernet is the best choice. Almost all Gigabit Ethernet switches are backward compatible with Fast Ethernet and regular Ethernet, so you can connect any standard Ethernet device to them. So even if your PC has only a Fast Ethernet port, a Gigabit Ethernet switch is a better choice than a Fast Ethernet switch—especially as your next PC will likely have a Gigabit Ethernet port.

To confirm that the switch is backward compatible, look for "10/100/1000" on it, indicating that it can run at 10 Mbps, 100 Mbps, or 1000 Mbps. Also, make sure the ports are auto-sensing. This enables different ports to run at different speeds, so that a single slower device doesn't drag the whole network down to its speed.

If you can get a great deal on a Fast Ethernet switch, or pick one up for free from someone who's upgrading to Gigabit Ethernet, go for it. Similarly, if someone offers you a regular Ethernet switch or hub for free, take it. Even regular Ethernet is perfectly workable for sharing any regular-speed broadband connections, such as a 2 Mbps DSL or a 6 Mbps cable connection, although transferring large files from one computer on the network to another will be slow. A regular Ethernet network will be a bottleneck only if the Internet connection delivers more than 10 Mbps. Most Internet connections are much slower than this.

Make the Connection to the Wired Network

To connect your PC to a wired network, you plug one end of an Ethernet cable into an Ethernet port on your PC and the other end into an Ethernet port on the network.

When you connect the PC to the network, Windows automatically tries to apply suitable settings. If your network is set up to provide the settings automatically, you won't need to change any settings: After a few seconds, Windows will have connected to the network, and you will be able to access both the networked computers and devices and the Internet (assuming the network shares an Internet connection).

Note If Windows is unable to apply the right network settings, you can apply them manually. See the section "Choose TCP/IP Settings for a Network Connection," later in this chapter, for instructions.

Protect the Wired Network Connection

When you connect your PC to a wired network, you need to protect the PC from attacks. There are two main threats:

- **The other computers on the network** If one of the other computers has a virus or other malware, that software can spread to your PC. Users of other computers on the network can also attack your computer, either accidentally or deliberately.
- **The Internet** Through the shared Internet connection, you have full access to the incredible range of attacks, viruses, and malware on the Internet.

To keep your PC safe on a wired network, you need to take two major precautions:

- **Turn on Windows Firewall** As discussed in Chapter 3, turn on Windows Firewall and check its configuration.
- **Run security software** Also as discussed in Chapter 3, install security software such as Microsoft Security Essentials on your PC and keep it updated. Scan your PC regularly for threats, and keep the real-time protection features turned on to detect Internet attacks.

Connect Safely to a Wireless Network

Wireless networks can be quick to set up and convenient, because you don't need to drill holes through the walls and floors and string cables like tripwires from room to room. Instead, you just set up the access point and then configure the computers to connect to it. But because wireless networks not only have wider reach than wired networks but also offer more ways for intruders to break in, you must spend more time and effort protecting them than wired networks.

In this section, we'll look first at how a wireless network works so that you understand the threats it poses. We'll then go through establishing the connection to the network. After that, I'll show you how to protect the wireless network connection.

Note For information on how to keep intruders out of your wireless network, see the section "Lock Down Your Own Wi-Fi Network Against Intruders," later in this chapter.

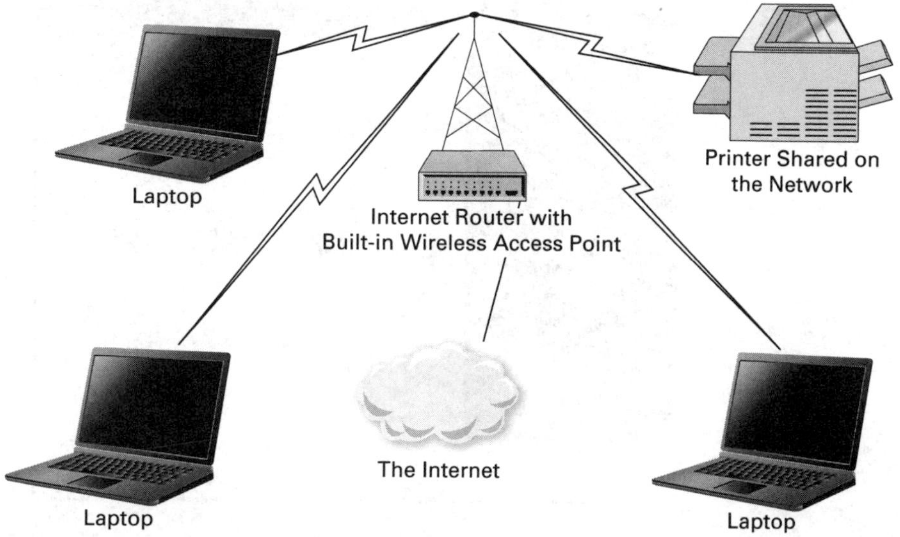

FIGURE 4-2 In a wireless network, the computers connect to the network and the Internet through a wireless access point. Many Internet routers have a wireless access point built in.

How a Wireless Network Works

A wireless network is built around a wireless access point. Each PC or device has a wireless network adapter that connects to the wireless access point via radio waves and transfers data through the air. Figure 4-2 shows a small wireless network that includes three laptops and a shared printer.

Note These days, most laptop PCs and many desktop PCs have wireless network adapters built in. If your PC doesn't, you can add a wireless network adapter via either USB or a PC Card.

Make the Connection to the Wireless Network

To make the connection to the wireless network, install a wireless network adapter if your PC doesn't already have one. If Windows displays a wizard—for example, the Found New Hardware Wizard on Windows XP (see Figure 4-3)—that asks you to let it install a driver for the wireless network adapter, follow the prompts to install it.

When the wireless network adapter is installed, follow the steps outlined in the next sections for the version of Windows you're using.

When establishing the network connection, Windows automatically tries to detect the network settings needed. If your network is set up to provide the settings automatically, you won't need to change any settings: After a few seconds, Windows will have connected to the network, and you will be able to access both the networked computers and devices and the Internet (assuming the network shares an Internet connection).

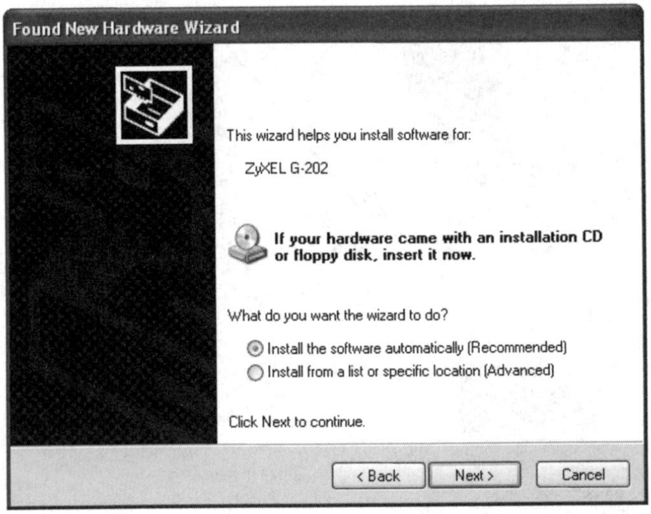

FIGURE 4-3 If you need to install a wireless network adapter before making the connection to the wireless network, allow Windows to install the driver for you.

Note If Windows is unable to apply the right network settings, you can apply them manually. See the section "Choose TCP/IP Settings for a Network Connection," later in this chapter, for instructions.

Connect to the Wireless Network on Windows XP

To connect to the wireless network on Windows XP, follow these steps:

1. If you need to turn on the wireless network adapter, do so.
2. When Windows notices the wireless network adapter, it searches for available wireless networks. If it finds some, it displays the Wireless Networks Detected pop-up balloon, as shown here.

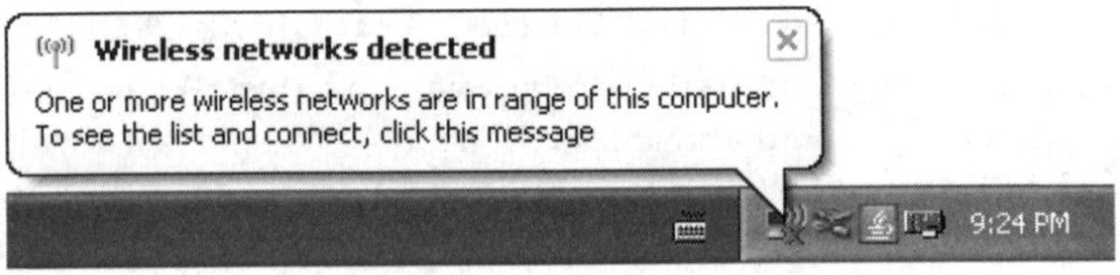

3. Click the balloon to display the Wireless Network Connection window (see Figure 4-4).
4. Click the network you want to connect to.

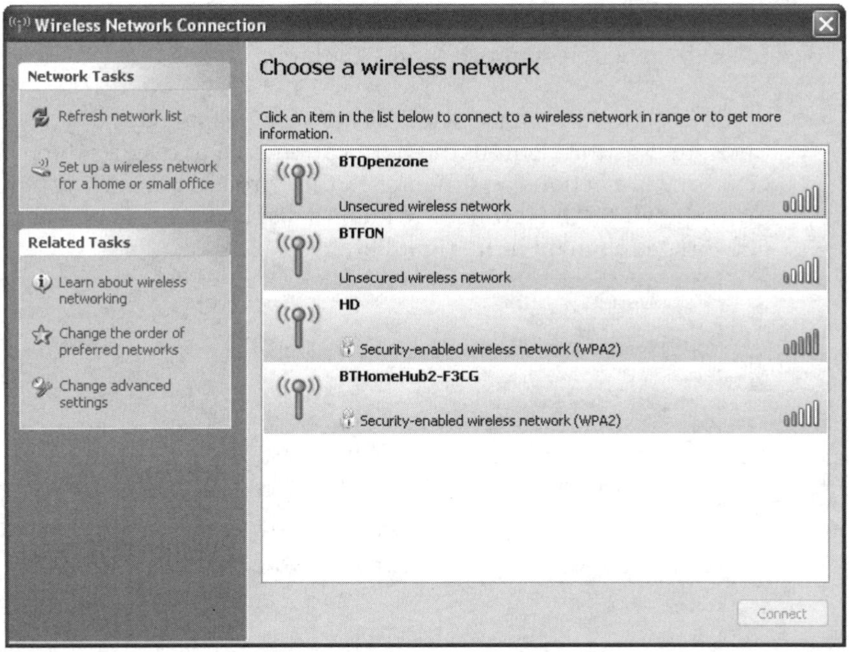

FIGURE 4-4 In the Wireless Network Connection window, click the network you want to connect to.

5. Click the Connect button. If the wireless network has security enabled (as most wireless networks do these days), Windows displays the Wireless Network Connection dialog box shown here, demanding the network key.

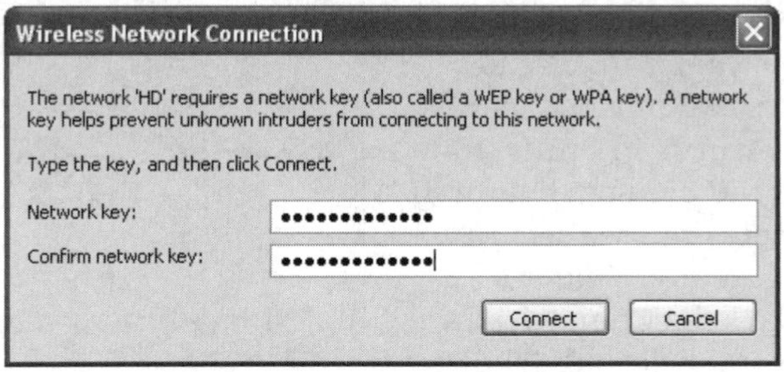

6. Type the key in the Network Key text box, press TAB, and then type the key again in the Confirm Network Key text box.
7. Click the Connect button. Windows tries to connect to the network using the key. If Windows succeeds in connecting to the network, it displays a star to the right of the network's name in the Wireless Network Connection window.
8. Click the Close button (the × button) to close the Wireless Network Connection window.

Connect to the Wireless Network on Windows 7

To connect to the wireless network on Windows 7, follow these steps:

1. If you need to turn on the wireless network adapter, do so.
2. Click the Network icon in the notification area to display the panel of available network connections and then click the wireless network you want to connect to, as shown on the left here. Windows displays controls for connecting to the network, as shown on the right here.

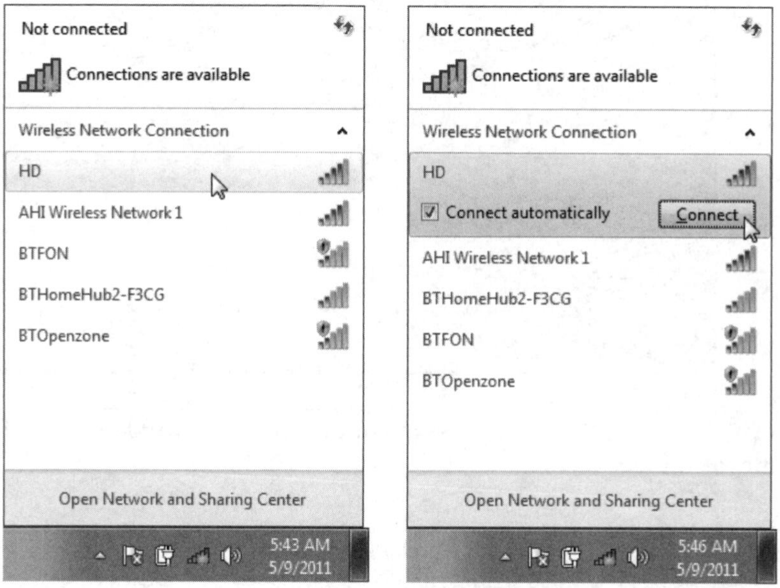

3. Select the Connect Automatically check box if you want Windows to connect automatically to this network in future.
4. Click the Connect button. If the network uses security (as most do), Windows displays the Connect To A Network dialog box, shown here.

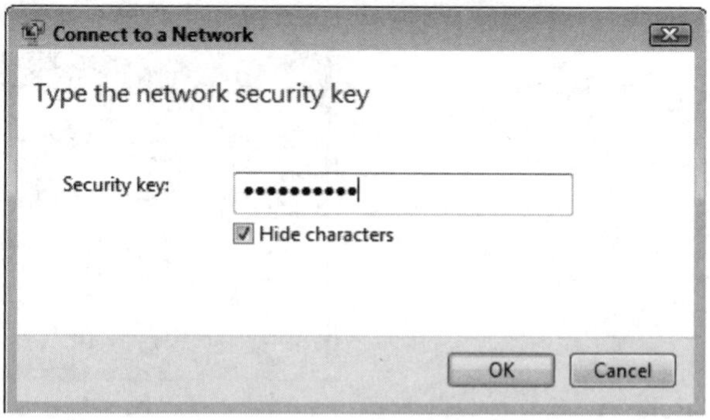

5. Select the Hide Characters check box if you want to prevent anyone looking over your shoulder from seeing the password.
6. Type the password in the Security Key text box.
7. Click the OK button. Windows connects to the network.

Protect the Connection to the Wireless Network

When you connect your PC to a wireless network, you expose it to the same threats as those on a wired network:

- Viruses, malware, and attacks from the other computers on the network
- The full malevolence and contagion of the Internet

So you need to protect your PC by turning Windows Firewall on and running security software such as Microsoft Security Essentials. (See Chapter 3 for instructions on both these moves.)

But a wireless network also exposes your PC to the threat of attackers who access your network from outside it. If such attackers are discreet, you may find it hard to detect them on the network.

Even though your wireless access point's range probably extends only a short way outside your home, an attacker can connect to the wireless network from much farther away by pointing an antenna at your network. The attacker typically needs a line of sight to your home, but in many places they can easily get a line of sight from a tall building or a hill.

Because a wireless network can be hacked into remotely like this, it's vital that you lock down your wireless network, as discussed in the section "Lock Down Your Own Wi-Fi Network Against Intruders," later in this chapter.

Choose TCP/IP Settings for a Network Connection

In most cases, Windows handles the network connection automatically. But with some network setups, you may need to choose TCP/IP settings manually in order to connect to the network. This section shows you how to do that.

Open the Network Connections Folder

First, you need to open the Network Connections folder. Here's what to do on the two versions of Windows discussed in this book:

- **Windows XP** Click the Start button, right-click My Network Places, and then click Properties on the context menu.

Note If the My Network Places item doesn't appear on the Start menu, choose Start | Control Panel to display a Control Panel window. If Control Panel opens in Category view, with Pick A Category at the top, click the Switch To Classic View link in the Control Panel box in the upper-left corner to switch to Classic view. Then double-click the Network Connections icon to display the Network Connections window.

- **Windows 7** Click the Network icon in the notification area and then click the Open Network And Sharing Center link to open a Network And Sharing Center window. In the left column, click the Change Adapter Settings link.

Open the Connection and Choose the Settings

Now take the following steps to open the connection and choose settings for it:

1. Right-click the network connection you want to configure and then click Properties on the context menu. Windows displays the Properties dialog box for the connection. At first, the General tab appears at the front, as shown on the left in Figure 4-5 for a wired network connection on Windows XP.
2. Double-click the Internet Protocol (TCP/IP) item or Internet Protocol Version 4 (TCP/IPv4) item to display the General tab of its Properties dialog box (shown on the right in Figure 4-5).
3. Select the Use The Following IP Address option button instead of the Obtain An IP Address Automatically option button. The controls in the Use The Following IP Address group box become available. Windows also automatically selects the Use The Following DNS Server Addresses option button instead of the Obtain DNS Server Address Automatically option button, which was selected before.
4. In the IP Address text box, type the IP address you want to assign your PC. The IP address is typically a number in the 10.0.*n*.*n* range (for example, 10.0.0.22) or a number in the 192.168.*n*.*n* range (for example, 192.168.1.23).
5. In the Subnet Mask text box, type the mask that defines the subnet the PC is on. The most common subnet mask is 255.255.255.0, but your network may use another mask.

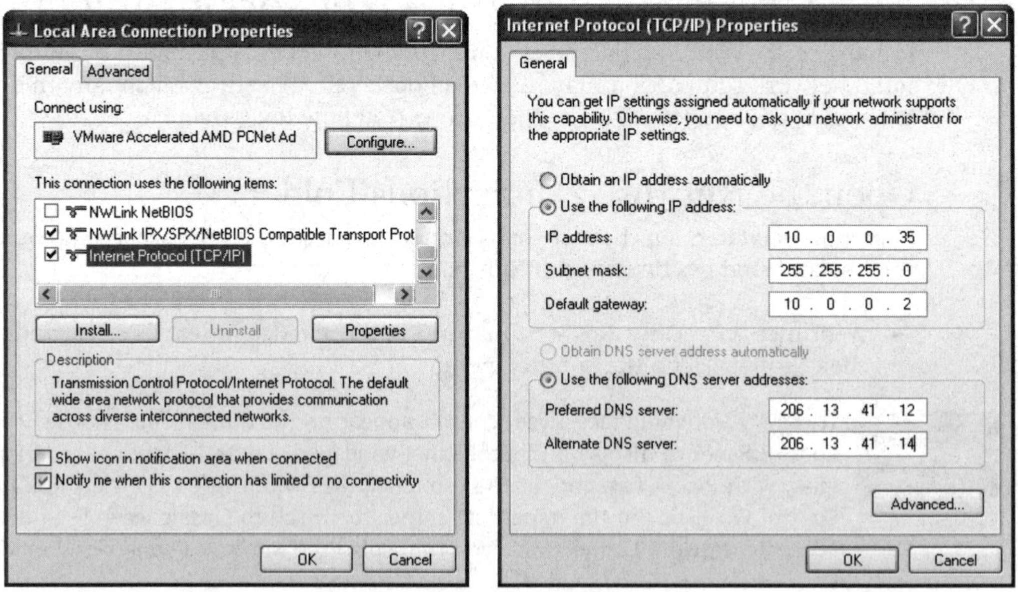

FIGURE 4-5 On the General tab of the connection's Properties dialog box (left), double-click the Internet Protocol (TCP/IP) item or Internet Protocol Version 4 (TCP/IPv4) item to display the General tab of its Properties dialog box (right).

6. In the Default Gateway text box, type the IP address of the gateway computer that connects the PC to the network. For home networks, this IP address is often the IP address of your network's router—for example, 10.0.0.2 or 192.168.0.1.
7. In the Preferred DNS Server text box, type the IP address of the primary DNS server. If your ISP gave you two IP addresses for DNS servers, this is the first of the two.
8. In the Alternate DNS Server text box, type the IP address of the secondary DNS server. If your ISP gave you two IP addresses for DNS servers, this is the

Understanding IP Addresses, DHCP, and DNS

Each computer on a network must have a unique Internet Protocol address, or IP address, to identify it. Your wired network or wireless network is separate from the Internet and is considered a *private network*. The Internet is a *public network*.

The Internet Protocol version 4 (IPv4) has several ranges of addresses used for private networks. The two ranges most commonly used for home networks are the 192.168.*x*.*x* range and the 10.*x*.*x*.*x* range, where each *x* represents a number in the range 0–255. Many home routers use the 192.168.0.1 address or the 10.0.0.2 address by default. Either works fine. (Technically, the 10.*x*.*x*.*x* range can support much bigger networks—but the 192.168.*x*.*x* range has plenty of IP addresses for all home networks.)

Because these address ranges are for private networks only, all private networks can use them. So both you and your neighbor can use the same 192.168.*x*.*x* addresses, because your networks don't connect directly to each other.

Your broadband router has both a private IP address on the local network and a public IP address on the Internet. When a computer on the network sends data to the Internet, the router sends the data from its public IP address.

The normal way of assigning IP addresses within a private network is called Dynamic Host Configuration Protocol (DHCP). When your PC starts up, Windows looks for a DHCP server—a computer or device allocating IP addresses. On your private network, your Internet router normally runs the DHCP server. Your PC requests an IP address from the DHCP server and then uses that address until you shut it down. After that, the DHCP server reclaims the address so that it can issue it to another computer or device.

Sometimes you may want to make sure that one or more computers on your network have specific IP addresses—for example, so that you can set your Internet router to pass along remote-access requests to a particular IP address. Some routers enable you to match an IP address to a computer's name so that the computer always has the same address. It's worth consulting your router's documentation to see if your router has this feature. If not, you can assign IP addresses manually to one or more computers, as discussed in the main text of this chapter.

To find a particular address on the Internet, a computer looks it up using the Domain Name System, or DNS. The computer consults a DNS server, which returns the address the computer needs to contact to reach the address. Normally, you use your ISP's DNS servers to look up addresses. Most ISPs give you a primary DNS server address and a secondary DNS server address; Windows automatically uses the secondary address when the primary address is busy or unavailable.

second address. Having two DNS servers for the connection is optional, but because DNS servers sometimes go down for the count, you should enter the secondary server if you have its address.

9. Click the OK button. Windows closes the Internet Protocol (TCP/IP) Properties dialog box, returning you to the Local Area Connections Properties dialog box.
10. Click the OK button. Windows closes the Local Area Connection Properties dialog box and applies your settings.

Now make sure the connection is working. The easiest way to do this is to open your web browser and ensure it displays a web page. For example, choose Start | Internet on Windows XP, or click the Internet Explorer button on the taskbar in Windows 7.

Control Which Items Your PC Is Sharing on the Network

After setting up your wired or wireless connection to the network, make sure that your PC is sharing only the items you want on the network.

Windows can share many items, such as files, printers, your PC's Public folder, and your music files. Sharing can be great for working with others or simply enjoying media, but it exposes parts of Windows to the network. So you should turn off any types of sharing you don't use. And if you don't use sharing at all, turn it off altogether.

Control Whether Windows XP Is Sharing Files and Printers

To control whether Windows XP is sharing files and printers on the network, you run the Network Setup Wizard. Follow these steps:

1. Choose Start | All Programs | Accessories | Communications | Network Setup Wizard to launch the Network Setup Wizard.
2. On the Welcome To The Network Setup Wizard screen, click the Next button.
3. On the Before You Continue screen, complete the steps listed: installing the network cards and cables, turning on all the computers and devices, and connecting to the Internet. You've probably done all this already. When you have done all this, click the Next button.
4. On the Select A Connection Method screen (see Figure 4-6), select the option button that describes your Internet connection. If you have a broadband connection, you'll normally want the This Computer Connects To The Internet Through A Residential Gateway Or Through Another Computer On My Network option button. Then click the Next button.

Note A "residential gateway" is one computing term for the Internet connection a broadband router provides. The term didn't catch on, perhaps because it sounds threateningly domestic.

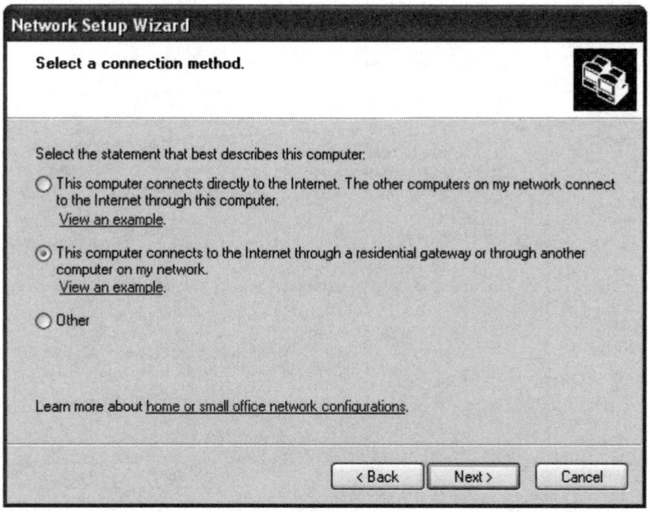

FIGURE 4-6 **On the Select A Connection Method screen, you'll normally want to select the This Computer Connects To The Internet Through A Residential Gateway Or Through Another Computer On My Network option button.**

5. On the Give This Computer A Description And Name screen, leave the text in the Computer Description box and the Computer Name box alone unless you need to change it. Click the Next button.
6. On the Name Your Network screen, type the workgroup name you're using for your network. There's a bug that makes Windows revert to the MSHOME workgroup name, so you need to type the right name even when you're just running the Network Setup Wizard to turn file and printer sharing on or off. Click the Next button to move along.
7. On the File And Printer Sharing screen (see Figure 4-7), select the Turn On File And Printer Sharing option button or the Turn Off File And Printer Sharing option button, as appropriate. Click the Next button.
8. On the Ready To Apply Network Settings screen, check through the settings and then click the Next button if they're okay.
9. On the You're Almost Done screen, select the Just Finish The Wizard; I Don't Need To Run The Wizard On Other Computers option button. Click the Next button.
10. On the Completing The Network Setup Wizard screen, click the Finish button.

Control Which Items Windows 7 Is Sharing

To control which items Windows 7 is sharing on the network, follow these steps:

1. Choose Start | Computer to open a Computer window.
2. In the left column, right-click the Network item and then click Properties on the context menu to open the Network And Sharing Center window.

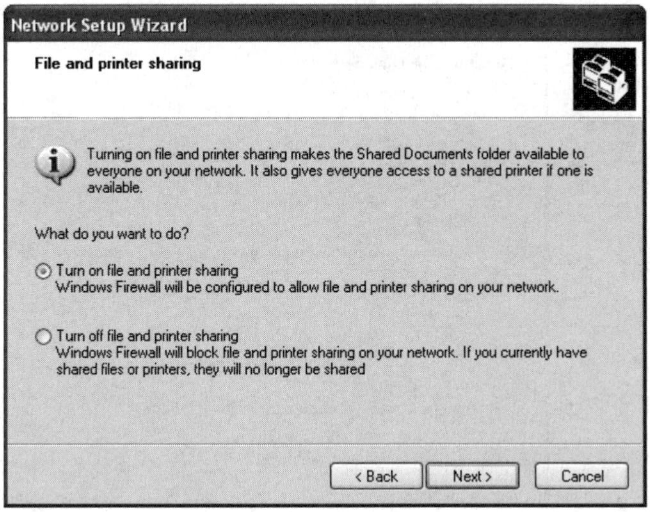

FIGURE 4-7 On the File And Printer Sharing screen of the Network Setup Wizard, choose whether to turn file and printer sharing on or off.

3. In the left column, click the Change Advanced Sharing Settings link to display the Advanced Sharing Settings window (shown here).

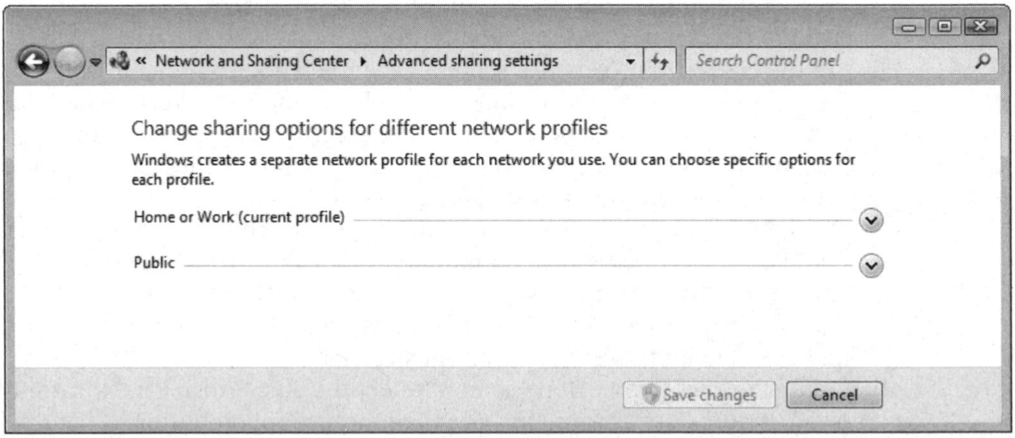

4. Click the down-arrow button on the Home Or Work line to display the sharing options (see Figure 4-8).
5. If you want your PC to be visible on the network, select the Turn On Network Discovery option button. To hide your PC, select the Turn Off Network Discovery option button.
6. If you want to share your files and printers with other people on the network, select the Turn On File And Printer Sharing option button. Otherwise, select the Turn Off File And Printer Sharing option button.

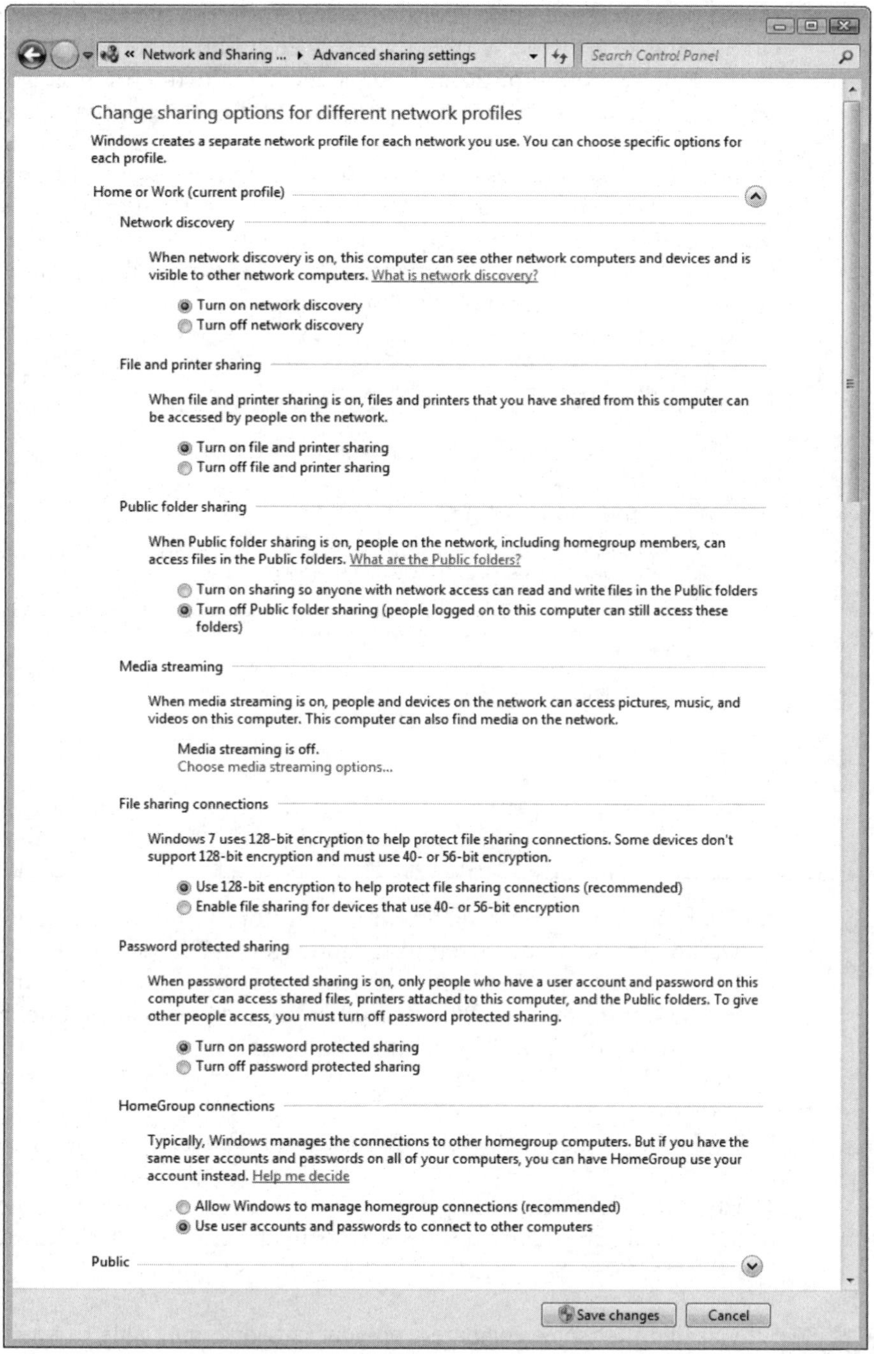

FIGURE 4-8 In the Advanced Sharing Settings window, you can control exactly which items Windows 7 shares on your Home or Work profile and your Public profile.

7. If you want to share your PC's Public folder on the network, select the Turn On Sharing So Anyone With Network Access Can Read And Write Files In The Public Folders option button. If not, select the Turn Off Public Folder Sharing (People Logged On To This Computer Can Still Access These Folders) option button.
8. If you want to share music, video, and picture files, see whether the readout in the Media Streaming area says Media Streaming Is On or Media Streaming Is Off. If it's off, follow these steps to set up media streaming:
   a. Click the Choose Media Streaming Options link to display the Media Streaming Options window, shown here.

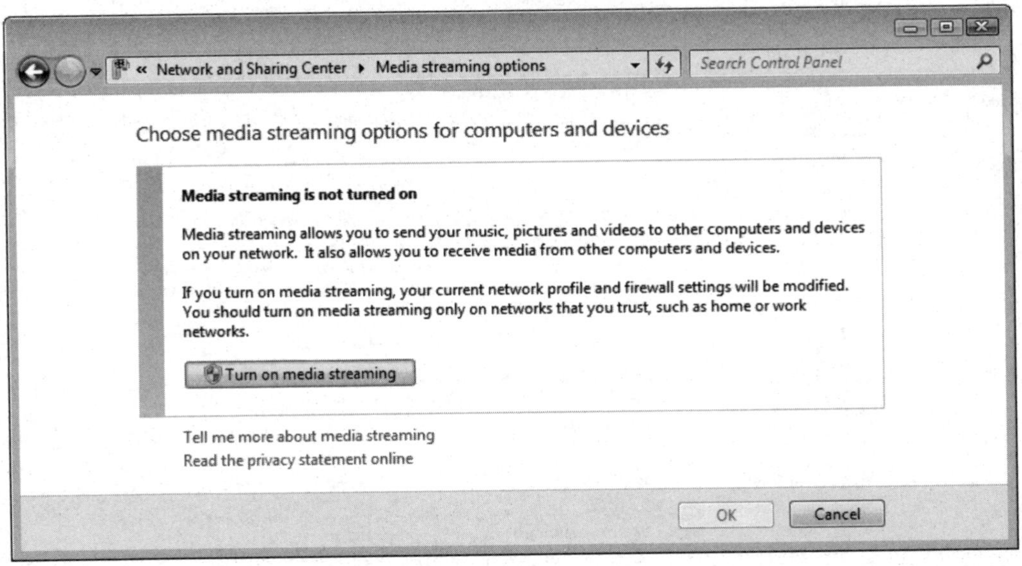

   b. Click the Turn On Media Streaming button. Windows displays a different version of the Media Streaming Options window (see Figure 4-9).
   c. In the Name Your Media Library box, type the name you want your shared media library to have. The default setting is your user name, but you may want to go for something snappier.
   d. In the Show Devices On drop-down list, make sure Local Network is selected.
   e. In the list box, select each item and then choose Allowed or Blocked, as needed.
   f. Click the OK button to return to the Advanced Sharing Settings window.
9. In the File Sharing Connections area, select the Use 128-Bit Encryption To Help Protect File Sharing Connections option button.

Note If you find that some computers on your network aren't able to access your shared files, go back to the File Sharing Connections area and select the Enable File Sharing For Devices That Use 40- Or 56-Bit Encryption option button. Click the Save Changes button to save the change.

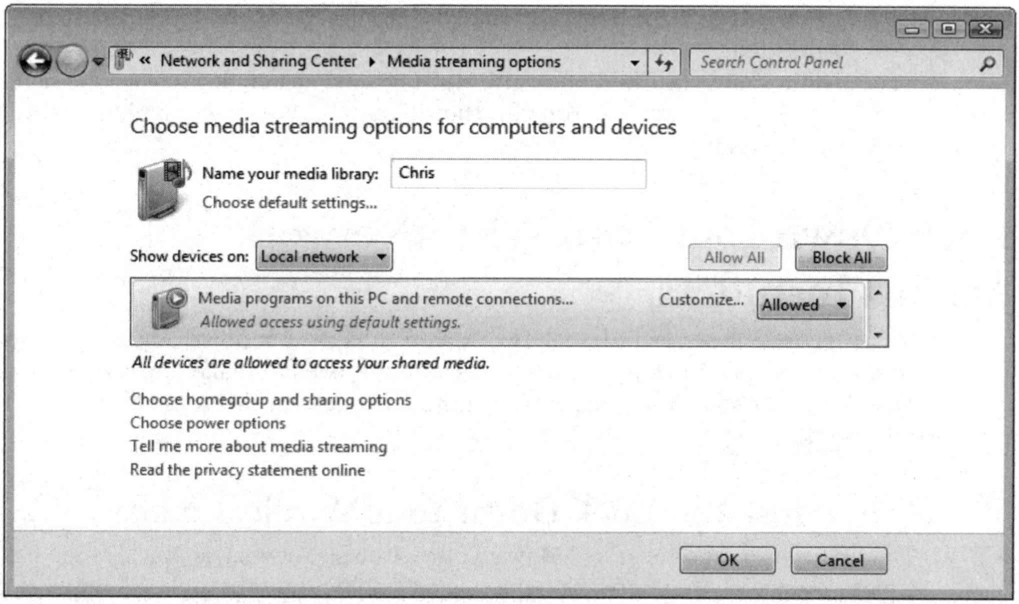

FIGURE 4-9 In the Media Streaming Options window, choose which media programs and remote connections to allow and which to block.

10. If you want to limit access to your shared files, printers, and the Public folder to only those people who have a user account and password on your PC, select the Turn On Password Protected Sharing option button. If you want anyone on the network to be able to access the shared items, select the Turn Off Password Protected Sharing option button.
11. In the HomeGroup Connections area, it is usually best to select the Allow Windows To Manage Homegroup Connections option button. The alternative is to select the Use User Accounts And Passwords To Connect To Other Computers option button, which requires you to do more setup.
12. Click the down-arrow button on the Public line to display the sharing options for public networks. These are broadly similar to the settings for private networks, so we won't go through them in full detail—but briefly, these are the settings you'll usually want:
    - **Network Discovery** Select the Turn Off Network Discovery option button.
    - **File And Printer Sharing** Select the Turn Off File And Printer Sharing option button.
    - **Public Folder Sharing** Select the Turn Off Public Folder Sharing (People Logged On To This Computer Can Still Access These Folders) option button.
    - **Media Streaming** Don't turn this on.
    - **File Sharing Connections** Select the Use 128-Bit Encryption To Help Protect File Sharing Connections option button.

- **Password Protected Sharing** Select the Password Protected Sharing option button.

13. When you've finished choosing sharing settings, click the Save Changes button to save your changes. You can then close the Windows Explorer windows you've opened.

Lock Down Your Own Wi-Fi Network Against Intruders

If you have your own wireless network, you must lock it down so that intruders can't break in. This section shows you five essential moves to make your wireless network more secure. It also discusses why making a wireless network totally secure is almost impossible.

Why Must You Lock Down Your Wireless Network?

The first reason you must lock down your wireless network is that it is too easy to attack. Unlike a wired network, which is accessible only through the network's cables and the Internet connection, a wireless network typically extends beyond the building that contains it. Worse, a wireless network automatically broadcasts its name, so any device within range knows the network is there. Worse still, an attacker can connect to the network from a distance by pointing an antenna at the network from anywhere he or she can establish a line of sight.

After connecting to the network, the attacker can attempt to access data on the computers within the network. Only you know what embarrassments your personal files contain—but we all have reasons for wanting to keep sensitive things private.

Even if you protect your computers against intrusion from computers that connect to the network, an attacker can still use your shared Internet connection. This is another worry, because all the activity that takes place on the Internet connection appears to originate from you. So if an attacker uses your connection to attack other computers, to con people, or to download unsavory files, you'll appear to be the perpetrator—and you'll have a hard time proving that you weren't.

So if you have a wireless network, you must actively take steps to prevent unauthorized people from accessing it.

Note The laws that cover wireless networks are unclear, and the courts interpret them in different ways. But as things stand at this writing, it's a mistake to leave your wireless network unsecured or demonstrably poorly secured. If other people can easily use your network, you may be held responsible.

This section discusses five essential moves you can make to protect your wireless network against unauthorized use. None of these measures is a panacea, but if you implement them all, your network will be reasonably secure. Perhaps more importantly, you will be able to demonstrate that if anybody hacks into your network, they have done so deliberately and skillfully rather than because of your negligence.

Note Locking down your wireless network is like installing a burglar alarm: The measures you can implement are a deterrent to casual would-be intruders, but unless you go to the extreme of implementing a virtual private network (as discussed on this book's website), a determined intruder can still break into your wireless network. Similarly, installing an alarm and window bars will prevent opportunistic thieves from breaking into your house, but a determined attacker with a wrecking ball will still be able to break in. You might look at wireless network security as trying to move casual intruders on to lower-hanging fruit rather than to ensure total security.

Change the Password on Your Wireless Access Point

Your first step is to change the password on your wireless access point. Most wireless access points come with a standard password set that provides a minimal level of security. The problem is that anyone can look up the standard password for any model of wireless access point on the Internet in seconds, which would enable them to take control of the wireless access point and change its settings to do what they want.

So your first move after getting a wireless access point should be to change its password. Set a new strong password (see the nearby Note) and make sure you remember it. The method for setting the access point's password varies depending on the device's model, so either log into your access point and see what you find, or consult the router's documentation.

Note A *strong* password is one that is impossible to guess and very difficult to break with a dictionary attack—an attack that tries to find the password by supplying the words in a list (called a *dictionary)* one at a time. To create a strong password, use eight characters or more; don't use any real word in any language; and include at least one number and one symbol (for example, ! or *).

Implement WPA Security

Your next step in securing your wireless network is to use Wi-Fi Protected Access (WPA)—preferably WPA2 if your wireless access point supports it. WPA is a security protocol that provides good levels of security for a wireless network. WPA usually uses a pre-shared key (PSK) to encrypt the data.

To use WPA, you specify WPA as the security type when setting up the network and then provide a suitable password to use.

Caution Don't use Wired Equivalent Privacy (WEP) to secure your wireless network. WEP has known flaws, and an attacker can easily break in. Most wireless access points include WEP for backward compatibility, but it's not strong enough to keep your wireless network safe.

Change the Name and Password for the Wireless Network

Each wireless network has a name to identify it. The name is more formally called a *service set identifier,* or SSID for (relatively) short. The SSID can be descriptive (for example, WarehouseOne) or generic (for example, belkin54g).

To enable users to get the wireless network set up quickly, each wireless access point comes with a default SSID and a default password. Anyone can look up these default names and passwords on the Internet, so it's important that you change both the SSID and the password. If you don't change the name, an attacker can tell which kind of wireless access point you have. He can then try to break in using the default password—and if you haven't changed the password, he'll be connected to the network in moments.

You can change the SSID and password in any of several ways:

- **By using the wireless access point's configuration program** Many wireless access points include configuration programs for setting up and maintaining the access point.
- **By using the wireless access point's configuration screens** Most wireless access points have a web-based interface you can access through any web browser.
- **By using a wizard in Windows** Windows provides a wizard for setting up a wireless network. For example, in Windows XP, choose Start | All Programs | Accessories | Communications | Wireless Network Setup Wizard to display the Wireless Network Setup Wizard. Figure 4-10 shows the Create A Name For Your Wireless Network screen of the Wireless Network Setup Wizard. On this screen, you specify the SSID for the network. You then save the wireless network's settings to a USB drive, plug it into the wireless access point to configure the access point, and then plug it into each PC in turn to configure that PC.

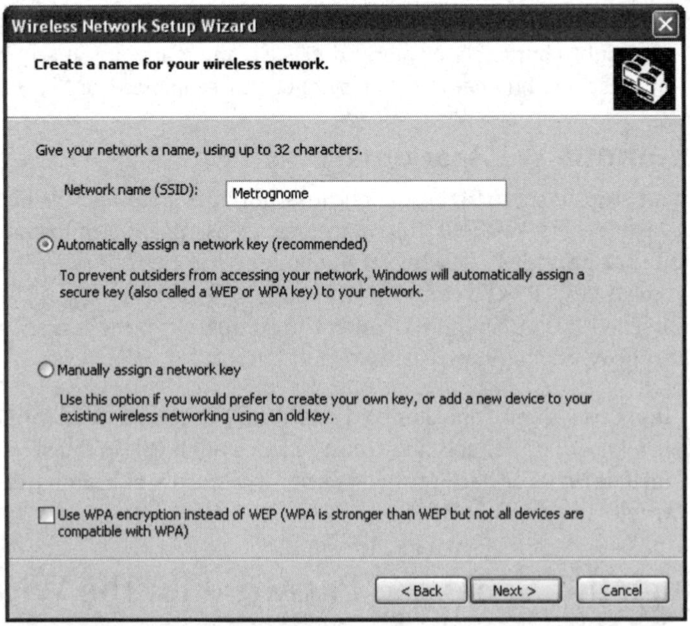

FIGURE 4-10 When setting up a new network, you can use the Wireless Network Setup Wizard in Windows XP to assign an SSID to your wireless access point.

Make the Wireless Network Closed

Your next move to protect your wireless network is to set your wireless access point to not broadcast its SSID. As you read earlier in this chapter, a wireless network broadcasts its SSID by default to let other devices know it's there.

You already know that the wireless network is there, so you don't need these broadcasts. So use your wireless access point's configuration program or configuration screens to turn off SSID broadcasts.

The only downside to making the network closed is that each time you add a PC or device to the network for the first time, you have to type in the network name. This is because the PC or device can't pick up the network name automatically.

Caution Turning off SSID broadcasts is only a moderately effective security measure. This is because each time a device connects to the wireless network, it sends the network name across the air unencrypted. A determined attacker with a wireless sniffer tool can capture the transmission and learn the network's name. But turning off SSID broadcasts will keep out opportunistic intruders, so it's well worth doing.

Restrict the Hardware Addresses Allowed to Access Your Wireless Network

Each wireless network adapter has a unique hardware address called a Media Access Control address, or MAC address for short. ("MAC" is written in uppercase to differentiate it from Apple's Mac computers, not to indicate shouting.)

On most wireless access points, you can set up a list of MAC addresses that are allowed to connect to the wireless network. If a device whose MAC address isn't approved tries to join the network, the wireless access point refuses the connection, even if the device provides the right authentication information.

To set up the list of allowed MAC addresses, you use your wireless access point's configuration program or configuration screens. This depends on the wireless access point, but most configuration tools include a list of the MAC addresses of the computers and devices connected to the network, together with a way of adding some or all of those addresses to the approved list.

The easiest way to get the list of MAC addresses is by connecting the devices to the wireless network one at a time. As you see each new MAC address appear in the list, you know which device it belongs to, and you can choose whether to allow it.

You can also find the MAC address by looking on the computer or device itself. This section shows you how to find the MAC address in Windows XP and Windows 7.

Caution Restricting access to only specific MAC addresses would be a great security measure—but determined attackers can circumvent this measure too. By using a sniffer, the attacker learns which MAC addresses are allowed to connect. The attacker then uses a program to *spoof* (pretend to be) the MAC address of an approved device when that device isn't connected to the network.

Find the MAC Address in Windows XP

To find the MAC address in Windows XP, follow these steps:

1. Choose Start | Control Panel to open a Control Panel window.
2. If Control Panel opens in Category view, with Pick A Category at the top, click the Switch To Classic View link in the Control Panel box in the upper-left corner to switch to Classic view.
3. Double-click the Network Connections icon to display the Network Connections window.
4. Double-click the connection for your wireless network to display its Status dialog box.
5. Click the Support tab to display its contents.
6. Click the Details button to display the Network Connection Details dialog box (see Figure 4-11).
7. Click the Close button to close the Network Connection Details dialog box.
8. Click the OK button to close the Status dialog box.

Tip You can press CTRL-C to copy all the contents of the Network Connections Details list, including the Physical Address readout. You can then paste this information into a text document (for example, in Notepad) and then copy only the MAC address.

Find the MAC Address in Windows 7

To find the MAC address in Windows 7, follow these steps:

1. Right-click the wireless network icon in the notification area and then click Open Network And Sharing Center on the context menu. The Network And Sharing Center window opens.

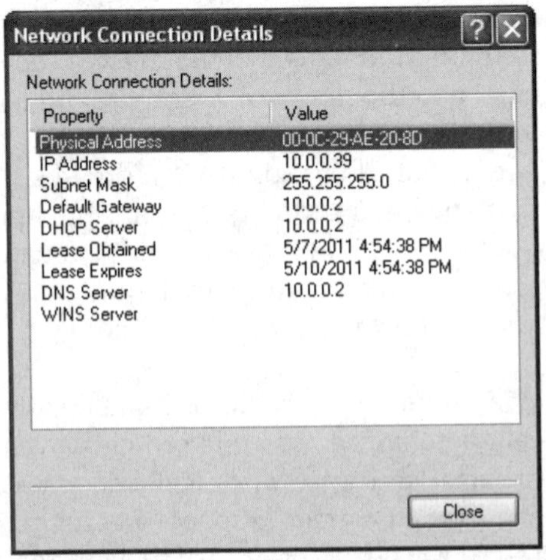

FIGURE 4-11 The Physical Address readout in the Network Connection Details dialog box shows the MAC address on Windows XP.

2. In the left pane, click the Change Adapter Settings link. The Network Connections window opens.
3. Double-click the connection for your wireless network to display the Status dialog box.
4. Click the Details button to display the Network Connection Details dialog box (see Figure 4-12).

Tip You can press CTRL-C to copy all the contents of the Network Connections Details list, including the Physical Address readout. You can then paste this information into a text document (for example, in Notepad) and then copy only the MAC address.

5. Click the Close button to close the Network Connection Details dialog box.
6. Click the Close button to close the Status dialog box.

Note The security measures described in this chapter are enough to prevent casual intruders from accessing your network. But because a wireless network's traffic goes across the air rather than along a wire, a determined attacker may still be able to access your network. If you need to ensure that none of the data you send across the wireless network can be read by an attacker, you can implement virtual private networking (VPN) on the wireless network. This subject is beyond the scope of this book, but you'll find instructions on the companion website.

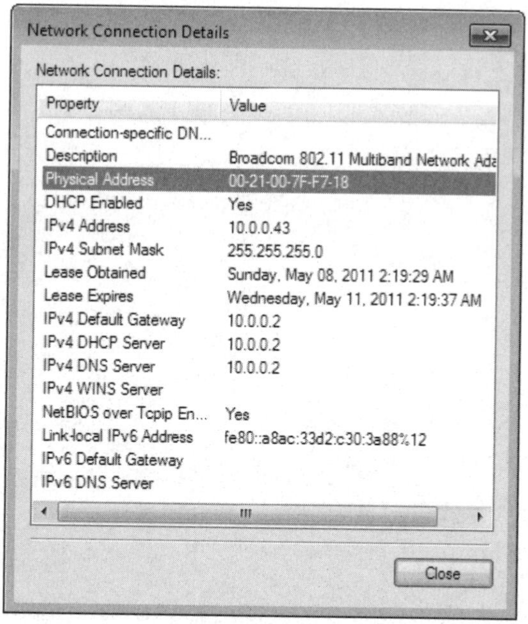

FIGURE 4-12 The Physical Address readout in the Network Connection Details dialog box shows the MAC address on Windows 7.

5 Connect Safely to the Internet

If you want to see a security expert start gibbering in terror, all you need do is show him an unprotected Windows PC connected to the Internet. He'll be petrified because he knows exactly what can happen to that PC—in fact, what has almost certainly happened already.

A few years ago, a study showed that a PC with a fresh installation of Windows and no antivirus software would pick up a virus, malware, or spyware infection within 20 minutes of being connected to the Internet. This makes clear both why such vast numbers of Windows PCs on the Internet are infected with malware and why it's so essential that you protect your PC.

In this chapter, we'll discuss how to connect safely to the Internet. I'll assume you've taken the security measures discussed in Chapters 3 and 4: keeping Windows updated, installing security software and making sure its real-time protection features are turned on, turning on Windows Firewall, and making sure Windows isn't sharing anything on the network that you don't want it to share.

We'll start by making sure you understand the threats the Internet poses to your PC, to your privacy and identity, and to your future. After all, if you're not worried about security, why bother protecting your PC at all? (Many people don't—but many of them end up regretting it.)

We'll then discuss the various types of Internet connections available, so that you can choose the best connection if you don't already have one or if you need to upgrade from your current connection.

Then we'll look at how to protect your Internet connection by "hardening" your Internet router, making sure its firewall is on and suitably configured for your needs. I'll show you an easy way to check your security by using an online tool that tries to probe the network.

Finally, we'll use an online tool to see how fast your Internet connection actually is. If you want to find this out first so that you know how your existing Internet connection compares to other options, jump to the end of the chapter and find out.

Understand the Threats from the Internet

In this section, we'll run quickly through the most direct threats the Internet poses to your PC and yourself. This is just a short exploration to convince you that protecting your PC is not only worthwhile but essential; it's not a laundry list of all the threats your PC faces. We'll explore other threats, such as spam and e-mail scams, in later chapters, together with ways to identify them and counteract them.

Now that more than a billion people are online, the Internet offers malefactors and criminals opportunities several orders of magnitude greater than ever before. By exploiting you or your PC, an attacker can increase his power, wealth, influence, or all three—so it's no wonder there are plenty of attackers.

The following list explains six direct threats the Internet poses to your PC. You'll notice that you need to take a specific action to trigger some threats—for example, you may need to download and run a file. But other threats either require no action on

"There's Nothing Valuable on My PC. Why Do I Need to Protect It?"

Many people ask this question, and it's a fair one. Let's go over why it's vital that you protect your PC.

First, a PC *does* usually contain valuable or at least sensitive data, such as the following:

- Your personal information (useful for *identity theft*—in other words, impersonation)
- Your financial information (useful for attacking your bank accounts or for phishing)
- Your contacts, including their e-mail addresses, phone numbers, and real-world addresses (useful for phishing or *social engineering*—trying to persuade someone to do something you want them to do)
- Your bookmarks and web-surfing history (useful for learning what you're interested in and what kinds of spam or offers might tempt you to respond)
- Your login information for shopping and financial websites (useful for attacks such as shopping on your credit cards)
- Login information for your Internet router (useful for breaking into it)

But let's say you don't bank or shop online, surf the Web, or send e-mail—so your PC really contains no sensitive or valuable data.

Do you still need to protect your PC?

Yes—you absolutely must protect it. That's because an attacker can take control of your PC and then use it to attack other PCs. The attacker can be anywhere in the world that he can get an Internet connection. Likewise, his targets can be anywhere in the world.

If anyone detects the attacks and traces the attacker, the tracks come back to you—as does the responsibility for them.

Similarly, if you have a gun, you know that you need to keep it safe. The issue isn't simply what *you* might do with the gun. It's what others might do with it.

your part or have much subtler triggers that are easy to pull unintentionally. Others yet may succeed because of *inaction* on your part—for example, because you have not installed security software, implemented Windows Firewall, or hardened your Internet router.

These are the six direct threats you need to protect against:

- **Intrusion** If you take your PC onto the Internet without a firewall and other protection, an attacker can break in across the Internet connection and copy sensitive information. You may not be able to detect such an intrusion. (An attacker could also delete your files, but you'd likely notice pretty soon—and there probably wouldn't be much in it for the attacker.)
- **Identity theft** If an attacker can access your PC, she may be able to learn enough information to enable her to impersonate you—"identity theft," as the newspapers call it. (The term "identity theft" is catchy but inaccurate because nobody can steal your identity—it's part of you. But someone who learns your identifying details can certainly impersonate you.)
- **Remote control** If you take your PC onto the Internet unprotected, an attacker can break into your PC across the Internet connection. If the attacker can gain remote control of your PC, she can take any actions remotely with the PC that you can take when sitting at the keyboard. If the attacker uses the PC when you're not using it, you may have no indication that she has used the PC—so she can continue to use it freely.
- **Drive-by attack** You go to a website—and it attacks your PC. You don't need to click anything on the website or download any files from it. Just going to the website launches a script that tries to exploit known weaknesses in Windows. A drive-by attack can install remote-control software on your PC that enables an attacker to take control of it remotely at will, or make it part of a botnet (discussed next).
- **Botnet** An attacker gaining remote control of your PC can install software that lets him use it to attack other computers, send spam, or share illegal files. Again, all this can happen without you being aware of it. The owners of most botnet computers, which are also called *zombie computers* or simply *zombies,* remain blithely unaware of the crimes their computers are committing in the dead of night or other supposed downtime.
- **Viruses and malware hidden in downloads** As you know, you can download vast amounts of free stuff from the Internet—everything from useful programs to screen savers, from celebrity pictures to videos of celebrities behaving bizarrely. Lots of the files are fine, but others are just a way to sneak malicious software onto your PC. So every time you download a file, you need to scan it to see if it's harboring malware. If you're running Microsoft Security Essentials, as I recommended in Chapter 3, make sure the real-time protection features are turned on; they can detect problems in files you download.

Caution Messages coming into your mailboxes can also contain attacks. A message created the right way can attack your PC when you do no more than open the message to see what it's about or what it contains.

Get the Best Type of Internet Connection for Your Needs

In the dark days of the early 1990s, a dial-up modem was the regular way for consumers to connect to the Internet. Modem speeds gradually crawled up from 14.4 kilobits per second (14.4 Kbps) to 56 Kbps maximum, but stuck there.

Note The reason modems are slow is that they convert digital data to sound, transfer the sound over a phone line, and then convert the sound back to digital data. This is a cumbersome process that's best avoided unless you have no alternative. (In case you're wondering, fax machines do the same thing—hence the same screeching sounds. But fax machines transfer data at even slower speeds.)

In most places these days, you can get a much faster connection than a modem. Faster connections are generally referred to as *broadband connections*.

This section walks you through the commonly available Internet connection technologies, starting with the slowest and speeding up to the fastest. Once you know your options, you'll be able to decide which connection type makes sense for you.

Choose the Right Type of Internet Connection

Table 5-1 provides a generalized summary of widely available connection options in descending order of preference—in other words, with the best connections first.

Dial-Up Connections

A dial-up connection using a modem is normally the slowest form of Internet connection, but it works almost anywhere you can find a phone line and is usually reliable. On the downside, a dial-up connection is not only slow at transferring data but also slow to connect, typically taking 10–30 seconds to establish a connection.

TABLE 5-1 Typical Internet Connection Options in Descending Order of Preference

Location	Connection Types
Urban or suburban	1. Fiber 2. DSL or cable 3. Wireless 4. Satellite 5. ISDN 6. Dial-up
Rural	1. DSL (if near to a substation) 2. Satellite 3. ISDN 4. Dial-up

These days, a dial-up connection is practical for e-mail or text-only instant messaging, but for most other Internet activities you will find its limitations difficult. See the sidebar "Optimize a Dial-Up Connection" for suggestions on maximizing the use of a dial-up connection while minimizing the irritation its slowness can cause.

The fastest dial-up connection you can get is 53.6 Kbps using a 56 Kbps modem. However, even this speed requires a good-quality telephone line and suitable equipment at the exchange. In practice, speeds of 33.6 Kbps to 48 Kbps are normal. The longer the distance from your modem to the ISP, and the greater the number of devices between the two, the slower the connection is likely to be.

Optimize a Dial-Up Connection

If you're stuck with a dial-up connection, first make sure that your connection is working as well as possible. Here are three suggestions:

- **Keep your connection open** Get a flat-rate ("all you can eat") connection from your ISP and telephone provider. Configure Windows never to drop the connection and to redial if the connection does get dropped (for example, if the ISP drops it or if there's a problem on the phone line). Turn off call waiting so that incoming calls don't knock you offline. You'll need a second phone line or a cell phone if you want to be able to make phone calls as well.
- **Ensure your modem is tuned correctly** Type **modem tune-up** into your favorite search engine to find recommendations for configuring a modem manually or modem-boosting utilities that do the tweaking for you.
- **Bond two or more modems together** If you'll be using dial-up long term and you have (or can get) two or more phone lines, consider bonding two or more modems together to form a single faster connection. There's some overhead on such connections, so you don't get the full bandwidth of the first modem plus the full bandwidth of each other modem—but you should see a considerable improvement. (For example, bonding two modems, each capable of a 48 Kbps connection, might yield a 90 Kbps connection.) Your operating system, your modems, and your ISP all need to support modem bonding.

Next, make sure your Internet applications are using your meager bandwidth sensibly. Here are four suggestions:

- **Web browser** Turn off as much multimedia—pictures, sounds, and videos—as you can bear. For example, if you're using Internet Explorer 8, follow these steps:
  1. Choose Tools | Internet Options. Internet Explorer displays the Internet Options dialog box.
  2. Click the Advanced tab and then scroll down to the Multimedia section (about halfway down).
  3. Clear the Play Animations In Web pages check box if you can dispense with animations.
  4. Clear the Play Sounds In Web pages check box if you can do without sounds.
  5. Select the Show Image Download Placeholders check box to make Internet Explorer display placeholders for images.

(Continued)

6. Clear the Show Pictures check box if you can dispense with pictures. (You can display a picture by right-clicking its placeholder and choosing Show Picture.)
7. Click OK. Internet Explorer closes the Internet Options dialog box.
8. If you cleared the Play Animations In Web pages check box in step 3, close and restart Internet Explorer.

- **E-mail** If possible, set up your e-mail program so that it consults you before downloading attachments greater than a certain size (for example, 50KB). You can then decide whether to download the latest picture of your aunt's dog rather than have it hog your Internet connection when you need to retrieve time-critical messages. Some e-mail programs offer this option, while others do not. Depending on your e-mail service provider, you may also be able to read your e-mail on the Web. This allows you to choose which e-mail headers to open and avoid downloading all the spam along with genuine messages.
- **Queue your downloads** Rather than downloading files while you're performing other activities online, schedule your downloads for a time when you won't be using the computer—for example, when you're usually asleep. Some web browsers provide download managers. Alternatively, use a third-party download manager such as GetRight (www.getright.com).
- **Close Internet applications you're not using** If you're not using an Internet program, close it to make sure it's not using your bandwidth surreptitiously. For example, instant-messaging clients such as Windows Live Messenger tend to lurk in the background, checking in to the IM server to see if there's anything new for you.

ISDN Connections

ISDN, which stands for Integrated Services Digital Network but is usually referred to by its abbreviation, is a digital telephone line that provides modest speeds but greater range than DSL (discussed later in this section) from the telephone exchange.

A normal consumer-grade ISDN line provides two 64 Kbps bearer channels and a delta channel that's used mostly for signaling. Depending on your ISP and phone company, you can use one bearer channel, use both bearer channels (giving 128 Kbps), or use the first bearer channel and add the second bearer channel on the fly when the first channel becomes busy.

Because the phone line is digital, connections take only moments to set up—so even if you don't keep the line open, you can establish a connection much more quickly than with a modem. If you do keep one channel open all the time (as you will probably want to do if you're paying a flat rate for the ISDN connection), you'll find that even though 64 Kbps sounds slow, it's adequate for e-mail and web browsing. However, downloading large files will be slow, even if you add the second channel for the duration of the download.

Consider ISDN only if you can't get a faster type of connection.

DSL Connections

DSL, which stands for Digital Subscriber Line but is also usually referred to by its abbreviation, is a digital telephone line. DSL comes in various implementations, but most consumer ones are variations of ADSL—asymmetrical DSL—in which download (or *downstream*) speeds are much higher than upload (or *upstream*) speeds. This means you can download data to your PC much more quickly than you can send data to another PC.

A typical DSL implementation splits off a part of the analog telephone line for digital use, leaving the still-analog part of the phone line for voice use—so with DSL, you don't need to get a second phone line to be able to make phone calls while you're online. However, DSL works only within a certain distance of the telephone exchange (the exact distance depends on the implementation), so DSL is not usually available in rural areas.

DSL speeds vary depending on the implementation, with downstream speeds of 384 Kbps to 6 Mbps being common. High-speed DSL, which typically is available only in cities, can provide up to 24 Mbps. Most DSL connections are "always on"—once you've configured and powered up the DSL router, it maintains the Internet connection permanently or until a problem occurs.

DSL can be great for home connections and small offices, because there is enough bandwidth to have multiple computers accessing the Internet at the same time. In many cases, your main choice will be between DSL and a cable connection.

Cable Connections

If you have cable television (or can get it), you can probably get cable Internet as well from your cable provider. Cable connection speeds vary depending on the cable company and its hardware and how far your house is from the cable connection point. But in general, speeds are comparable with DSL—for example, from 512 Kbps up to several megabits per second.

Like DSL connections, cable connections are "always on" and provide a good solution for home connections and small offices, with enough bandwidth for multiple computers to connect to the Internet simultaneously.

Wireless Connections

Wireless Internet connections are very convenient, especially if you need to be able to connect from any point within the area covered by the wireless network. At this writing, many coffee shops, libraries, and similar institutions provide wireless Internet access for their patrons. Some municipal bodies provide wireless access throughout their areas. Examples include El Paso (Texas), Houston (Texas), Pacifica (California), and Philadelphia (Pennsylvania), but there are many others.

Satellite Connections

Satellite tends to be the most expensive form of Internet connection, but it is worth considering if you are in a rural area where the only alternatives are ISDN and dial-up—or perhaps only dial-up. For example:

- StarBand (www.starband.com) offers a 512 Kbps service for $49.99 a month, a 1 Mbps services for $69.99 a month, and a 1.5 Mbps service for $99.99 a month.
- HughesNet (www.hughesnet.com) offers a 1 Mbps service for $59.99 a month, a 1.5 Mbps service for $79.99 a month, and a 2 Mbps service for $109.99 a month.

Fiber-Optic Connections

If your building or street is wired for fiber-optic connections, you should jump at the chance to get one. This is the fastest form of connection, providing bandwidth of 100 Mbps or so. You'll probably be sharing the circuit with your neighbors, but even so, you'll get great performance.

The drawback to fiber-optic connections is that they are normally available only in new communities or refitted buildings (for example, apartment blocks). However, they are gradually becoming more widespread.

Order Your Internet Connection

Once you've decided which Internet connection type will suit you best, research Internet service providers (ISPs) who offer that connection type where you live. Here are some pointers:

- To find out which broadband technologies are available where you live, put your area code into a broadband search engine. For example, use the Find Broadband Service Now page on DSLReports.com to search for broadband services by U.S. ZIP code.
- Consult your neighbors, colleagues, or friends about what Internet connection type they have, how well it works, and whether they're happy with it.
- If you've decided to get a cable connection, you may find that your only choice is your existing cable company—in which case, the decision-making process shouldn't take long.

After selecting a provider, order the service and either install it yourself or have it installed. What you need to do varies depending on the technology, but broadband providers try to make the process as straightforward and user friendly as possible. After all, they don't need unhappy customers any more than other businesses do.

Cable routers and DSL routers are the two types of routers you're most likely to use. There are two usual setups for these types of routers:

- **Router on the network** The Internet router is connected to your network. These days, this is the most common setup for home networks. In many cases, the Internet router has a built-in switch on which you can base the wired portion of the network, as shown in Figure 5-1. The router may also have a built-in wireless access point you can use for the wireless portion of the network. If the router doesn't have a built-in switch or wireless access point, you use a separate switch or wireless access point to create the network; the router connects to this switch or access point, as shown in Figure 5-2. In either case, your PC connects to the Internet by connecting to the network.
- **Router attached to one computer** If you have only one PC rather than a network, the router connects to the PC (see Figure 5-3) rather than to a network switch or wireless access point. The router may attach to the PC via a USB cable or via an Ethernet cable.

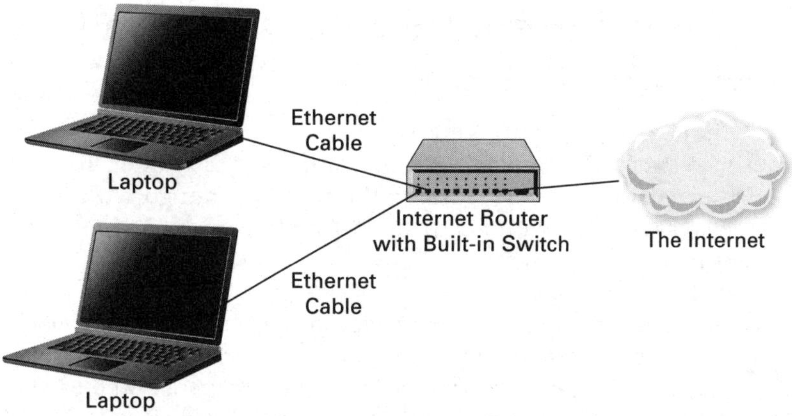

FIGURE 5-1 A typical home network these days uses a router connected to the Internet, often with a built-in switch for a wired network and a built-in wireless access point for a wireless network.

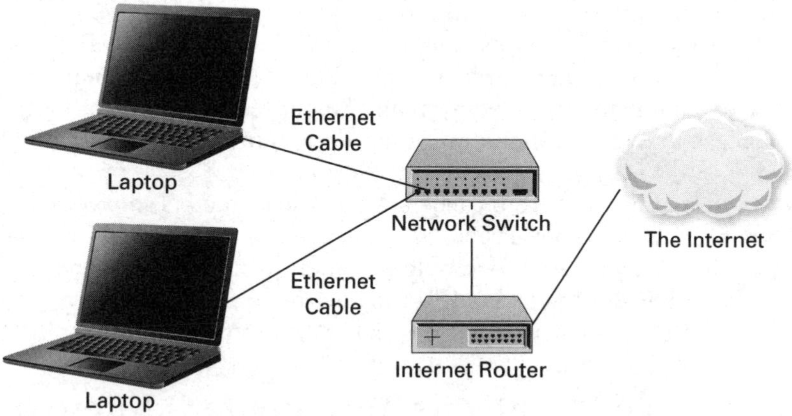

FIGURE 5-2 You can also share a stand-alone Internet router by using a network switch (as shown here) or a wireless access point.

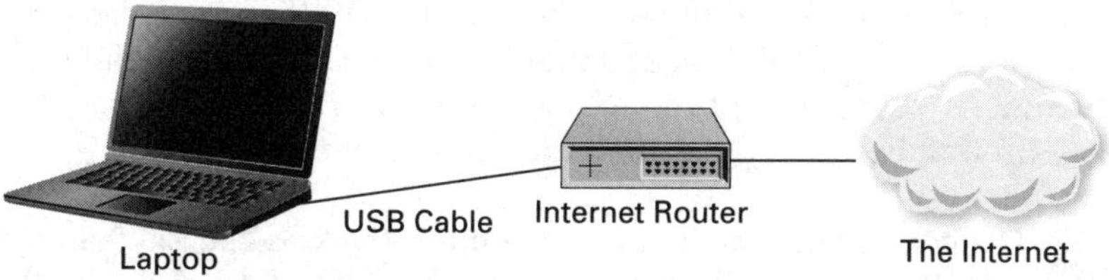

FIGURE 5-3 If you don't have a network, the router connects directly to your PC via either USB or Ethernet.

Turn On Your Internet Router's Firewall and Harden the Router

Next, you need to configure your Internet router to be as hard a nut as possible for an attacker to crack. This process is called *hardening* the router. To harden the router, you change its default password, turn on the firewall, configure it for maximum protection (or at least as much as you need), and turn off features that may make the router easier to attack.

Note How you configure your router depends on which make and model it is and what type of configuration interface it provides. Usually, you'll use either a custom program that came with the router or a configuration web page on the router. The configuration web page is more typical, and I'll show you an example of one.

Change the Router's Default Password

Most routers ship with a default password set. You need to enter this password to access the router in the first place. These passwords are widely available on the Internet, so they offer minimal protection.

The first time you access the router, change the password. As usual, create a strong password by using at least eight characters (12 characters or more is much stronger), not using a real word in any language, including both lowercase and uppercase letters, and including at least one number and one symbol.

Note Default passwords are dangerous—but some routers ship without any password at all. The aim is presumably to encourage you to apply your own password rather than lazily accept the default password. This could be a good idea if implemented properly. But some models let you leave the router without any password at all, which is even more dangerous than having a default password.

Turn On and Configure Your Router's Firewall

As you'll remember from Chapter 3, a firewall is a protective barrier that prevents unauthorized communications from crossing a network connection. A firewall typically uses a list of types of data to determine what is allowed to pass. Anything that's not on the permitted list, the firewall blocks.

Almost all Internet routers include a firewall. If your Internet router has a firewall, you must turn it on and make sure it's configured suitably to protect your network. (If your Internet router doesn't have a firewall, you need to install a third-party firewall between the router and the Internet connection.)

Note Chapter 3 shows you how to turn on the Windows Firewall feature in Windows to protect your PC. You need to turn on your router's firewall as well. The router's firewall prevents threats from the Internet from getting onto the network. On the PC, Windows Firewall prevents threats from your network from getting onto your PC.

Turn On Your Internet Router's Firewall

To turn on your Internet router's firewall, follow these general steps:

1. Open the router's configuration program or configuration web page. You'll need to authenticate yourself unless Windows or your browser has stored your credentials.
2. Click the Firewall button or link.
3. Select the option for turning on the firewall.
4. Click the button to apply the changes—for example, an OK button, an Apply button, or a Save Changes button.

Configure Your Internet Router's Firewall

Next, configure your Internet router's firewall to protect your network. Again, which settings are available and what they're called depends on your Internet router, so you'll need to look at your router's configuration program or configuration screens—and likely consult its documentation—to learn the possibilities.

Figure 5-4 shows the DoS Defense Setup screen for a DrayTek Vigor router. "DoS" there stands for Denial of Service, not the ancient Disk Operating System that you may remember from 1980s PCs. This is a full-featured router, and as you can see in the figure, it offers more than a dozen options for deflecting attacks.

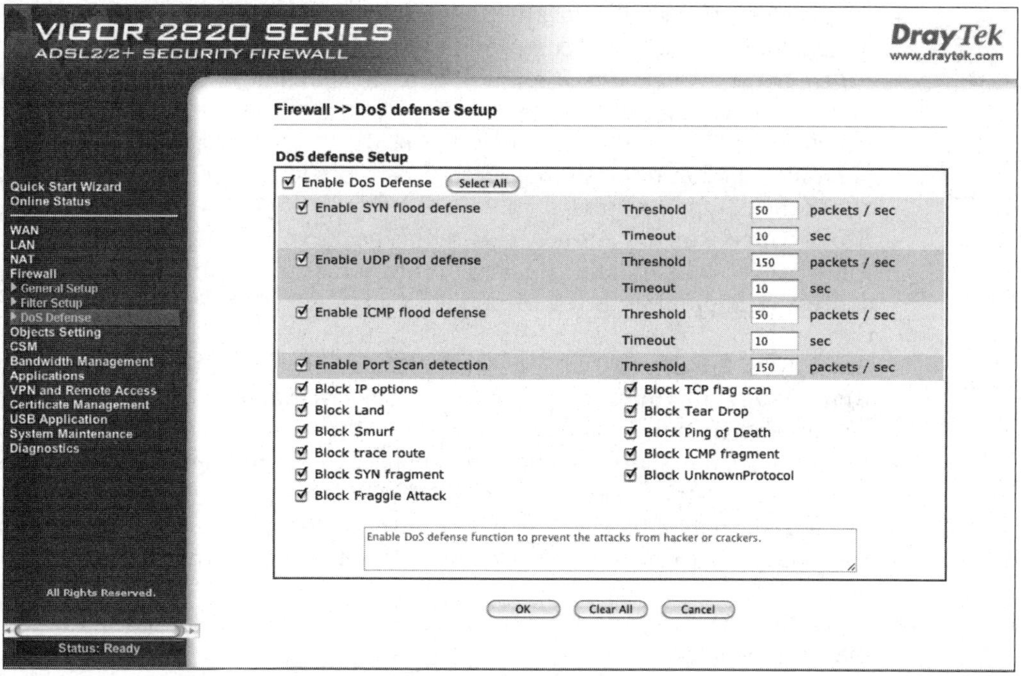

FIGURE 5-4 Locate the firewall-configuration screen in your router's configuration program or configuration screens, and then investigate your options for blocking attacks.

Let's dig into these options so you have an idea of the types of protection you can apply. Your router will probably include at least some of these options, even if they have different names.

First, there are three "flood defenses"—SYN Flood Defense, UDP Flood Defense, and ICMP Flood Defense—to protect against a flood of a particular type of data packet. A SYN flood is when an attacker sends a stream of synchronize (SYN) requests and ignores the acknowledgment (ACK) replies your router sends. The router gets stuck dealing with the SYN requests—much as you would if a dozen people decided to keep phoning you, yelling "Hello? Hello?" but ignoring your replies, and then hanging up. Similarly, a UDP flood sends a surfeit of User Datagram Protocol (UDP) packets, and an ICMP flood sends an overload of Internet Control Message Protocol (ICMP) packets.

Note A *protocol* is a set of rules for transmitting data electronically between devices.

Next, the Enable Port Scan Detection feature makes the router detect when someone runs a port scan. A *port scan* probes the router to see which of its ports have services running. For example, if the port scan shows that some of the ports for sending and receiving e-mail are open, the attacker can try to attack those ports.

The remaining options are for blocking specific attacks:

- **Block IP Options** Blocks any packet that contains IP options in its addressing information. These packets represent a potential security risk.
- **Block Land** A *land attack* sends SYN packets that have the same source address and destination address.
- **Block Smurf** A *smurf attack* uses the ICMP protocol to ask your router to reply to an information request—but directs the reply to another address in order to attack the computer there.
- **Block Trace Route** A *trace route* request asks your router to respond to a trace route packet, which determines the route across the Internet to a particular address. The problem is that replying to the request shows that your router is there.
- **Block SYN Fragment** Fragmented SYN packets can be the sign of an attack.
- **Block Fraggle Attack** A *fraggle attack* is a variation on the smurf attack, discussed earlier.
- **Block TCP Flag Scan** A *TCP flag scan* uses different flag (option) settings on TCP packets to try to determine how TCP/IP is set up on the target and so how the attacker may attack it. The flag settings on the TCP packets sent are unusual. For example, a *Christmas tree packet* is "lit up like a Christmas tree" with all its options set.
- **Block Tear Drop** A *tear drop attack* uses an overlong ICMP packet to try to crash the target machine.

- **Block Ping Of Death** The *ping of death* sends overlapping packets that the target machine will struggle to reconstruct. This can crash the target machine.
- **Block ICMP Fragment** Fragmented ICMP packets can be the sign of an attack.
- **Block Unknown Protocol** Protocols that the router doesn't recognize can be the sign of an attack.

Reading through this list, you can probably see that it's pretty safe to block all these possible attacks. For this router, you can simply click the Select All button at the top to select all the check boxes, turning all the defenses and blocking on. Your router likely has a similar control.

The one problem is that blocking everything may block some aboveboard traffic. This is relatively unlikely, but it does happen. The usual victims are instant messaging and multiplayer Internet games, but other traffic may fall foul of the firewall, too.

If you find that the firewall features you've enabled prevent some traffic you need from reaching your network, experiment with different firewall settings until the traffic is able to pass again. But keep as many of the firewall features as possible turned on to protect your network against the wide variety of attacks that malefactors can run.

Note For a normal home network, your router doesn't need to answer requests from the Internet. By turning off the acknowledgment of data packets that try to probe a network, you prevent an attacker from determining that there's a router at your IP address. So the attacker is less likely to try to break in than if she's sure that a router is there and that it has open ports that may provide a way in.

Check Your Defenses

Now it's time to check your defenses by using the ShieldsUP!! tool on the Gibson Research Corporation website. Follow these steps:

1. Choose Start | Internet to open a window of Internet Explorer or your default web browser.
2. Click the Address box to select its contents.
3. Type the address **www.grc.com** and press ENTER. The home page of the Gibson Research Corporation website appears.
4. Click the ShieldsUP!! link
5. Scroll down to the Hot Spots area and then click the ShieldsUP!! link to display the ShieldsUP!! page (see Figure 5-5).
6. Read through the information and make sure you want to go ahead with the test. (It's harmless and helpful.) Then click the Proceed button if you want to go ahead.

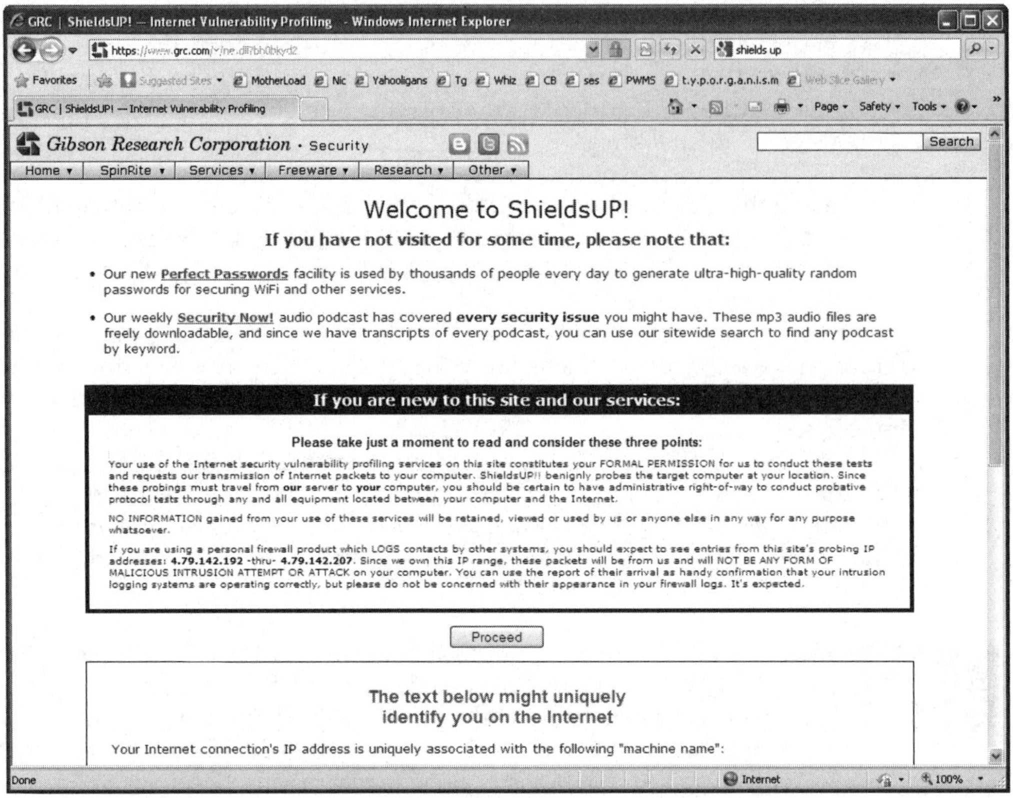

FIGURE 5-5 On the ShieldsUP!! page, read the information and then click the Proceed button.

7. On the ShieldsUP!! page that appears (see Figure 5-6), go to the ShieldsUP!! Services box and then click the File Sharing button.
8. ShieldsUP!! tries to probe your PC, displaying a progress readout as it does so. It then displays the results, as shown in Figure 5-7.
9. Note any open ports you need to block and then scroll down to the bottom of the window, where you'll find the ShieldsUP!! Services box.
10. Click the Common Ports button to run that test. Figure 5-8 shows the result of this test—my network has some ports open that I would be well advised to close.
11. Repeat the process with the other buttons in the ShieldsUP!! Services box to identify ports you may need to block.

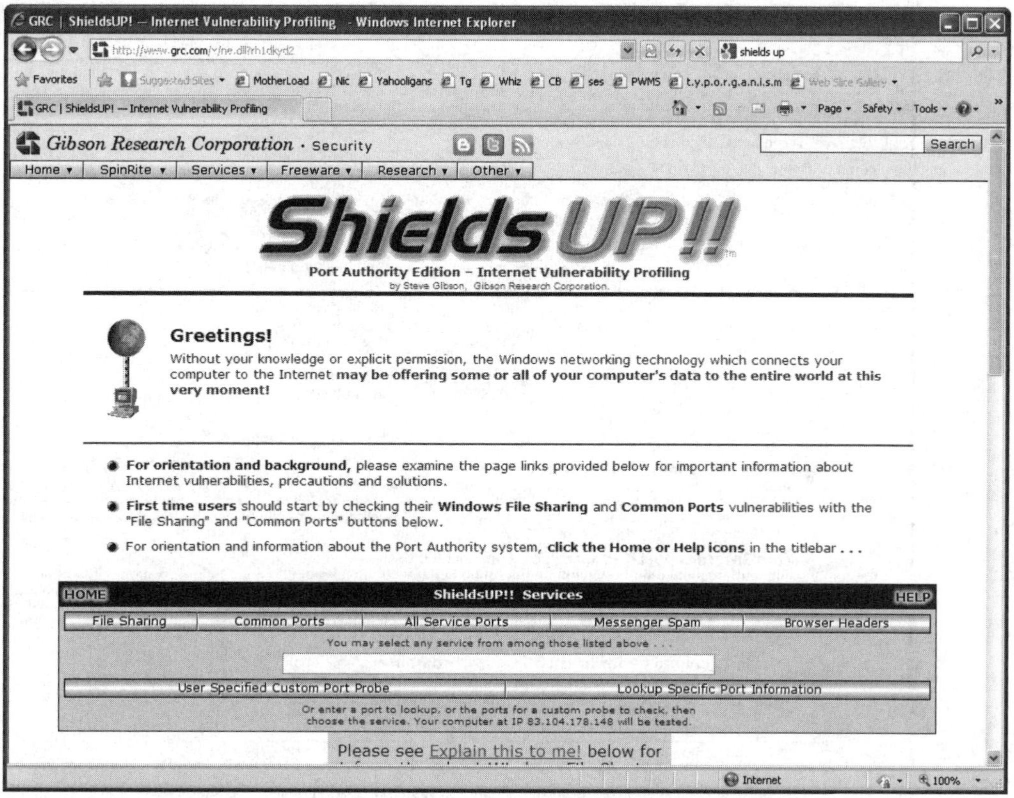

FIGURE 5-6 Start your probe of your PC by clicking the File Sharing button in the ShieldsUP!! Services box.

When you've finished testing, open your Internet router's configuration program or configuration screens again, and see what you can do to block the open ports. Then go back to ShieldsUP!! and try probing the network again.

Find Out How Fast Your Internet Connection Is

Now that you've established your Internet connection and locked it down as best you can, you'd probably like to find out how fast it is. You can find various utilities and sites on the Internet for checking connection speed and throughput. Here, we'll use one of the easiest sites, the CNET Bandwidth Meter, which doesn't require you to install any extra software on your PC.

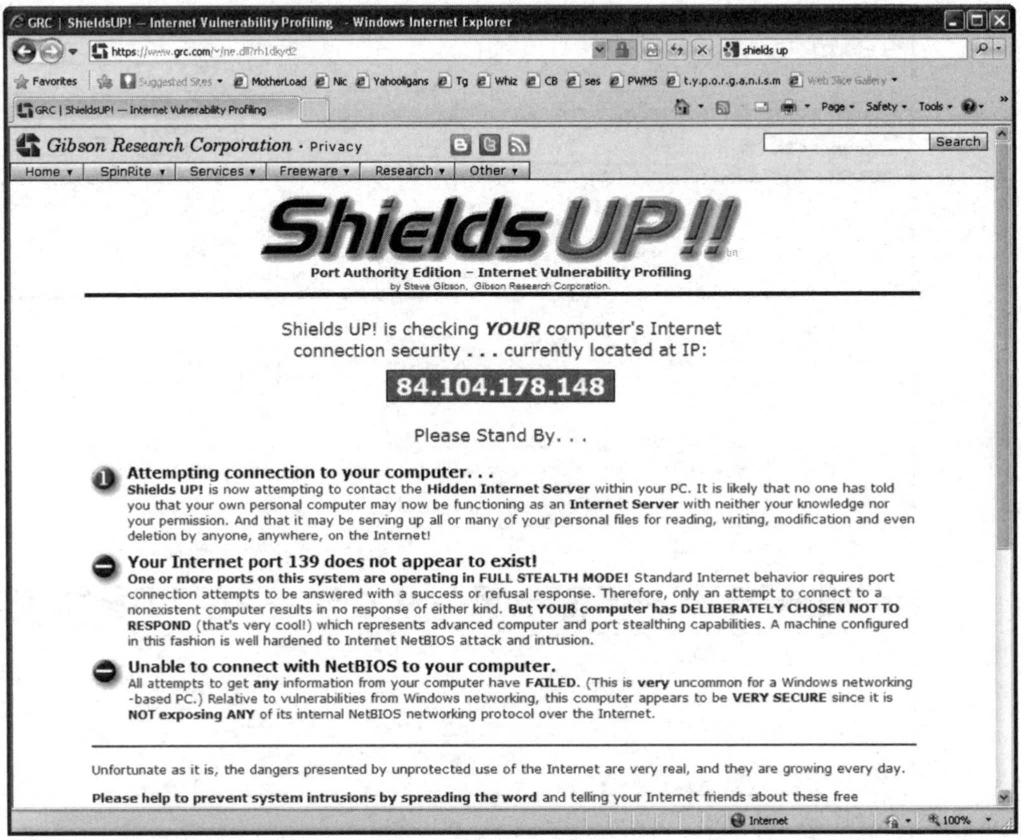

FIGURE 5-7 ShieldsUP!! tries to probe your PC. The No Entry signs indicate that you've blocked entry to particular ports.

To use the Bandwidth Meter, follow these steps:

1. Launch your web browser and go to http://reviews.cnet.com/internet-speed-test.
2. In the Select Your Location box, click the At Home button, the At Work button, the At School button, or the Other button to tell the Online Speed Test roughly what kind of connection you're using. Clicking the button also starts the test.
3. The Bandwidth Meter runs the test (see Figure 5-9), during which it displays an information screen and then displays the results page.
4. Run the test a few more times to see if you get consistent results.

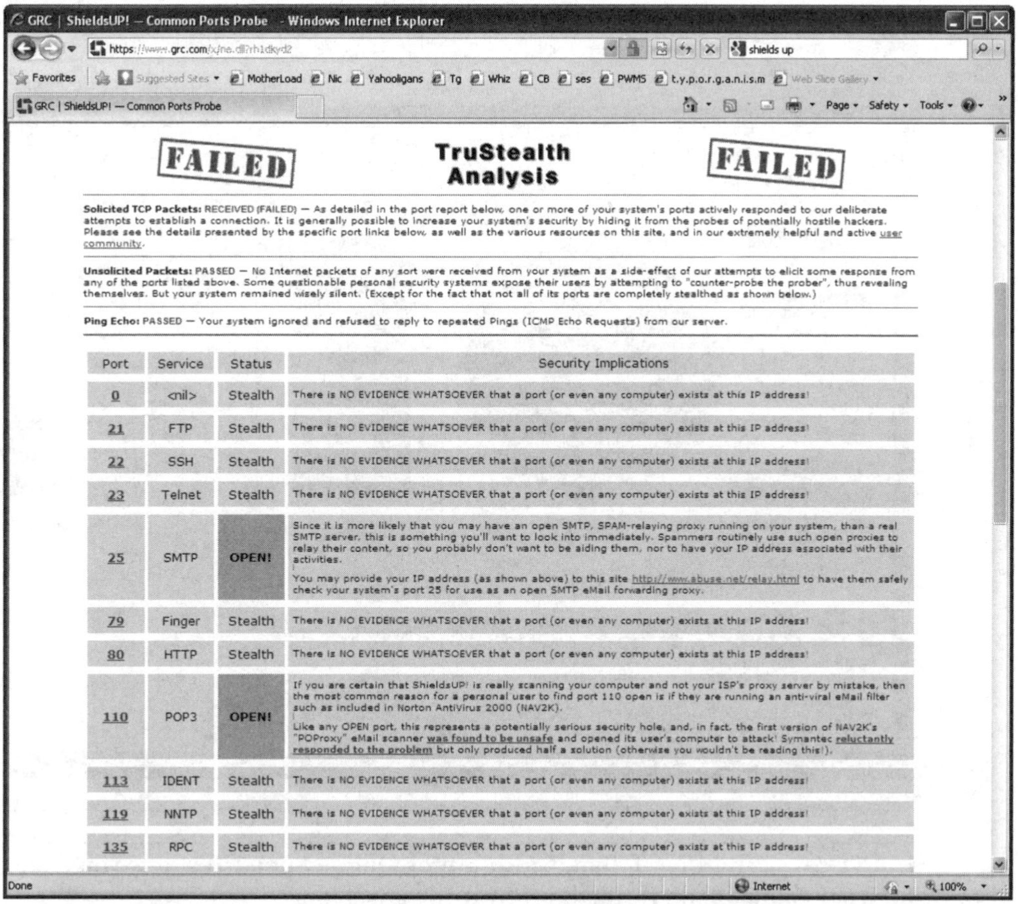

FIGURE 5-8 The Common Ports scan on ShieldsUP!! can help you identify open ports that you need to block.

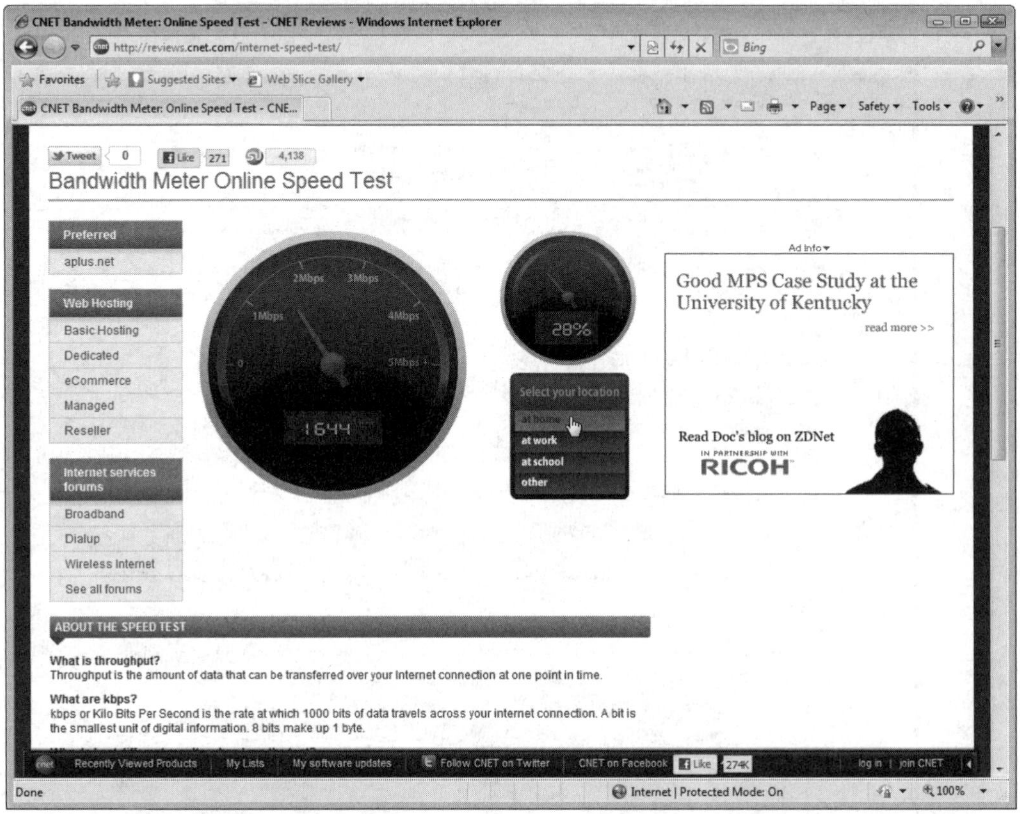

FIGURE 5-9 The CNET Bandwidth Meter Online Speed Test lets you check your Internet connection's throughput by using a web page.

6 Surf the Internet Safely

If you've followed the instructions in Chapters 4 and 5, your PC should have an Internet connection at this point. Your next move in keeping your PC healthy is to learn to use the Internet safely.

As you saw in Chapter 5, the Internet poses a wide range of threats to everyone who uses it: You can easily stumble upon a malicious web page that attacks your PC without you doing anything more than visiting the site; you can accidentally download a virus or other malware; or an attacker can try to break into your PC from the other side of the world. And unless you're highly unusual, your PC contains private, confidential, or otherwise sensitive data that you need to protect from people who want to exploit you or impersonate you.

In this chapter, I'll show you how to surf the Web safely using Internet Explorer, the Microsoft-developed browser that comes with most versions of Windows.

We'll start by going over how to keep Internet Explorer updated with fixes and patches that protect against the latest attacks. We'll then configure Internet Explorer to make sure it's secure against online threats. After that, I'll guide you through browsing the Web safely. And at the end of the chapter, I'll show you several other browsers you may want to try if you don't like Internet Explorer or find it doesn't meet your needs.

Note Internet Explorer used to come with all versions of Windows, but as a result of various antimonopoly actions by the U.S. Department of Justice and the European Commission, some versions of Windows now come either without Internet Explorer or with a choice of browsers, of which Internet Explorer is one. If your PC doesn't have Internet Explorer, you can download it from the Microsoft Download Center, www.microsoft.com/downloads.

Keep Internet Explorer Updated

More and more people are using the Web for banking, shopping, and other activities that involve transferring financial, private, or otherwise sensitive data. Criminals want to exploit the opportunities the Web offers, so malicious hackers are constantly trying to figure out new ways of attacking web browsers and gaining information from them.

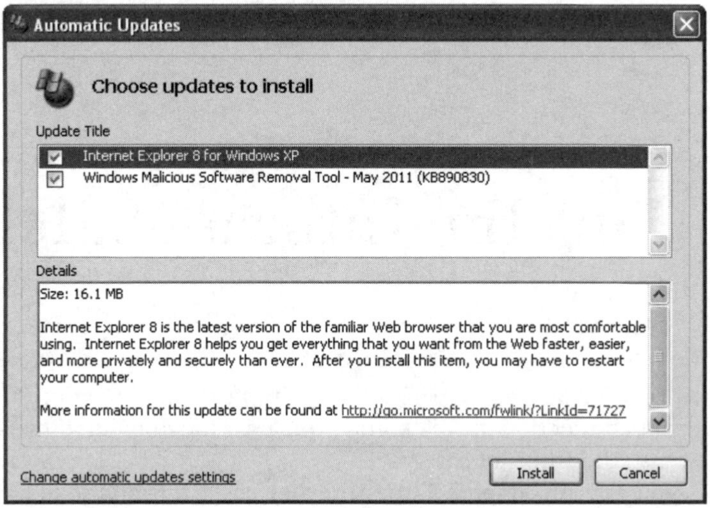

FIGURE 6-1 Automatic Updates (on Windows XP) or Windows Update (on Windows 7) helps you keep Internet Explorer up to date.

Because Internet Explorer is still the most widely used web browser overall, it's a popular target for attacks. This means you must keep Internet Explorer updated with the latest fixes and patches to keep your information out of the hands of hackers and criminals.

Keeping Internet Explorer up to date is easy, because Automatic Updates (on Windows XP) and Windows Update (on Windows 7) can automatically check for updates.

Note See the section "Keep Windows Updated with the Latest Patches and Fixes" in Chapter 3 for instructions on making sure Automatic Updates or Windows Update is configured to check for updates automatically.

When Automatic Updates or Windows Update notifies you that updates are available, install them. Figure 6-1 shows Automatic Updates ready to upgrade Windows XP to Internet Explorer 8.

Secure Internet Explorer Against Online Threats

Updating Internet Explorer to the latest version is a good start to staying safe on the Web, but you must also make sure that Internet Explorer has suitable settings for handling security threats, cookies, pop-up windows, and other Web-based threats.

To choose settings, you work in the Internet Explorer Properties dialog box or the Internet Options dialog box. This is the same dialog box with two different names. It's called Internet Properties dialog box when you open it from Control Panel but Internet Options dialog box when you open it from Internet Explorer.

Why It's Important to Update to the Latest Version of Internet Explorer

To keep your PC protected and enable yourself to browse the Web safely, you need to keep Internet Explorer updated. Usually, it's a good idea to install the latest version of Internet Explorer soon after Microsoft releases it.

Internet Explorer version 6 had many security holes that compromised not only its safety and that of any data you transferred with it, but also the safety of Windows as a whole. So if you are still running Internet Explorer 6, update it immediately to the latest version of Internet Explorer for the version of Windows you're running. Internet Explorer 8 is the latest version for Windows XP, whereas Internet Explorer 9 is the latest version of Windows 7.

The easiest way to get the latest version of Internet Explorer is by using Automatic Updates (on Windows XP) or Windows Update (on Windows 7). You can also go to the Microsoft Download Center (www.microsoft.com/downloads/), which contains prominent links to the latest versions of Internet Explorer.

Open the Internet Properties Dialog Box or Internet Options Dialog Box

To configure Internet Explorer's options, open the Internet Properties dialog box as follows:

- **Windows XP** Choose Start | Control Panel to open a Control Panel window. If Control Panel opens in Category view, with Pick A Category at the top, click the Switch To Classic View link in the Control Panel box in the upper-left corner to switch to Classic view. Then double-click the Internet Options icon.
- **Windows 7** Choose Start | Control Panel to open a Control Panel window. Open the View By drop-down list and choose Large Icons or Small Icons. Then click the Internet Options link.

Note If Internet Explorer is already running, you can also choose Tools | Internet Options from Internet Explorer to display the Internet Options dialog box. But if Internet Explorer isn't already running, setting the Internet options from Control Panel is marginally more secure and may save you the trouble of restarting Internet Explorer to make certain changes take effect.

Choose Suitable Security Levels for Each Security Zone

Now that you've opened the Internet Properties dialog box, click the Security tab to bring it to the front (see Figure 6-2). On this tab, you choose the security settings that Internet Explorer uses for different types of websites.

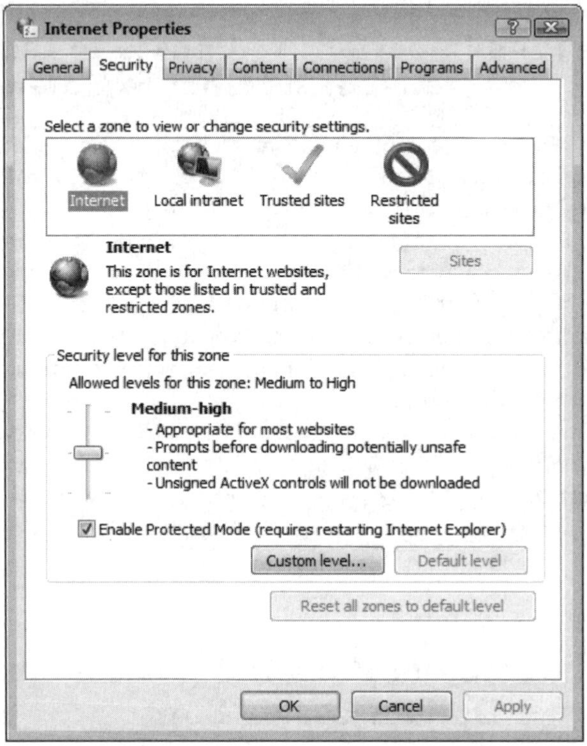

FIGURE 6-2 On the Security tab of the Internet Properties dialog box, make sure Internet Explorer is using high enough security levels for the Internet zone, Local Intranet zone, Trusted Sites zone, and Restricted Sites zone.

Understand Internet Explorer's Security Zones

To provide different levels of security for different types of websites, Internet Explorer uses *security zones*—areas of websites that have the same security level. Table 6-1 explains the four predefined security zones Internet Explorer uses.

Note Security zones give you (or whoever administers your PC) a great deal of flexibility in how you handle different websites. If someone else administers your PC (for example, on a work network), you may find that the controls in the Security Level For This Zone box on the Security tab of the Internet Properties dialog box are disabled.

Apply the Default Settings to Your Security Zones

Usually the best approach for home users is to use the default settings for the security zones. You can do this quickly by clicking the Reset All Zones To Default Level button on the Security tab. If the Reset All Zones To Default Level button is dimmed and unavailable, but the Custom Level button is available, your security zones are already using the default settings, so you don't need to do anything.

TABLE 6-1 Internet Explorer's Security Zones

Security Zone	Explanation	Default Security Level
Local Intranet	Sites that you access on your local area network. Local Intranet sites are mostly for businesses, which have internal websites that people access via the local area network. On a home network, you probably won't have an internal website.	Medium-Low
Internet	All sites that your computer doesn't access on a local area network and that aren't explicitly trusted or restricted. This is the security zone that you need to configure most carefully.	Medium-High
Trusted Sites	Sites that you (or an administrator) have explicitly designated as being trusted by Internet Explorer.	Medium
Restricted Sites	Sites that you (or an administrator) have explicitly restricted users from accessing.	High

Make Sure That Protected Mode Is On

Next, make sure the Enable Protected Mode check box is selected. Protected mode runs Internet Explorer with restricted privileges to limit the actions that a rogue website can take against your PC.

Note The Enable Protected Mode check box doesn't appear on Windows XP. Only Windows 7 and Windows Vista have Protected mode.

Tighten Up Security Beyond Internet Explorer's Default Levels

If you want to tighten up your security to protect your PC more than the default settings do, take the steps in the following list. You can also lower your security levels if you really want, but as you can imagine, I don't recommend it.

1. In the Select A Zone To View Or Change Security Settings list box, click the zone for which you want to set the security level. For example, click Local Intranet.
2. Drag the Security Level For This Zone slider to the appropriate position.
3. Make sure the Enable Protected Mode check box is selected.
4. If you want to choose custom settings for the security level, click the Custom Level button to display the Security Settings dialog box for the zone. For example, Figure 6-3 shows the Security Settings – Internet Zone dialog box, in which you can choose exactly the settings you want for the Internet security zone. Click the OK button when you've made your choices.

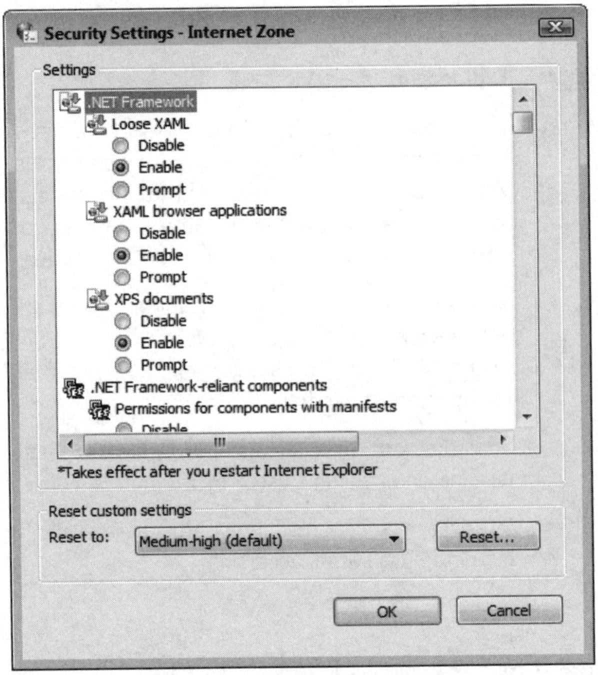

FIGURE 6-3 When you need a custom security level for a zone, you can choose exactly the options you want in the Security Settings dialog box.

Caution Choose custom settings in the Security Settings dialog box only if you're familiar with the settings this dialog box offers. Usually, it's best to use the default settings for a security zone. If you want to undo changes you've made in the Security Settings dialog box, open the Reset To drop-down list, choose the default security level—for example, Medium-High (Default)—click the Reset button, and then click the Yes button in the confirmation dialog box.

5. Click the Apply button to apply the settings you've chosen.

Specify Trusted Sites and Restricted Sites

If there are particular websites you want your PC to trust, you can add them to the Trusted Sites list. Similarly, if there are websites you want Internet Explorer to treat with extreme caution, you can add them to the Restricted Sites list.

To set up your list of trusted sites, follow these steps:

1. Click the Trusted Sites zone in the Select A Zone To View Or Change Security Settings box.
2. Click the Sites button to display the Trusted Sites dialog box (shown on the left in Figure 6-4).

Wouldn't It Be Safer to Set the Security Level for the Internet Zone to High?

Looking at the Security Level For This Zone setting for the Internet zone, you may well wonder whether it wouldn't be better to set the slider to High rather than to Medium-High.

The answer is—yes, it would be more secure. But the High level of security disables some features that many websites use. That prevents many websites from functioning properly.

When this happens, it's often not obvious that your security settings are causing the problem. Instead, you may get the impression that Internet Explorer is not displaying the web page correctly, that a link or button on the page doesn't work, or that the web server isn't responding. This ambiguity tends to be a frustrating waste of time. So usually it's better to use the Medium-High security setting for the Internet zone rather than the High setting.

3. Type the first trusted website's address in the Add This Website To The Zone text box.

Note If you leave the Require Server Verification (https:) For All Sites In This Zone check box selected (as it is by default), all trusted sites must use the Hypertext Transfer Protocol Secure (HTTPS) rather than the regular HTTP protocol. You can tell which sites use HTTPS easily because their URLs start with **https://** rather than **http://**.

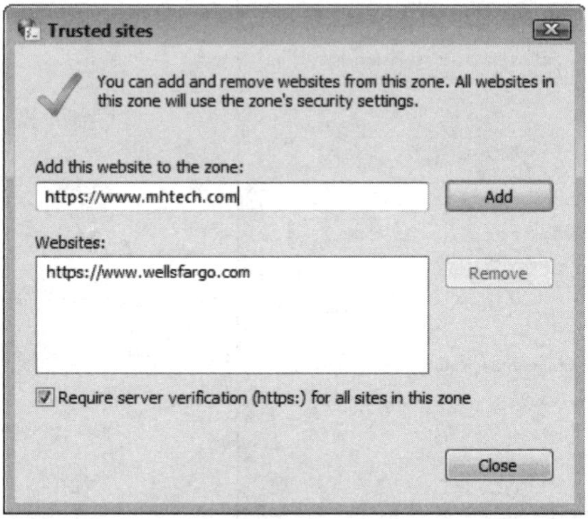

FIGURE 6-4 Use the Trusted Sites dialog box (left) to set up a list of the websites you want Internet Explorer to treat as trusted. Use the Restricted Sites dialog box to build a list of restricted sites.

4. Click the Add button.
5. Repeat steps 3 and 4 for each other website you want Internet Explorer to trust.
6. Click the Close button.

Similarly, you can set up your list of restricted sites like this:

1. Click the Restricted Sites zone in the Select A Zone To View Or Change Security Settings box.
2. Click the Sites button to display the Restricted Sites dialog box (shown on the right in Figure 6-4).
3. Type the first restricted site's URL in the Add This Website To The Zone text box.
4. Click the Add button.
5. Repeat steps 3 and 4 for each other website you want Internet Explorer to restrict.
6. Click the Close button.

Tell Internet Explorer How to Handle Privacy Issues

Now click the Privacy tab to display its controls (see Figure 6-5). On this tab, you can choose how to handle cookies, pop-up windows, and InPrivate Browsing.

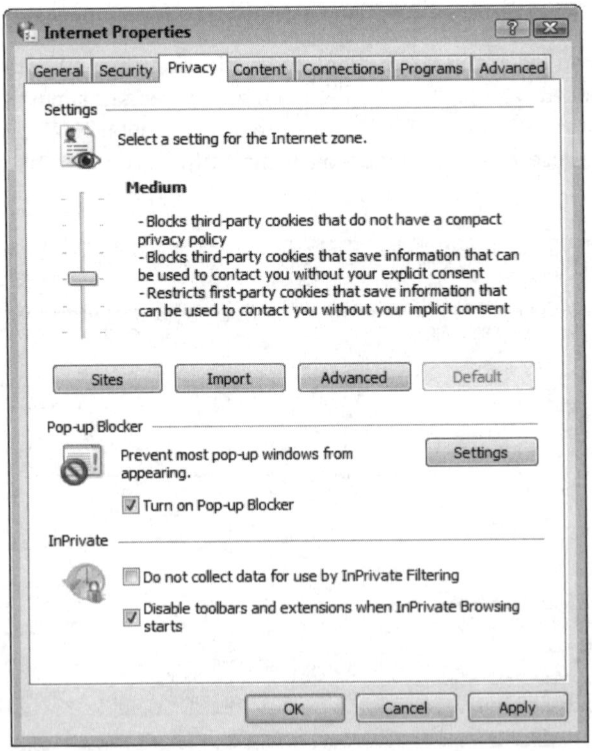

FIGURE 6-5 Choose how to handle cookies, pop-up windows, and InPrivate Browsing on the Privacy tab of the Internet Properties dialog box.

What Are Cookies? Are They Bad for Me?

A cookie is a small text file that contains details of your interactions with a particular website (or a bunch of affiliated websites). For example, if you browse the amazon.com site, the amazon.com servers will cause Internet Explorer to store a cookie named *yourname*@amazon.txt, where *yourname* is your user name.

The cookie stores only information you've provided to that website. You can provide this information either directly—for example, by creating a user account with the site—or indirectly (for example, by browsing from page to page or by performing searches). The cookie can't grab data from files on your computer. Only the site that creates the cookie can access the cookie.

By using cookies, a website can identify you (by your user account) each time you access that site. The site can track which pages you visit, which items you search for, which advertisements seem to interest you, and so on. Cookies benefit you, because they enable the site to give you more targeted information, by being able to tell that you've visited a specific link before, and by you not needing to identify yourself manually to the site. But cookies also mean that the companies that run websites can build up information about your actions and preferences. The bigger the website—or if a company owns several sites that use the same cookie—the more information the company can learn about you and your preferences.

Cookie files are stored in the Cookies folder in your user profile. You can access this folder and view the cookies (in a text editor such as Notepad), but usually a cookie's contents aren't intelligible unless you know the inner workings of the website the cookie refers to.

When you're choosing how to deal with cookies, the big difference is between first-party cookies and third-party cookies. *First-party cookies* are those from sites to which you navigate deliberately. For example, when you go to amazon.com, Amazon can set a first-party cookie. First-party cookies are usually helpful, so you will normally want to accept them.

By contrast, *third-party cookies* come not from sites to which you navigate, but from sites associated with those sites. Third-party cookies tend to try to track your movement from one website to another in order to gather details of what you appear to be interested in. Third-party cookies can sometimes be helpful to you, but you will often want to block them.

Choose How to Handle Cookies

Your first order of business on the Privacy tab of the Internet Properties dialog box is choosing how to handle cookies.

The quick way to control how Internet Explorer handles cookies is to drag the Settings slider in the upper half of the Privacy tab. Table 6-2 explains the settings you can choose and the effects they have. Before you read the table, you should know that a *compact privacy policy* is a way of claiming that the site is safe.

TABLE 6-2 Cookie Settings and What They Allow and Block

Setting	First-party Cookies	Third-party Cookies	Notes
Block All Cookies	Blocked	Blocked	Websites can't read cookies they've already set.
High	Blocked unless the site has a compact privacy policy	Blocked	Blocks cookies that save your contact information without your consent.
Medium-High	Allowed	Blocked unless the site has a compact privacy policy	Blocks cookies that save your contact information without your consent.
Medium	Allowed	Blocked unless the site has a compact privacy policy	Restricts first-party cookies that save your contact information without your consent.
Low	Allowed	Blocked unless the site has a compact privacy policy	Restricts third-party cookies that save your contact information without your consent.
Accept All Cookies	Allowed	Allowed	There's no good reason to use this setting.

Normally, you'll want to choose either the High setting or the Medium-High setting. You can also choose specific settings for certain sites or custom settings for handling cookies as a whole.

Tip Tighten up your cookie-handling settings as much as possible. Websites use cookies cunningly, and the results may surprise you. For example, a web page can display different prices or interest rates depending on the information the web server learns from your cookies.

If you want to choose which sites can set cookies and which can't, click the Sites button. In the Per Site Privacy Actions dialog box (see Figure 6-6), type a site's URL in the Address Of Website text box and then click the Block button or the Allow button, as appropriate.

The normal reason you'll want to set cookie actions for individual sites is when you've set a restrictive level of cookie handling overall but you need to do business with a site that your settings are blocking. (You can also use the custom settings to block a particular site that's exploiting the loose settings you've chosen, but this approach is neither safe nor recommended.)

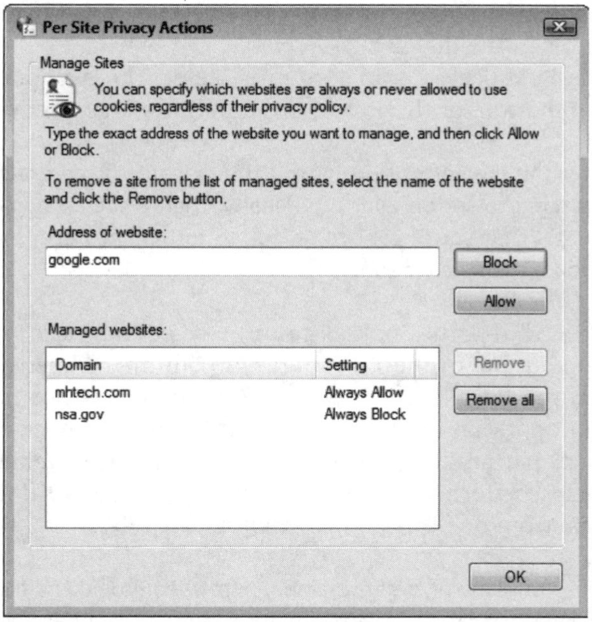

FIGURE 6-6 Use the Per Site Privacy Actions dialog box to control exactly which sites can set cookies on your PC and which cannot.

The six cookie-handling settings work pretty well for most needs, but if you don't like any of the combinations, you can choose custom settings. Follow these steps:

1. Click the Advanced button to display the Advanced Privacy Settings dialog box (see Figure 6-7).

FIGURE 6-7 In the Advanced Privacy Settings dialog box, you can choose custom settings for handling first-party cookies, third-party cookies, and session cookies.

2. Select the Override Automatic Cookie Handling check box to enable the other controls in the dialog box.
3. In the First-party Cookies column, select the Accept option button, the Block option button, or the Prompt option button, as needed.

Tip Select the Prompt option button if you want to see exactly which cookies websites are asking to set on your PC. Usually, there's such a bombardment of cookie requests that you'll want to switch to either the Accept option button or the Block option button very soon.

4. In the Third-party Cookies column, select the Accept option button, the Block option button, or the Prompt option button, as needed.
5. Select the Always Allow Session Cookies check box if you want Internet Explorer always to use session cookies, whether they come from first parties or third parties. Session cookies are temporary cookies that are deleted when you close Internet Explorer, so they're relatively safe—the information doesn't persist from one browsing session to the next.

Note If the company or organization you're with provides a cookie-handling policy, you can import it by clicking the Import button on the Privacy tab of the Internet Properties dialog box, selecting the policy file in the Privacy Import dialog box, and then clicking the Open button.

Set Internet Explorer to Block Pop-up Windows

Many websites use pop-up windows to display extra information to you. Some pop-up windows are helpful—for example, displaying extra information about a configuration option on a computer you're choosing specifications for. But many pop-up windows try to display extra information you don't want to see, such as advertisements, adult content, and fake warning dialog boxes. Figure 6-8 shows a mild example—a pop-up window from the Groupon discount site.

To block pop-up windows, select the Turn On Pop-up Blocker check box in the Pop-up Blocker area of the Privacy tab of the Internet Properties dialog box.

Selecting this check box gives you a moderate level of protection against pop-up windows. If you want to crank up the protection level or specify sites that are allowed to show you pop-ups, follow these steps:

1. Click the Settings button to display the Pop-up Blocker Settings dialog box (see Figure 6-9).
2. Open the Blocking Level drop-down list at the bottom of the dialog box and then choose the setting you want:
   - **High: Block All Pop-ups** Gives you the most protection. This is usually the best choice. When you want to override the blocking, CTRL-ALT-click the link or button that produces the pop-up window.
   - **Medium: Block Most Automatic Pop-ups** Blocks pop-ups that try to open automatically but allows pop-ups that you open deliberately. This setting is

FIGURE 6-8 Blocking pop-up windows helps keep advertisements and worse out of your face.

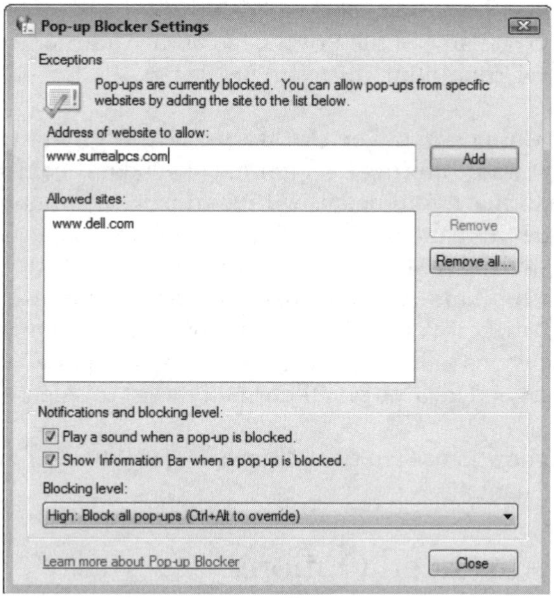

FIGURE 6-9 In the Pop-up Blocker Settings dialog box, you can choose the High level of protection in the Blocking Level drop-down list. You can also build a list of exceptions—websites that are allowed to display pop-up windows.

good in theory, because the automatic pop-ups are usually the ones you don't want to see. But pop-up creators are cunning beasts, and they tend to find ways around this blocking.
- **Low: Allow Pop-ups From Secure Sites** Blocks pop-ups from sites to which you don't have a secure connection but allows pop-ups from sites where the connection is secure. But because you can establish a secure connection to a malevolent site, it's best not to use this setting.

3. If you want to allow a particular site to display pop-ups, type its name into the Address Of Website To Allow box and then click the Add button. Repeat this move to add as many sites as needed to the Allowed Sites box.
4. In the Notifications And Blocking Level area, choose whether Internet Explorer should alert you when it blocks pop-up windows:
   - **Play A Sound When A Pop-up Is Blocked** Select this check box if you want Internet Explorer to play a sound when it blocks a pop-up window. If you find the chiming annoying, clear this check box.
   - **Show Information Bar When A Pop-Up Is Blocked** Select this check box if you want to be able to use the Information Bar to override blocking. I'll show you the Information Bar in just a minute.
5. Click the Close button to close the Pop-up Blocker Settings dialog box.

Choose Options for InPrivate Browsing

Internet Explorer's InPrivate Browsing feature minimizes the amount of information that Internet Explorer stores about your web browsing and reduces the options that websites have for tracking you through your browsing. You can switch on InPrivate Browsing at any point by choosing Safety | InPrivate Browsing.

The InPrivate area of the Privacy tab of the Internet Properties dialog box contains two options for controlling InPrivate Browsing:

- **Do Not Collect Data For Use By InPrivate Filtering** Select this check box if you don't want Internet Explorer to collect data about which of the websites you visit try to share your details with third-party content providers. Usually it's helpful to provide this data to Microsoft. (This option isn't about Microsoft tracking what *you* do—it's about Microsoft tracking what the websites you visit do.)
- **Disable Toolbars And Extensions When InPrivate Browsing Starts** Select this check box if you want InPrivate Browsing to automatically disable toolbars and extensions (add-on features to Internet Explorer). Disabling these items is usually a good idea, so you'll normally want to select this check box.

To learn how to use InPrivate Browsing, see the section "Use InPrivate Browsing," later in this chapter.

Choose Advanced Options

To keep Internet Explorer's security tight, you need to make sure that the settings in the Security section of the list on the Advanced tab of the Internet Properties dialog

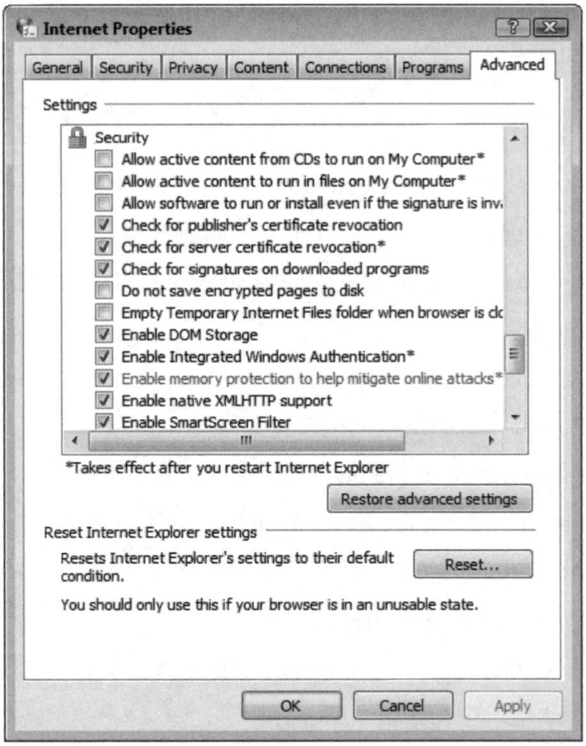

FIGURE 6-10 Check that the Security settings on the Advanced tab of the Internet Properties dialog box are set securely enough.

box are set either to their defaults or to even more secure settings. Click the Advanced tab to display its contents, and then scroll down until you see the Security section, as shown in Figure 6-10.

> **Tip** If you haven't deliberately changed any of the settings on the Advanced tab, you can quickly reset all the Advanced settings to their defaults by clicking the Restore Advanced Settings button. If you do this, you don't need to check through the Security settings one by one—but you do lose any other customizations you've made to the Advanced settings.

Table 6-3 lists the Security settings from the Advanced tab. The table gives the default settings and indicates some higher-security settings you may want to try instead. The table doesn't explain what the settings do, as most of the explanations are complex.

TABLE 6-2 Default and Higher-Security Settings for Internet Explorer's Advanced Security Settings

Check Box Name	Default State	Higher-Security Setting
Allow Active Content From CDs To Run On My Computer	Cleared	N/A
Allow Active Content To Run In Files On My Computer	Cleared	N/A
Allow Software To Run Or Install Even If The Signature Is Invalid	Cleared	N/A
Check For Publisher's Certificate Revocation	Selected	N/A
Check For Server Certificate Revocation	Selected	N/A
Check For Signatures On Downloaded Programs	Selected	N/A
Do Not Save Encrypted Pages To Disk	Cleared	Selected
Empty Temporary Internet Files Folder When Browser Is Closed	Cleared	Selected
Enable DOM Storage	Selected	N/A
Enable Integrated Windows Authentication	Selected	N/A
Enable Memory Protection To Help Mitigate Online Attacks	Selected	N/A
Enable Native XMLHTTP Support	Selected	N/A
Enable SmartScreen Filter	Cleared	Selected
Use SSL 2.0	Cleared	Selected
Use SSL 3.0	Selected	N/A
Use TLS 1.0	Selected	N/A
Use TLS 1.1	Cleared	Selected
Use TLS 1.2	Cleared	Selected
Warn About Certificate Address Mismatch	Selected	N/A
Warn If Changing Between Secure And Not Secure Mode	Cleared	Selected
Warn If POST Submittal Is Redirected To A Zone That Does Not Permit Posts	Selected	N/A

Tip The Advanced setting you'll benefit most from changing is the Enable SmartScreen Filter check box. By default, this check box isn't selected, but I recommend you select it, because it can help you avoid bumping into malicious websites by accident. SmartScreen checks each website address against a list of websites that have been reported to be unsafe and warns you about any that may be dangerous. If you choose not to use SmartScreen Filter all the time like this, you can check an individual site manually at any point.

If you're working in the Internet Options dialog box, you may need to restart Internet Explorer to make some of these changes take effect. If you're not sure whether you've set any such settings, restart Internet Explorer anyway just to be safe.

If you're working in the Internet Properties dialog box and Internet Explorer isn't running, the changes take effect the next time you start Internet Explorer.

Close the Internet Properties Dialog Box

When you've finished choosing Security settings, Privacy settings, and Advanced settings, click the OK button to close the Internet Properties dialog box.

Browse the Web Safely

Now that you've got Internet Explorer updated to the latest version, patches and fixes applied, and security settings chosen, you're ready to browse the Web.

This section shows you five essential moves for browsing. You'll learn to do the following:

- Recognize dangerous websites.
- Deal with pop-up windows while browsing the Web.
- Download files.
- Make sure you've got a secure connection before parting with information.
- Use InPrivate Browsing to hide your traces.

Recognize Dangerous Websites

If you want to stay safe on the Web, it's best to avoid dangerous websites. But how do you know which websites are dangerous and which aren't?

Internet Explorer's built-in SmartScreen Filter feature provides a way of identifying websites that other people have reported as posing threats. If you selected the Enable SmartScreen Filter check box on the Advanced tab in the Internet Properties dialog box, SmartScreen Filter warns you of any potentially dangerous websites you try to go to.

If you chose not to enable SmartScreen Filter, you can check the current website at any point by choosing Safety | SmartScreen Filter | Check This Website. The SmartScreen Filter dialog box opens and tells you whether the site is known to contain threats or not, as shown here.

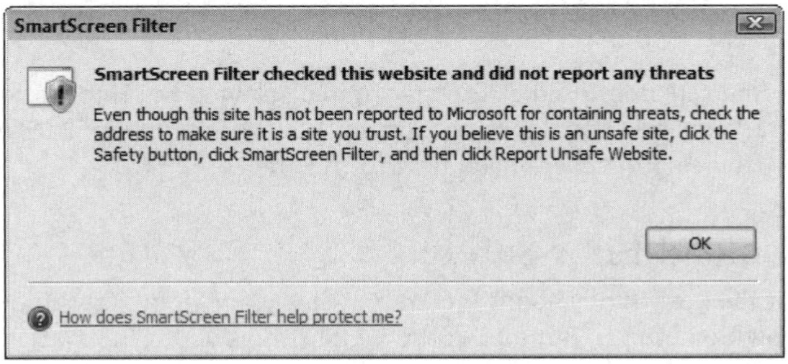

Note If you notice a website try to attack your PC—for example, by displaying unwanted pop-up windows or by attempting to install software—you can report it to SmartScreen Filter. To do so, choose Safety | SmartScreen Filter | Report Unsafe Website. On the Report A Website page that Internet Explorer displays, select the I Think This Is A Phishing Website check box or the I Think This Website Contains Malicious Software check box, as appropriate, and choose the website's language in the Language Used On This Website drop-down list. Then type the characters in the challenge box (to prove you're human rather than a program) and click the Submit button.

Apart from SmartScreen Filter, and any warnings from Microsoft Security Essentials or other security software you're running, you need to rely on your own common sense to identify dangerous websites. Generally speaking, avoid the following:

- Any website that tries to install software on your PC
- Any website that displays pop-up windows or dialog boxes you're not trying to open
- Any website that offers illegal items
- Any website that offers for free items you know aren't free, such as free downloads of commercial software or videos

If in doubt, err on the safe side. If the website offers anything that seems too good to be true, it probably is. For example, if the website claims you can win an iPad by clicking the button in a dialog box, avoid the site like the plague.

Deal with Pop-up Windows While Browsing the Web

When Internet Explorer blocks a pop-up window, it displays the Information Bar at the top of the window to let you know. (If you've cleared the Show Information Bar When A Pop-up Is Blocked check box in the Pop-up Blocker Settings dialog box, you won't see the Information Bar. But you'll hear a sound—unless you've cleared the Play A Sound When A Pop-up Is Blocked check box as well.)

If you want to see the pop-up window, click the Information Bar and then click Temporarily Allow Pop-Ups on the menu that appears (see Figure 6-11). If you want to see all pop-ups from this site, click the Information Bar and then click Always Allow Pop-ups From This Site.

If you don't want to see the pop-up window or allow this site to display pop-ups, click the Close button (the × button) to close the Information Bar.

Note You can stop Internet Explorer from displaying the Information Bar by clicking the Information Bar, choosing Settings | Show Information Bar For Pop-ups, and then removing the check mark next to this item.

Download Files Safely

One of the best things about the Web is that you can quickly find the files you need and download them. But one of the worst things about the Web is that you can quickly

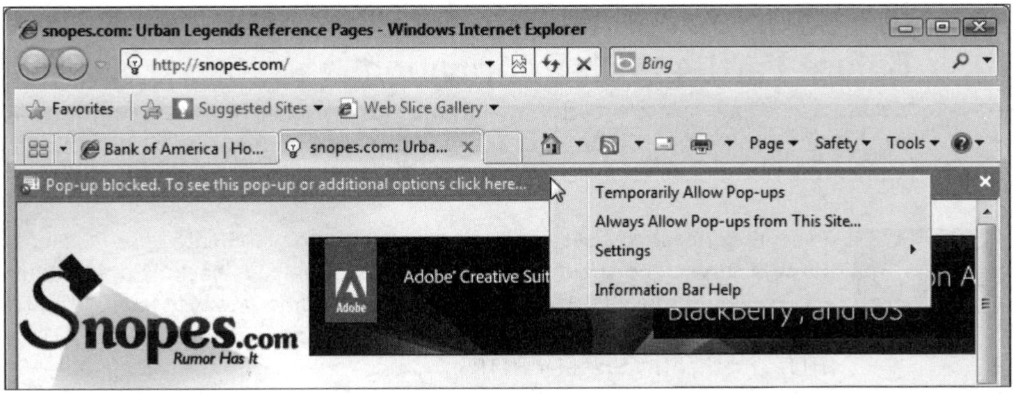

FIGURE 6-11 When Internet Explorer displays the Information Bar to tell you it has blocked a pop-up, you can click to open the menu and then either temporarily allow pop-ups or always allow this site to display them.

find files containing viruses and malware, download them in seconds, and compromise not only your PC and your data but also your personal information.

This means you must take care when downloading files from the Web. Follow these three main principles:

- **Learn to recognize dangerous file types** Avoid downloading any file with the file extension .bat, .com, .pif, or .scr, because these are executable programs—when you open them, they run, and can take actions on your PC. Watch out for files that have two extensions—for example, Rihanna.jpg.bat. The .jpg part of the name appears to be a file extension and suggests that the file is a JPEG picture, but the .bat is really the file extension—so if you try to open the "picture" file, the batch file runs.
- **Download software only from sites you know and trust** You're safe downloading software from sites such as the Microsoft Download Center (www.microsoft.com/download/), CNET Download.com (http://download.cnet.com), and other major sites. But before downloading software from sites you don't know, think twice—and then think better of it.
- **Keep your security software's real-time protection features running** To protect you against downloaded files, keep the real-time protection features of Microsoft Security Essentials running or your other security program running. The security program can alert you to any nasties in files you download.

Caution Be especially careful about downloading other people's copyrighted content without permission. First, such files are popular vectors for malware—by hiding a Trojan horse program in an attractive file such as a popular movie, an attacker can spread the program easily. Second, downloading copyrighted content without permission can expose you to legal consequences.

Establish a Secure Connection Before Parting with Information

When you use a website on which you enter any private or sensitive information, you must make sure your web browser is using a secure connection rather than a regular connection.

Note A secure connection uses encryption to ensure that the data your PC sends to the web server, and the data that the web server sends back, is unintelligible to anyone who intercepts it in transit. A secure address always starts with https:// rather than http://. The https:// indicates that the connection uses HTTP Secure (HTTPS) rather than regular HTTP.

To establish a secure connection, make sure the URL you use starts with https://. When Internet Explorer displays the web page, make sure the padlock icon appears in the Address box, as shown here.

For some sites, Internet Explorer changes the background of the Address box to green to indicate that it has verified the site's identity. The name of the company or organization associated with the website appears to the right of the padlock icon.

Caution Don't treat a secure connection as a panacea. If a malicious website accepts HTTPS connections, you can establish a secure connection to it. If the website contains scripts or code that attack your PC, they run as normal. The only difference is that the data being transferred back and forth is encrypted.

Check a Site's Digital Certificate

Each secure website uses a digital certificate to prove its identity. A digital certificate is a small chunk of encrypted code that contains information identifying the web server. The digital certificate is secured in such a way that its contents can't be tampered with, so you can be sure the information the certificate contains is genuine.

Note Digital certificates come from *certificate authorities,* or CAs. The three biggest CAs are VeriSign, Comodo, and GoDaddy.

If you've established a secure connection to a website, but you want to find out more about the site before parting with any information, you can check the site's certificate. To get quick information about the certificate, hold the mouse pointer over the certificate, and you'll see a ScreenTip showing the CA that provided the digital certificate—for example, Bank of America Corporation [US] Identified by VeriSign, as shown here.

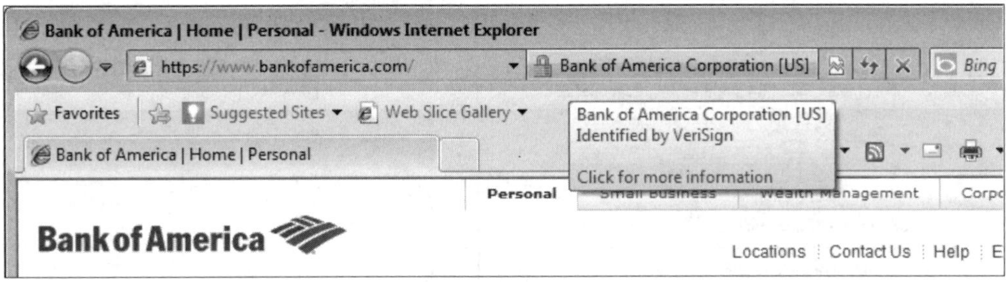

Click this ScreenTip if you want to see more information in the Website Identification pane, shown here.

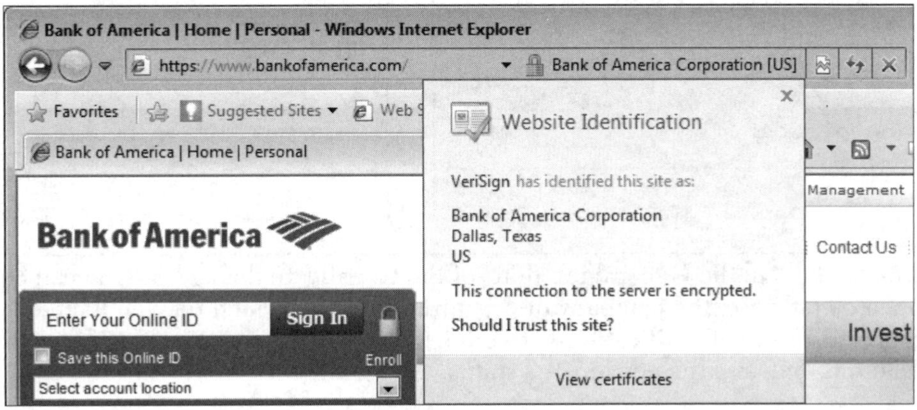

You can click the Should I Trust This Site? link to open a Help window giving you general principles for deciding whether to trust websites. Clicking this link doesn't give you the kind of definitive answer—for example, "Yes" or "You're kidding, right?"—that the question might suggest.

To help you decide whether to trust the site, you can click the View Certificates link to display the digital certificate the server running the website is using. The Certificate dialog box opens with the General tab at the front. In the left screen in Figure 6-12, you see the General tab for the certificate for www.bankofamerica.com.

On the General tab, you can check four things:

- **What the certificate is for** This certificate's purpose is "Ensures the identity of a remote computer," which is what we need in this case.
- **Whom the certificate was issued to** This certificate was issued to www.bankofamerica.com.
- **Who issued the certificate** The VeriSign Class 3 Extended Validation SSL certificate authority issued the certificate.
- **What the certificate's validity period is** This certificate is valid from 2/4/2011 to 3/7/2012.

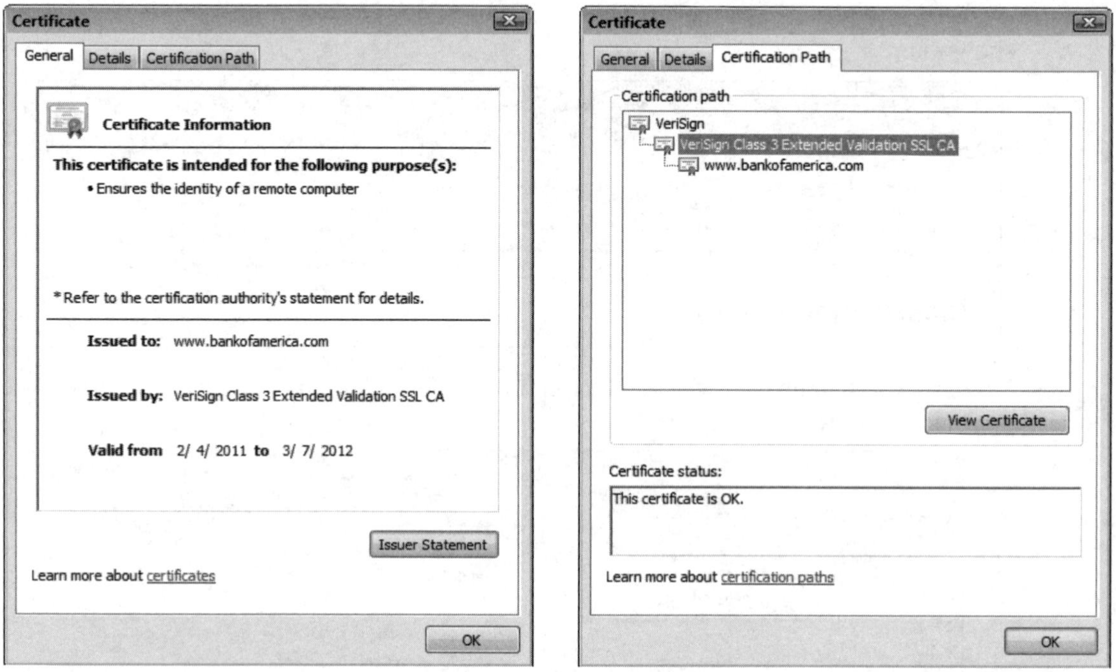

FIGURE 6-12 On the General tab (left) of the Certificate dialog box, you can check the certificate's purpose, the company or organization it was issued to, who issued it, and its valid period. On the Certification Path tab (right), you can see the chain of certificates that leads to this one, and the certificate's status.

You can click the Details tab to display its contents, but they're best left to techies, so I'll skip over them. Instead, click the Certification Path tab to display its contents, as shown on the right in Figure 6-12. Here, you can see the certificate path from the certificate authority to the company or organization that holds the certificate. Generally speaking, the shorter the path, the better. You can also see the certificate's status—in this case, "This certificate is OK."

Tip You can click another certificate in the path and click the View Certificate button to display that certificate.

From looking at this certificate, we can see that I've reached the right website. So I can click the OK button to close the Certificate dialog box and start logging into the website.

Note If after viewing the certificate you're still not sure whether to trust the site, don't trust it.

Use InPrivate Browsing

When you want to browse without Internet Explorer storing the details of where you've been, switch to InPrivate Browsing by choosing Safety | InPrivate Browsing or pressing CTRL-SHIFT-P.

Note Many people refer to InPrivate Browsing as "porn mode" because—well, the nickname says it all. But InPrivate Browsing has many more salubrious uses too, especially in countries where the government or the authorities monitor what citizens do online. If you use InPrivate Browsing, remember that anyone with a warrant may be able to learn the details of your browsing history from your Internet service provider (ISP).

When you switch to InPrivate Browsing, Internet Explorer opens a new window and adds the InPrivate indicator to the left end of the Address box, as shown here.

You can then browse much as normal. Internet Explorer stores essential information about browsing temporarily so that standard features work. For example, Internet Explorer stores cookies in memory so that web pages work correctly, and it keeps the path of web pages you browse so that you can move backward and forward along it as usual. But Internet Explorer gets rid of this information at the end of your InPrivate session rather than saving the cookies and the history information permanently.

When you're ready to stop InPrivate Browsing, close the InPrivate window.

Meet Other Web Browsers You May Want to Try

Almost every version of Windows comes with Internet Explorer as the default web browser. This is because—as I'm sure you know—Internet Explorer is Microsoft's web browser, and Microsoft would prefer you to use Internet Explorer rather than another browser. The U.S. Department of Justice and the European Commission have taken various antimonopoly shots at Microsoft, but Internet Explorer still comes as the default web browser on most PCs.

If you don't like Internet Explorer, find it too slow, or are concerned about the many security problems it has had in the past, you can choose from a wide variety of other web browsers. Here are the essentials on the four leading alternatives to Internet Explorer that you may want to consider: Firefox, Google Chrome, Safari, and Opera. All are free, so the only cost to trying them is time.

Should You Use Internet Explorer or Another Browser?

Earlier versions of Internet Explorer had horrendous security holes, but the current versions at this writing—Internet Explorer 8 for Windows XP, and Internet Explorer 9 for Windows 7 and Windows Vista—are about as secure as their rivals. Security experts can argue endlessly about the details (it's their job), but for most practical purposes, they're pretty close.

The latest versions of Internet Explorer also have much the same functionality as their rivals. Sure, each browser outdoes the other browsers in some areas—but it typically lags behind in other areas. Again, the experts sweat the details so that you don't have to.

What this means is that choosing which browser you'll use is often not so much a question of security or utility as it is of philosophy. Many people don't want to use Internet Explorer either because Internet Explorer used to be dangerous (true) or because Microsoft is too big and powerful (debatable, and perhaps irrelevant).

If you're not worried about these issues, and Internet Explorer is on your PC, use it and see how it suits you. And if you find that Internet Explorer works well for you, keep right on using it.

If curiosity takes you, try one or more of the other browsers. But don't feel compelled to switch to another browser until you're positive that it offers you advantages over Internet Explorer.

Note All four browsers—Firefox, Google Chrome, Safari, and Opera—make claims about how fast they are. All four perform well on a PC that's running well. Just which is fastest depends on exactly which task the browsers are performing. But unless you're planning to sit there timing your browser with an accurate stopwatch, chances are you won't notice much difference. Unless your PC needs a tune-up (in which case, see Chapters 1 and 2), any of these browsers should run pretty well.

Each browser lets you open multiple tabs within the same window, with each tab containing a web page. You can also open multiple browser windows. Use tabs when you want to be able to switch easily from page to page but view only one page at once. Use multiple windows when you want to compare two or more pages side by side, when you need to separate your browsing by topic (a different topic in each window), or when you simply need to open too many tabs to fit into a single window.

Note See this book's companion website for information about installing and using Firefox, Google Chrome, Safari, and Opera.

FIGURE 6-13 Firefox is a stable and full-featured web browser.

Firefox

After Internet Explorer, Firefox is the most widely used browser on the Internet. Whereas Internet Explorer runs only on Windows, Firefox comes in versions for all three major operating systems: Windows, Mac OS X, and Linux.

Firefox is stable and easy to use. You can customize it extensively by installing add-on components called *extensions*. Figure 6-13 shows Firefox running on Windows 7.

At this writing, Firefox is a mature and full-featured web browser and has relatively few disadvantages. You may find the occasional website that expects every visitor to be using Internet Explorer, and which causes Firefox display problems as a result, but such sites are pretty rare these days.

To get Firefox, take your current web browser to the Mozilla Firefox Web Browser page, www.mozilla.com.

Google Chrome

Google Chrome is a sleek web browser created by Google. Chrome runs quickly and displays web pages quickly. As you can see in Figure 6-14, Chrome has a stripped-down

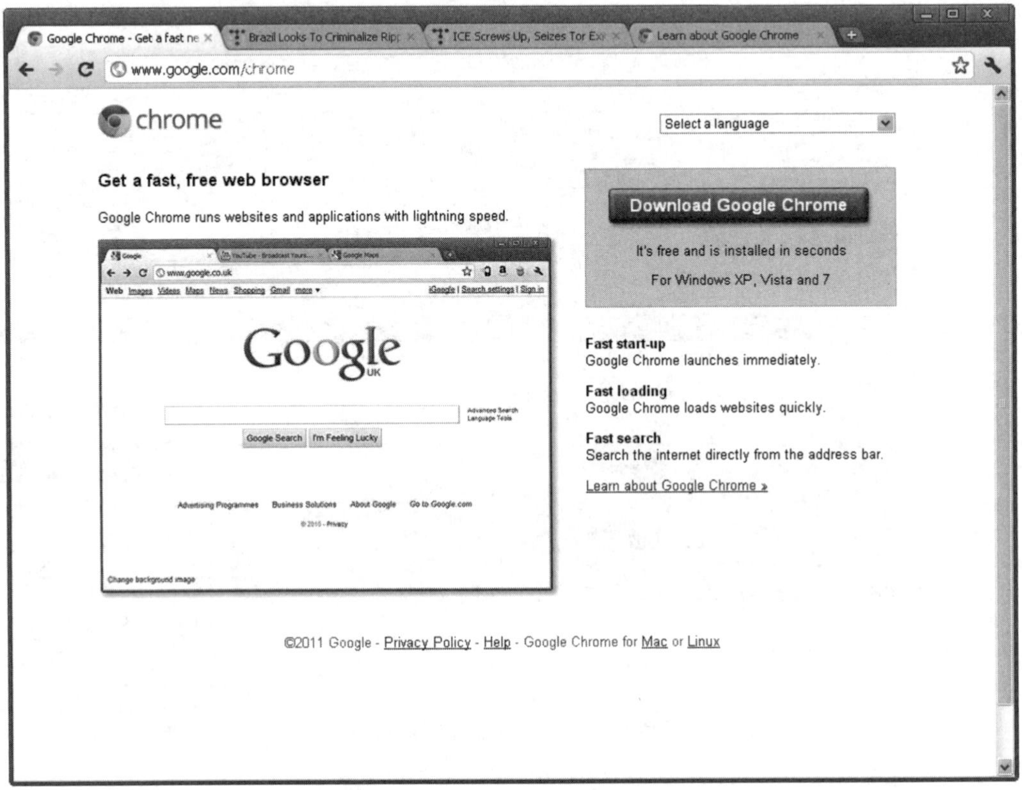

FIGURE 6-14 **The Google Chrome web browser has a stripped-down user interface and runs fast.**

user interface with no menus except the menu that appears when you click the wrench icon.

Apart from speed and sleekness, Google Chrome's other main selling point is stability. Whereas most browsers run all their tabs as part of a single Windows process, Google Chrome runs each tab as a separate process. This may sound arcane and trivial, but it means that when one tab crashes, you can shut down just that one tab (by shutting down its process) rather than having to shut down all the tabs. When you're browsing extensively, and have opened many tabs that you want to look at later, this extra stability can make a huge difference.

You can get Google Chrome from www.google.com/chrome.

Safari

Safari is Apple's web browser. Developed first for Macs, Safari is now available for Windows and for iOS devices—the iPhone, iPad, and iPod touch. Safari has a clean

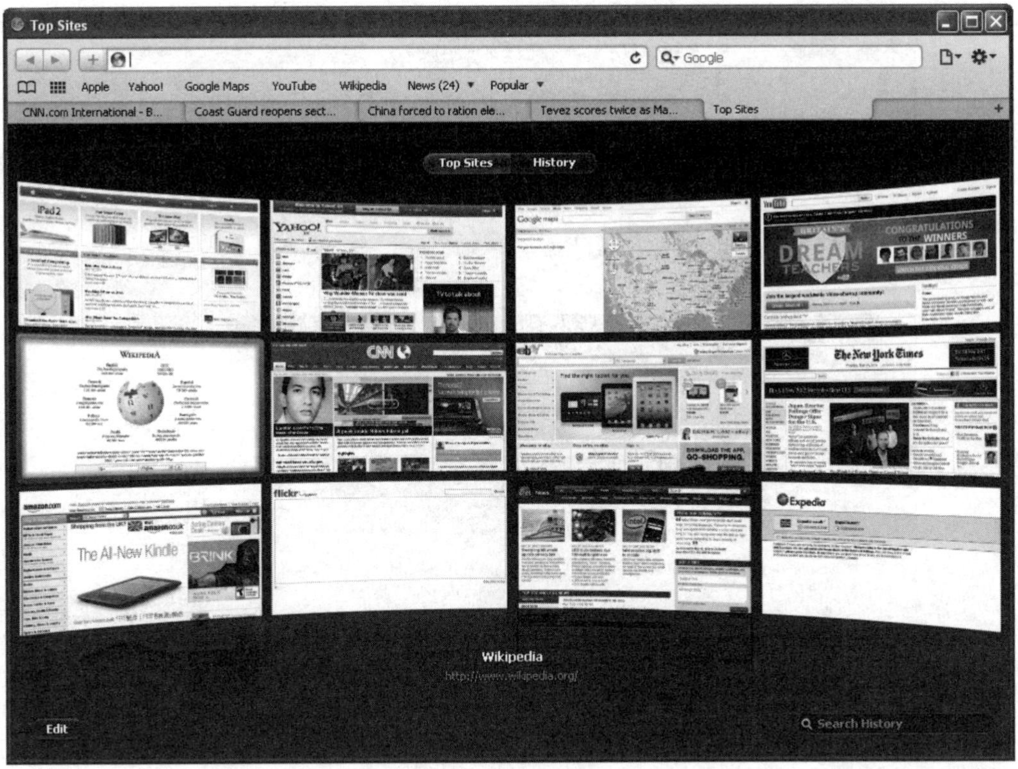

FIGURE 6-15 Apple's Safari web browser's Top Sites feature gives you an easy way to navigate to the sites you visit most frequently.

user interface and useful features such as the Top Sites screen (shown in Figure 6-15) and its Reader view, which eliminates distractions from the web page you're reading. Safari is less customizable than Firefox.

To get Safari, go to www.apple.com/safari/download.

Opera

Opera (see Figure 6-16) is a fast and sleek web browser with several standout features, including these:

- **Tab stacking** You can create groups of tabs by dragging one tab on top of another. This enables you to open more tabs in the same window without each tab becoming too small to identify.

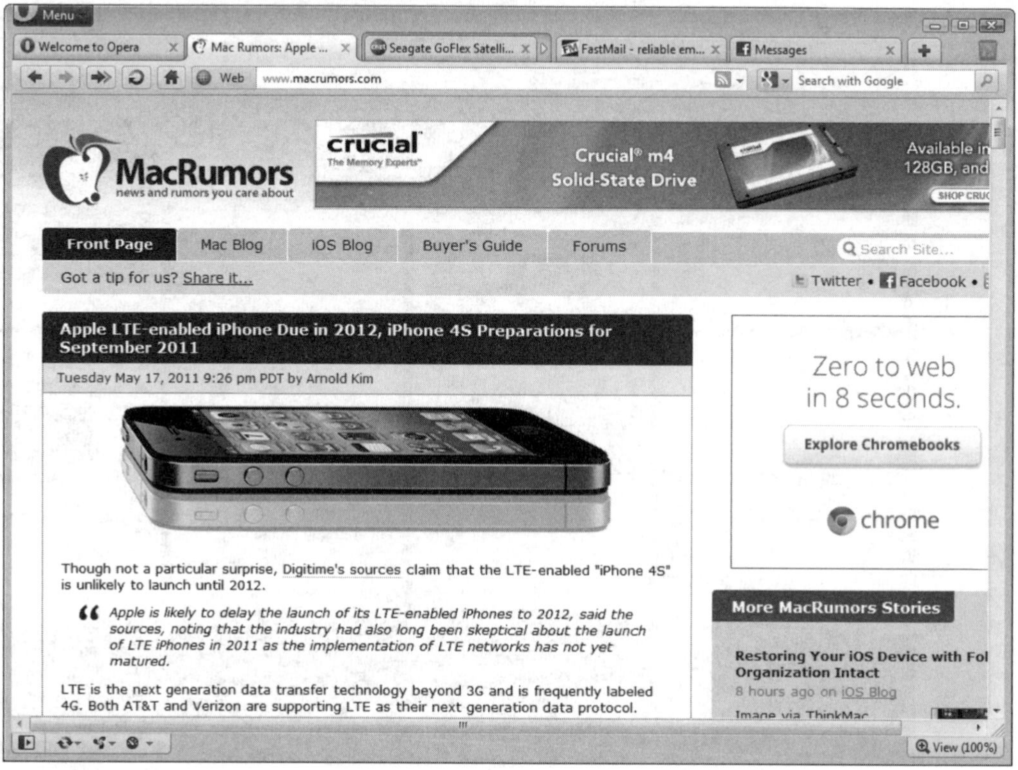

FIGURE 6-16 Opera's features include tab stacking, the Speed Dial screen, and mouse gestures.

- **Speed Dial** This screen presents a quick list of your favorites sites, like Safari's Top Sites feature. Each time you open a new tab in Opera, the Speed Dial screen appears, giving you quick access to these sites. (You can go to another site instead if you want.)
- **Mouse gestures** You can perform common actions, such as moving forward or back, by flicking your mouse.

To get Opera, go to www.opera.com.

7 Enjoy E-mail, Instant Messaging, and Social Networking Safely

E-mail was the original "killer application" for the Internet—the reason why people found they couldn't do without the Internet. And it's still a killer application today. Most people who are on the Internet use e-mail every day—and many of us use it all day, every day.

Several years ago, instant messaging became the next killer application, providing an easy way to communicate in real time with your friends, family, and contacts. Better still, you could chat not only with text but also with audio and video.

At this writing, social networking—for example, keeping up with your friends on Facebook or "tweeting" your latest news on Twitter—is the latest killer application. And you can be sure there'll be further killer applications to come, even if we have little or no idea at the moment of what they might be.

In this chapter, I'll show you how to enjoy e-mail, instant messaging, and social networking safely. We'll consider what each of the technologies is for, then look at the different threats you face and discuss the best ways to deal with them. As you'll see, much depends on your taking a sensible approach to these killer applications rather than getting excited and going overboard with them.

This chapter concentrates on the programs you're most likely using for e-mail and instant messaging on Windows: the e-mail programs Outlook Express and Windows Live Mail as well as the Windows Messenger and Windows Live Messenger instant-messaging programs. We won't look at a particular program for social networking, as it mostly takes place via websites rather than in dedicated programs.

Note Chapter 8 shows you how to protect your children online by using parental controls.

Use E-mail Safely

Almost everybody on the Internet uses e-mail. That puts almost everyone on the Internet at risk from the threats that e-mail poses.

In this section, we'll look at what e-mail is for (briefly, because I'm betting you already know), what threats it poses to you and your PC, and what you should do to counteract these threats.

Understand What E-mail Is For

As you know, e-mail is for sending and receiving messages from one computer to another.

You can also send and receive files attached to messages. E-mail can be a great way of getting files from point A to point B, as long as the files aren't so big that mail servers reject them and bounce them back to you.

E-mail is also an easy way of distributing information from one person to many specific people. For example, popular e-mail newsletters go out to many thousands of people who have signed up and provided their e-mail addresses.

Understand the Dangers of E-mail

Because so many people use e-mail constantly, e-mail is a great way for malefactors to attack both people and their computers. That means you always need to be on your guard when using e-mail.

The seven main dangers of e-mail are spam, phishing and spear-phishing, dangerous attachments, links to sites other than the apparent destination, scripts, web bugs, and hoaxes. The following subsections explain what these dangers are. The following sections tell you how to deal with them.

Note Some e-mail attacks are borne simply from malice and mischief, but most attacks try to make money for the perpetrators.

Understand What Spam Is

Spam is unwanted e-mail, usually trying to sell you something—performance-enhancing pills, mail-order brides, or other items you wouldn't care to ask for in a store. (Or, in many cases, items that you had never imagined existed.)

Spam may also try to make you take an action you wouldn't otherwise take. For example, many messages encourage you to buy a penny stock on which the spammer is running a pump-and-dump maneuver, getting the price to rise so that he can sell his holdings at a profit before the price falls again.

Understand What Phishing and Spear-Phishing Are

Phishing (pronounced "fishing") is an attempt to trick you into providing sensitive or valuable information that the phisher can exploit.

For example, many phishing messages claim to come from eBay, PayPal, Amazon, or a major bank. These messages tell you that there is a security problem, such as that someone else has tried to access your account, and that you need to log in to fix the problem. The message contains a link that appears to go to eBay (or wherever) but actually takes you to a fake login page that captures your credentials.

These phishing messages tend to be pretty obvious—for example, using a generic greeting (such as "Dear Valued Customer") rather than your real name. I'll give you examples of how to spot them later in the chapter.

What's much more dangerous is *spear-phishing,* a variant on phishing in which an attacker targets you directly rather than dangling a general lure in front of however many e-mail addresses he has handy. A spear-phishing message is tailored to you, so usually it will address you by your name rather than using a generic greeting. It will usually be carefully written by a native speaker of English, and it will try to hook you with a specific attack that the attacker believes will work for you personally rather than for Joe or Jane Public. The attack may be trying to get your bank details, trying to get you to open a dangerous attachment such as a Word document that contains auto-running macros, or another action—exactly what doesn't matter. But it's targeted at you specifically.

Here's a classic example of spear-phishing from a couple of years back.

One Monday, about 20,000 executives opened their inboxes and found a message that claimed to be a subpoena commanding them to appear before a federal grand jury.

Each message addressed the executive by his or her correct name, and had the right company name, address, and telephone number.

The message provided a handy link to view the full subpoena.

More than 2,000 of those executives clicked that link. They saw a screen that told them they needed to install a browser add-on to view it. They clicked the Yes button for the installation... and installed a keystroke logger on their PCs.

That gave the tech support divisions of those companies a king-size headache—once they realized that keystroke loggers were loose on their networks.

Understand What Dangerous Attachments Are

E-mail is a great way of transferring files from one computer to another, but it's also a great way for an attacker to sneak dangerous files onto your PC. So you need to treat all files attached to e-mail messages as guilty until proven innocent.

The main danger is that you may receive a file containing a program or other active content that runs automatically when you open the file. Active content types include the following:

- Script files, which have the .scr file extension
- Batch files, which have the .bat file extension
- Microsoft Office files, some of which can contain macros
- Command files, which have the .com file extension
- Program information files, which have the .pif file extension

To protect yourself against dangerous attachments, run security software such as Microsoft Security Essentials (discussed in Chapter 3) and keep the real-time protection features enabled.

It's best to check every file you receive via e-mail for viruses and other threats. If you're expecting to receive a file from someone you know via e-mail, you may be tempted to assume that the file is safe. But you should check it anyway, because the sender's computer may be infected with malware and may have included that malware in the file.

Most people these days are wary of files attached to e-mail messages from people they don't know, so attackers try to trick us into opening the files. There are too many tricks to warn you about all of them, but here are two examples of dangerous attachments:

- **E-card file** If you receive a message claiming someone has sent you an e-card, be very cautious. Some of these are real, and display a card—but others attack your PC. Some get bonus points by displaying a card to distract you while they attack your PC.
- **Package Delivery Failure file** If you receive a message claiming to be from FedEx, UPS, or another delivery company saying that you need to fill in a document to get a delivery you missed, don't open the document.

If you're not sure that a file is the type it claims to be, save it to your desktop and then right-click the file and choose Properties from the context menu to display the Properties dialog box for the file. Then look at the Type Of File readout (see Figure 7-1).

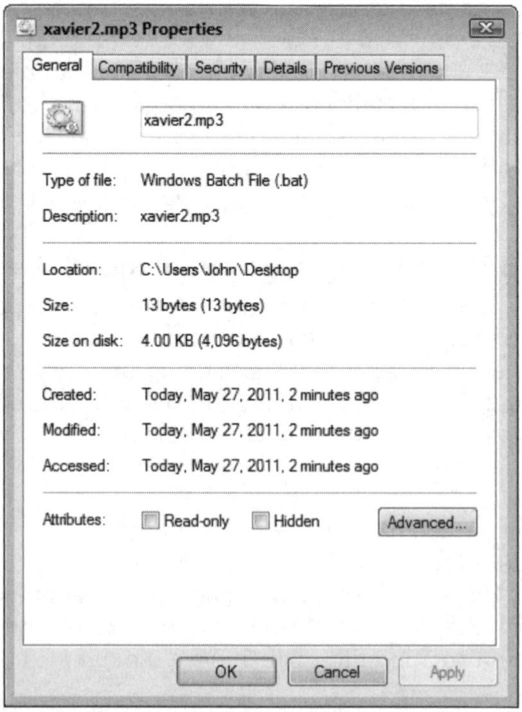

FIGURE 7-1 Check the Type Of File readout in the Properties dialog box for a file to see for sure what type of file it is.

Caution Watch out for files given two file extensions to make them look harmless. For example, the filename "Lady Gaga.jpg.exe" contains the text .jpg, which looks like the file extension for the JPEG image file type. But the actual file extension is .exe, the file extension for an executable program that will run when you open the file. Depending on your settings, Windows may hide the real file extension, so the file looks as though the apparent file extension (in this case, .jpg) is the actual file extension.

Understand What Links to Different Destinations Are

A formatted e-mail message is a document formatted with the HyperText Markup Language (HTML) just like a web page, so formatted e-mail messages can contain links. As on a web page, a link in an e-mail message has text or an object (for example, a graphic) that you click to open the associated web page in a browser window.

The problem is that the associated web page doesn't necessarily have anything to do with the destination that the text or object seems to show. So an attacker can include a link that appears to go to your bank's website but that actually takes you to a replica site run by the attacker.

Understand What Scripts Are

Apart from any scripts that come attached to e-mail messages, your PC can also be attacked by scripts that run automatically when you open a message. A script is a sequence of instructions in a programming language. Once set running, the script can perform just about any actions automatically on your PC that you can take when working normally. (In fact, scripts can take some actions automatically that you *can't* take when working normally.)

You can protect yourself against this kind of script also by running security software such as Microsoft Security Essentials (discussed in Chapter 3) and keeping the real-time protection features enabled.

Understand What Web Bugs Are

A *web bug* is an image linked to an e-mail message but stored on a server on the Internet rather than sent as part of the message. When your e-mail program opens the message, it requests the image from the server, so that it can display the full message to you. The server can log the request, which tells the sender that you have opened the e-mail message. The sender also knows that your e-mail address is active rather than abandoned.

Because of web bugs, most e-mail programs block the loading of images in any message suspected of being spam or phishing. I'll show you how to make sure this setting is on in Outlook Express and Windows Live Mail later in this chapter.

Understand What E-mail Hoaxes Are

Less of a threat than the other attacks I've just mentioned, e-mail hoaxes can still be a waste of time, effort, and Internet bandwidth. Hoaxes take as many forms as malefactors can dream up, but here are three examples:

- **Postcard for a dying child** The e-mail urges you to send a postcard to a child with a terminal disease so that he or she can get into the Guinness Book of Records. Some variants ask you to send a greeting card. This e-mail is based on several real-life requests from dying children to get cards—but the requests were made long ago. (One boy ended up receiving more than 30 million cards and recovered from his cancer after an operation.)
- **Bill Gates giving away money** As you probably know, Bill Gates and his wife Melinda run a charitable foundation called the Bill and Melinda Gates Foundation, which does great work on improving healthcare and reducing poverty. But—as you might suspect—even Bill Gates doesn't give away large sums of money if you forward a particular e-mail to ten people (or more, depending on the variant of the hoax message).
- **Some new threat or other** Many hoaxes identify a new threat—for example, that a particular e-mail message will destroy the files on your computer. The message encourages you to forward it to as many people as possible. All this does is generate more useless e-mail traffic, which helps nobody.

Deal with Spam

To deal with spam, you need first to understand your two lines of defense against it. You then need to choose settings in your e-mail program to deal with spam that gets past the first line of defense. And when spam arrives in your inbox, you can either simply get rid of it or tell your e-mail program how to handle it in the future.

Let's take it from the top.

Understand Your Lines of Defense Against Spam

Your first line of defense against spam is the spam filters that your ISP almost certainly uses. Most ISPs turn on these filters by default but let you turn them off if you want to (for example, because the filters are blocking legitimate messages sent to you). Make sure these filters are on. How you do this depends on your ISP, so consult your ISP's help system and find out how to check whether the filters are on or off.

Note ISPs use various techniques to determine what's spam and what isn't—but here's a clever one: They set up mailboxes for e-mail addresses that don't exist. Any messages that end up in these mailboxes are by definition spam—so the ISP can block these messages for everyone else too.

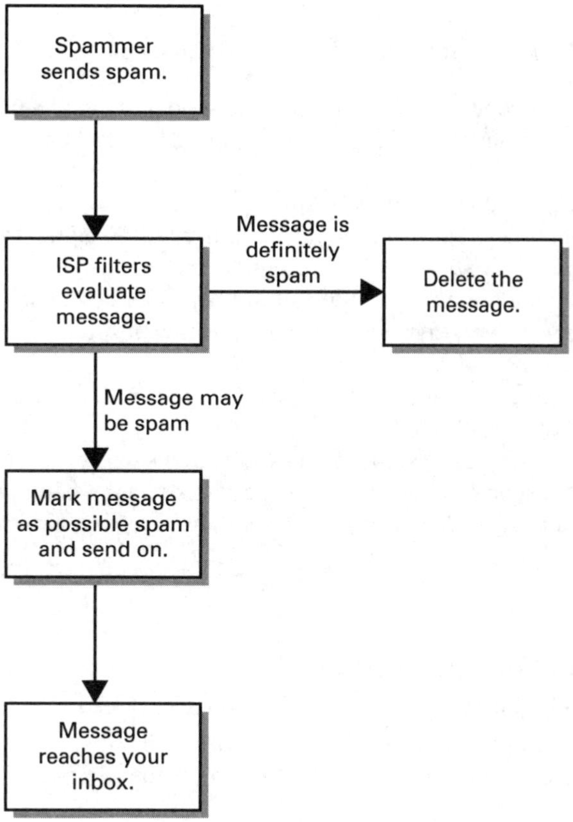

FIGURE 7-2 Your ISP's spam filters remove many spam messages, preventing them from reaching your inbox. After that, you're the one who has to deal with the spam.

If a message is definitely spam, your ISP's filters typically remove it, so you never see it. If a message *may* be spam, the ISP either marks it with a spam-warning flag and passes it on to you for you to decide, or simply passes it along to you without comment. Figure 7-2 illustrates this process.

Your second line of defense against spam is your e-mail program's junk mail filter, if it has one. Windows Live Mail does have a junk mail filter, but Outlook Express (in Windows XP) doesn't. The next section shows you how to make sure Windows Live Mail's junk mail filter is turned on and set to give a suitable level of protection.

When your e-mail program retrieves your e-mail messages from the server, it typically analyzes the messages to see if they're junk mail. If it suspects a message of being junk mail, it flags the message as suspected junk. Depending on the settings you've chosen, the e-mail program either puts the message in your inbox or in the Junk Mail folder.

Why It's Almost Impossible to Defeat Spam

If nobody responded to spam, the spammers would stop, wouldn't they? Eventually, anyway. The spammers wouldn't get any money, so they'd have no reason to keep spamming.

So—surely nobody responds to spam?

You'd hope that'd be the case. But in 2009 the Messaging Anti-Abuse Working Group (MAAWG) did a survey. MAAWG is a group of Internet service providers who manage more than a billion e-mail accounts altogether, so MAAWG knows all about spam.

The survey showed that one in six e-mail users responded to messages that they thought might be spam.

That's worth saying again: These people thought the message might be spam—*but they replied to it anyway.*

Given these figures, it's no wonder that spam keeps on coming. Security experts calculate that spammers need a response rate of only a handful in a thousand to make money—and the MAAWG survey suggests they're getting a much higher response rate than that.

Make Sure Your Junk Mail Filter and Anti-Phishing Features Are Turned On

If your e-mail program has a junk mail filter, make sure it's turned on and has suitable settings. Also turn on any anti-phishing features the e-mail program offers.

Note Outlook Express doesn't have a junk mail filter.

To set up the junk mail filter and anti-phishing features in Windows Live Mail, follow these steps:

1. Click the Windows Live Mail button to display the main menu. The Windows Live Mail button is the button to the left of the Home tab.
2. Click Options to display the submenu and then click Safety Options to display the Safety Options dialog box. This dialog box opens with the Options tab (shown on the left in Figure 7-3).
3. Select the appropriate option button:
   - **No Automatic Filtering. Mail From Blocked Senders Is Still Moved To The Junk Email Folder** Usually it's best not to use this setting.
   - **Low: Move The Most Obvious Junk Email to the Junk Email Folder** This setting is the best bet for general use. If you find too much spam gets through with this setting, move up to the High setting.
   - **High: Most Junk Email Is Caught, But Some Regular Mail May Be Caught As Well. Check Your Junk Email Folder Often** This setting's name does what it says on the tin. Try it if you're having a problem with spam.

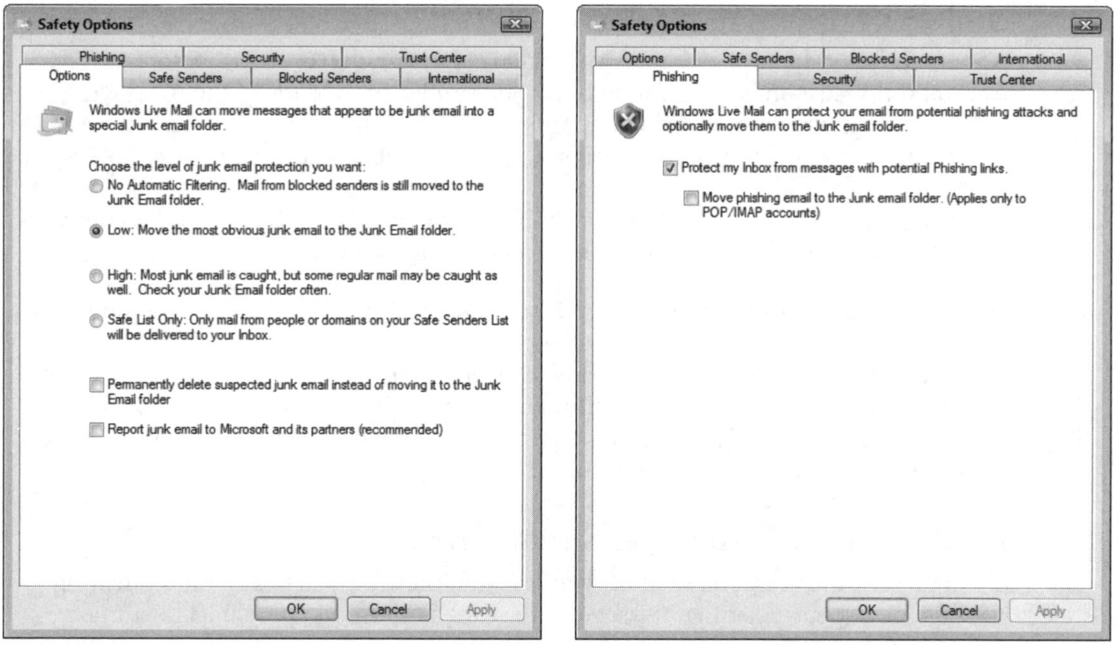

FIGURE 7-3 On the Options tab of the Safety Options dialog box, make sure that Windows Live Mail's junk mail filter is turned on and set to a suitable level of protection. On the Phishing tab, select the Protect My Inbox From Messages With Potential Phishing Links check box.

- **Safe List Only: Only Mail From People Or Domains On Your Safe Senders List Will Be Delivered To Your Inbox** This setting gives the most protection, but you need to add each approved sender to the list on the Safe Senders tab of the Safety Options dialog box. Usually, this is practicable only for people who have few contacts—for example, young children.

Note On the Options tab of the Safety Options dialog box, you can select the Permanently Delete Suspected Junk Email Instead Of Moving It To The Junk Email Folder check box if you want Windows Live Mail to adopt a shoot-on-sight policy toward spam. Usually, it's better to review your spam and delete it manually to make sure the junk mail filter hasn't caught anything that isn't spam.

4. Select the Report Junk Email To Microsoft And Its Partners check box if you want to report junk mail.
5. Click the Phishing tab to display its contents (shown on the right in Figure 7-3).
6. Select the Protect My Inbox From Messages With Potential Phishing Links check box.
7. Select the Move Phishing Email To The Junk Email Folder check box if you want Windows Live Mail to put suspected phishing messages in the Junk Email folder.
8. Click the OK button to close the Safety Options dialog box.

Deal with Spam in Your Inbox

When you find a spam message in your inbox, you can delete it. But before you do, you can tell your e-mail program to block the sender or to identify the message as junk. Which options are available depends on the e-mail program you're using.

In Outlook Express, select the message in your inbox and then choose Message | Block Sender.

In Windows Live Mail, right-click the message, click Junk Email on the context menu (see Figure 7-4), and then click the command you want:

- **Add Sender To Blocked Sender List** Blocks all messages from this sender (for example, jon@hundredpercentspam.com).
- **Add Sender's Domain To Blocked Sender List** Blocks all messages from this sender's domain (for example, all messages from hundredpercentspam.com).
- **Mark As Junk** Marks the message as junk to help the Junk Mail Filter identify spam more accurately in the future.

Deal with Phishing and Spear-Phishing

If you've read the previous section, you already know how to deal with a phishing message or a spear-phishing message: The straightforward approach is to simply

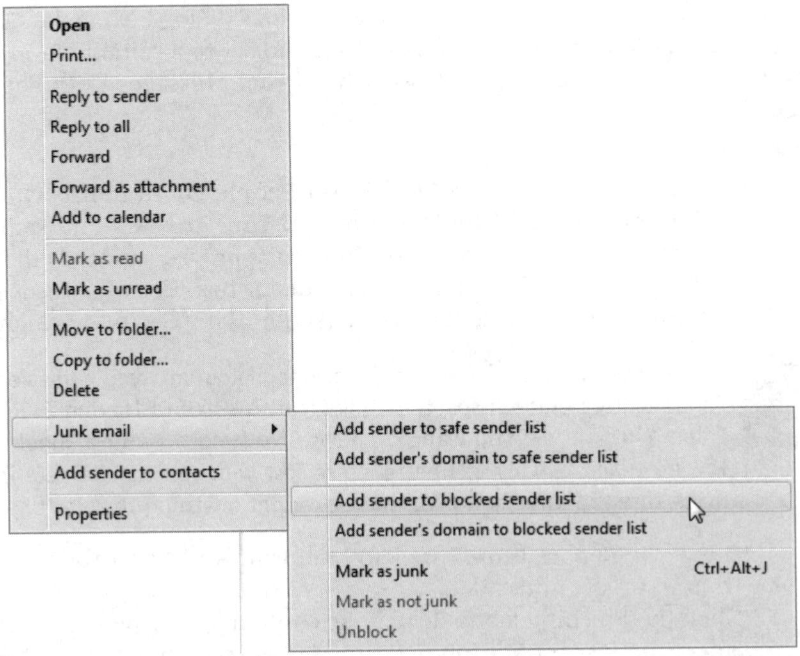

FIGURE 7-4 Use the Junk Email submenu on the context menu in Windows Live Mail to block the message's sender or the sender's domain, or to mark the message as junk mail.

Never Ask to Be Removed from a Spammer's List

Many spam messages include an address to which you can send a message asking to be removed from the spammer's mailing list.

Never use these links: All your "remove me" message does is tell the spammer that your e-mail address is live. The spammer can then sell your address to other spammers as a live address, which is worth more than an address that may be dormant or defunct.

Don't send a message insulting or abusing the spammer either. He won't read it, so all it does is prove your e-mail address is live.

Use the Remove links in e-mail messages only for legitimate companies with which you've done business.

delete the wretched thing. Alternatively, you can block the sender or the sender's domain, or mark the message as junk mail, and then delete the message.

Before that, though, you need to recognize the phishing message. Aye, there's the rub... so let's dig in a bit.

Many phishing messages are obvious. For example, here are the highlights of a phishing message I received while writing this chapter:

```
From:          Mr. Phillips Oduoza
Subject:       Dear: Sir/Madam.Your USD10.5Million.

Dear: Sir/Madam.Your USD10.5Million.

I am Mr Ben Tomllison, Chief Executive Officer, President and Member
of Operating Committee, set up to fight against scam and Fraudulent
activities worldwide.
...
You are being legally contacted regarding the release of your long awaited
fund. After a detailed review of your file, our new president ( PRESIDENT
GOOD-LUCK JONATHAN ) has mandated REV: EMMANUEL SCOTT to release your fund
immediately, The sum of US USD$10.5Million has been approved in your favor
via my desk. This payment will be effected to you through ATM-CARD or WIRE
TRANSFER immediately upon confirmation of your responds.
...
You are advised to contact REV: EMMANUEL SCOTT with his email
(revemmannuelscot@live.com ) and Include the following information. Your
Full Name? Your Address? Your Private Cell Phone Number? Your Age/ Marital
Status? a Copy of your International Passport or Valuable Drivers License?
for recorganization to avoid wrong delivery of your package to another
person, Note that the above fund has been cleared from terrorist or fraud
related Activities.

Your Prompt Co-operation is highly imperative.
...
```

You'll quickly see five main giveaways here:

- The message has a generic greeting—"Dear: Sir/Madam"—rather than addressing me by name.
- The name in the From line and the name given in the introduction don't match.
- The English is atrocious—grammar, word choice, sentence structure, and so on. This is not a native speaker of English writing. Some spams have better command of the language than this, but generally do not have professional quality.
- The message asks for enough identifying information for someone to attempt to impersonate you.
- The entire premise is absurd. Nobody goes around handing out $10 million to people they don't know.

This message is clearly phishing. Others are less obvious—but you can use the same techniques to identify them. These are the three key tests:

- Is the message sent to your e-mail address? If so, you'll be able to see the address in the To field. (If not, it's phishing.)
- Is the message addressed to you by name? (If not, it's phishing.)
- Does the message offer you something for nothing? (If so, it's usually phishing.)

Most phishing messages fail all three of these tests, so they're easy to identify.

Spear-phishing messages are much harder to pick out. Because, by definition, a spear-phishing message is sent to the right e-mail address and is addressed to you by name, you must evaluate the message's bona fides (or lack thereof) by the context alone.

As usual—if in doubt, err on the side of caution.

Deal with Dangerous Attachments

When you receive e-mail attachments you're not sure are what they appear to be, don't open them.

If the attachment comes from someone you know, contact that person and make sure that he or she has sent you the attachment. If so, let your security software scan it for viruses or malware, and open it only if it seems to be safe.

If the attachment comes from someone you don't know, it's usually best to delete it.

Deal with Links to Different Destinations

Before you click on any link in an e-mail message, see where it goes. To do so, hold the mouse pointer over the link and then look at the status bar, as shown here. If the link goes to an address wildly different from the site it should go to, don't click the link. Even if the link's address appears legitimate, don't click if you have any doubts.

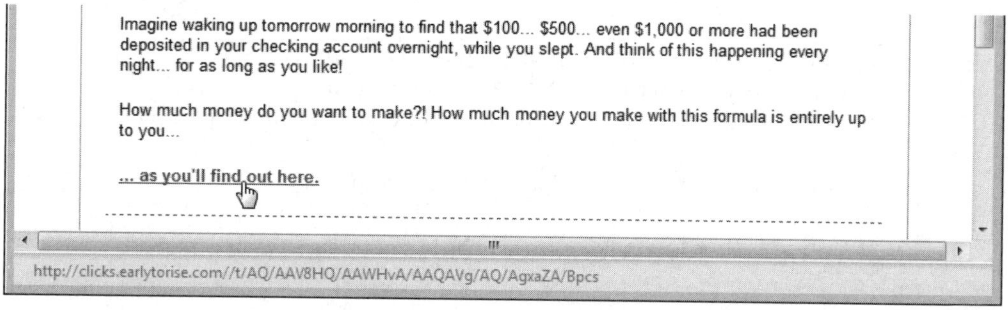

Deal with Scripts

The best way to deal with scripts attached to e-mail messages is to run security software such as Microsoft Security Essentials and keep the real-time protection features enabled. (I know—I keep mentioning the same thing. But it's vital.)

Another security measure you can take is to turn off the Preview pane in Outlook Express or the Reading pane in Windows Live Mail, because displaying a message in this pane can run a script without your actually opening the message.

To turn off the Preview pane in Outlook Express, take these steps:

1. Choose View | Layout from the menu bar to display the Window Layout Properties dialog box.
2. In the Preview Pane area, clear the Show Preview Pane check box.
3. Click the OK button to close the Window Layout Properties dialog box.

To turn off the Reading pane in Windows Live Messenger, choose View | Layout | Reading Pane | Off.

Deal with Web Bugs

To deal with web bugs, you must first tell your e-mail program not to request the images for potentially dangerous messages. If you decide the message is safe, you can click the Show Images link on the Information Bar that appears at the top of the message window, as shown here.

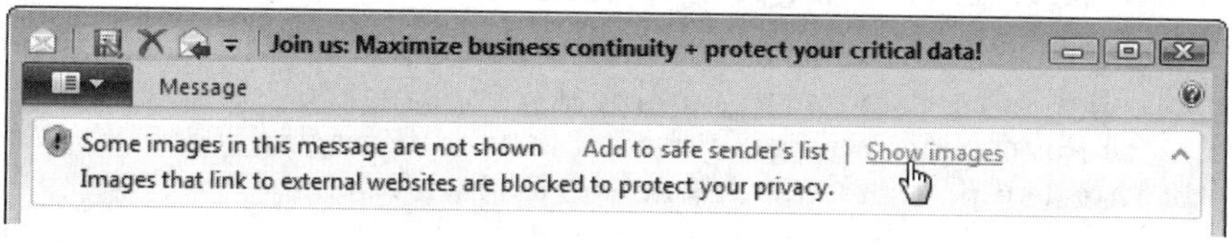

Tell Outlook Express Not to Request Images

To tell Outlook Express not to request images in HTML messages, follow these steps:

1. Choose Tools | Options to display the Options dialog box.
2. Click the Security tab to bring it to the front.
3. Select the Lock Images And Other External Content In HTML E-mail check box.
4. Click the OK button to close the option button.

Tell Windows Live Messenger Not to Request Images

To tell Windows Live Mail not to request images in HTML messages, follow these steps:

1. Click the Windows Live Mail button to display the main menu. The Windows Live Mail button is the button to the left of the Home tab.
2. Click the Options item to display the Options submenu, and then click the Safety Options button to display the Safety Options dialog box.
3. Click the Security tab to bring it to the front.
4. In the Download Images area, select the Block Images And Other External Content In HTML Email check box.
5. If you want Windows Live Mail to display images and external content in messages from addresses you've added to the Safe Senders list, select the Show Images And External Content Sent From Email Addresses In My Safe Senders List check box.
6. Click the OK button to close the Safety Options dialog box.

Deal with E-mail Hoaxes

If you receive a hoax e-mail message, just delete it.

If a friend has sent on the hoax message to you, tell him or her how to identify hoax messages. Lend him or her this book. Or—better—get him or her to buy a copy.

Tip If you're not sure whether a message you've received is a hoax or not, look on a site such as Hoax-Slayer (www.hoax-slayer.com).

Use Instant Messaging Safely

Instant messaging can be a great way to communicate with people who matter to you—but it opens you up to a different set of dangers.

In this section, we'll go over what instant messaging is good for. We'll then look at the threats it poses and discuss how to deal with them.

Understand What Instant Messaging Is For

Instant messaging enables you to communicate in real time with one or more other people. You can send text messages, chat via audio, or chat via video. The limits depend on the program you're using, but typically a text chat can contain scores or hundreds of participants, an audio chat can include up to a dozen people, and a video chat can have two, three, or four people.

While chatting, you can transfer files to other participants.

You can hold multiple separate text chats at once. Most instant messaging programs limit you to one audio chat or video chat at a time to avoid your mouth and face having to multitask.

Understand the Dangers of Instant Messaging

If we leave aside time wasting, gossip, and indiscretions, instant messaging has four main dangers:

- **Spam** A spammer can send spam via instant messaging, just as she can via e-mail.
- **Dangerous links** Text messages can contain dangerous links.
- **Dangerous files** You can receive dangerous files via file transfer in instant messaging sessions.

Note *Social engineering* is when someone tries to get you to part with valuable information unintentionally or cause you to take an action that will benefit them—for example, giving them remote control of your PC by offering help via Windows' Remote Assistance feature. *Grooming* is when an adult develops a younger person's trust in order to exploit or abuse that person.

- **Social engineering and grooming** When you're chatting via text, it's vital to make sure you know who you're communicating with. You should never give out personal information to anyone you don't know.

Note Microsoft frequently changes the settings in Windows Live Messenger and Windows Messenger, so the settings in the version you're using may be different from those described here. If you can't find the specific option I mention, look for one with a similar name or similar functionality.

Protect Yourself Against Instant-Messaging Spam

To protect yourself against instant-messaging spam, you can limit the people who can contact you. You can do this in several ways:

- **Limit a new contact's access to your information** When you get a new contact request and select the Yes, Add As A Friend option button (as shown here), you can select the Limit The Access This Person Has To My Stuff And My Info check box in Windows Live Messenger.

- **Choose the Limited setting or the Private setting in Privacy Options** In Windows Live Messenger, follow these steps:
  1. Click the main menu (the one with your name) and then click More Options to display the Options dialog box.
  2. Click the Privacy tab to display its contents.
  3. Click the Edit Settings button in the Settings area to open a browser window to the Privacy Options screen (see Figure 7-5).
  4. Select the Limited option button or the Private option button, as needed. Read the explanations of who these settings permit to search for you, see your status, send you friend invitations, and so on.
  5. Click the Save button to save your settings.
  6. Click the Close button (the × button) to close the browser window.
  7. Click the OK button to close the Options dialog box.
- **Block anyone you don't want to chat with** In Windows Messenger, right-click the contact and then click Block on the context menu. In Windows Live Messenger, right-click the contact and then click Appear Offline To This Person on the context menu.

Protect Yourself Against Dangerous Links

The only way to protect yourself against dangerous links—links to sites that threaten your PC—is not to click them.

Caution Be very careful about clicking links in instant-messaging programs, even when links come from people you know and trust.

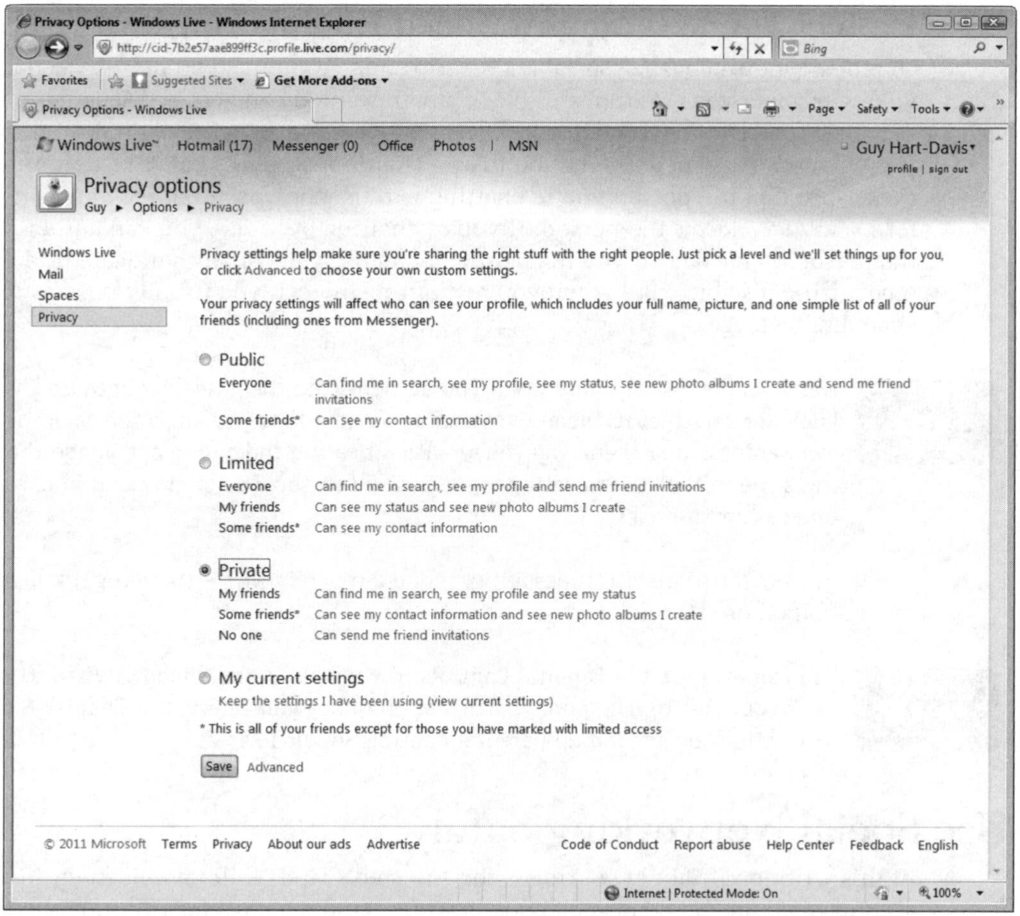

FIGURE 7-5 On the Privacy Options screen, select the Limited option button or the Private option button to help protect yourself against instant-messaging spam.

Protect Yourself Against Dangerous Files

To protect yourself against dangerous files, follow these guidelines:

- Accept file transfers only from people you know and trust.
- Always run security software such as Microsoft Security Essentials, and keep its real-time protection features running.
- Before opening any file you have received via file transfer, make sure you know what type of file it is. Right-click the file in a Windows Explorer window or on your desktop and then click Properties on the context menu to display the Properties dialog box. Then look at the Type Of File readout (look back to Figure 7-1, earlier in this chapter).

Protect Yourself Against Social Engineering and Grooming

To protect yourself against social engineering and grooming, you mostly need to keep your wits about you. You can also block any unwanted contacts as discussed in the section "Protect Yourself Against Instant-Messaging Spam," a little earlier in this chapter.

When you accept an invitation to an instant-messaging chat, take a minute to make sure that the person you're chatting with is who you think they are—in security terms, to *authenticate* the person. If you're chatting by video, you can authenticate the person by his face; if you're chatting by audio, you can authenticate him by recognizing his voice. But when you're chatting by text, you usually need to rely on shared knowledge.

Note Many people take it amiss when you authenticate them, mainly because they know for sure they're themselves and so assume that you know the same. To avoid awkwardness, tell them why you're authenticating them, and encourage them to do the same in their chats with people. Just a few seconds of checking in can avoid unpleasant surprises.

If your kids use instant messaging, make sure they know the dangers of grooming by pot-bellied predators.

Note You can also use the Parental Controls in Windows 7 and Windows Vista to limit your kids to using only particular programs you select. See Chapter 8 for instructions on setting up parental controls in Windows 7.

Use Social Networking Safely

At this writing, social networking is the Internet's latest killer application. In this section, we'll look at what social networking is and what it's for, examine the threats it poses, and discuss what you can do about them.

Understand What Social Networking Is and What It's For

Social networking enables you to publish your personal information and news quickly and easily, and to keep up with the information and news shared by the people you're interested in.

Each social networking site or service is based on an Internet site that you can access using either a web browser or a program designed for that site or service. For example, you can access Facebook by displaying the Facebook website in your web browser (such as Internet Explorer) or via a Facebook program such as the Facebook app for the iPad and iPhone.

At this writing, these are the main social networking sites and services:

- **Facebook** Facebook (www.facebook.com) is the largest social network, with more than 750 million active users as of Summer 2011. Facebook focuses on personal users, but many businesses have a Facebook presence too.

- **LinkedIn** LinkedIn (www.linkedin.com) is a business-oriented social network with more than 100 million registered users as of March 2011. Most LinkedIn members use the site for professional networking.
- **Twitter** Twitter (www.twitter.com) is a micro-blogging service on which users send short messages called *tweets.* Each tweet can be up to 140 characters of text and goes out to the user's followers. As of early 2011, Twitter claimed more than 200 million users.

Note Other social networking sites include Bebo (personal), Myspace (personal), Orkut (personal; based in Brazil but popular in India too), and Plaxo (professional).

- **Flickr** Flickr (www.flickr.com) is an image-hosting website and online community. Users can post photos on Flickr either for viewing directly on the website or for embedding in blog posts or web pages. As of September 2010, Flickr had more than five billion images.

Note Most mainstream social-networking sites don't allow children under 13 to join. This is because any website or online service that collects data from children under 13 must comply with the provisions of the Children's Online Privacy Protection Act (COPPA), which are much stricter than those about collecting data from adults. But as most social-networking sites only ask for a birth date without verifying it, children can easily join such sites. Don't let your children do this if they are under 13.

Understand the Dangers of Social Networking

Social networking exposes you to a variety of dangers, including loss of privacy, identity theft, phishing and scams, and malware attacks.

Let's consider each of these in detail, because most people usually don't consider them until too late.

Deal with the Threat to Privacy

The first and most obvious threat social networks pose is to your privacy.

Understand the Root of All Social-Networking Evil

Money is the root of all evil in social networking—as it is of most other things.

Consumer-oriented social networks present a cuddly image, but they're run by huge companies. For example, Facebook is a large company with a huge market valuation. Like any other company, Facebook's primary goal is to make money for its shareholders.

Facebook accounts are free, so Facebook makes most of its money by selling information to advertisers. This means Facebook has a strong motivation to get users to share as much information as possible. That way, the advertisers can target them more accurately and get better results.

All social networks pile the pressure on you to share information online, to increase your number of friends or followers, and to keep coming back when there's something new to read (however mundane or inane it may be).

The more information you post online, the more other people can learn about you. If it's the right people learning about you, that can be fine. But scammers and identity thieves can also learn about you. Colleagues, employers, and potential employers can also learn things you don't want them to know.

The first way to deal with the threat to your privacy is simply not to post private or confidential information online. You don't have to sign up for a Facebook account. And even if you do sign up, you don't have to post your intimate thoughts or embarrassing photos to it.

If you do post those thoughts or photos, you must use the second way of dealing with the threat to your privacy: Choose suitably tight settings for sharing information with others. For example, in Facebook, click the Account drop-down button and then click Privacy Settings to display the Choose Your Privacy Settings screen (see Figure 7-6).

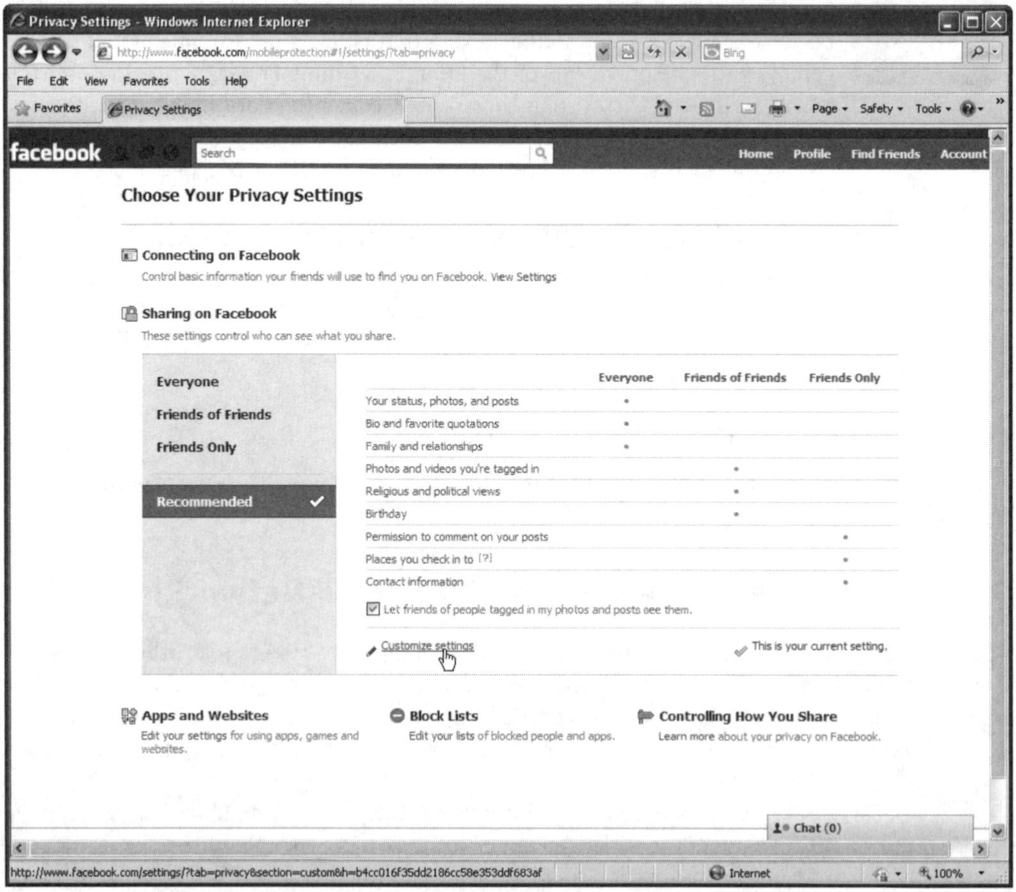

FIGURE 7-6 On the Choose Your Privacy Settings screen, check whom you're sharing the different categories of information with.

Here you can see whom you're sharing different categories of information with—for example, sharing your Family information and Relationships information with Everyone.

If you need to tighten up the settings, click the Customize Settings link to display the Choose Your Privacy Settings: Customize Settings screen (see Figure 7-7). Here you can open each drop-down list and choose the specific setting:

- **Everyone** Choose this setting only if you want anyone on Facebook to be able to see your information.
- **Friends Of Friends** Choose this setting if you want not only your friends but also all their friends to be able to see your information. This setting is widely popular, but if you're a typical Facebook user, it shares your information with hundreds or thousands of people you don't know and have no reason to trust.

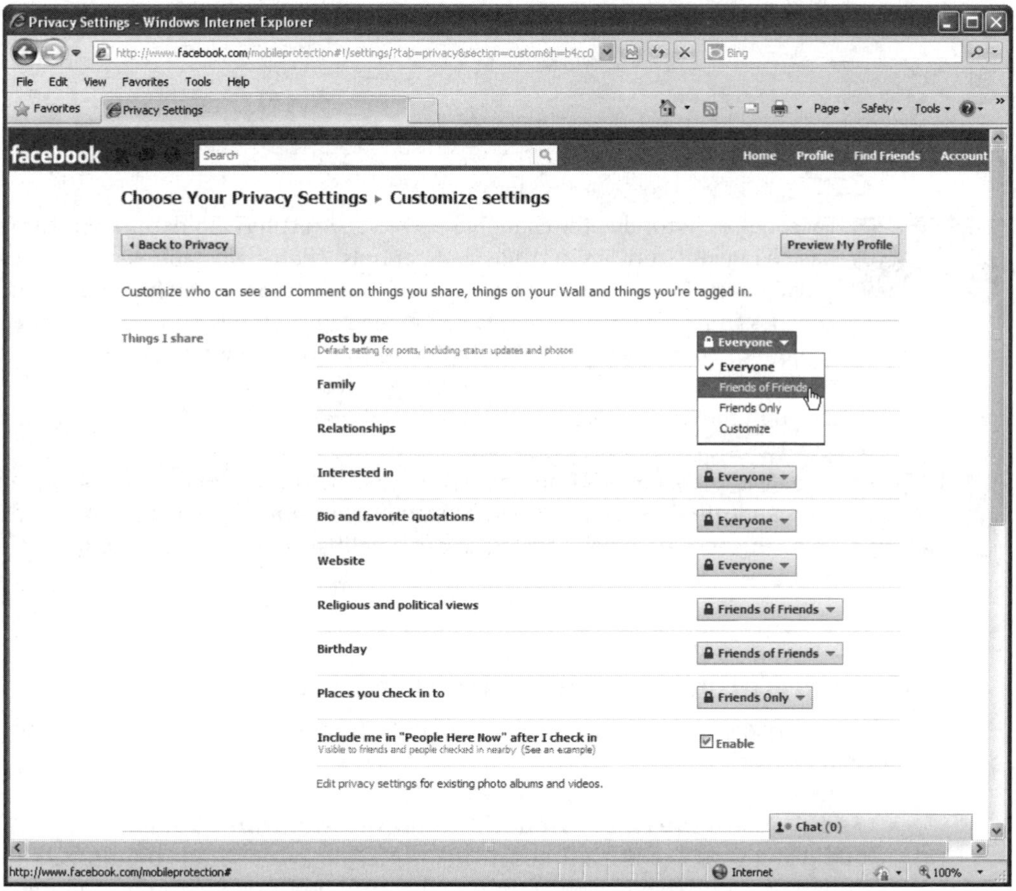

FIGURE 7-7 Use the controls on the Choose Your Privacy Settings: Customize Settings screen to tighten up your privacy settings.

- **Friends Only** Choose this setting to restrict the information to people you've accepted as friends on Facebook. This is the best choice for any information that's not in the public domain.
- **Customize** Choose this setting to display the Custom Privacy dialog box (shown here), in which you can choose to share the category of information with specific people but not with others. You may want to use this functionality sometimes, but it's cumbersome.

Caution: Facebook is notorious for changing its privacy settings. To date, when Facebook has changed its privacy settings and controls, the new default settings have usually been looser than before. So every time Facebook notifies you about changes in its settings, or makes you agree to new terms and conditions, you need to go into your privacy settings and make sure they protect your privacy.

After you change your settings, save the changes to make them take effect.

Note: To reduce the amount of information that social-networking sites hold about you, communicate directly via e-mail or instant messaging rather than communicating through social networks. Alternatively, go old-school and use voice or text messages.

Protect Yourself Against Identity Theft

You can protect yourself against identity theft (impersonation) on social networks in two main ways:

- **Avoid posting private or confidential information** I doubt you'd even dream of putting your credit card numbers or bank account details online. Similarly, don't post your social security number or full address. Share your phone number only with those friends you want to be able to contact you.

Tip When deciding what to post to your social-networking site, follow this guideline: *Post only material that you're happy to publish on the Internet permanently.* This is because even a passing post or off-color joke can come back to haunt you later—for example, when a would-be employer views your Facebook page. Many companies now ask for details of social-networking accounts as part of the interview process, so it's better to be safe than to be sorry.

- **Choose tight privacy settings** As discussed in the previous section, go into the social-networking site's privacy settings and choose carefully which information to share with whom.

Note LinkedIn is substantially different from Facebook. To use LinkedIn effectively, you normally need to build a business profile containing detailed information on your skills and employment history—otherwise, you might as well not bother joining. Then again, the temptation to publish inappropriate party photos on LinkedIn is minimal.

Protect Yourself Against Phishing and Scams

To protect yourself against phishing and scams, follow these three suggestions:

- **Choose tight privacy settings** As discussed in the previous two sections, visit the site's privacy settings and restrict the sharing of your information.
- **Make sure you're accessing the social-networking site itself** That may sound dumb, but a popular attack is to send a phishing message containing a link to a look-alike site—for example, a clone of the Facebook login page—that captures your username and password. Avoid clicking such links. Instead, go to the social-networking site by entering its address in your web browser (or using a favorite or bookmark).
- **Keep your wits about you** As usual, if any offer seems too good to be true, it probably *is* too good to be true. Similarly, treat any e-mail messages saying your social-networking account has been compromised with suspicion, and don't click links in them. Go to the site via your browser and log in. If there's a security problem, the site will tell you when you log in.

Protect Yourself Against Malware Attacks

To protect yourself against malware attacks from social-networking sites, follow these two suggestions:

- **Run security software** I know I sound like a broken record—but run security software such as Microsoft Security Essentials all the time, and make sure its real-time protection features are enabled.

- **Be wary of new features** In Spring 2011, many Facebook users followed instructions to enable a new Dislike button as a counterpart to the ubiquitous Like button. To enable the button, they had to copy a chunk of JavaScript code, paste it into the Address box, and then press ENTER—which ran the malicious code on their computers. Make sure you don't fall for tricks like this.

In the next chapter, I'll show you how to keep your children safe online by using the parental control settings built into Windows 7. Turn the page when you're ready to get started.

8 Protect Your Children with Parental Controls

As you've seen in the past couple of chapters, the Internet brings a wide range of threats to you and your PC along with its many benefits.

Everyone who goes online needs to keep their wits about them. This is doubly important for children, many of whom are easier to fool than adults, because they're still learning how to deal with other people and figure out whom to trust.

To keep your children safe online, you need to limit the actions they can take. You may also need to track what they do online—which websites they visit, whom they contact, and so on—so that you can identify dangers or topics you need to discuss with them.

This chapter shows you how to set up Windows' Parental Control features to help keep your children safe online. We'll start by discussing what the Parental Controls are and what you can do with them; then we'll cover how you set them up.

Understand What Parental Controls Offers

Windows 7 has a feature called Parental Controls built in. You can use it to set time limits for using the PC, choose which games the user can play, and control which programs the user can run. You manage these Parental Control features through Control Panel and store the settings on your PC.

Although Windows 7 doesn't have web filtering capabilities or activity reports to see what the user has been doing, you can add them by installing the Family Safety program, which is part of Microsoft's Windows Live Essentials web-based software suite. What's confusing is that when you install and turn on Family Safety to get these extra features, you then need to manage *all* the Parental Controls through Family Safety's web-based interface rather than managing them on your PC—even if you've already set them up on your PC.

Windows XP doesn't have Parental Control features as such, but you can shut out some unsuitable content by setting up the Content Advisor feature. To provide full-on Parental Controls, you need to install third-party software. I'll mention a couple of possibilities at the end of this chapter.

Caution As you'll see in this chapter, Parental Controls can help you prevent a child (okay, or a parent) from taking certain unwanted actions on a PC. But Parental Controls can't keep a child safe. So even if you apply Parental Controls and choose tight settings, you must still police the child's use of the PC.

Set Up Windows 7's Built-in Parental Controls

In this section, we'll look at how to set up the Parental Controls features built into Windows 7. We'll look at three features in particular: setting time limits for using the PC, choosing which games the user can play, and controlling which programs the user can run.

Open the Parental Controls Window

To set up Parental Controls, you first open the Parental Controls window. You can open the Parental Controls window in various ways, but this way is usually the easiest:

1. Click the Start button to display the Start menu.
2. Click your picture at the top of the Start menu to display a User Accounts window (see Figure 8-1).
3. Click the Parental Controls link in the lower-left corner to display the Parental Controls window (see Figure 8-2).

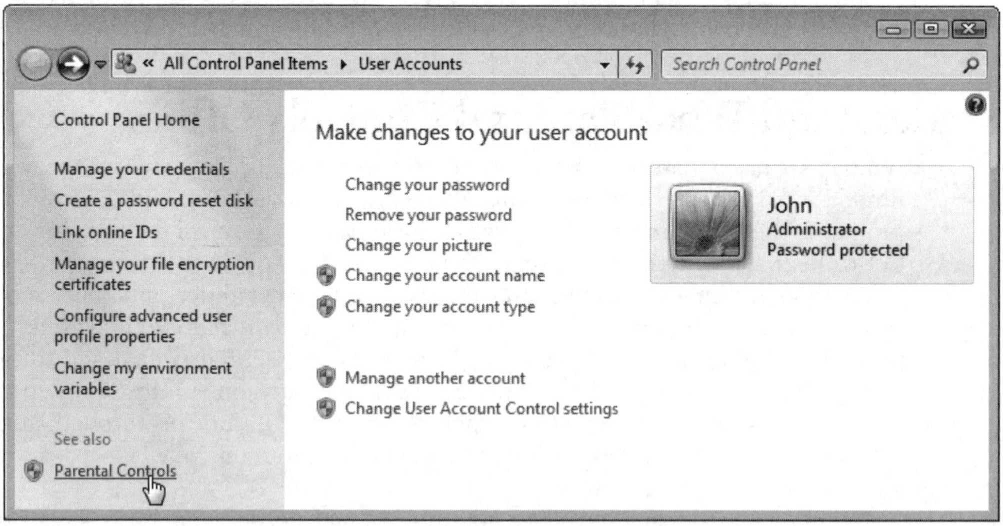

FIGURE 8-1 Click the Parental Controls link in the lower-left corner of the User Accounts window to display the Parental Controls window.

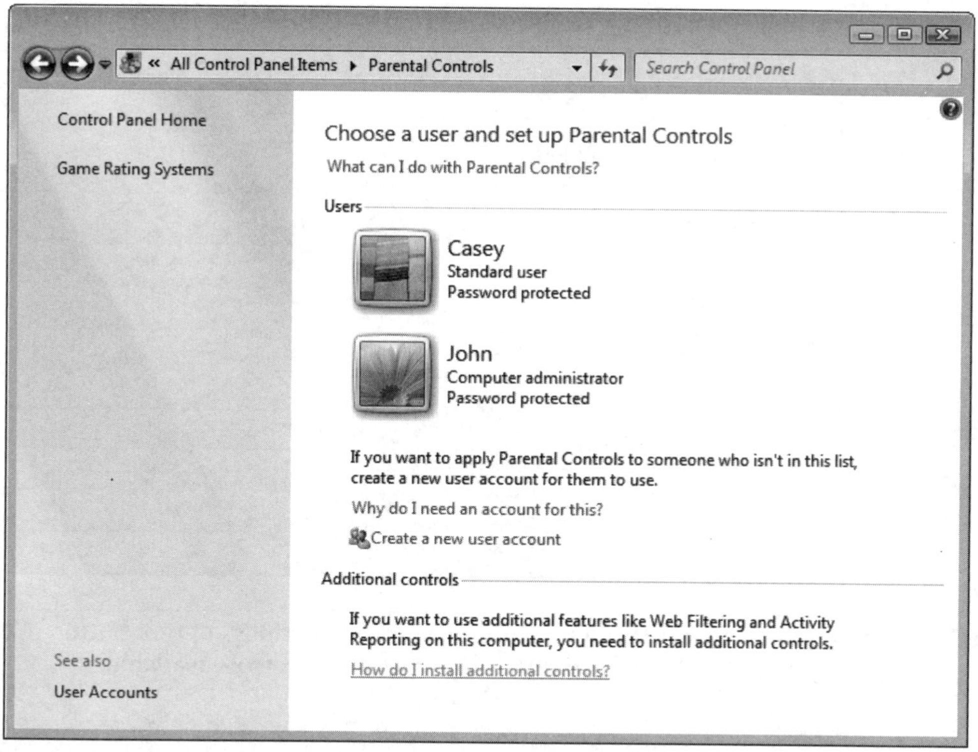

FIGURE 8-2 From the Parental Controls window in Control Panel, you can start setting up Parental Controls. Before you do, you may need to install additional controls by clicking the link at the bottom of the window.

Note If the user doesn't already have his or her own user account, you can create one by clicking the Create A New User Account link and following through the screens that appear. Make sure you create a Standard account rather than an Administrator account, because you can apply Parental Controls only to a Standard account.

4. In the Users list, click the user account you want to apply Parental Controls to. Windows displays the User Controls window.
5. In the upper-left area, select the "On, Enforce Current Settings" option button to make the controls in the Windows Settings area available (see Figure 8-3).
6. You can now set the Time Limits settings, the Games settings, and the Allow And Block Specific Programs settings, as discussed in the following sections.

Set Time Limits for the User

To restrict the times the user can use the PC, click the Time Limits link in the Windows Settings area. In the Time Restrictions window (see Figure 8-4), click and drag through the hours you want to block, turning their squares blue. When you've made your selections, click the OK button to return to the User Controls window.

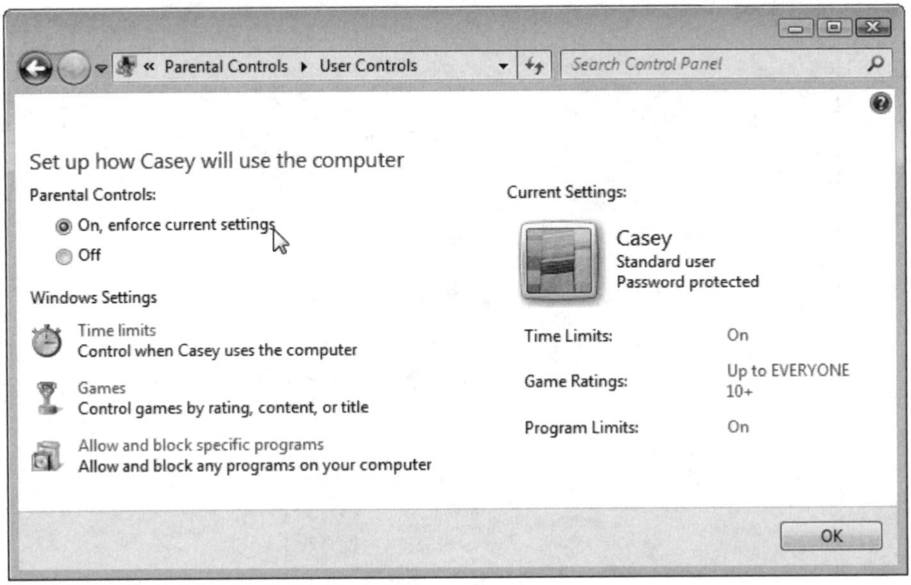

FIGURE 8-3 Select the "On, Enforce Current Settings" option button in the User Controls window to make the Windows Settings controls available.

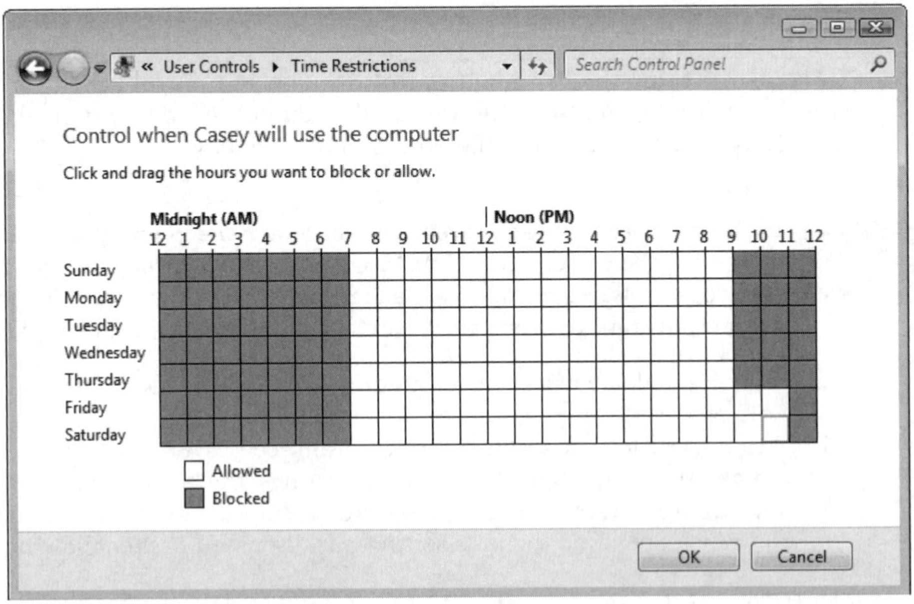

FIGURE 8-4 In the Time Restrictions window, select the box for each hour during which you want to block the user from using your PC. Here, the user is blocked from 9 P.M. to 7 A.M. from Sunday to Thursday and 11 P.M. to 7 A.M. on Friday and Saturday.

Set Games Controls for the User

To choose which games the user can play, click the Games link in the Windows Settings area of the User Controls window. In the Game Controls window (see Figure 8-5), choose settings as follows:

1. In the Can *User* Play Games? area, select the Yes option button or the No option button, as needed. If you select the No option button, skip ahead to step 10, because you don't need to set game ratings or block or allow specific games.
2. In the Block (Or Allow) Games By Rating And Content Types area, click the Set Game Ratings link to open the Game Restrictions window. Figure 8-6 shows the top part of the Game Restrictions window.
3. In the If A Game Has No Rating, Can *User* Play It? area, select the Allow Games With No Rating option button or the Block Games With No Rating option button, as appropriate.
4. In the Which Ratings Are OK For *User* To Play? area, select the highest game rating the user may play—for example, Everyone 10+ or Teen.
5. In the Block These Types Of Content area, select the check box for each context type you want to block, even if the game's rating allows it. The types of content range from Alcohol And Tobacco Reference to Violence and Violent References.

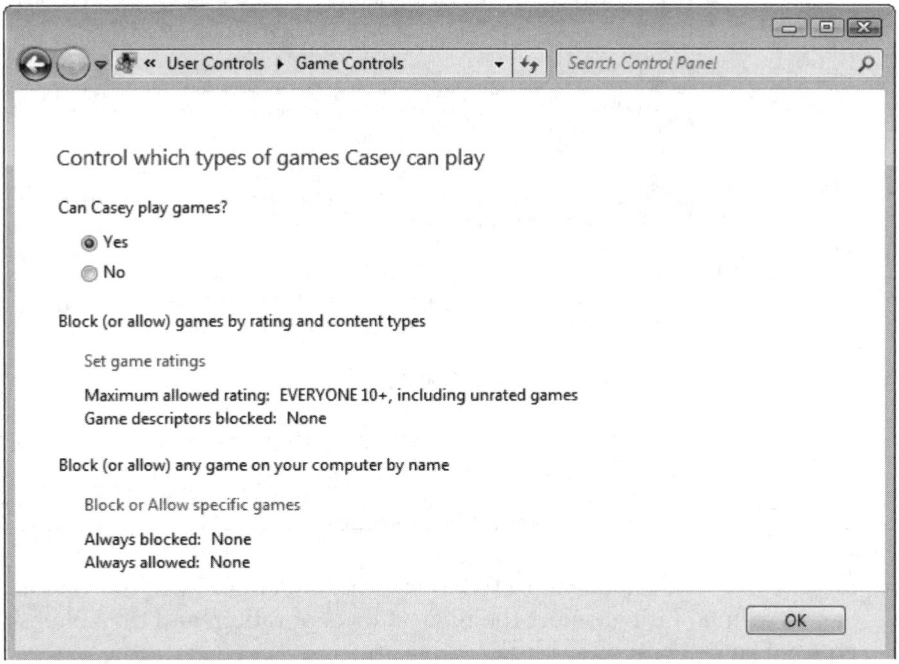

FIGURE 8-5 In the Game Controls window, choose whether the user may or may not play games. You can then block or allow games by rating or content type as well as block or allow games by name.

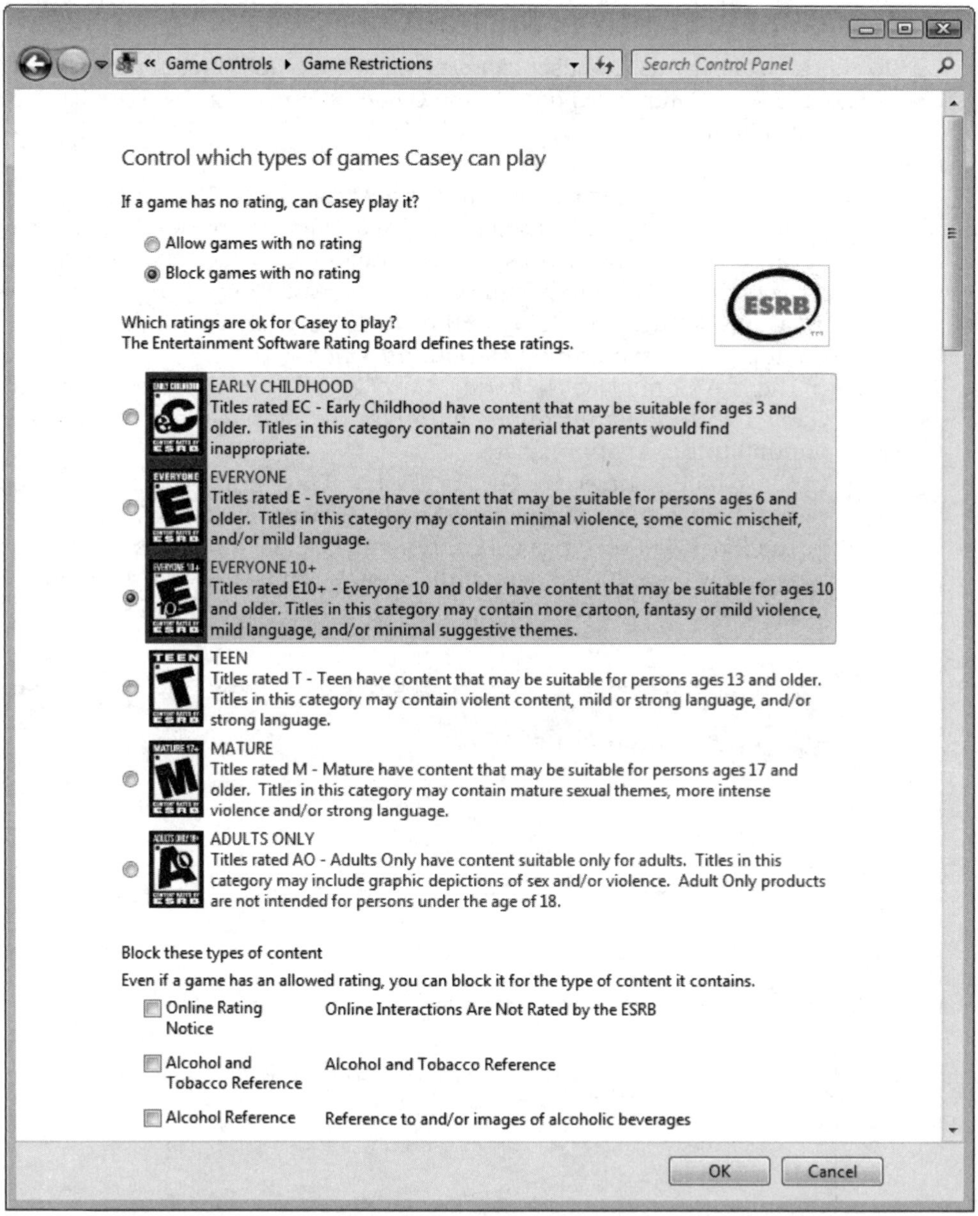

FIGURE 8-6 In the Game Restrictions window, choose whether the user can play games with no rating, select the highest level of rating, and then choose which types of game content to block.

6. Click the OK button when you've finished choosing settings in the Game Restrictions window.
7. In the Block (Or Allow) Any Game On Your Computer By Name area, click the Block Or Allow Specific Games link to display the Game Overrides window (shown in Figure 8-7 with settings chosen).
8. For each game, select the appropriate option button:
   - **User Rating Setting** Select this option button to let the user ratings you've set control whether the user can play the game.
   - **Always Allow** Select this option button to override the user rating setting and allow the user to play the game.
   - **Always Block** Select this option button to override the user rating setting and always block the user from playing the game.
9. Click the OK button to return to the Game Controls window.
10. Click the OK button to return to the User Controls window.

Caution Blocking works only for games created by developers who submit their games for ratings. Many independent games are unrated, so the blocking doesn't work for them. Flash-based games on websites aren't blocked either, but you can prevent users from playing them by blocking the websites. If you need to police your child's game play tightly, block games with no rating, choose a low rating, and permit specific games that you've reviewed for suitability.

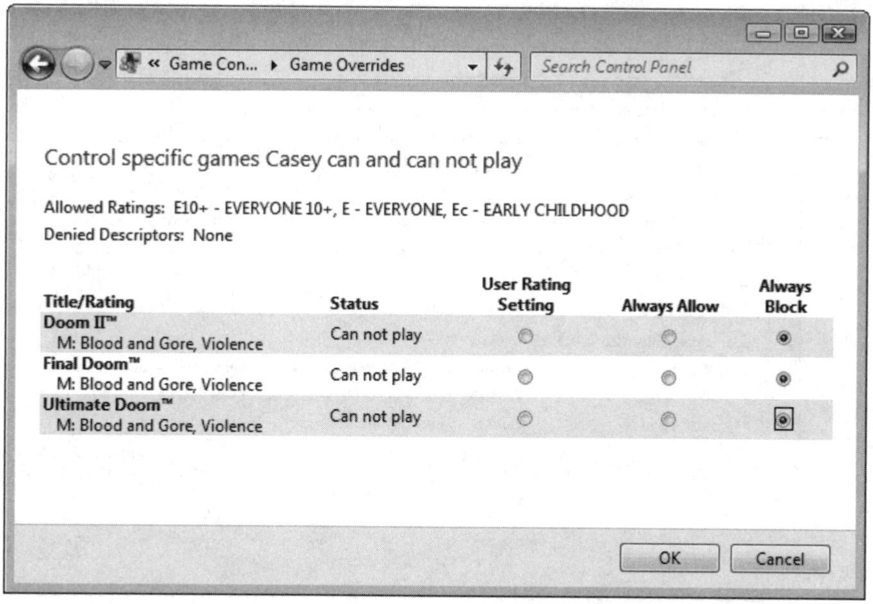

FIGURE 8-7 In the Game Overrides window, select the User Rating Setting option button, the Always Allow option button, or the Always Block option button for each game, as needed.

Limit the Programs the User Can Run

The third type of Parental Control you can apply in the User Controls window is to control which programs the user can run and which they cannot run. To control programs, follow these steps:

1. In the User Controls window, click the Allow And Block Specific Programs link to display the Application Restrictions window (see Figure 8-8). When you click this link, Windows has to scare up a list of all the programs on your PC; this may take several minutes.
2. In the Which Programs Can *User* Use? area, select the *User* Can Only Use The Programs I Allow option button.
3. Click the Uncheck All button at the bottom to clear all the check boxes in the Check The Programs That Can Be Used list box.

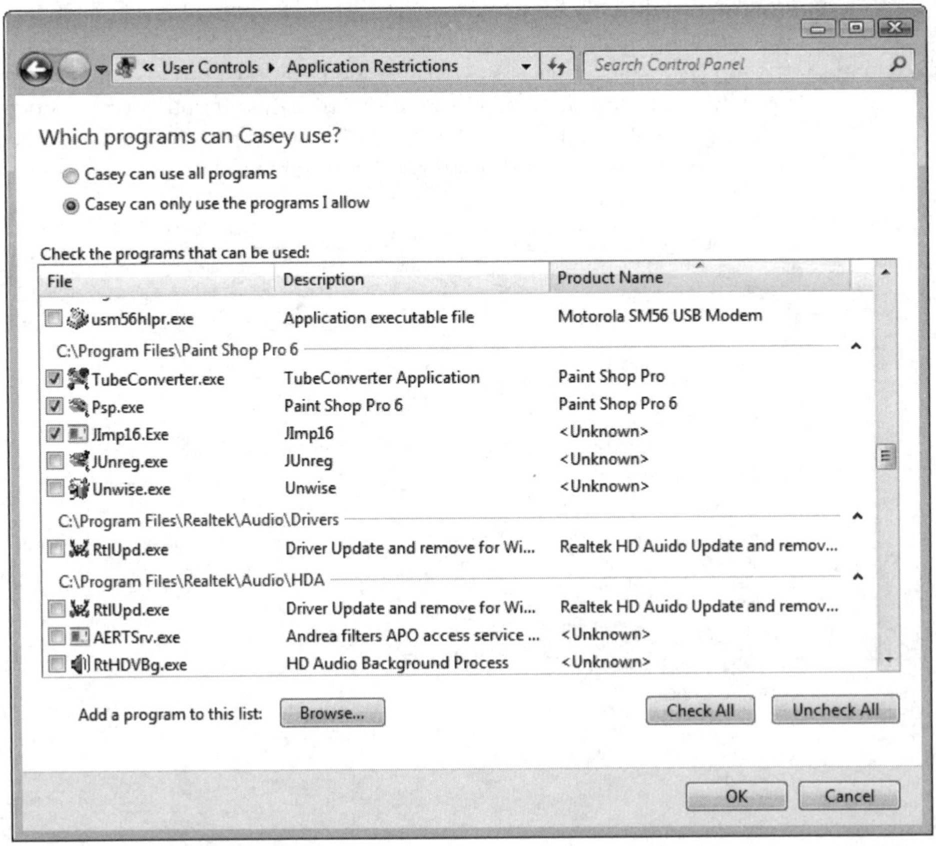

FIGURE 8-8 In the Application Restrictions window, select the *User* Can Only Use The Programs I Allow option button and then select the check box for each permitted program.

4. Select the check box for each program you will let the user run. This is a long list, so you'll need to scroll up and down through it.

Note Each group of programs appears in a section that shows its folder name. You can collapse each section by clicking the up-arrow button at its left end, and expand the collapsed section by clicking the down-arrow button that replaces the up-arrow. You can click a column heading to sort the contents of the section by that heading—by File (the file name), Description, or Product Name.

5. If you need to allow the user to use a program that doesn't appear in the list, click the Browse button, click the program in the Open dialog box that appears, and then click the Open button.
6. Click the OK button to return to the User Controls window.

Choose Family Safety Settings in Windows Live Essentials

If you need more extensive Parental Controls than those built into Windows 7, you can download, install, and use the Family Safety program that Microsoft provides as part of Windows Live Essentials.

When you use Family Safety, you manage all the Parental Control settings through Family Safety rather than through Control Panel's Parental Controls applet. You must have a Windows Live ID (such as a Windows Live account or a Hotmail account) to use Family Safety, and your Family Safety settings are stored on the Web.

Install the Family Safety Program of Windows Live Essentials

To install the Family Safety program of Windows Live Essentials, open your web browser and go to the Windows Live Essentials site (http://windows.microsoft.com/en-US/windows7/products/features/windows-live-essentials).

Note If you've already installed all the Windows Live Essentials programs, Family Safety is already on your PC.

From this page, click the Download button in the Family Safety area if you want to install just the Family Safety programs of Windows Live Essentials. If you want to install other programs as well, click the Download link for the whole shebang. Either way, the Windows Live Essentials installer runs, and it gives you the option of installing all the programs or just some of them (see Figure 8-9).

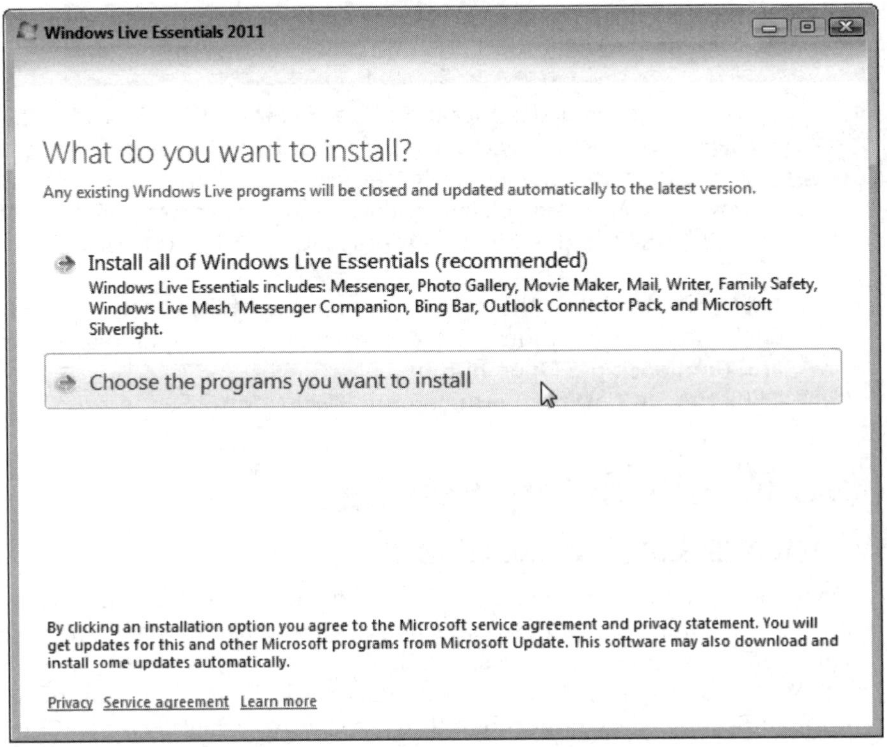

FIGURE 8-9 **If you want to install only the Family Safety program of Windows Live Essentials, click the Choose The Programs You Want To Install button on the What Do You Want To Install? screen.**

If you want to install just the Family Safety program, or just some programs, click the Choose The Programs You Want To Install button, choose the programs on the Select Programs To Install screen (see Figure 8-10), and then click the Install button. Otherwise, click the Install All Of Windows Live Essentials button.

The Done! dialog box appears when the installation is complete. Click the Close button.

Open the Family Safety Web Page

To choose Family Safety settings, first open the Family Safety web page as described here. You can then choose settings as described in the following sections.

1. Click the Start button to display the Start menu.
2. Click your picture at the top of the Start menu to display a User Accounts window.

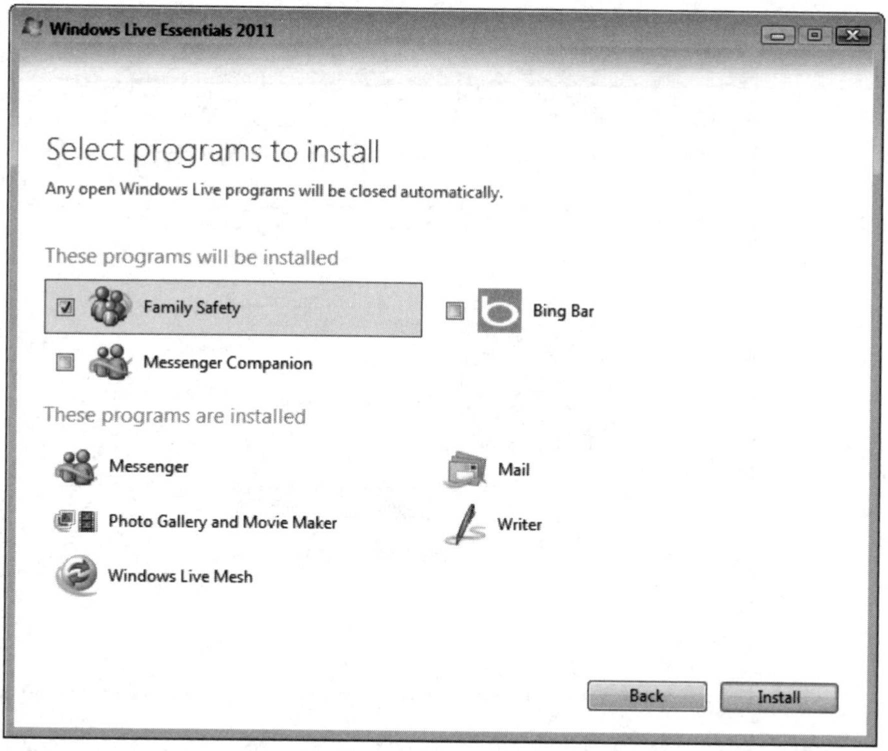

FIGURE 8-10 On the Select Programs To Install screen, select the check box for each program you want to install.

3. Click the Parental Controls link in the lower-left corner to display the Parental Controls window.
4. In the Additional Controls area, open the Select A Provider drop-down list and then click Windows Live Family Safety.
5. Click the name of the user you want to control. Windows displays the Windows Live Family Safety sign-in dialog box (see Figure 8-11).
6. Type your Windows Live ID and password and then click the Sign In button. The Select The Windows Accounts You Want To Monitor On This Computer window opens (see Figure 8-12).
7. Select the Monitor Account check box for the user's account.
8. Click the Save button. Windows then sets up Family Safety and displays the Go To The Family Safety Website To Customize Settings window (see Figure 8-13).

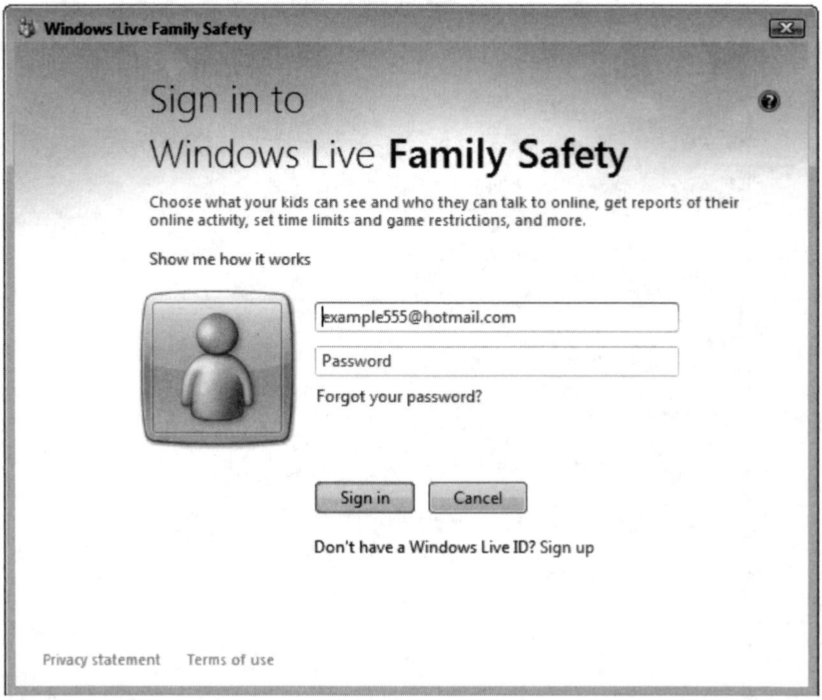

FIGURE 8-11 You must sign into Windows Live Family Safety using your Windows Live ID before you can configure Family Safety settings on your PC.

9. Click the Go To The Family Safety Website link to open a browser window showing the Family Safety web page (see Figure 8-14).
10. Click the Edit Settings link for the user you want to control. The browser window displays the Family Safety page for that user (see Figure 8-15).

Choose Web Filtering Settings

To choose web filtering settings, follow these steps:

1. Click the Web Filtering link to display the Web Filtering page (shown in Figure 8-16 with settings chosen).
2. Select the Turn On Web Filtering option button.
3. Drag the slider to choose the level of blocking to apply:
   - **Allow List Only** Lets the user access only those sites you've added to the Allow list.
   - **Child-Friendly** Lets the user access sites rated as child-friendly as well as sites in the Allow list.

FIGURE 8-12 In the Select The Windows Accounts You Want To Monitor On This Computer window, select the check box for the user account you want to affect.

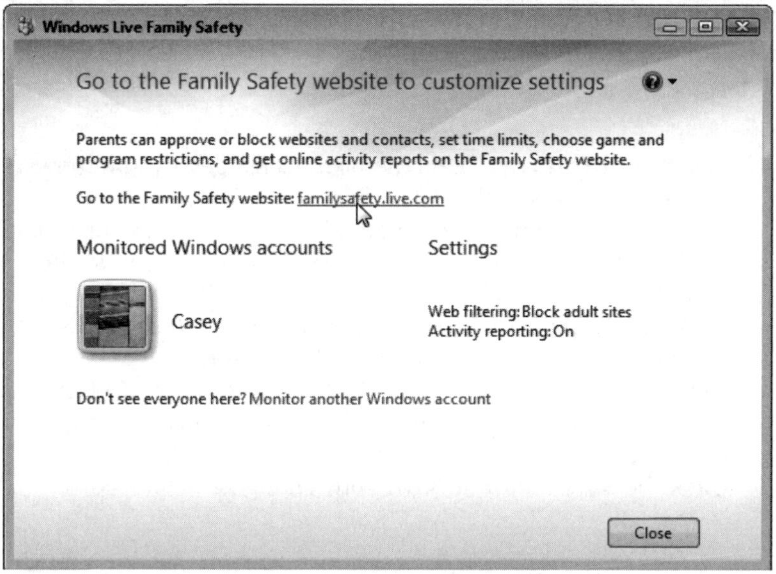

FIGURE 8-13 In the Go To The Family Safety Website To Customize Settings window, click the Go To The Family Safety Website link.

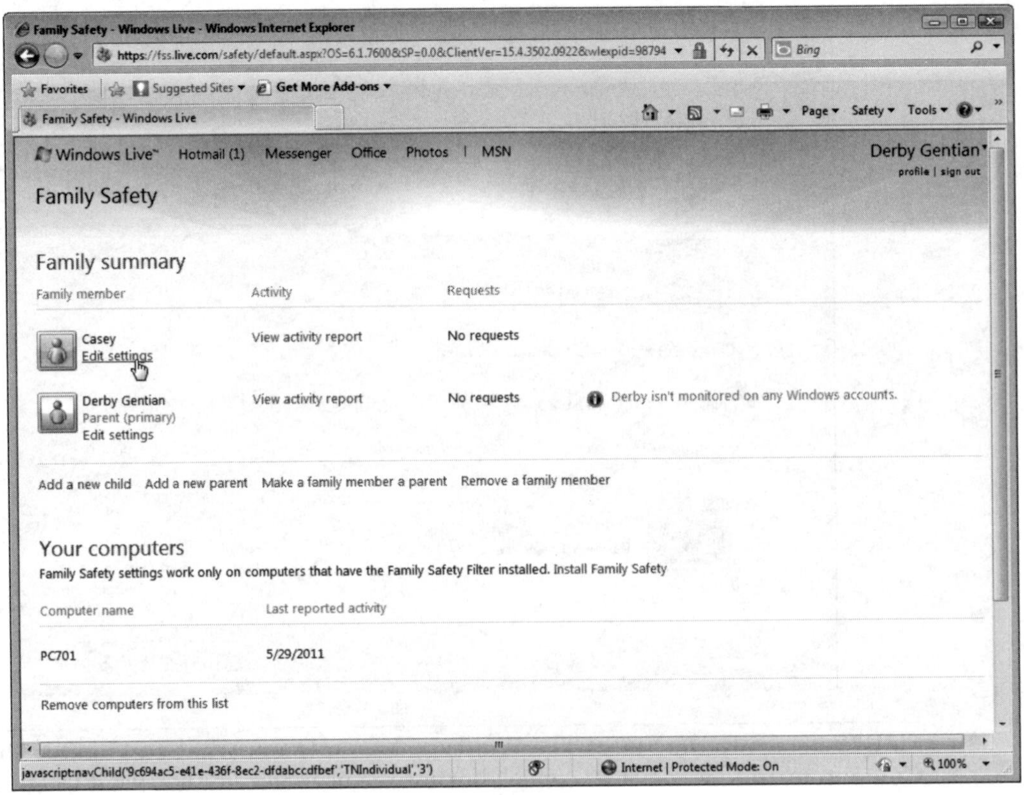

FIGURE 8-14 On the Family Safety website, click the Edit Settings link for the user you want to control.

- **General Interest** Lets the user access general-interest sites, child-friendly sites, and sites in the Allow list.
- **Online Communication (Basic)** Lets the user use social networking web chat and web mail, as well as access general-interest sites, child-friendly sites, and sites in the Allow list.
- **Warn On Adult** Lets the user access all sites, but displays a warning before displaying a site that contains adult material.

4. In the File Downloads area, select the Allow *User* To Download Files Online check box if you want to allow the user to download files. Otherwise, clear this check box.
5. Click the Save button to save your changes.

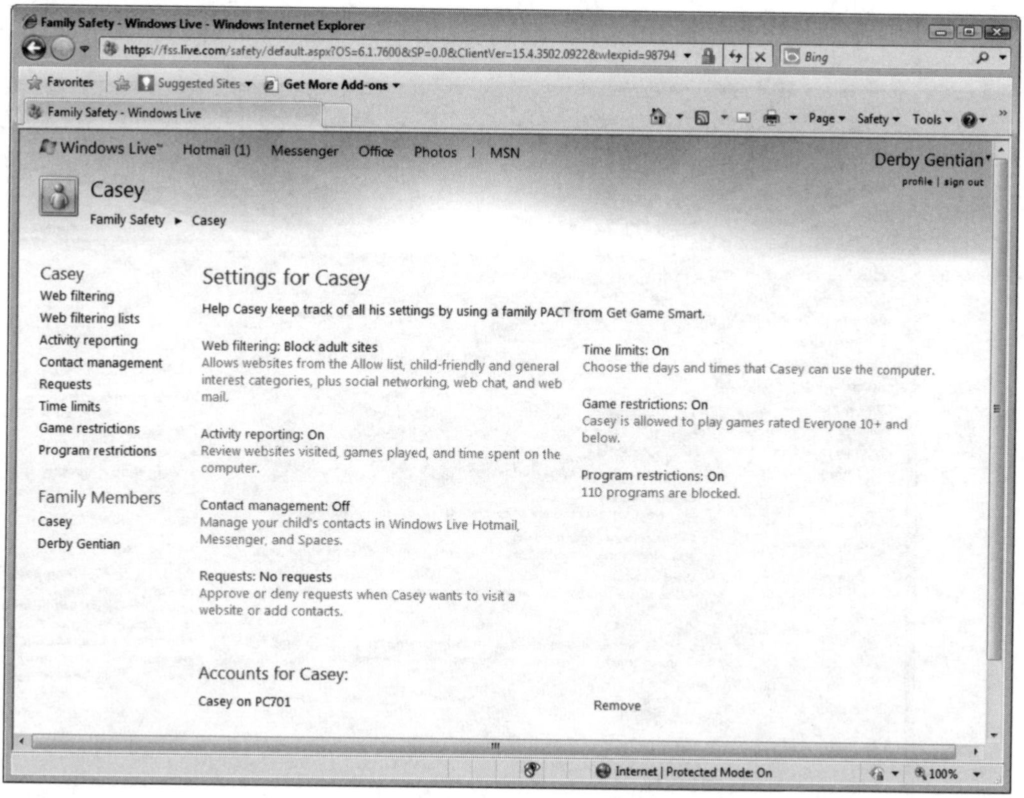

FIGURE 8-15 From the Family Safety page for a user, you can access the different categories of Parental Controls.

Set Up Your Web Filtering Lists

Next, set up your web filtering lists—the list of sites you want to allow the user to access, and the list of sites you want to block the user from accessing. Follow these steps:

1. In the left column, click the Web Filtering Lists link to display the Web Filtering Lists page, shown in Figure 8-17 with settings chosen.
2. Click in the text box and type or paste the URL of the first website you want to allow or block.
3. In the drop-down list on the right side, choose For This Person Only or For Everyone, as needed.
4. Click the Allow button or the Block button, as appropriate.
5. Add further sites as needed.
6. Click the Save button to save your changes.

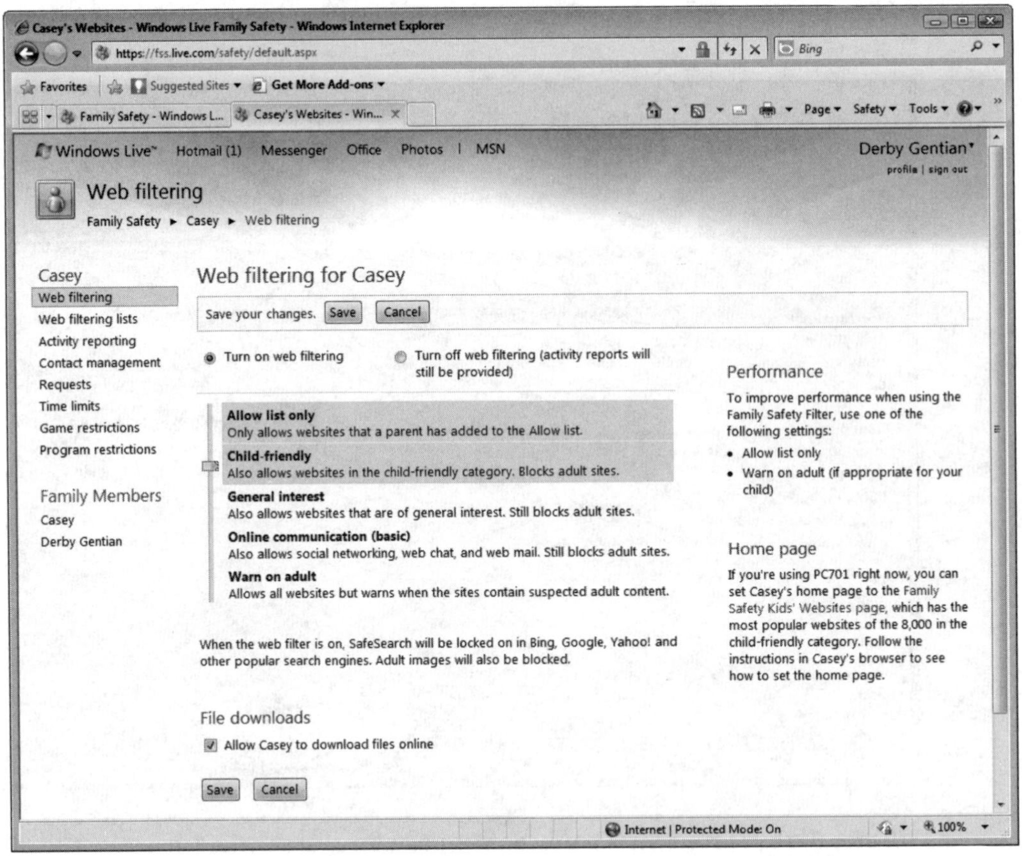

FIGURE 8-16 On the Web Filtering page, turn on web filtering, choose what to allow and block, and decide whether the user may download files.

Choose Contact Management Settings

If your child has a Windows Live ID, you can choose which contacts the child may communicate with. To do so, follow these steps:

1. In the left column, click the Contact Management link to display the Contact Management page (shown in Figure 8-18 with settings chosen).
2. Near the top of the page, select the Parent Manages The Child's Contact List option button instead of the Child Manages Their Own Contact List option button.
3. In the *User* Can Use area, select or clear the Windows Live Messenger check box, the Windows Live Hotmail check box, and the Spaces On Windows Live check box, as needed.

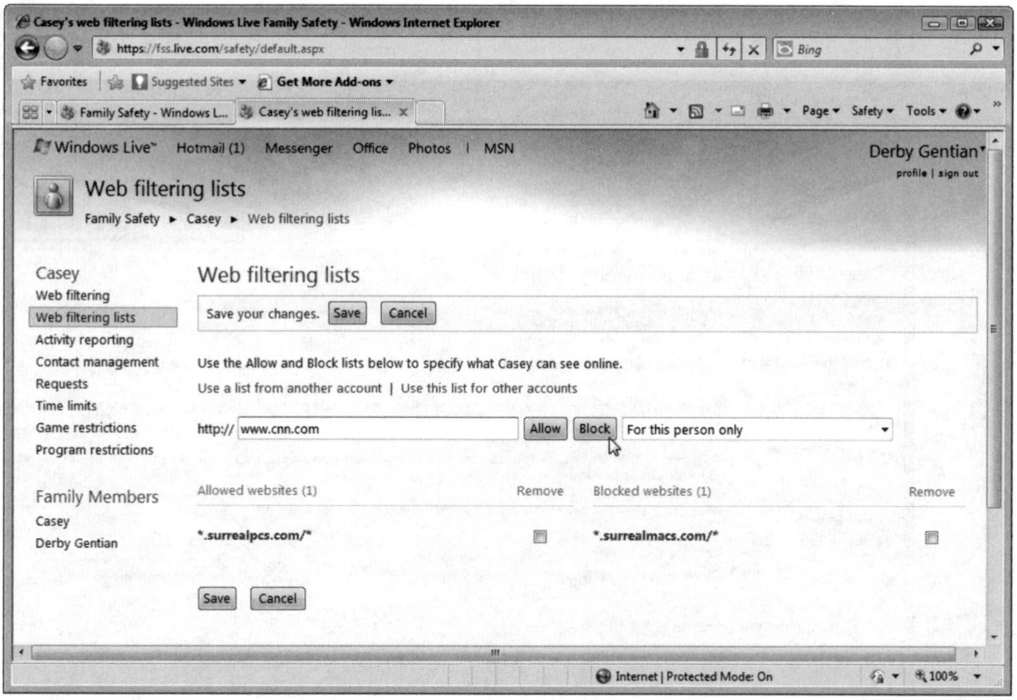

FIGURE 8-17 Set up your lists of allowed websites and blocked websites on the Web Filtering Lists page. You can allow or block a site for this person only or for everyone.

4. In the Contacts For *User* area, type each contact's name and e-mail address, in turn, and then click the Add button to add each contact to the list.
5. Click the Save button to save your changes.

Choose Time Limits

To set time limits for the user, follow these steps:

1. In the left column, click the Time Limits link to display the Time Limits page (see Figure 8-19).
2. Select the Turn On Time Limits option button.
3. Select the box for each hour you want to block the user from using the PC. You can click and drag through the boxes to select several or many at once.
4. Click the Save button to save your changes.

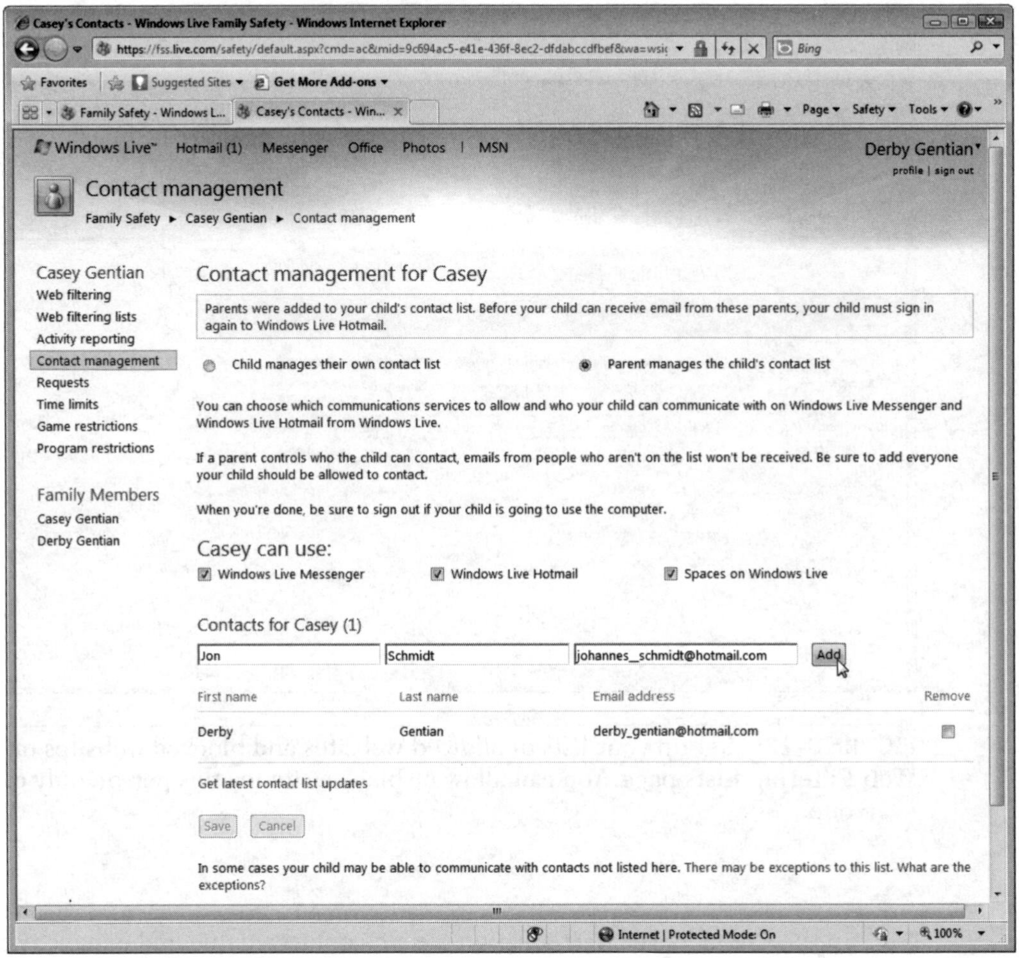

FIGURE 8-18 On the Contact Management page, choose which communications tools your child may use, and set up the contacts list.

Choose Game Restrictions

To choose game restrictions for the user, follow these steps:

1. In the left column, click the Game Restrictions link to display the Game Restrictions page (shown in Figure 8-20).
2. Select the Turn On Game Restrictions option button.

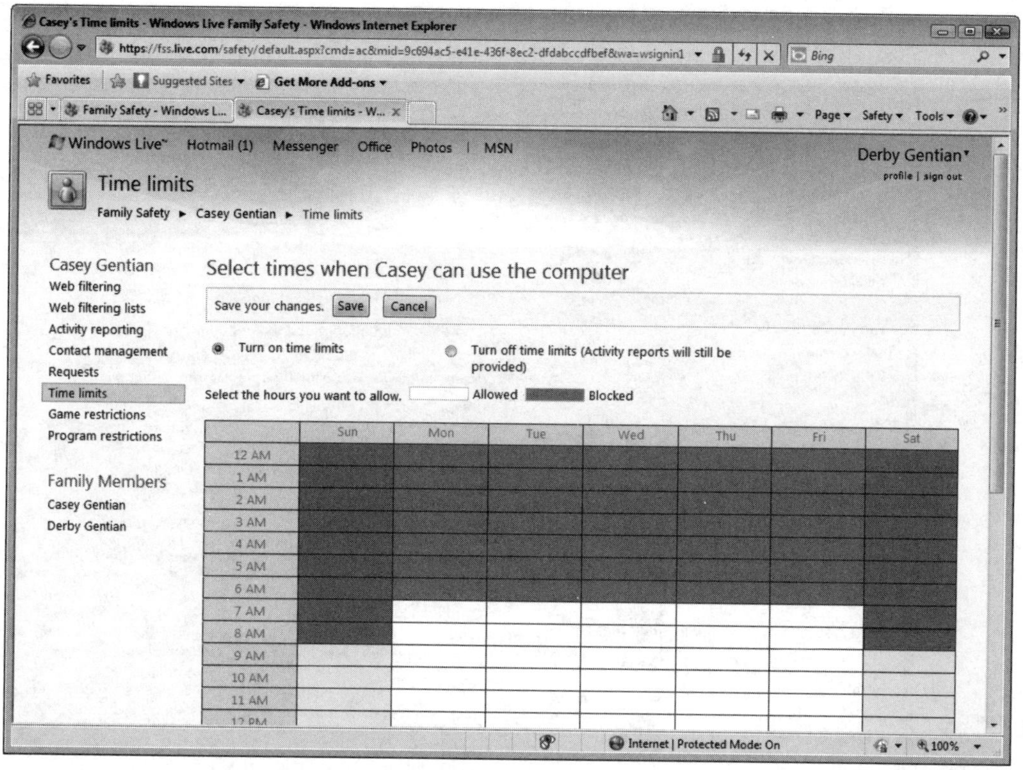

FIGURE 8-19 On the Time Limits page, select the box for each hour during which you want to block the user from using your PC.

3. Clear the Allow Games That Aren't Rated check box unless you want the user to be able to play unrated games.
4. Drag the slider up or down to the maximum rating for games the user may play—for example, Everyone 10+ or Teen.
5. If you want to block or allow specific games, click the Block Or Allow Specific Games link to display the Manage Games page. For each game, select the Use Game Rating option button, the Always Allow option button, or the Always Block option button, and then click the Save button to return to the Game Restrictions page.
6. Click the Save button to save the changes you've made to game restrictions.

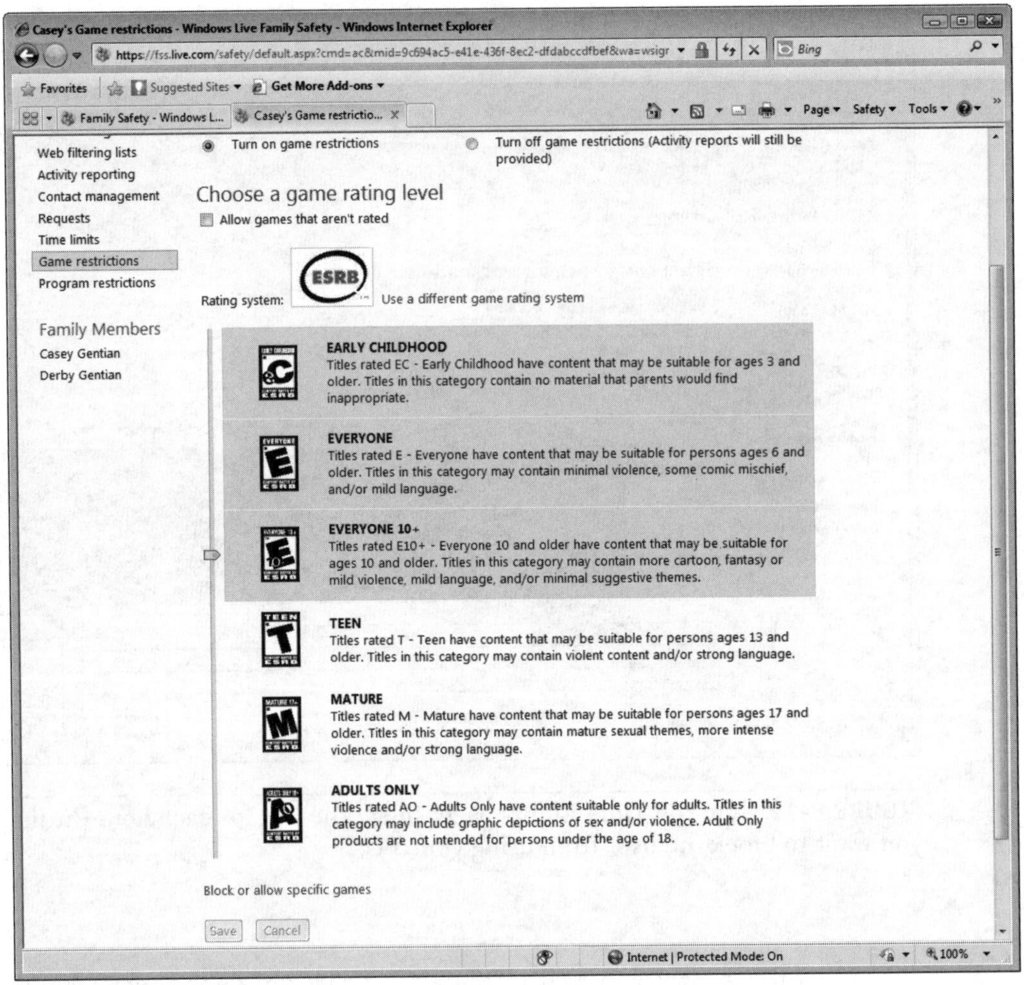

FIGURE 8-20 On the Game Restrictions page, select the Turn On Game Restrictions option button, choose the highest level of games the user can play, and decide whether to permit unrated games.

Choose Program Restrictions

To restrict the programs the user can run on the PC, follow these steps:

1. In the left column, click the Program Restrictions link to display the Program Restrictions page (see Figure 8-21).

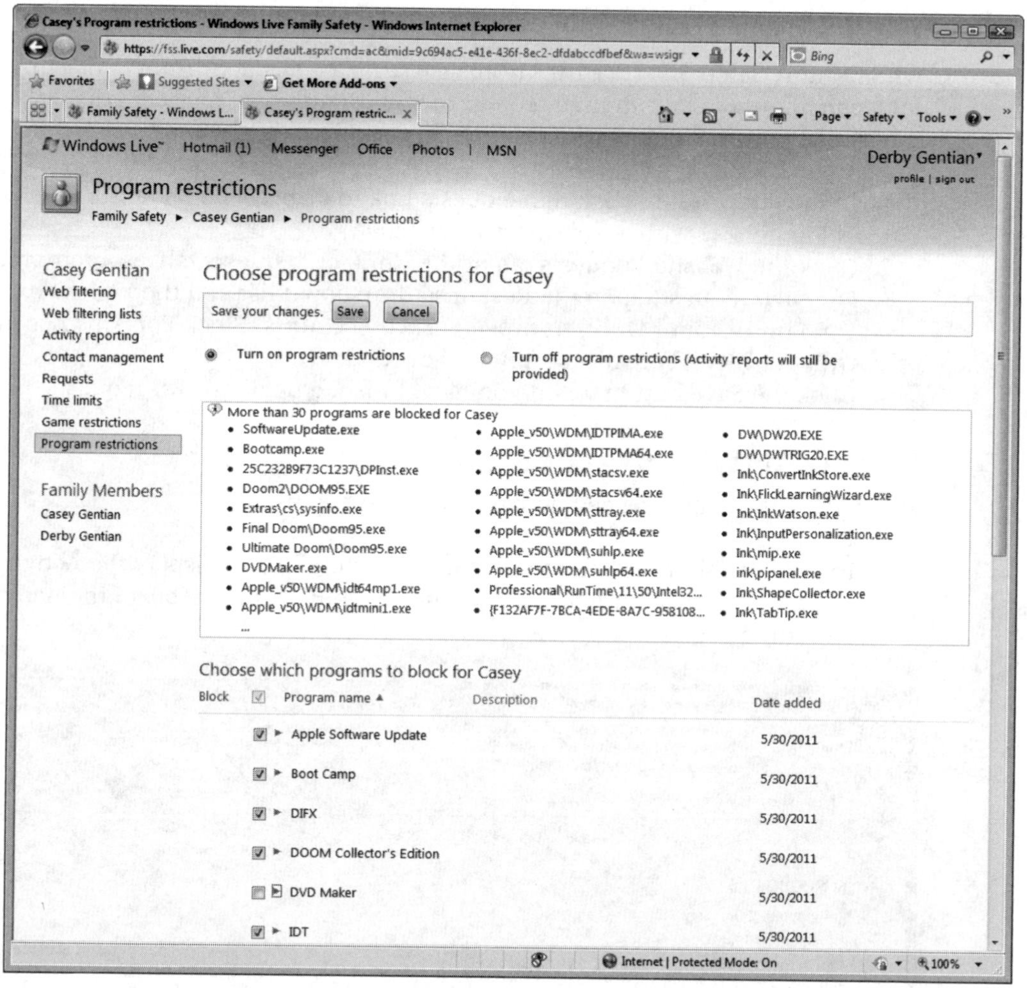

FIGURE 8-21 On the Program Restrictions page, select the Turn On Program Restrictions option button and then choose which programs to block for the user.

2. Select the Turn On Program Restrictions option button.
3. In the Choose Which Programs To Block For *User,* select the check box for each program you want to block. You can click the gray disclosure triangle to expand or collapse an item in the list.
4. Click the Save button to save your changes.

Deal with a User's Requests

When Family Safety blocks a user from accessing a website or from contacting someone, the user can submit a request to you for approval to access the website or contact the person. To deal with these requests, follow these steps:

1. In the left column, click the Requests link to display the Requests page (shown in Figure 8-22 with a website request active).
2. Click the Website Requests tab or the Contact Requests tab, as appropriate.
3. For each request, open the Response drop-down list and then click Approve For This Account Only, Approve For All Accounts, Block For This Account Only, or Block For All Accounts, as needed.
4. Click the Save button when you have finished dealing with requests.

Get an Activity Report

To see what the user has been doing, follow these steps:

1. In the left column, click the Activity Reporting link to display the Activity Reporting page. Figure 8-23 shows the Computer Activity tab of the Activity Reporting page.

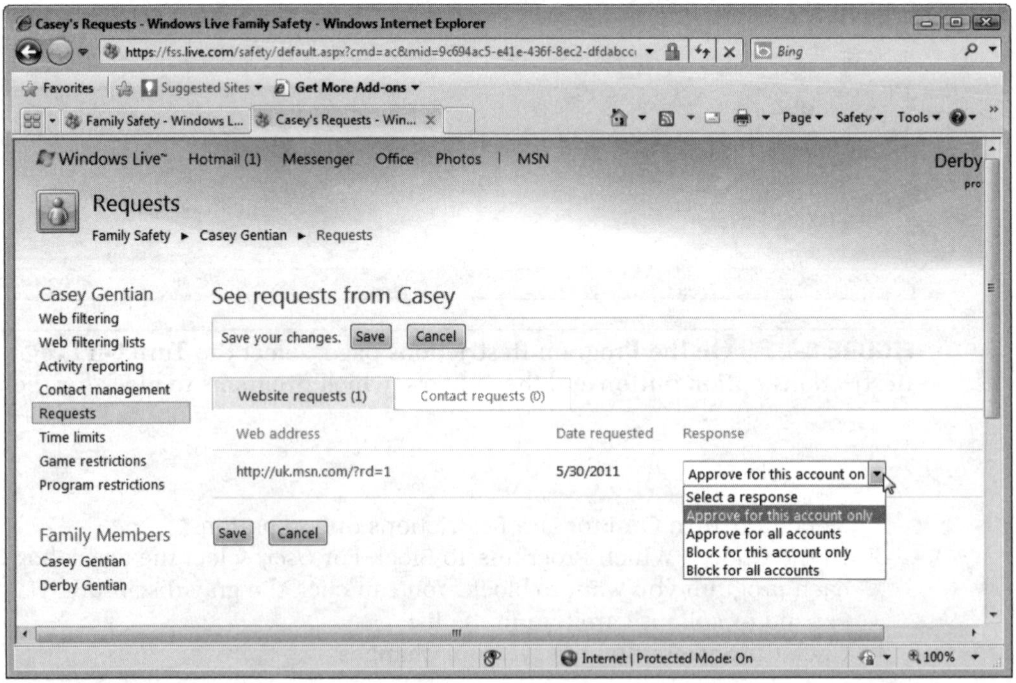

FIGURE 8-22 On the Requests page, choose whether to approve or block website requests and contact requests.

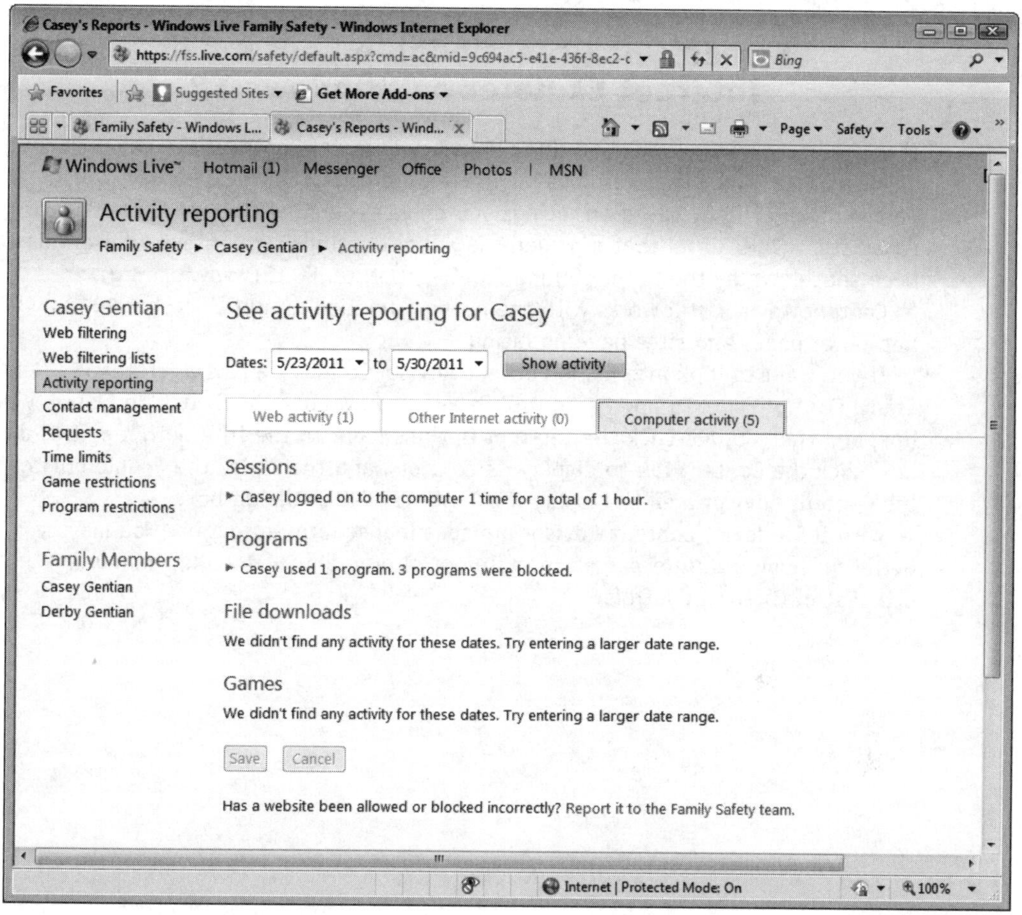

FIGURE 8-23 On the Activity Reporting page, choose the date range, click the Show Activity button, and then click the Web Activity tab, the Other Internet Activity tab, or the Computer Activity tab.

2. In the Dates box, choose the starting date for the period whose activity you want to view.
3. In the To box, choose the ending date for the period.
4. Click the Show Activity button to display activity for that period.
5. Click the Web Activity tab, the Other Internet Activity tab, or the Computer Activity tab.
6. Click a gray disclosure triangle to expand or collapse the items below it.
7. If you make changes, such as blocking or allowing a website or contact, click the Save button to save the changes.

Screen Out Objectionable Content in Internet Explorer on Windows XP

If you're using Windows XP, you don't have the Parental Controls features built into Windows 7. Internet Explorer does have a feature called Content Advisor, which helped block content based on ratings you chose—but the Internet Content Rating Association (ICRA) tool that provided the website ratings for Content Advisor has now been shut down by the Family Online Safety Institute, FOSI (www.fosi.org).

Content Advisor still works with the ratings supplied up until October 2010 by ICRA, but newer pages and sites have no rating.

If you want to look into using Content Advisor to provide partial protection, choose Start | Control Panel to open a Control Panel window, click the Switch To Classic View link, and then double-click the Internet Options icon. In the Internet Properties dialog box, click the Content tab to display its controls, and then click the Enable button in the Content Advisor area to display the Content Advisor dialog box.

With ICRA down, Content Advisor provides inadequate protection. You may be better off buying a third-party parental-control program such as Net Nanny or CyberPatrol Parental Controls.

PART III Upgrade Your Hardware and Operating System

9 Upgrade Your PC's Memory and Hard Drive

In this chapter, we'll look at two ways of upgrading your PC's hardware: first, adding memory; second, replacing the hard drive or adding another internal hard drive.

If your PC doesn't have as much memory as you need, or at least as much as it can hold, adding memory can give it a great performance boost. As long as your PC can contain more memory, and the memory is accessible, adding the memory is usually a straightforward operation.

Replacing the hard drive is harder, requires more preparation, and takes longer. Because the hard drive contains your PC's operating system and your files, you need to transfer all that data to the new hard drive. But with the right preparation, you can manage the hard drive replacement without either technical assistance or disaster.

Adding an extra hard drive is faster and easier than replacing the existing hard drive—as long as your PC has space for another drive.

Add Memory to Your PC

Adding memory is usually the quickest and easiest way to get your PC running better. Although your PC may have had enough RAM when you bought it, computing demands increase year by year, if not month by month, as programs and documents grow larger and we open more and more of each at once.

When your PC runs low on memory, it starts using hard disk space as virtual memory, and your PC slows down more than enough for you to notice. If this is happening, adding memory can be a quick fix.

In this section, I'll show you how to find out how much memory your PC currently has and how much it can have. You'll also learn how to find suitable memory and install it.

How Much Memory Does Your PC Need to Run Windows Well?

To run Windows at all, your PC needs:

- **Windows 7** 1GB
- **Windows XP** 128MB

These are absolute minimum requirements. Both Windows 7 and Windows XP operating systems run far better with much more RAM.

The minimum RAM figures cover pretty much only what Windows itself needs. But each application you run requires RAM, too, as does each file you open. And if you run two or more user sessions at the same time, by using the Fast User Switching feature, you'll need enough RAM for all the applications and documents each user has opened.

Table 9-1 shows memory recommendations for good performance. The "Several Concurrent Users" columns show recommendations for when you're using Fast User Switching.

Memory generally comes in modules of 128MB, 256MB, 512MB, 1GB, 2GB, and 4GB. At this writing, 2GB modules are generally the best value.

Note 4GB is the maximum amount of memory that 32-bit PCs can use. If you have a 64-bit PC and a 64-bit version of Windows, you should be able to use far more RAM. In theory, a 64-bit PC can use up to 16 exabytes (16 billion gigabytes) of RAM, although current hardware makes 32GB a practical maximum for any PC that's still recognizable as a PC.

Find Out How Much Memory Your PC Has

To check quickly how much RAM your PC has, open the System Properties dialog box on Windows XP or the System window on Windows 7. Follow these steps:

1. Click the Start button to display the Start menu.
2. Right-click the My Computer item (on Windows XP) or the Computer item (on Windows 7) to display the context menu.
3. Click the Properties item.

TABLE 6-1 Memory Recommendations for Good Performance on Windows 7 and Windows XP

Operating System	Single User, Few Programs	Single User, Many or Large Programs	Several Concurrent Users	Several Concurrent Users, Many or Large Programs
Windows 7	2GB	4GB	4GB	4GB
Windows XP	512MB	1GB	1GB	2–4GB

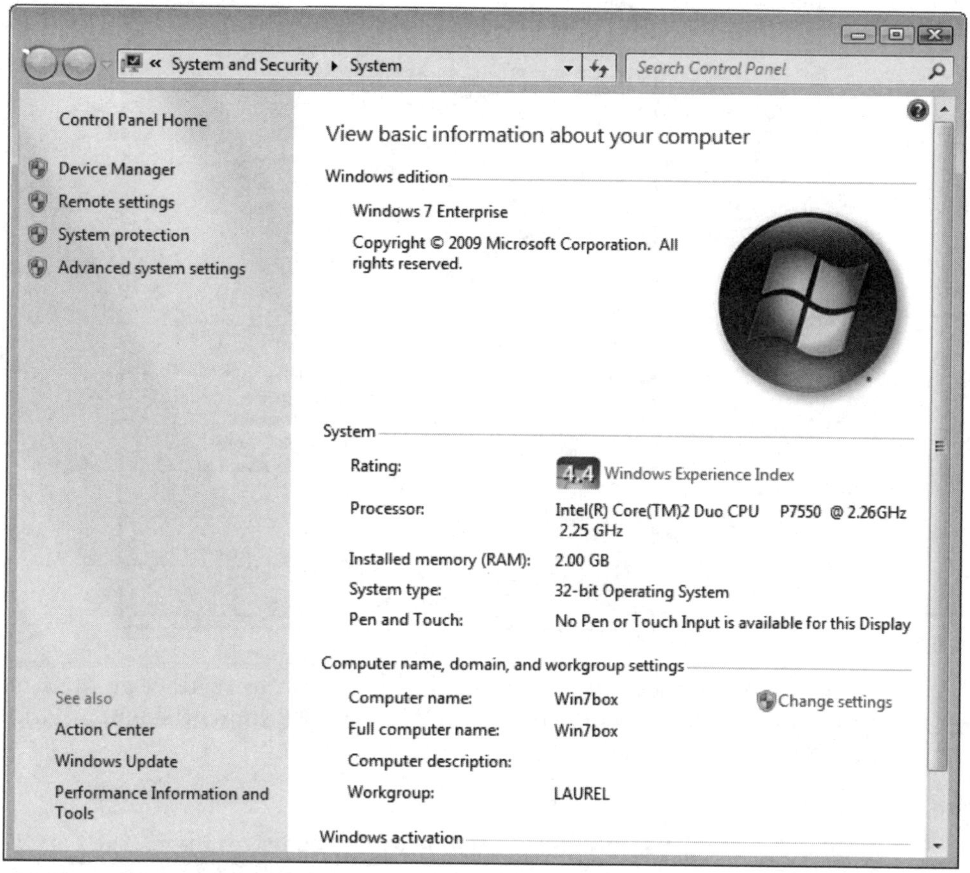

FIGURE 9-1 The Installed Memory (RAM) readout in the System window for Windows 7 shows the amount of RAM in your PC.

Figure 9-1 shows the System window for Windows 7. The Installed Memory (RAM) readout shows the amount of RAM: 2GB. Figure 9-2 shows the System Properties dialog box for Windows XP. The second-to-last line of the readout in the Computer section shows the amount of RAM: 1GB.

If you've found your PC contains 4GB of RAM, you can stop at this point: Unless it's a 64-bit PC, it can't take any more.

If your PC contains less than 4GB of RAM, read on.

Find Out Which Memory Modules Are in Which Memory Slots

If your PC contains less than 4GB of RAM, or less RAM than you want, find out which memory modules are in which memory slots on your PC. The hard way is to open

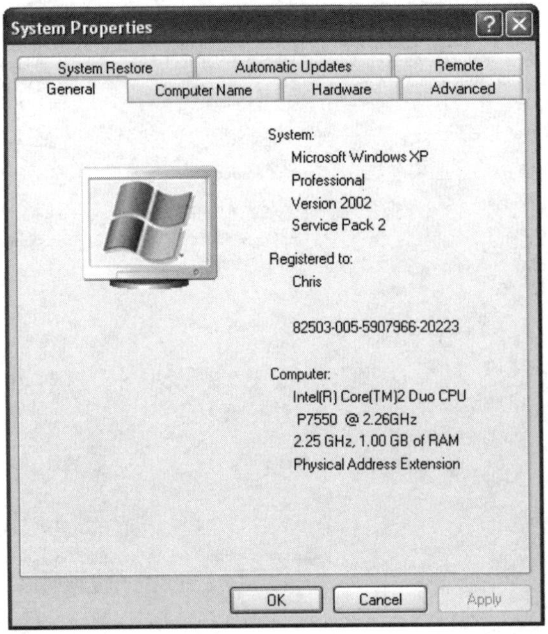

FIGURE 9-2 The second-to-last line of the Computer readout on the General tab of the System Properties dialog box in Windows XP shows the amount of RAM in your PC.

up the PC, peer at the modules, and look up the codes on them. The easy way is to download and install the CPU-Z program and then run it.

Download and Install CPU-Z

To download and install CPU-Z, follow these steps:

1. Open your web browser and navigate to the CPUID website, www.cpuid.com.

Tip You can also download CPU-Z from other sites, such as CNET's Download.com site.

2. Click the link to download the latest version of the CPU-Z application.
3. If Windows displays the File Download dialog box, prompting you to decide whether to open the file or save it, click the Save button and then choose the folder in which to save the file. For example, you might save the file in the Downloads folder in your user account.
4. When Windows has finished downloading the file, it displays the Download Complete dialog box. Click the Open button.

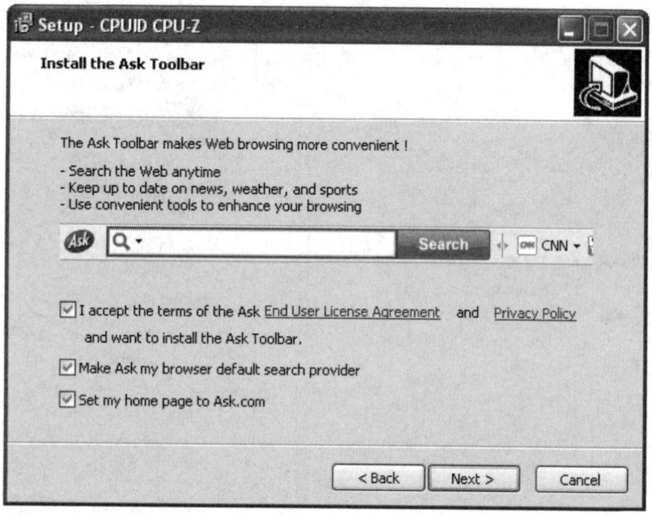

FIGURE 9-3 Clear the check boxes for any extra options that the CPU-Z setup routine offers but that you don't want.

5. Follow through the setup routine for CPU-Z. This is straightforward except for two things:
   - Watch out for any options that the CPU-Z setup routine may try to install. Figure 9-3 shows an example of such a screen, which tries to install a toolbar, change your search provider, and change your home page. You don't need any of these, and you probably don't want any of them either. If you encounter such a screen, clear the check boxes for any extra items you don't want to install.
   - The setup routine may offer to create a desktop shortcut for CPU-Z. You probably don't need one, as you can easily run CPU-Z from the Start menu—and you've probably got enough clutter on your desktop already.

Run CPU-Z and Find Out About Your PC's Memory

To use CPU-Z, follow these steps:

1. Open the Start menu and click the CPU-Z icon. The CPU-Z window appears.

Note If you allowed the CPU-Z setup routine to create a desktop shortcut, you can double-click that shortcut to launch CPU-Z.

2. Click the Memory tab to display its contents (shown on the left in Figure 9-4), and then look at the Size readout in the General group box at the top. This is the total amount of RAM—in the figure, this is 2048MB, or 2GB. (1GB equals 1024MB.)

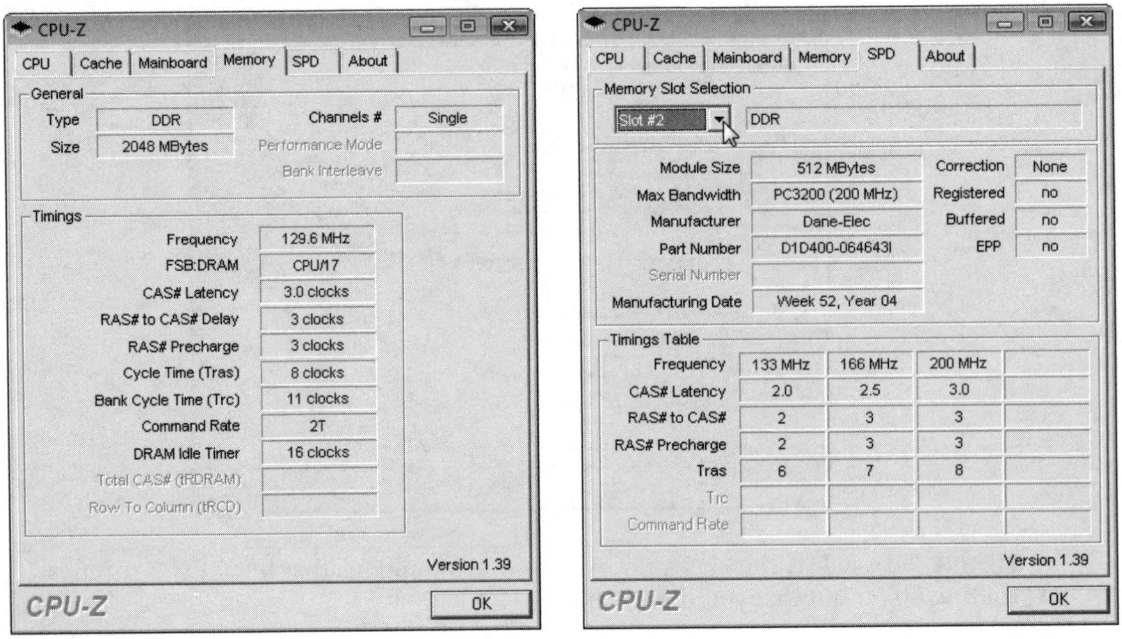

FIGURE 9-4 The Size readout near the top of the Memory tab in the CPU-Z window shows the total amount of RAM installed in your PC. The SPD tab in the CPU-Z window lets you examine the size and type of each memory module. Use the Memory Slot Selection drop-down list to select the module you want to view.

3. In the upper-left corner of the General group box, check whether the Channels readout says Single or Dual.
   - **Single** If your PC uses single-channel memory, you can safely put different-sized memory modules in different slots. Provided that the memory is compatible, the only issue is the total amount of memory installed.
   - **Double** If your PC uses dual-channel memory, you may need to install identical memory modules in each pair of memory slots to get the best performance. If your PC has four memory slots, you can have different-capacity memory modules in each pair—for example, 512MB modules in one pair, and 1GB modules in the other pair.
4. Click the SPD tab to display its contents (shown on the right in Figure 9-4). The Memory Slot Selection drop-down list should show the first memory slot that contains memory. Note the details of the memory module:
   - **Module Size** This readout shows the size of the memory module—for example, 512 MBytes (512MB) or 1024 MBytes (1GB).
   - **Max Bandwidth** This readout shows the memory's speed and its "PC" rating—for example, "PC3200" or "PC5300." This is one of the terms you'll use when searching for memory.

Note Depending on your PC's configuration, CPU-Z may not be able to detect any memory information on the SPD tab except the module size.

- **Manufacturer** This readout shows the name of the memory manufacturer. You may need this information to identify the type of memory your PC needs.
- **Part Number** This readout shows the part number of the memory. You may need this information when searching for more memory.

5. In the Memory Slot Selection drop-down list, select the next memory slot and then note the details of the memory module. Repeat the process for each of the memory slots.

Note Most laptops have two memory slots, whereas most desktops have two, three, or four memory slots. Some ultraportable laptops and tiny desktops have a single memory slot.

Use Other Information Sources If Necessary

If CPU-Z can't tell you which type of memory your PC needs, use one of these two approaches:

- **Consult your PC's documentation** This will tell you both the type of memory and the PC's maximum capacity. If you've lost the documentation, search the manufacturer's website for it.
- **Use a tool such as those provided by Micron Technology, Inc.'s, Crucial memory division:**
  1. Open your web browser and go to www.crucial.com.
  2. To find out which memory is installed on your PC, click the Scan My System button, and then agree to the terms and conditions. The Crucial System Scanner displays a recommendation of compatible upgrades together with details of your current memory and configuration.

Figure Out Your Memory Options

From what you've learned in the previous sections, figure out whether you can add more memory to your PC. Here are examples of two configurations you may run into.

Laptop PC, Two Slots, 512MB RAM in One Slot Say you have a laptop PC with two memory slots. Each memory slot can contain a module up to 1GB. At the moment, one slot contains a 512MB memory module, and the other slot is empty. You have four choices for increasing the memory:

- **Add 512MB to the second slot** By installing a 512MB memory module in the second slot, you get 1GB RAM. This is an inexpensive upgrade that will improve your PC's performance significantly.

- **Replace the 512MB module with a 1GB module** If your PC uses double-channel memory, you may not be able to install different-capacity modules in different slots. In this case, replacing the 512MB slot with a 1GB module gives you 1GB RAM with the option of adding another 1GB module in the other memory slot later.
- **Add 1GB to the second slot** By installing a 1GB memory module in the second slot, you get 1.5GB RAM. This upgrade is more expensive than the first option, but you'll be able to run even more programs. If your PC uses double-channel memory, you may not be able to do this.
- **Switch to two 1GB modules** To get the most RAM, you must remove the 512MB memory module and install a 1GB memory module in each slot. This upgrade gives you the best possible performance but is also the most expensive. Treat the surplus memory module gently, and you may be able to sell it on eBay.

Desktop PC, Three Slots, 512MB in Each of Two Slots Say you have a desktop PC with three memory slots, two of which contain a 512MB memory module each. The third memory slot is empty. Here, you have four main choices for increasing the memory:

- **Add 512MB to the third slot** By installing a 512MB memory module in the third slot, you get 1.5GB RAM. This is an inexpensive upgrade that will give your PC an appreciable performance boost, but it makes sense only if your PC requires double-channel memory and your budget is limited. If not, use one of the other ways to get a greater amount of RAM.
- **Add 1GB or 2GB to the third slot** By installing a 1GB memory module in the third slot, you double the memory to 2GB; by installing a 2GB memory module in the third slot, you triple the memory to 3GB. Either of these is an affordable upgrade that will make a big difference without your needing to discard any of the existing memory.
- **Add 1GB or 2GB to the third slot and replace one or two of the 512MB modules** If 2GB memory isn't enough, you not only need to add a 1GB memory module or 2GB to the third slot but also replace either one or both of the 512MB memory modules. You can go to 2.5GB, 3GB, or 4GB total. Again, you may be able to sell the memory modules you remove—or, better, use them in another of your PCs.
- **Add 2GB to two slots, removing the existing memory** The best way to get the PC's full complement of RAM is to remove the existing memory and put in two 2GB memory modules. This takes the PC to the 4GB limit.

Buy the Memory

Armed with the information you've gathered so far, you're ready to buy the memory for your PC. Your local PC paradise will probably have suitable memory, but you'll almost certainly find a wider selection—and perhaps better prices—online, either from a major online retailer such as CDW (www.cdw.com) or PC Connection (www.pcconnection.com) or directly from a memory company such as Crucial (www.crucial.com) or Kingston Technology Company (www.kingston.com).

Get the Most Bang for Your Memory Buck

Here are two strategies for getting the maximum amount of memory for the money you pay:

- **Max out the memory when you buy** If you have enough money, get the maximum amount of memory installed when you buy the PC. This way, you'll enjoy the best possible performance from the start, and you can be sure that you'll never need to discard memory modules in order to upgrade. Also, you won't need to open up your PC and poke at its innards.
- **Leave some memory slots free** If you can't max out the memory when you buy your PC, don't fill up the memory slots with low-capacity modules. Instead, put higher-capacity modules in one or more of the slots, and leave the remaining slot or slots empty until you can afford to stuff high-capacity modules into them. For example, if you buy a laptop that has two memory slots, it's better to buy a 2GB module for one slot (and then be able to upgrade to 4GB by adding another 2GB module) than to reach 2GB by putting 1GB in each of the slots and needing to discard one or both modules when you upgrade.

Install the Memory

With the memory in hand, you're ready to install it:

- **Desktop PC** For a desktop PC, the installation process is usually straightforward, as shown in the first example. However, if you have a small or specially shaped PC, you may have to remove some components in order to access the RAM.
- **Laptop PC** Laptops have widely varying designs. If you're lucky, your laptop's memory is in an easily accessible location—for example, under a screwed-down hatch on the bottom of the laptop, as in the second example. If you're unlucky, you may have to partly disassemble the PC to install the memory—for example, flipping back the keyboard and then removing components under it. Consult your PC's user guide to learn the details.

Tip Check YouTube for videos by PC hobbyists who have not only replaced the memory in your model of PC but recorded themselves doing so. By watching a few videos, you can learn how to get around problems that the user guide skips past.

Install the Memory in a Desktop PC

To install the memory in a desktop PC, follow these general steps:

1. Shut down Windows, turn off your PC, and disconnect all the cables.
2. Put your PC on a table or other suitable surface.

3. Open the side opposite the motherboard. For example, you may need to undo a latch, unscrew a couple of thumb-screws (the knurled kind you turn with your fingers, not the kind that mangle your fingers), or unscrew case screws with a screwdriver.
4. Touch a metal part of the PC's case to discharge any static from your body.
5. If you need to remove one of the existing memory modules:
   - Lay down a sheet of paper or an antistatic bag (the kind PC components come in) so that you have somewhere to put the module.

Tip If you have a digital camera or a phone that takes photos, take some of the memory in your PC before you attack it. Also, take photos of any connections you need to disconnect. It's all too easy to lose track of which piece goes where, or which way around a connection goes.

   - Press down and out with a thumb on each of the spring clips at the ends of the socket, as shown in Figure 9-5. When the clips release, they pull the memory module up and out.
   - Remove the module using your fingers and then put it on the bag or sheet of paper.
6. Insert the new memory module:
   - Remove the memory module from its protective bag.
   - Align the memory module with the memory slot, making sure the notch in the module matches the break in the socket, as shown in Figure 9-6.
   - Press the memory module down gently but firmly, so that it slides into the socket and the spring clips engage.
7. Close the PC, restore it to its normal place, and then reconnect the cables.

FIGURE 9-5 Normally you press down on a spring clip at each end of the memory socket to release the memory module.

FIGURE 9-6 Place the memory module's corners in the guides in the spring clips so that you can press it down into place.

Tip While your PC is open, you might want to give it a quick Spring clean—especially if the fan is as dusty as the fan in the figures.

Install the Memory in a Laptop PC

To install the memory in a laptop PC, follow these general steps:

1. Shut down Windows, turn off your PC, and disconnect any cables.
2. Remove the battery if it's removable.
3. Touch a metal object to discharge any static from your body.
4. Following the instructions in the PC's documentation, open the memory area.
5. If you need to remove one of the existing memory modules:
   - Lay down a sheet of paper or an antistatic bag (the kind PC components come in) so that you have somewhere to put the module.
   - Press out with a thumb or finger on each of the spring clips at the ends of the socket. (If the space is confined enough to make using your hands awkward, use the eraser ends of a couple of eraser-tipped pencils.) When the clips release, they push the memory module up and out.
   - Remove the module using your fingers and then put it on the bag or sheet of paper.
6. Insert the new memory module:
   - Remove the memory module from its protective bag.
   - Align the memory module with the memory slot, making sure the notch in the module matches the break in the socket. For many laptop memory slots, you need to insert the memory module at an angle, as shown in Figure 9-7.
   - Press the memory module down gently but firmly, so that the spring clips engage. Figure 9-8 shows an example.
7. Close the laptop, replace the battery, and then reconnect any cables needed.

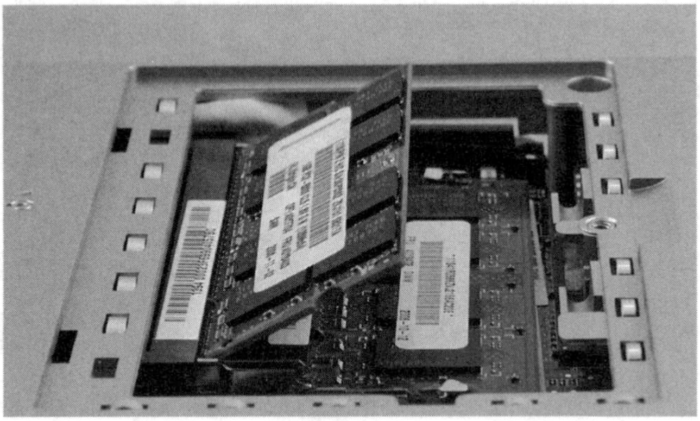

FIGURE 9-7 Insert the memory carefully. Usually it goes in at an angle, like this.

Restart Your PC and Verify It Recognizes the Memory

Next, restart your PC and verify that it recognizes the memory you have added. The easiest way to do this is to open the System Properties dialog box or System window again after Windows has loaded.

1. Click the Start button to display the Start menu.
2. Right-click the My Computer item (on Windows XP) or the Computer item (on Windows 7) to display the context menu.
3. Click the Properties item.

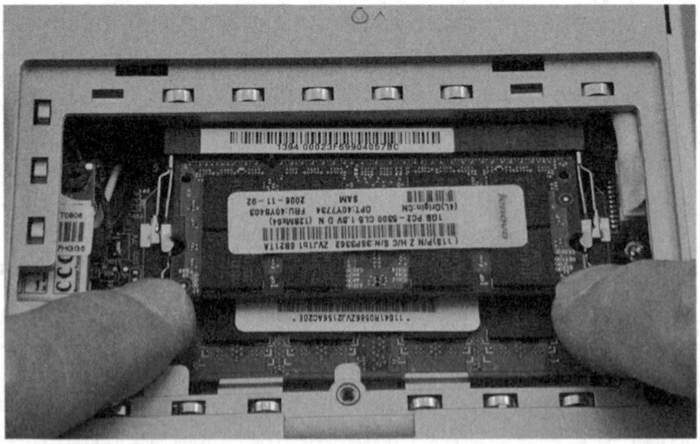

FIGURE 9-8 Press the memory module into place. The spring clips are the shiny metal pieces just above each fingernail.

Replace Your PC's Hard Drive or Add an Extra Drive

Chances are that all too soon, you'll find yourself running out of space on your computer. When this happens, you can attach an external hard drive via USB easily enough, but in many cases a better solution is to add a new internal hard drive to your computer.

If your computer can contain only one hard drive, you'll need to replace the existing drive—and then either reinstall Windows on the new drive or clone your existing operating system installation to the new drive. But if you can add a hard drive to your existing drive, the upgrade is faster and more convenient—and you'll end up with even more hard drive space.

Check How Many Hard Drives Your Computer Has—and How Many It Can Have

Your first step is to check how many hard drives your computer currently has—and how many hard drives it can hold.

If you have a laptop, you can probably skip this step, because almost all laptops contain only a single hard drive. If you have one of the monster laptops that can contain two or more hard drives, you probably already know about this feature.

Similarly, if you have a standard model of desktop computer, most likely it has a single drive. But if you're not sure, or if you want to make sure that the hard drive doesn't contain unused space on which you could create another drive, follow these steps:

1. Open the Disk Management window (see Figure 9-9):
   - **Windows XP** Choose Start | Run to display the Run dialog box. Type **diskmgmt.msc** and press ENTER or click the OK button.
   - **Windows 7** Click the Start button to open the Start menu. Type **diskmgmt.msc** in the Search box and then press ENTER.
2. In the lower part of the window, look at each Disk readout. The figure shows one disk, called Disk 0 (because computer counting starts at zero rather than one), which is divided into three drives (100GB, 100GB, and 98.09GB). There's also a drive called CD-ROM 0, which is the first optical drive on the system. As the DVD designation indicates, this optical drive is actually a DVD drive rather than a CD drive.
3. Click the Close button (the × button) or choose File | Exit to close the Disk Management window.

So that's how many drives your computer currently holds. But how many *can* it hold?

At this point, we're probably talking about a desktop rather than a laptop. If you have the computer's documentation at hand (or if you can locate it on the Web), look up the number of drive slots or bays. Otherwise, shut down Windows, turn the

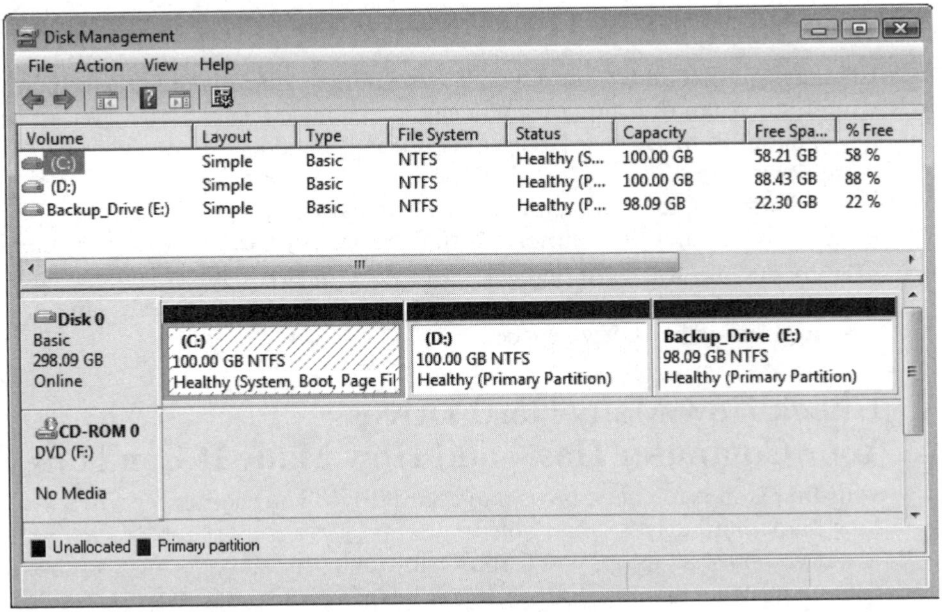

FIGURE 9-9 The Disk Management window lets you see both how many hard drives (and other types of drives) are installed on your computer and how they are partitioned.

computer off and disconnect the cables, open the case, and take a look. Figure 9-10 shows an example of what you may see in a sparsely populated case.

The first thing you're looking for here is an empty drive bay. It may be either 3.5 inches wide (the width of most desktop hard drives) or 5.25 inches (the width of optical drives and some heavyweight hard drives). It's easiest to mount a 3.5-inch drive in a 3.5-inch bay, but you can also mount it in a 5.25-inch bay if you buy mounting rails.

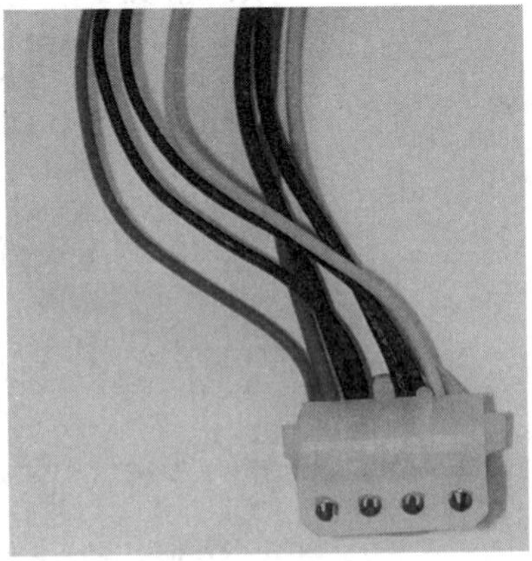

The second thing you're looking for is a power connector, a plug that probably looks like this. Unless your computer is loaded with drives and extras, you'll probably find several power connectors available—though they may be wrapped up in a tight bundle with a plastic tie.

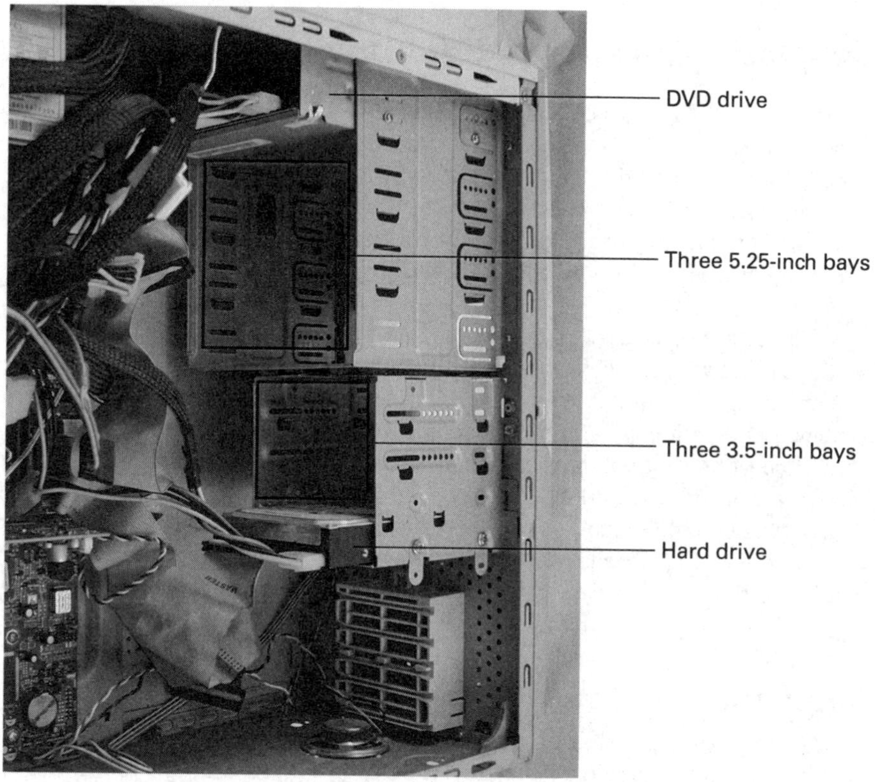

FIGURE 9-10 Most tower-style computers offer you the choice of 3.5-inch bays for hard drives or 5.25-inch bays that can contain optical drives, hard drives, or other components.

The third thing you're looking for is a drive cable with a free connector. Drive cables are the flat, wide ribbons that go from the hard drive and optical drive to the motherboard. Usually, you'll find a connector free.

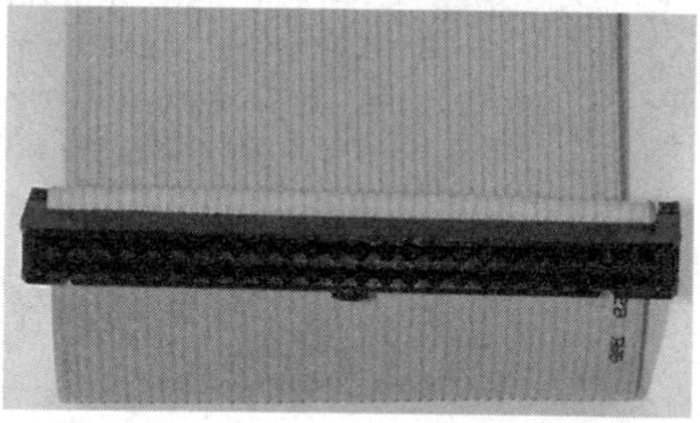

Decide Whether to Add a Drive or Replace the Existing Drive

By this point, you have the knowledge to decide whether you're adding a hard drive to your computer or replacing the existing hard drive. (If your computer can contain only one hard drive, you have had no choice all along.)

If you haven't yet decided, you're probably better off adding a drive, because you don't need to reinstall Windows or transfer your data—you simply get the extra storage space that the new drive provides.

Replacing a Laptop's Hard Drive Can Be a Nightmare

Before you commit to replacing the hard drive on a laptop, it's a good idea to check how serious an operation the drive replacement is. Some laptops are designed to be easy to maintain and upgrade, but others are designed to be opened only by trained technicians armed with special tools.

You can get the special tools yourself, but buying them increases the total cost of the upgrade. And if you end up wrecking your computer, the cost becomes far too high.

So consult your laptop's user guide and find out exactly what is involved. If you see the magical words "field replaceable unit" or "FRU" (its abbreviation) describing the hard drive, that's great news. If not, carefully review the steps involved in opening the computer. See if you can find a video on YouTube that goes through the steps.

If you find that you have to remove several internal components before you can even access the hard drive, you may want to save the time and effort and solve your disk-space problem another way. For example, you can archive older files or move seldom-used files to an external hard drive to make more space on the internal hard drive so that you don't need to replace it.

Buy the Hardware

Next, buy a suitable hard drive for your computer. Make sure it is the right physical size, has enough capacity for your needs, and a fast enough rotational speed (I'll explain rotational speed in a moment in the section "Choose the Drive's Rotational Speed"). You may also want to consider buying a solid state drive (SSD) instead.

Tip Remember to consider the amount of noise the hard drive makes. Given how close your laptop will normally be to you while you are using it, a quiet or silent hard drive is usually a good idea. Even on a desktop computer that will normally be several feet away from you, a quiet or silent hard drive can make the difference between peaceful work and struggling to concentrate through an irritating noise. SSDs make virtually no noise, as they have no moving parts. (They sometimes hum quietly, especially when bored.)

Choose the Drive's Physical Size

Most laptop computers use 2.5-inch drives. You'll find a wide variety of these at a good computer store. Some ultraportables use 1.8-inch drives. The selection of these tends to be smaller, capacities tend to be lower, and prices tend to be higher.

For a laptop, you must also check the drive height. Some slim-line laptops can use drives only up to 9mm high, whereas others accept 12mm drives. You can use a 9mm drive in a 12mm space easily enough, but the other way around doesn't fit.

Most desktop computers can use either 3.5-inch drives or 5.25-inch drives. 3.5 inches is normally the best choice, as you'll find a good range of drive capacities at affordable prices, but you may have to go to 5.25 inches if you want a monster drive.

Note You can put a hard drive designed for a laptop into a desktop if you want, as long as you get the right connectors and mounting hardware. But generally speaking, desktop hard drives are less expensive, faster, and more capacious than laptop hard drives. So the only time putting a laptop hard drive in a desktop normally makes sense is when you've got an extra laptop drive—for example, because you've upgraded your laptop.

Choose the Drive's Capacity

You may simply want to choose the highest-capacity drive you can afford, but typically you'll get the best value from buying a little way back from the cutting edge. For example, instead of buying a 750GB drive for a laptop, you might get a better deal on a 500GB drive.

In some cases, you will need to balance the drive's capacity against its rotational speed—if you want the highest capacity available, you may need to settle for a lower rotational speed.

Choose the Drive's Rotational Speed

The drive's rotational speed controls to a large extent how fast it can deliver data to the computer: the faster the rotational speed, the faster the data gets transferred. It also affects how much energy the drive uses, how hot it becomes, and how much noise it makes.

At this writing, 5400 rpm drives are the best choice for laptop computers unless you're trying to boost performance. 4200 rpm drives are less expensive but slower and are seldom worth buying; however, if your laptop uses a 1.8-inch drive, you may need to settle for a 4200 rpm drive. 7200 rpm laptop drives are also available, but they tend to have lower capacity than the largest 5400 rpm drives and produce more heat and noise. So unless performance is your main criterion, a 5400 rpm laptop drive may be a better choice than a 7200 rpm laptop drive.

For desktop computers, 7200 rpm drives are normally the best choice, giving good performance with high capacity. Many 7200 rpm 3.25-inch drives are also impressively quiet, which can be welcome when you need to concentrate. Faster drives (for example, 10,000 rpm or 15,000 rpm) are typically designed for servers and tend to be too noisy for desktop use.

Should You Buy a Hard Drive or a Solid State Drive—or a Bit of Both?

As you learned in Chapter 1, some PCs use solid state drives (SSDs) instead of hard drives. SSDs consist of memory modules rather than spinning platters, so they're more resistant to shock than hard drives. They also give better performance, consume less power, generate less heat, and make less noise.

All of that sounds perfect, but SSD capacities are lower than hard drive capacities, and SSDs are much more expensive than hard drives. So choosing between the two can be tough.

If you can afford an SSD capacious enough for your data, go for it.

If you can't afford an SSD, look for a hybrid hard drive—a spinning hard drive with extra memory modules to cache frequently used data and deliver it more quickly than the hard drive alone can.

Get Any Software You Need

If you're adding a hard drive to your computer, you won't need to buy any extra software, as your current operating system remains in place. But if you're replacing your hard drive, you will need to set up the new drive with your operating system.

There are two main ways of putting the operating system onto your new drive:

- **Reinstall Windows from scratch** The basic way is to reinstall Windows from scratch on the new hard drive. You'll then need to apply any Windows updates and install all the programs you use. To reinstall Windows, you'll need your Windows DVD.
- **Clone your computer's hard drive** Cloning your computer's existing operating system on to the new drive can save you plenty of time and effort, as you don't need to reinstall Windows and your programs. But to clone the drive, you need cloning software such as Macrium Reflect Free Edition (free; www.macrium.com/reflectfree.asp) or Acronis True Image Home Edition (around $50; www.acronis.com or any Internet retailer you trust).

Install the New Hard Drive

At this point, you should be ready to install the new hard drive in your computer. The procedure is different depending on whether you're adding the hard drive to the computer or replacing the existing disk.

The first of the next two sections shows the steps for adding a hard drive. This section uses a desktop computer as the example. The second section shows the steps for replacing the hard drive. That section uses a laptop computer as the example.

Add a Hard Drive to Your Computer

To add a hard drive to your computer, follow these steps:

1. Save any unsaved documents, close your programs, and shut down Windows.
2. Disconnect the cables from your computer and put the computer on a suitable work surface.
3. Open the case. What this involves depends on how your computer is designed and built, but here are three examples:
   - **Tower-style computer** Unscrew any retaining screws and then remove the side panel on the side of the case away from the motherboard. If you're not sure which side this is, look at the back of the computer and see which side the parts and expansion cards are up against. That side is where the motherboard is, so you want the other side.
   - **Desktop-style computer** Unscrew any retaining screws and then remove the top panel or the entire cover. In a miniature case, you may need to remove other components before you can access the hard drive. In this case, consult the computer's manual to see which computers you must remove and how to remove them.
   - **Laptop computer** Consult the documentation.

Deal with Masters, Slaves, and Jumpers

These days, you can often simply connect a disk to a drive cable without worrying about its configuration. This is because many computers and disks use the Cable Select method of choosing the disk's role. With Cable Select, the cable connection used to connect the disk determines the drive's role.

If your computer doesn't use Cable Select, you will need to check that the disk is set to the correct role: *master* (primary) or *slave* (secondary). To change the configuration, you use a *jumper* (a small connector) to connect two pins. The next illustration shows the back of a disk drive with a jumper in place connecting two pins.

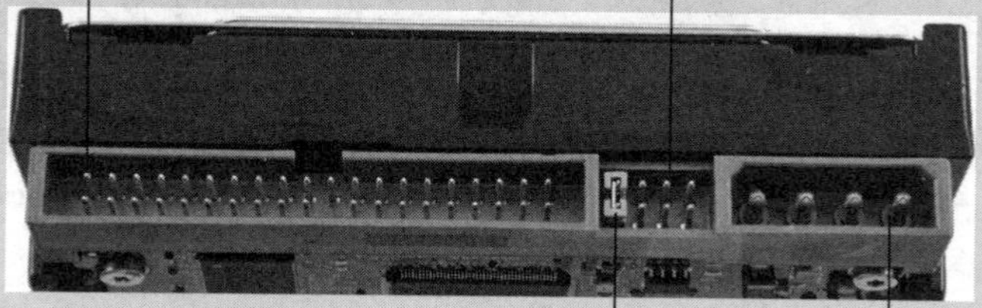

Normally, you'll find a small and confusing diagram on the disk's label indicating which jumper configuration means what. Sometimes, you'll need to consult the disk's documentation or the manufacturer's website to find that small and confusing diagram.

When you're adding a disk, check the existing disk's configuration to determine how to configure the new disk. For example, if you're adding a second disk on the same cable, and you find the existing disk is configured as a master, configure the second disk as a slave.

When you're replacing a disk, the best approach is normally to set the same type of jumper configuration on the new disk as on the old disk, and to connect the new disk to the same connector on the same cable. For example, if the old disk is jumpered to the Cable Select position, jumper the new disk to Cable Select, and use the same connector on the same drive cable. That should give you the correct result.

4. Identify a suitable drive bay, insert the drive, and then screw it in place. Figure 9-11 shows the second disk in place.
5. Connect a drive cable and a power cable to the drive.
6. Close the case again.
7. Restore your computer to its usual location and then reconnect the cables.
8. Start the computer and then log onto Windows.

FIGURE 9-11 If you have plenty of space, allow a gap between the disks rather than placing them right against each other.

Replace the Hard Drive in Your Computer

To replace the hard drive in your computer, follow these steps. (The computer in this example is a laptop.)

1. Save any unsaved documents, close your programs, and shut down Windows.
2. Disconnect the cables from your computer and put the computer on a suitable work surface. For a laptop computer, you may want to put down a cloth or a large mouse mat to prevent the computer from getting scratched.
3. Turn the laptop so that you can access the cover or hatch that allows access to the inside or the hard drive. The sample computer has hatches on the bottom for its field-replaceable units (see Figure 9-12), which makes the replacement procedure far easier.
4. Open the hard drive compartment, as in this example. Normally, the hard drive is obvious when you're in the right place.

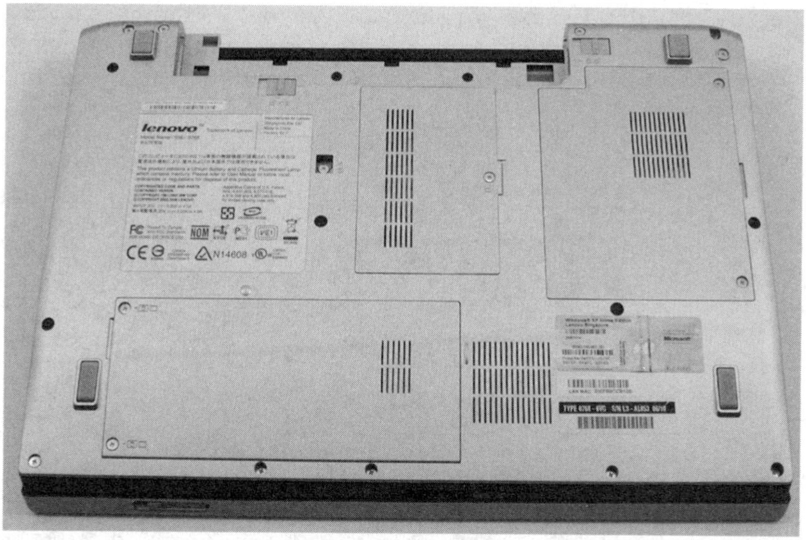

FIGURE 9-12 This laptop is designed to allow you to replace the hard drive and memory easily.

5. Detach the hard drive from its connector and then remove it. The next illustration shows an example of a drive that is held by its connector and by spring clips.

6. If the hard drive uses an enclosure, as in the example shown in the next illustration, unscrew any retaining screws and then remove the disk from the enclosure. Insert the replacement disk and then apply the retaining screws.

7. Insert the hard drive or enclosure in the bay or area that contains it and then secure its connector.
8. Close the case again.

Tip If you replaced your hard drive because it was too small rather than because it had begun to lose data, you can reuse the drive by turning it into an external drive. Buy a hard drive enclosure (also called a "hard drive caddy") of the right size and connection type, insert the drive, and then connect it to your PC like any other external drive.

After installing the new hard drive, you need to put Windows on it, either by reinstalling Windows from scratch or by copying across the cloned version of your previous drive that you created using imaging software.

10 Upgrade from Windows XP to Windows 7

If your PC is still running Windows XP, rest assured you're in good company: Hundreds of millions of other PCs around the world are still running Windows XP, too—and probably will be for several years to come.

As long as you've upgraded to Service Pack 3, Windows XP is a solid operating system. It has reasonably good security. And its hardware requirements are pretty modest by modern standards. If your PC is still running well, you likely feel no compelling reason to upgrade to Windows 7. In this case, skip this chapter for now.

But if you are thinking of upgrading from Windows XP to Windows 7, read on. You'll first need to work out whether your PC will be able to run Windows 7. Next, because the upgrade is awkward, you'll need to decide whether it makes sense to you. If you decide to go ahead, you'll need to transfer your data from Windows XP to a safe place, install Windows 7, and then transfer the data to Windows 7. And, finally, you'll need to install all your programs on Windows 7.

Note If you're thinking of upgrading from Windows XP, your only sensible choice is Windows 7. Don't upgrade from Windows XP to Windows Vista, as Windows Vista requires heavier hardware than Windows 7, is less secure, and is not as easy to use. Even if someone gives you a free copy of Windows Vista, upgrading from Windows XP makes little sense unless you're using Windows Vista as a stepping stone to upgrade to Windows 7 (more on this later in this chapter).

Understand Why Upgrading from Windows XP to Windows 7 Is Awkward

In an ideal world, you'd be able to upgrade straight from Windows XP to Windows 7, keeping all your programs and files where they were.

How Microsoft Moves Customers Along to New Versions of Its Software

Microsoft has two main ways of shunting customers along from older software to newer software.

The first way is by stopping sales of the older software. For example, nowadays most new PCs come with Windows 7 installed. If you want a new PC with Windows XP installed, you must not only jump through several hoops but also pay extra for the privilege.

The second way is by cutting off support for the older software. Microsoft ended support for Windows XP with Service Pack 2 on 32-bit computers on July 13, 2010, heavily encouraging customers to install Service Pack 3. At this writing, Microsoft has announced support for Windows XP with Service Pack 3 until May 2014.

Microsoft is also supporting Windows XP with Service Pack 2 on 64-bit computers until May 2014. This is because there's no Service Pack 3 for 64-bit versions of Windows XP.

Both of these ways of moving customers along work slowly, but they get the job done in the end. These days, very few people are running Windows 98, Windows NT 4.0, or other antiquated versions of Windows.

Upgrade Windows XP to Windows Vista and Then to Windows 7

If you decide the double upgrade will be preferable to installing Windows 7 and your programs from scratch, make sure you've got the right versions of Windows. If necessary, pick up an upgrade copy of Windows Vista; you can find plenty at bargain prices on eBay and similar sites.

Here are the versions you can upgrade to:

- **Windows XP Home Edition** You can upgrade to Windows Vista Home Basic Edition, Windows Vista Home Premium Edition, Windows Vista Business Edition, or Windows Vista Ultimate Edition.
- **Windows XP Professional Edition** You can upgrade to Windows Vista Business Edition or Windows Vista Ultimate Edition.
- **Windows Vista Home Basic Edition or Windows Vista Home Edition** You can upgrade to Windows 7 Home Premium Edition or Windows 7 Ultimate Edition.
- **Windows Vista Business Edition** You can upgrade to Windows 7 Professional Edition or Windows 7 Ultimate Edition.
- **Windows Vista Ultimate Edition** You can upgrade only to Windows 7 Ultimate Edition.

So for example, say you've got a home PC running Windows XP Home Edition. What you probably want to do is upgrade it to Windows Vista Home Edition and then to Windows 7 Home Premium Edition.

Similarly, if your PC is running Windows XP Professional Edition, your most direct upgrade route is to Windows Vista Business Edition and then to Windows 7 Professional Edition.

But as you already know, this world isn't ideal. And Microsoft has made it less so by deciding to prevent you from upgrading straight from Windows XP to Windows 7. Instead, Microsoft allows you to upgrade from Windows XP only to Windows Vista, and from Windows Vista to Windows 7.

For most people, this double upgrade is too expensive to contemplate. It also clutters up your PC's hard disk with an extra old version of Windows that you neither want nor need.

Find Out Whether Your PC Can Run Windows 7

The first thing you need to do is find out whether your existing PC can run Windows 7. You can get a quick idea by comparing your PC to the system requirements for Windows 7. If things look promising, you can run the Windows 7 Upgrade Advisor to make sure your PC's hardware is compatible with Windows 7.

Compare Your PC to Windows 7's System Requirements

To get a quick idea of whether your PC can handle Windows 7, compare your PC to this list of system requirements for Windows 7:

- **Processor** 1 GHz or faster
- **RAM** 1GB or more
- **Hard drive space** 16GB or more free
- **Graphics** DirectX graphics

If you're not sure how fast your PC's processor is or how much RAM it contains, press WINDOWS KEY–BREAK to display the System Properties dialog box (shown on the left in Figure 10-1). The readout in the lower-right corner of the General tab shows the processor speed and the amount of RAM.

To check the amount of free space on the hard drive, open its Properties dialog box like this:

1. Choose Start | My Computer to display a My Computer window.
2. Right-click the hard drive and then click Properties on the context menu.

The readout on the General tab of the Properties dialog box (shown on the right in Figure 10-1) shows the amount of free space.

Note If your PC doesn't have enough RAM for Windows 7, you may be able to add RAM. See Chapter 9 for instructions. If the hard drive doesn't have enough free space, you can free up space (as discussed in Chapter 2), replace the hard drive (as discussed in Chapter 9), or add another hard drive (also discussed in Chapter 9) and move some files to it.

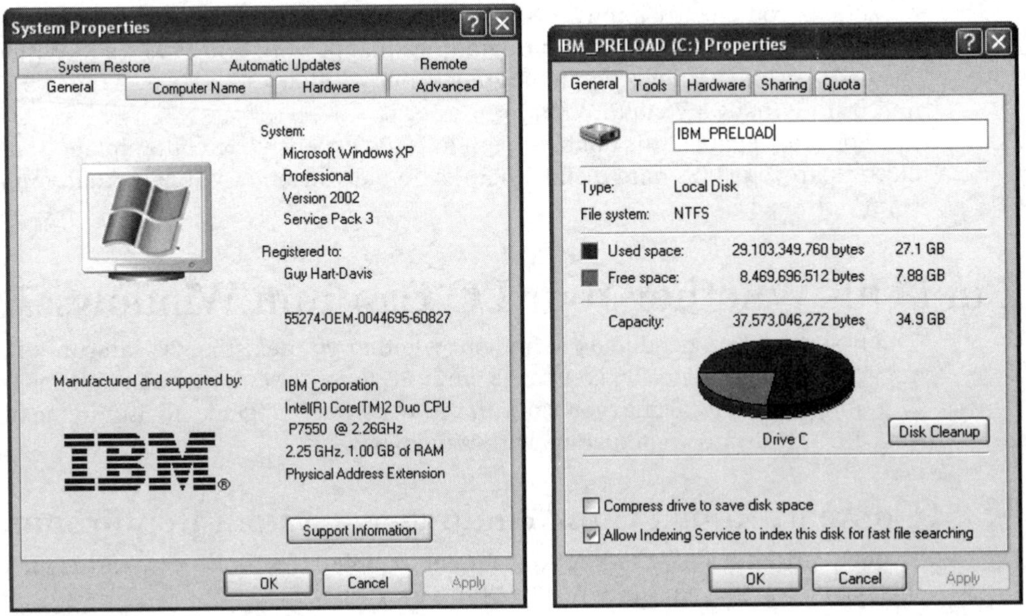

FIGURE 10-1 To see your PC's processor speed and RAM, look at the readouts near the bottom of the General tab of the System Properties dialog box (left). To see how much free space your PC's hard drive has, check the readout on the General tab of the Properties dialog box for the drive (right).

Install and Run the Windows 7 Upgrade Advisor

If your PC's specs look okay for Windows 7, you're ready for the next stage of checking: installing and running the Windows 7 Upgrade Advisor. The Upgrade Advisor checks all your PC's hardware and warns you about any items that Windows 7 doesn't support.

Download and Install the Windows 7 Upgrade Advisor

To download and install the Windows 7 Upgrade Advisor, follow these steps:

1. Choose Start | Internet to open your web browser.
2. Go to the Microsoft Download Center, www.microsoft.com/downloads.
3. Search for **windows 7 upgrade advisor** and then click the Tool link.
4. Click the Download button to start the download.
5. When Internet Explorer asks you what to do with the file, click the Save button.
6. When the file has downloaded, click the Open button to open the file. The Windows 7 Upgrade Advisor Setup Wizard launches.

7. Select the I Accept The License Terms option button and then click the Install button.
8. When the installation finishes, leave the Launch Windows 7 Upgrade Advisor check box selected and then click the Close button. Windows 7 Upgrade Advisor then launches.

Run the Windows 7 Upgrade Advisor

If you launched the Windows 7 Upgrade Advisor at the end of the installation process, as described in the previous section, the Upgrade Advisor is already running. If not, launch it by choosing Start | All Programs | Windows 7 Upgrade Advisor. You'll see the first Windows 7 Upgrade Advisor screen.

Make sure that all the hardware devices you want to use in Windows 7 are connected to your PC and powered on. You don't need to worry about your PC's innards (unless you've started eviscerating it), but connect any printers, scanners, external drives, and other external devices.

Note The Windows 7 Upgrade Advisor sends the details of your PC's hardware and software to a Microsoft website so that it can check which items will work with Windows 7 and which won't. This is fine and harmless, but if you have installed a firewall that monitors outbound traffic, it may light up like a Christmas tree fearing that a rogue program is shipping your identity data to Columbia and your financial details to the Bahamas. If this happens, reassure the firewall that all is well.

When all the hardware is present and correct, click the Start Check button. The Advisor displays the Checking Compatibility screen as it checks, which can take a while, depending on how complex or exciting your PC is. When the Advisor has finished checking, it displays its Report screens. Figure 10-2 shows an example of the first part of a Report screen.

Report screens contain three categories of information:

- **Information icons** The blue circles containing the letter *i* show information—for example, that you need to perform a custom installation of Windows 7 and then reinstall your programs.
- **Passed icons** The green check marks indicate that your PC has passed one or more requirements.
- **Issue icons** The yellow triangles containing exclamation points indicate items that you will need to deal with. For example, in Figure 10-2, the issue icon with the text "16 GB free hard disk space required" warns that my PC doesn't have enough space to install Windows 7. This is a showstopper.

Note If you're thinking of upgrading to the 64-bit version of Windows 7, click the 64-bit Report tab at the top of the Windows 7 Upgrade Advisor window. The 64-bit version of Windows 7 has different requirements than the 32-bit version, so this tab usually shows a different set of concerns—and often more of them.

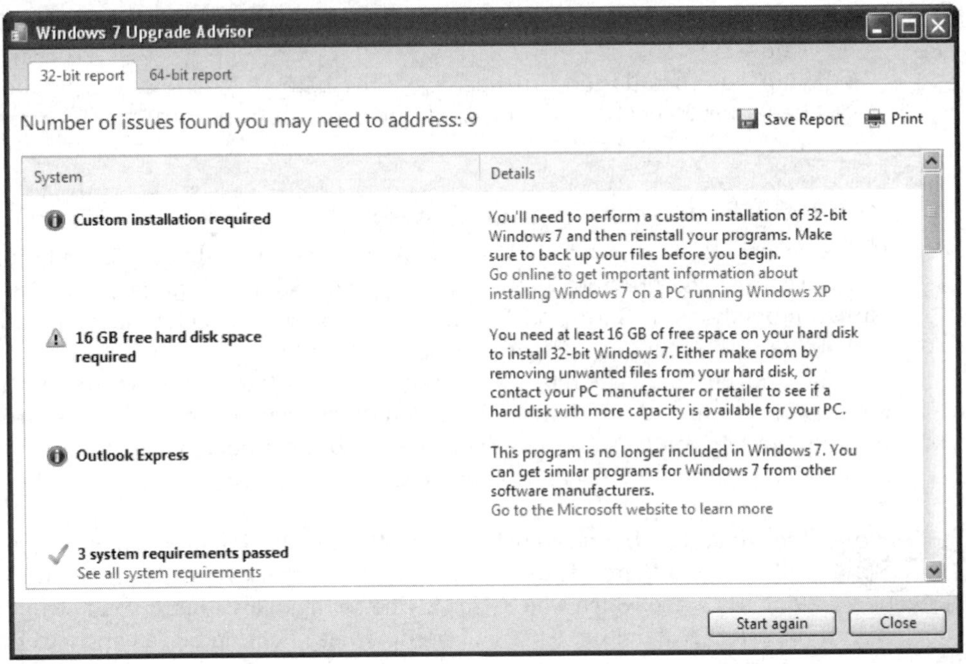

FIGURE 10-2 After the Windows 7 Upgrade Advisor runs, it displays a Report screen containing what you need to know about upgrading your PC to Windows 7.

Scroll down through the Report screens and assess whether installing Windows 7 on your PC is viable. If the Windows 7 Upgrade Advisor has flagged many issues, you can try to deal with them and then run the Upgrade Advisor again to see if all is well. But if your PC seems unsuited for Windows 7 right across the board, you're probably better off either staying with Windows XP or buying a new PC in due course. See this book's website for advice on buying a new PC.

Prepare for the Upgrade

If you've run the Windows 7 Upgrade Advisor and your PC seems able to handle Windows 7, your next move is prepare for the upgrade. Because installing Windows 7 doesn't pick up your Windows XP programs and settings the way you would like it to, you need to copy the files and settings to a safe place before installing Windows 7. The easiest way to do this is to use Microsoft's free Windows Easy Transfer program to transfer your programs and files to an external hard drive

Collect the Installation Files for All Your Programs

When you install Windows 7 over Windows XP, Windows 7 doesn't pick up your programs from Windows XP. To use your programs on Windows 7, you will need to install them on Windows 7.

You probably don't need me to spell out what this means: You must round up the programs' installation discs (CDs or DVDs) or distribution files and then run the installation routines to install the programs on Windows 7.

Rounding up the installation discs and distribution files is a pain—but it's necessary if you want to use the programs after installing Windows 7. What you should do at this point is think hard about which programs you actually need and which you can dispense with. Having a good clear-out of seldom-used programs will not only reduce the time you need to spend installing the programs on Windows 7 but will also give you a streamlined Program Files folder and Start menu.

Download and Install Windows Easy Transfer

To download and install Windows Easy Transfer, follow these steps:

1. Choose Start | Internet to open your web browser.
2. Go to the Microsoft Download Center, www.microsoft.com/downloads.
3. Search for **windows easy transfer xp 7** and then click the link for Windows Easy Transfer For Transferring From Windows XP (32-Bit) To Windows 7.

Note If you have the 64-bit version of Windows XP, click the Windows Easy Transfer For Transferring From Windows XP (64-Bit) To Windows 7 link instead.

4. Click the Download button to start the download.
5. When Internet Explorer asks you what to do with the file, click the Save button.
6. When the file has downloaded, click the Open button to open the file. The Software Update Installation Wizard launches.
7. Click the Next button and then follow through the installation process. You need to agree to the license agreement as usual, but that's the only decision.
8. On the Completing The Windows Easy Transfer For Windows 7 Installation Wizard screen, click the Finish button.

Transfer Files Using Windows Easy Transfer

To transfer files using Windows Easy Transfer, follow these steps:

1. Choose Start | All Programs | Windows Easy Transfer For Windows 7 to launch Windows Easy Transfer. The Welcome To Windows Easy Transfer screen appears.
2. Click the Next button to display the What Do You Want To Use To Transfer Items To Your New Computer? screen (see Figure 10-3).
3. Click the An External Hard Disk Or USB Flash Drive button. Windows Easy Transfer displays the Which Computer Are You Using Now? screen.
4. Click the This Is My Old Computer button. Windows Easy Transfer displays the Checking What Can Be Transferred screen as it checks what's on the computer. When it finishes, it displays the Choose What To Transfer From This Computer screen (see Figure 10-4).

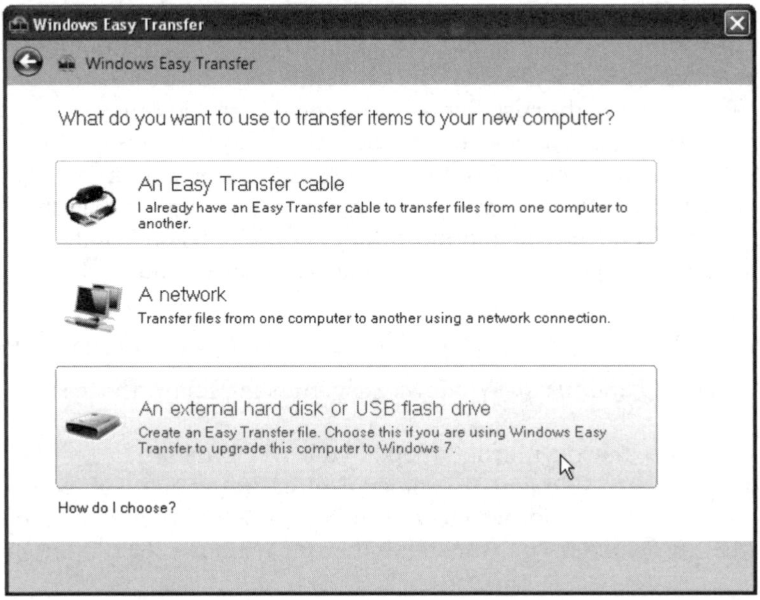

FIGURE 10-3 On the What Do You Want To Use To Transfer Items To Your New Computer? screen of Windows Easy Transfer, click the An External Hard Disk Or USB Flash Drive button.

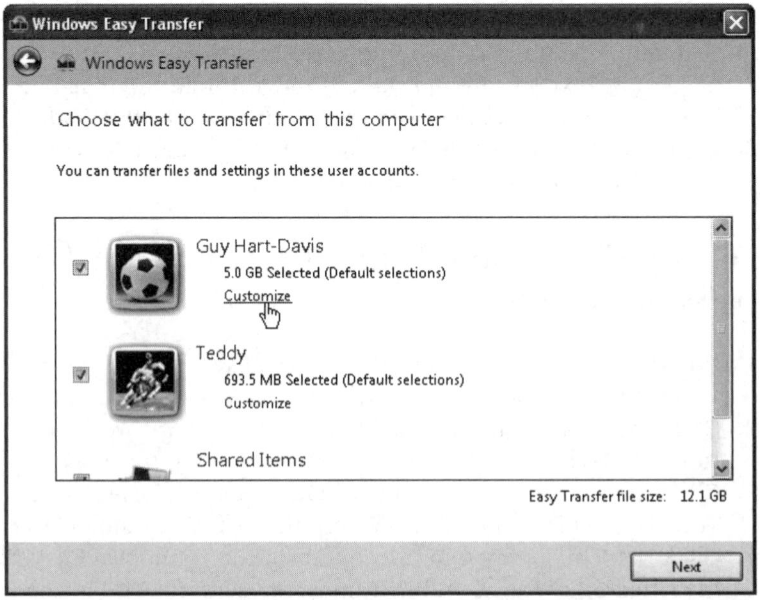

FIGURE 10-4 On the Choose What To Transfer From This Computer screen, select the check box for each item you want to transfer. Click the Customize link if you want to pick and choose the items to transfer.

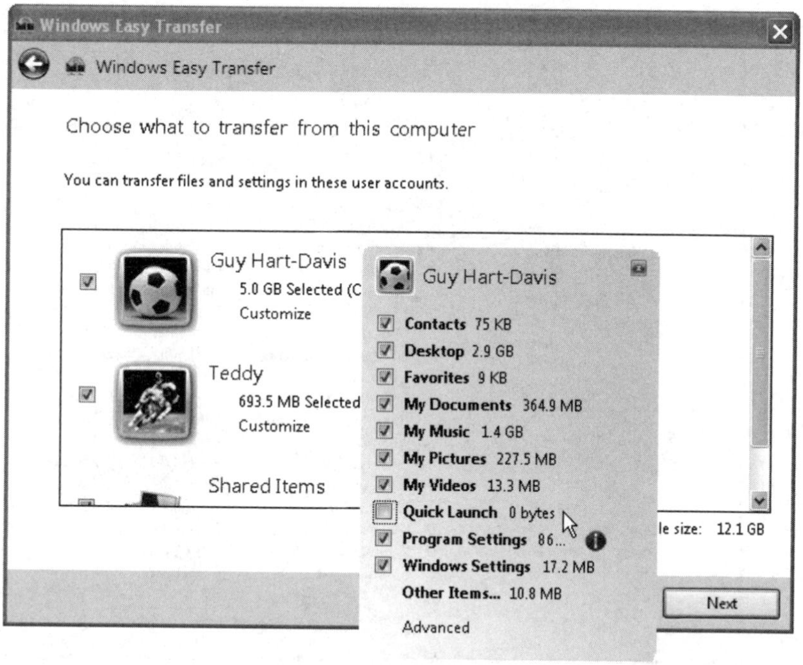

FIGURE 10-5 You can remove items from the transfer package by clearing their check boxes in the pop-up window.

5. Select the check box to the left of each item you want to transfer. Usually, you'll want to transfer everything—each of the user accounts (unless some of the users won't use the upgraded PC) and the Shared Items folder.
6. If you want to transfer only some of the items from an account or from the Shared Items folder, click the Customize link. Windows Easy Transfer pops up a window showing the details of what's set to transfer from the account or folder (see Figure 10-5).
7. Clear the check box for each item you don't want to transfer.
8. If you want to make further changes, click the Advanced link to display the Modify Your Selections window (see Figure 10-6).
9. Select the check boxes for the items you want to transfer, and make sure the check boxes for the items you don't want to transfer are cleared. As usual, you can click the + button next to an item to expand its listing, revealing its contents, or you can click the – button to collapse the listing, hiding its contents.
10. When you have finished choosing the items to transfer, click the Save button to close the Modify Your Selections windows, saving your changes.
11. On the Choose What To Transfer From This Computer screen, click the Next button. Windows Easy Transfer displays the Save Your Files And Settings For Transfer screen.
12. If you want to protect your files with a password, type the password.

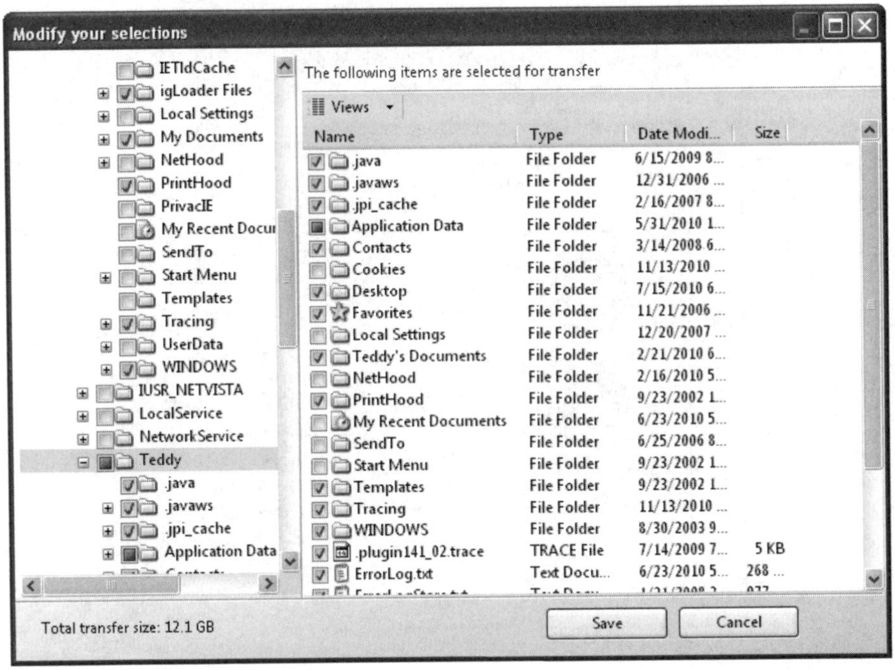

FIGURE 10-6 In the Modify Your Selections window, select the check box for each item you want to transfer. Clear the check box for any item that Windows has lined up for transfer but that you don't want.

13. Click the Save button. Windows displays the Save Your Easy Transfer File dialog box, which is a regular Save dialog box with a different name.
14. Choose the drive and folder you want to save the Windows Easy Transfer file in.
15. Optionally, change the filename in the File Name box. Windows Easy Transfer suggests a straightforward name, such as Windows Easy Transfer – Items From Old Computer, which works fine.
16. Click the Save button. Windows Easy Transfer then starts saving the files and settings to the file you chose, displaying the Saving Files And Settings screen with a progress readout as it does so.
17. If you see the message "Windows Easy Transfer encountered some errors," as shown here, click the Fix These Errors link to open a Windows Easy Transfer dialog box that lists the problem files (see Figure 10-7). Follow the instructions to solve the problem—for example, decrypting encrypted files—then select the check boxes and click the Retry button. If you don't need these files, select the check boxes and click the Skip button. Click the Close button to close the Windows Easy Transfer dialog box.

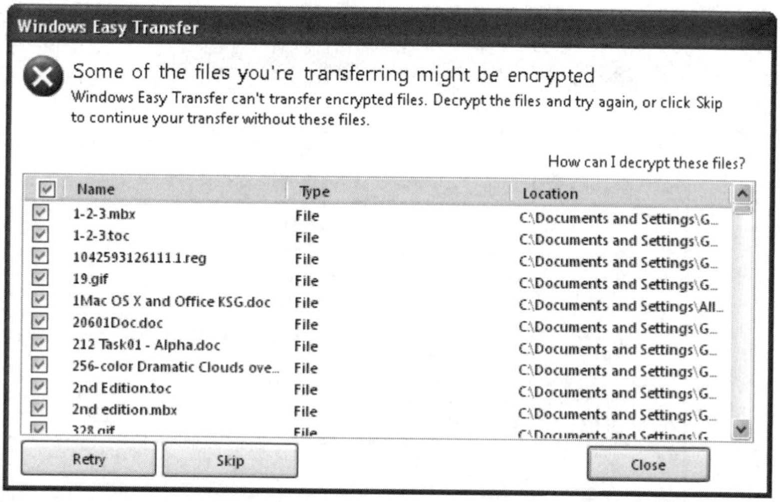

FIGURE 10-7 In this Windows Easy Transfer dialog box, follow the instructions for dealing with the problem files; then select their check boxes and click the Retry button. Alternatively, select the files' check boxes and then click the Skip button.

Tip Click the check box to the left of the Name header to select or clear all the check boxes at once.

18. When Windows Easy Transfer finishes transferring the files, it displays the These Files And Settings Have Been Saved For Your Transfer screen.
19. Click the Next button. Windows Easy Transfer displays the Your Transfer File Is Complete screen (see Figure 10-8), which gives instructions for using the file or files on your new computer.
20. Click the Next button. The Windows Easy Transfer Is Complete On This Computer screen appears.
21. Click the Close button. Windows Easy Transfer closes.

Install Windows 7

At this point, you're ready to install Windows 7. Follow these steps:

1. Close any programs you're running.
2. Insert the Windows 7 DVD in your PC's optical drive. The Install Windows dialog box opens (see Figure 10-9).
3. Click the Install Now button. Setup copies temporary files and then displays the Get Important Updates For Installation screen (see Figure 10-10).

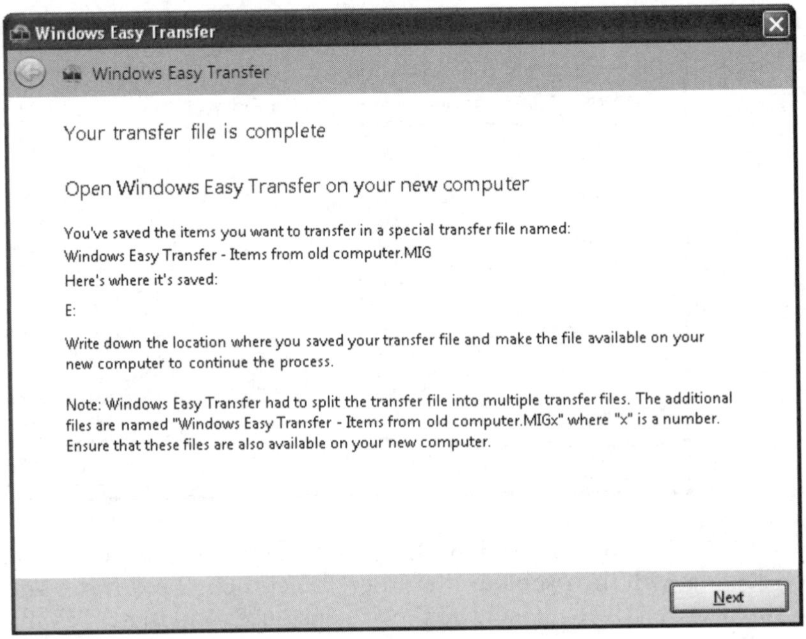

FIGURE 10-8 The Your Transfer File Is Complete screen gives you instructions on using the transfer file or files.

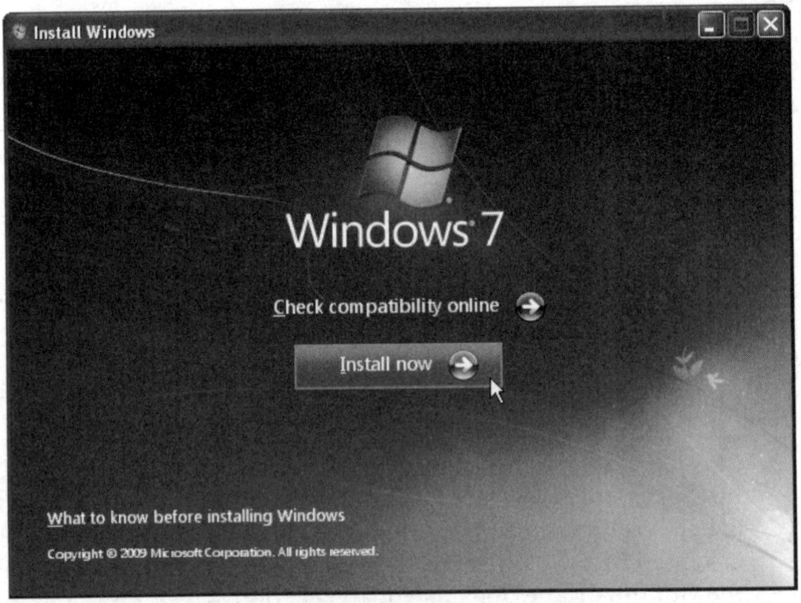

FIGURE 10-9 In the Install Windows dialog box, click the Install Now button.

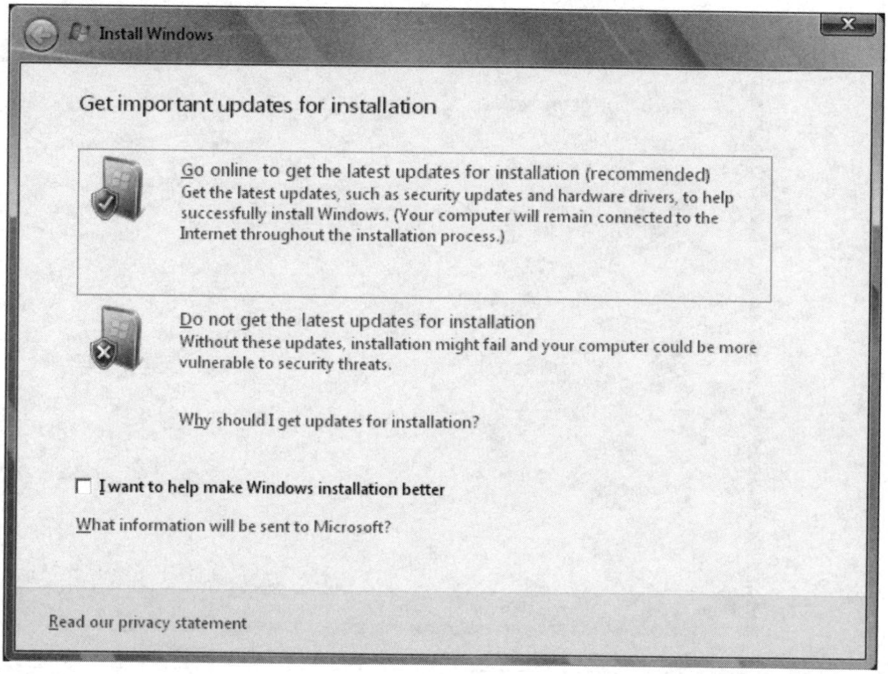

FIGURE 10-10 When Windows displays the Get Important Updates For Installation screen, click the Go Online To Get The Latest Updates For Installation button.

4. Click the Go Online To Get The Latest Updates For Installation button. Windows downloads the latest updates and then displays the Please Read The License Terms screen.

Note If you want to help Microsoft improve the installation process for Windows 7, select the I Want To Help Make Windows Installation Better check box. This makes the installation process send details to Microsoft about your PC's hardware configuration, how the install runs, and any entertaining errors that occur. This information is anonymous; Microsoft won't follow up with you about it.

5. Read the license terms, blench as needed, but then select the I Accept The License Terms check box and click the Next button if you want to proceed. The Which Type Of Installation Do You Want? screen appears (see Figure 10-11).
6. The Upgrade button looks tempting, but it won't work from Windows XP. So click the Custom button. The installer displays the Where Do You Want To Install Windows? screen (see Figure 10-12).
7. Windows 7 installs the files it requires and then restarts your PC one or more times as needed. When the installation is complete, follow the procedure for creating your account and logging in.

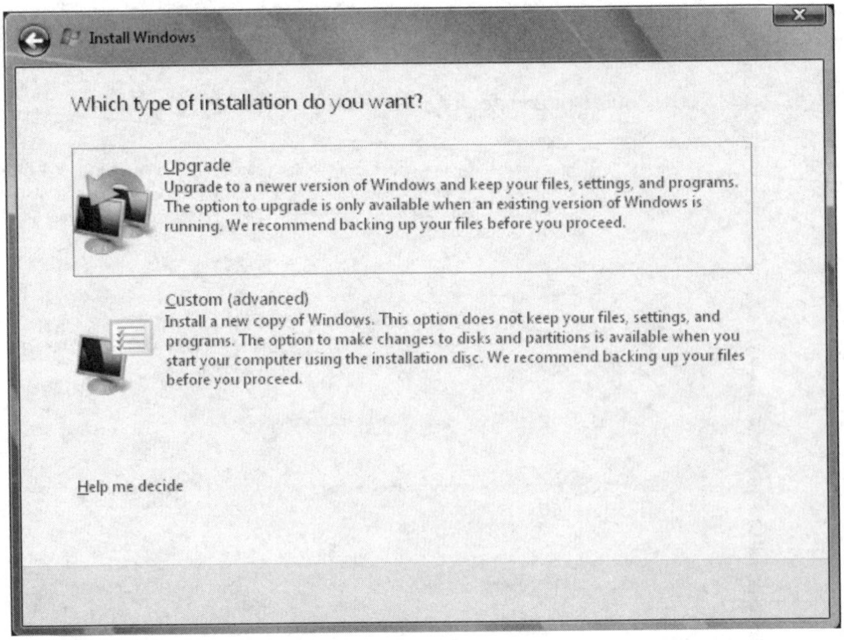

FIGURE 10-11 On the Which Type Of Installation Do You Want? screen, click the Custom button.

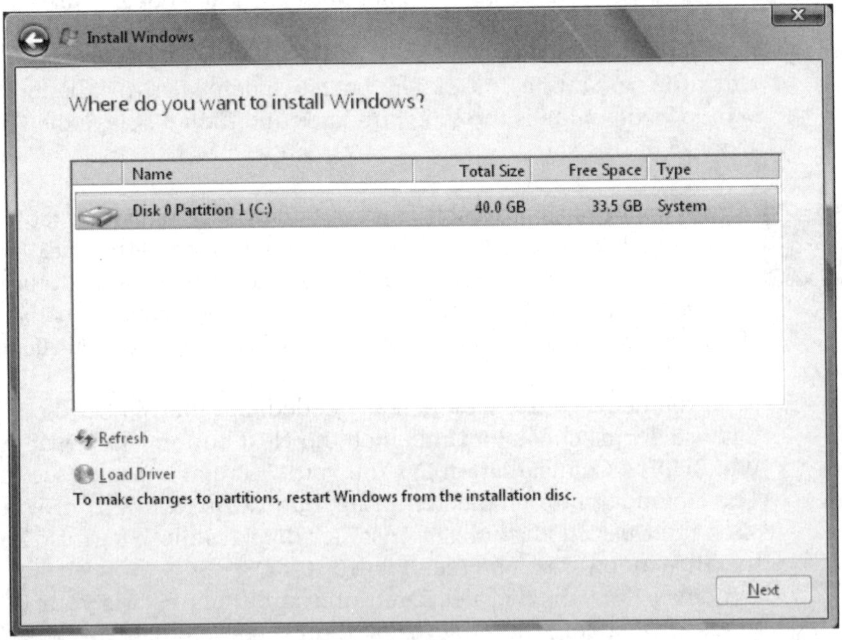

FIGURE 10-12 On the Where Do You Want To Install Windows? screen, click your existing hard drive and then click the Next button.

Note When you transfer your files using Windows Easy Transfer, you can transfer your user account information from the Windows XP PC to your new Windows 7 account.

Transfer Your Files and Settings to Windows 7

After you have logged in, you need to run Windows Easy Transfer to transfer the files and settings from the removable drive.

Run Windows Easy Transfer and Install Your Files

To run Windows Easy Transfer and transfer your files to Windows 7, follow these steps:

1. Connect the external drive on which you saved the Windows Easy Transfer files to your PC.
2. Click the Start button to open the Start menu.
3. Type **windows easy** in the Search box.
4. Click the Windows Easy Transfer search result that appears in the Programs list at the top of the Start menu. Windows Easy Transfer opens and displays the Welcome To Windows Easy Transfer screen.
5. Click the Next button to display the What Do You Want To Use To Transfer Items To Your New Computer? screen (shown in Figure 10-4, earlier in this chapter).
6. Click the An External Hard Disk Or USB Flash Drive button. Windows Easy Transfer displays the Which Computer Are You Using Now? screen (see Figure 10-13).
7. Click the This Is My New Computer button. Windows Easy Transfer displays the Has Windows Easy Transfer Already Saved Your Files From Your Old Computer To An External Hard Disk Or USB Flash Drive? screen (see Figure 10-14).
8. Click the Yes button. Windows Easy Transfer displays the Open An Easy Transfer File dialog box. This is a renamed version of the Open dialog box you're familiar with.
9. Navigate to the drive and folder in which you stored the Windows Easy Transfer file, click the file, and then click the Open button.
10. If you protected your Windows Easy Transfer file with a password, Windows Easy Transfer displays the Enter The Password You Used To Help Protect Your Transfer File And Start The Transfer screen.
11. Type your password and click the Next button. Windows Easy Transfer displays the Choose What To Transfer To This Computer screen (see Figure 10-15).
12. Choose what to transfer:
    - To transfer all of an item, select the check box to its left.
    - Click the Customize link to display a pop-up panel containing check boxes you can select or clear.
    - For further options, click the Advanced link at the bottom of the pop-up panel and then work in the Modify Your Selection dialog box. Click the Save button when you've finished making your choices.

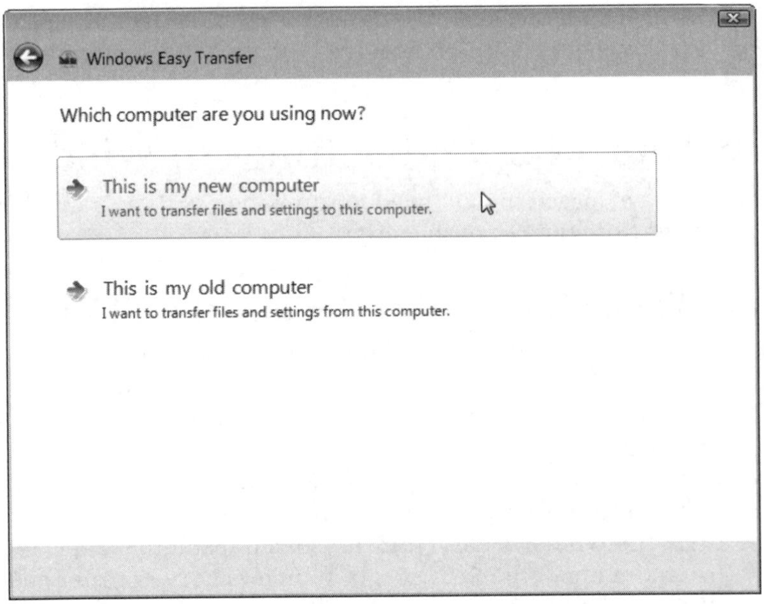

FIGURE 10-13 On the Which Computer Are You Using Now? screen, click the This Is My New Computer button.

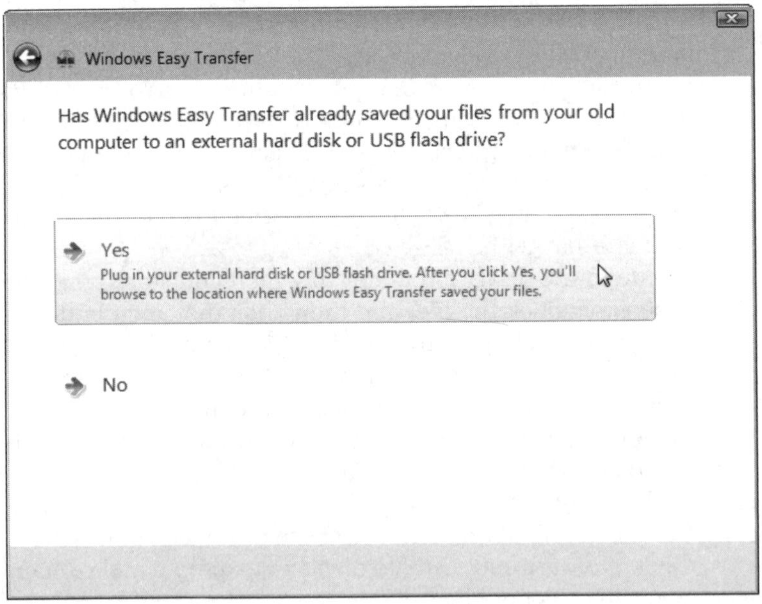

FIGURE 10-14 On the Has Windows Easy Transfer Already Saved Your Files From Your Old Computer To An External Hard Disk Or USB Flash Drive? screen, click the Yes button.

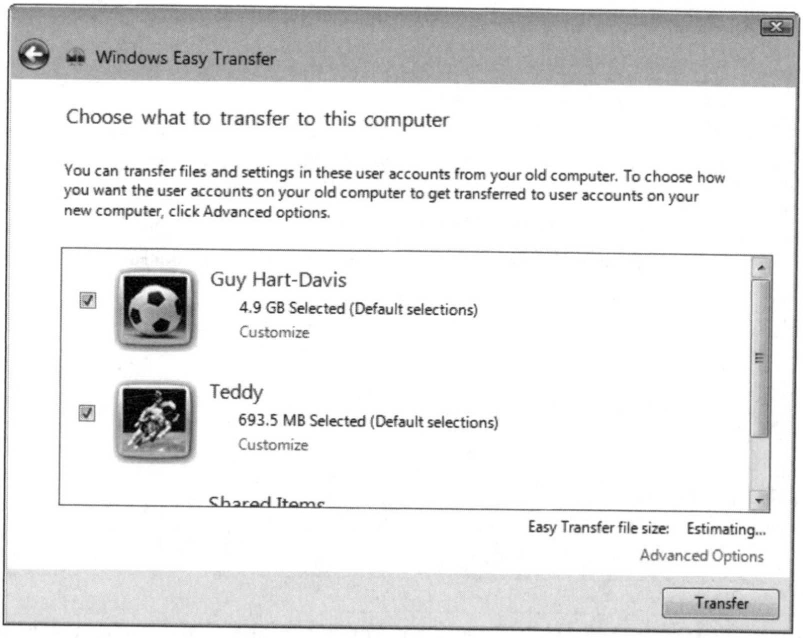

FIGURE 10-15 On the Choose What To Transfer To This Computer screen, select the check box for each item you want to transfer. You can customize the selection by clicking the Customize link.

13. Click the Advanced Options link in the lower-right corner of the Windows Easy Transfer window to display the Advanced Options dialog box. Figure 10-16 shows the Map User Accounts tab, on which you can map your incoming user account to your new user account in Windows 7.

Note On the Map Drives tab of the Advanced Options dialog box, you can map a drive from the old PC to a particular drive on the new PC. When you're transferring data to the same PC after installing Windows 7, you don't need to map drives.

14. In the User Account On The New Computer column, open the drop-down list on the row for your old account and then select the new account you want to map it to.

Note At this point, you can map other incoming user accounts to accounts you've created in Windows 7. But if you're transferring data to a fresh installation of Windows 7, you normally need to map only your account. You can let Windows create the other accounts automatically using the incoming data.

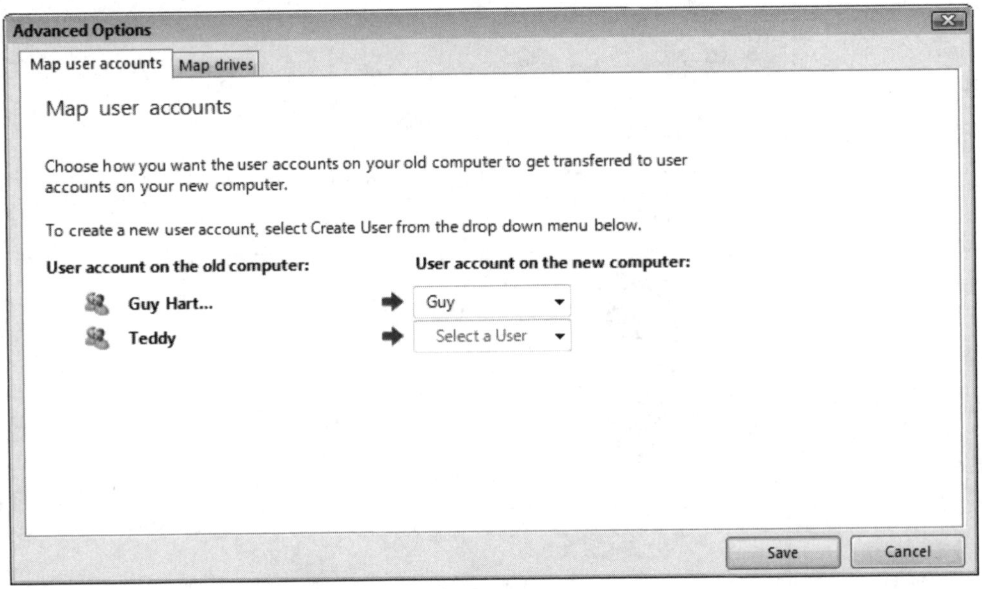

FIGURE 10-16 On the Map User Accounts tab of the Advanced Options dialog box, map your incoming user account to your Windows 7 user account.

15. Click the Save button to close the Advanced Options dialog box and return to the Windows Easy Transfer window.
16. Click the Transfer button to begin transferring the data. Windows Easy Transfer displays the Transferring Items To This Computer screen as it transfers the data.

Caution Don't use your PC while Windows Easy Transfer transfers the data to it.

17. If the Protected Content Migration dialog box (see Figure 10-17) appears, type your password and then click the Confirm My Account Information And Update Content Protection button.
18. When Windows Easy Transfer has finished transferring the files, it displays the Your Transfer Is Complete screen.
19. Click the See What Was Transferred button to open the Windows Easy Transfer Reports window. The Transfer Report tab, shown in Figure 10-18, lets you see the details of what you transferred.

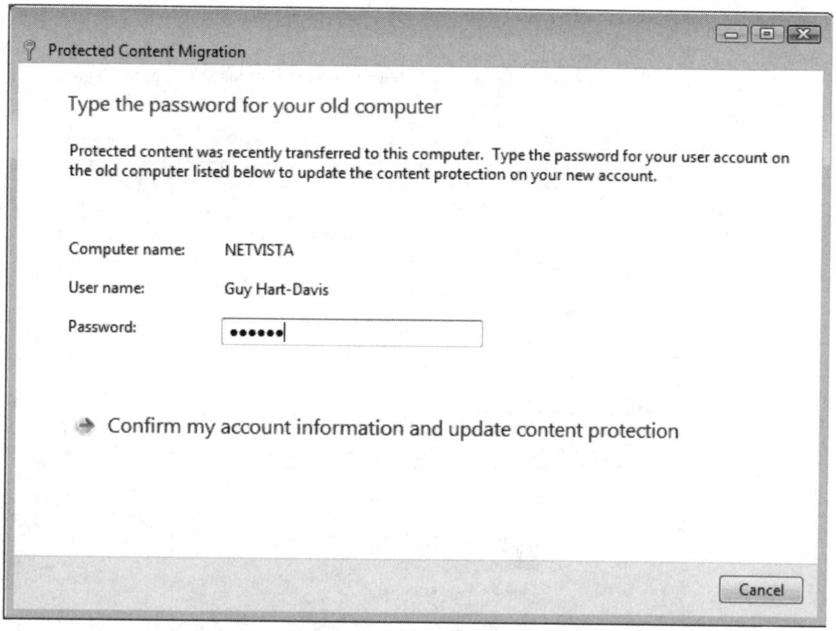

FIGURE 10-17 In the Protected Content Migration dialog box, type your password and click the Confirm My Account Information And Update Content Protection button.

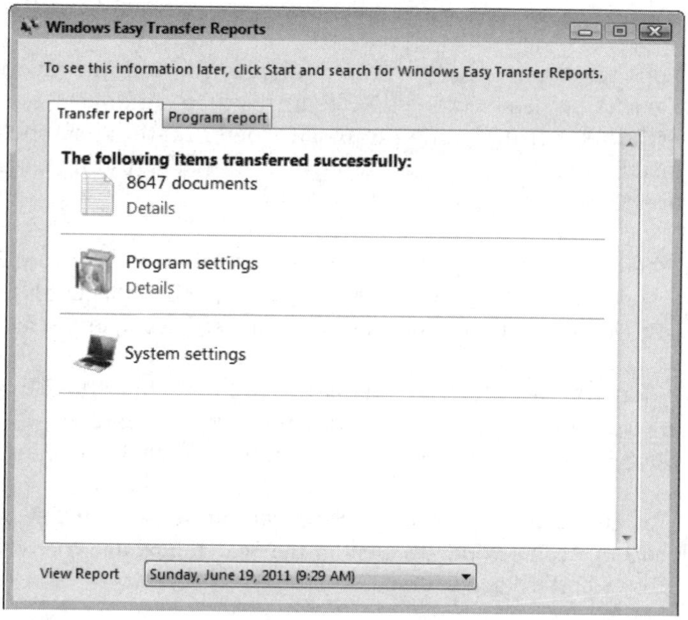

FIGURE 10-18 On the Transfer Report tab of the Windows Easy Transfer Reports window, you can see which items you transferred.

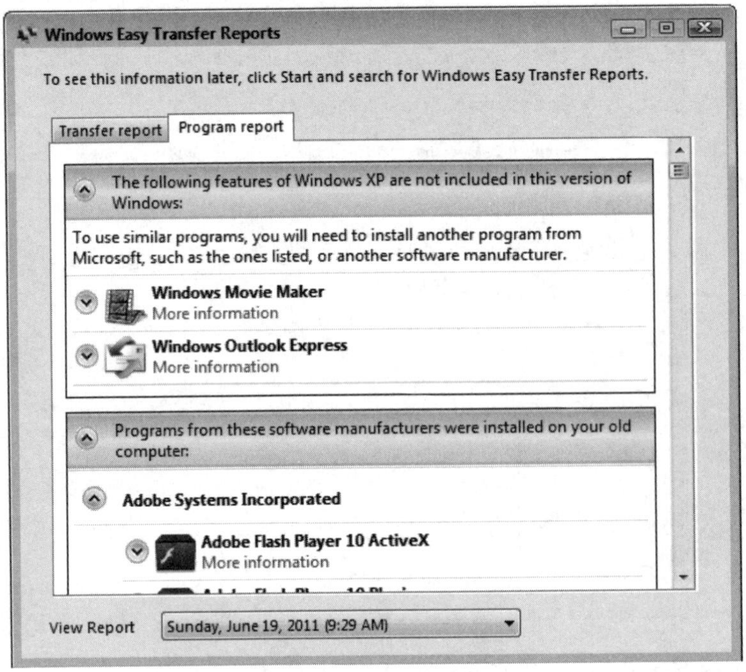

FIGURE 10-19 On the Program Report tab of the Windows Easy Transfer Reports window, you can see the list of programs that were installed on Windows XP.

20. Click the Program Report tab to display its contents (see Figure 10-19). The top section lists Windows XP features that Windows 7 doesn't include, together with links for replacing them. The lower section lists the programs that were installed on Windows XP. You can use this list to make sure you install all the programs you need on Windows 7.

Note You can also display the Program Report tab of the Windows Easy Transfer Reports window by clicking the See A List Of Programs You Might Want To Install On Your New Computer button on the Your Transfer Is Complete screen.

21. When you have finished using the reports, click the Close button (the × button) to close the Windows Easy Transfer Reports window.
22. Click the Close button to close Windows Easy Transfer.

Tip You can reopen the Windows Easy Transfer Reports window by clicking the Start button, typing **windows easy** in the Search box, and then clicking the Windows Easy Transfer Reports result.

You've now transferred your user accounts and files to Windows 7. But now you need to install your programs.

Install Your Programs on Windows 7

To install your programs on Windows 7, you need to run the installation routine for each program, just as you did when you installed them on Windows XP in the first place.

Insert the first CD or DVD in your PC's optical drive, or double-click the distribution file for a program you downloaded. Follow through the installation routine as usual, accepting the license agreement, entering serial numbers, and choosing options as necessary.

Caution Remember to install antivirus software on your new installation of Windows. See Chapter 3 for instructions on getting and installing Microsoft Security Essentials.

A Practicing Green Computing

Caught between sky-high energy prices and global warming, you'll probably want to keep both your utility bills and your consumer footprint as small as possible. To help, this appendix shows you how to choose power-saving settings for your PC, share printers and other peripherals on your network, go green when choosing a new PC, and dispose of your old PC in as eco-friendly a way as you can.

Choose Power-Saving Settings for Your PC

To save power, set up your computer to turn the monitor off and go to sleep as soon as makes sense. In most cases, you'll want to choose settings that will kick in after you leave the computer untouched for more than a few minutes. But if your work (or play) involves long pauses for thought, you'll want to make the kick-in delay longer.

In this section, we'll look at choosing power settings first on Windows XP and then on Windows 7.

Choose Power-Saving Settings on Windows XP

To choose power-saving settings on Windows XP, follow these steps:

1. Choose Start | Control Panel to open a Control Panel window.
2. If Control Panel opens in Category view, with Pick A Category at the top, click the Switch To Classic View link in the Control Panel box in the upper-left corner to switch to Classic view.
3. Double-click the Power Options icon to display the Power Options Properties dialog box.
4. If the Power Schemes tab doesn't already appear at the front, click it. The left screen in Figure A-1 shows the Power Schemes tab.
5. In the Power Schemes drop-down list, select the power scheme you want to customize. For example, choose Home/Office Desk for a desktop PC or Portable/Laptop for a laptop. The controls in the Settings For box show the values for that power scheme.

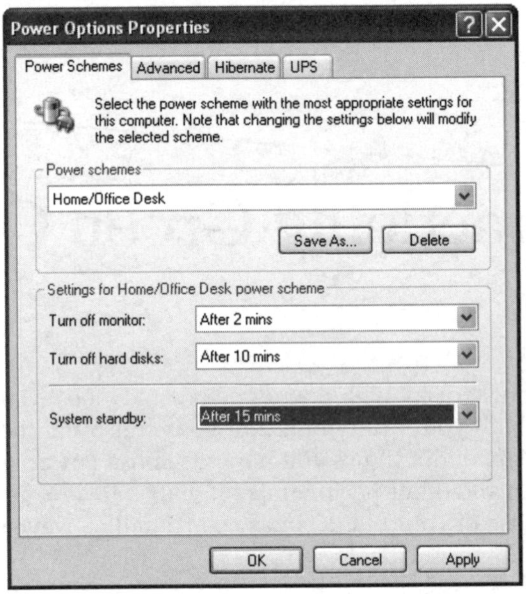

FIGURE A-1 Use the controls on the Power Schemes tab of the Power Options Properties dialog box to reduce your PC's power demands to a minimum.

6. In the Turn Off Monitor drop-down list, choose how long the PC should wait without input before turning off the monitor. Choose as short a time as is practicable, because even an LCD monitor goes through plenty of power. For example, choose After 2 Mins.
7. In the Turn Off Hard Disks drop-down list, choose how long to wait before turning off the hard disk. Normally, you'll want this interval to be longer than the Turn Off Monitor interval. For example, choose After 10 Mins.
8. In the System Standby drop-down list, choose how long to wait before putting the whole PC into standby. This interval must be as long as or longer than the Turn Off Hard Disks interval. For example, choose After 15 Mins.
9. Click the OK button to close the Power Options Properties dialog box and apply your choices.

Choose Power-Saving Settings on Windows 7

To choose power-saving settings on Windows 7, follow these steps:

1. Choose Start | Control Panel to open a Control Panel window.
2. In the View By drop-down list, choose Large Icons or Small Icons (whichever you prefer).
3. Click the Power Options icon to display the Power Options window (see Figure A-2).

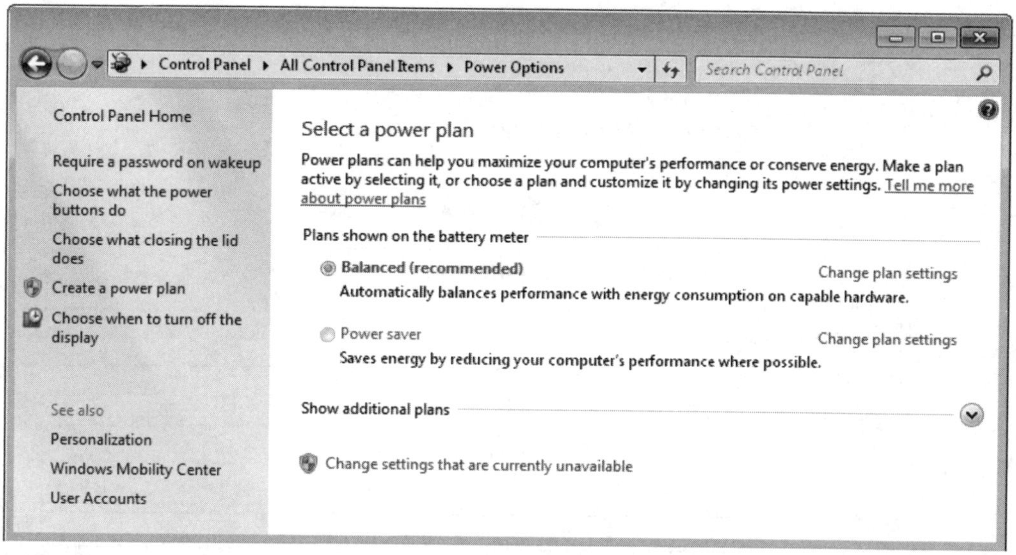

FIGURE A-2 Click the Change Plan Settings link in the Power Options window to reach the Edit Plan Settings screen.

Note In the Power Options window, you may need to click the Change Settings That Are Currently Unavailable link before you can change the power settings.

4. Click the Change Plan Settings link for the plan you're currently using (the plan whose option button is selected). Windows displays the Edit Plan Settings screen (see Figure A-3).
5. In the Turn Off The Display drop-down list, choose how long the PC should wait without input before turning off the screen. Choose as short a time as is practicable—for example, 5 Minutes. For a laptop, you can choose different settings for when it is running off the battery and for when it is plugged in.
6. Click the Change Advanced Power Settings link to display the Power Options dialog box (see Figure A-4).
7. Expand the Hard Disk item and then choose settings in the Turn Off Hard Disk After area. For a laptop, you can choose different settings for when it is running off the battery and for when it is plugged in.
8. Expand the Sleep item to display its contents.
9. Expand the Hibernate After item and then choose how long to wait before hibernating. Again, for a laptop, you can choose different settings for when the laptop is running off the battery and for when it is plugged in.
10. Click the OK button to close the Power Options dialog box. Windows returns you to the Edit Plan Settings window.
11. Click the Save Changes button. Windows applies the changes.

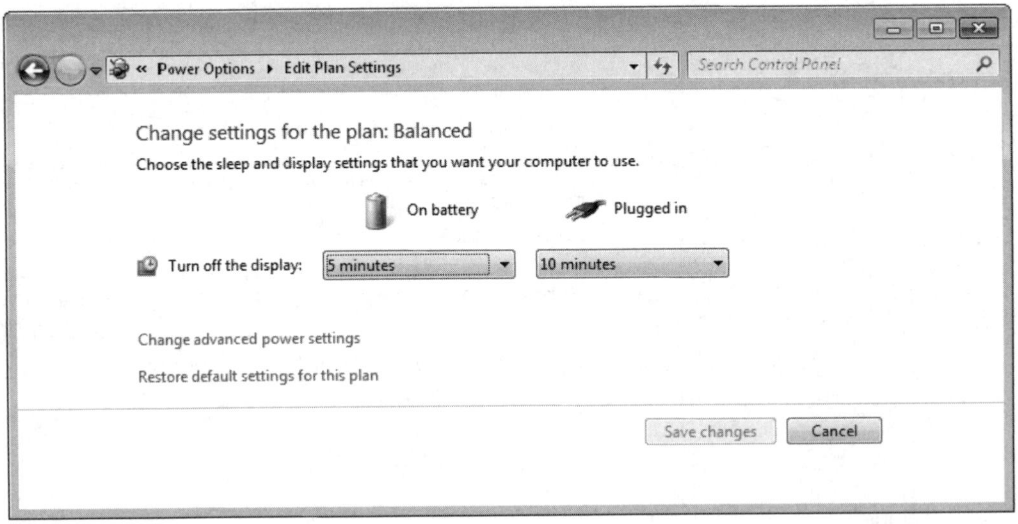

FIGURE A-3 On the Edit Plan Settings screen, choose how long to wait before turning off the display.

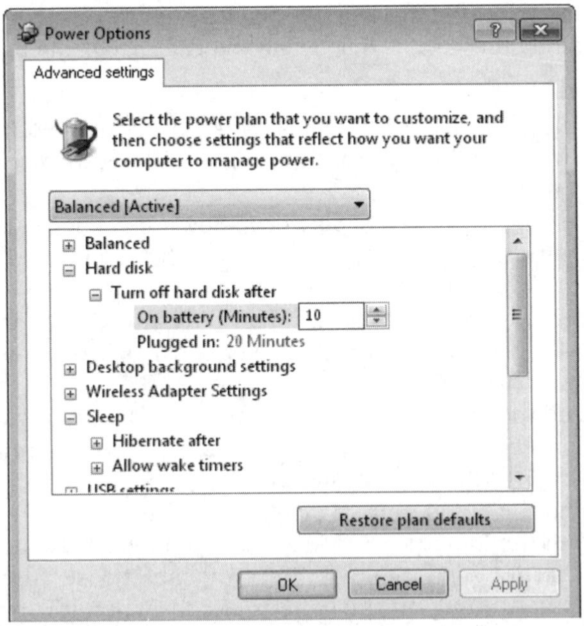

FIGURE A-4 In the Power Options dialog box, choose how long to wait before turning off the hard disk and before sleep.

Share Printers and Other Peripherals

In the days before networks became affordable and easy to set up, each PC that needed to print documents required a printer of its own. These days, you can easily share a single printer among all the computers on your network.

Note If you haven't already set up a network, follow the instructions in Chapter 4. This chapter also explains how to turn on printer sharing.

Share a Printer on Windows XP

To share a printer on Windows XP, follow these steps:

1. Choose Start | Printers And Faxes to open a Printers And Faxes window.
2. Right-click the printer you want to share and then click Properties on the context menu to display the Properties dialog box for the printer.
3. Click the Sharing tab to bring it to the front (see Figure A-5).
4. Select the Share This Printer option button.
5. Type the name for the shared printer in the Share Name text box. This is the name that people using other computers will see.
6. Click the OK button. Windows shares the printer.

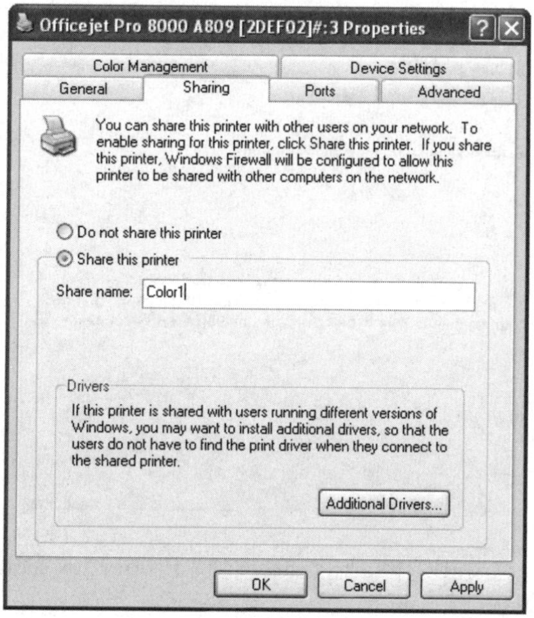

FIGURE A-5 To share a printer on Windows XP, select the Share This Printer option button and then type the name under which to share the printer.

Share a Printer on Windows 7

To share a printer on Windows 7, follow these steps:

1. Choose Start | Devices And Printers to open a Devices And Printers window.
2. Right-click the printer you want to share and then click Printer Properties on the context menu to display the Properties dialog box for the printer.
3. Click the Sharing tab to bring it to the front (see Figure A-6).
4. Select the Share This Printer check box.
5. Type the name for the shared printer in the Share Name text box. This is the name that people using other computers will see.
6. Select the Render Print Jobs On Client Computers check box if you want the other computers to process their print jobs rather than making your PC do the work. This is usually a good idea.
7. Click the OK button. Windows shares the printer.

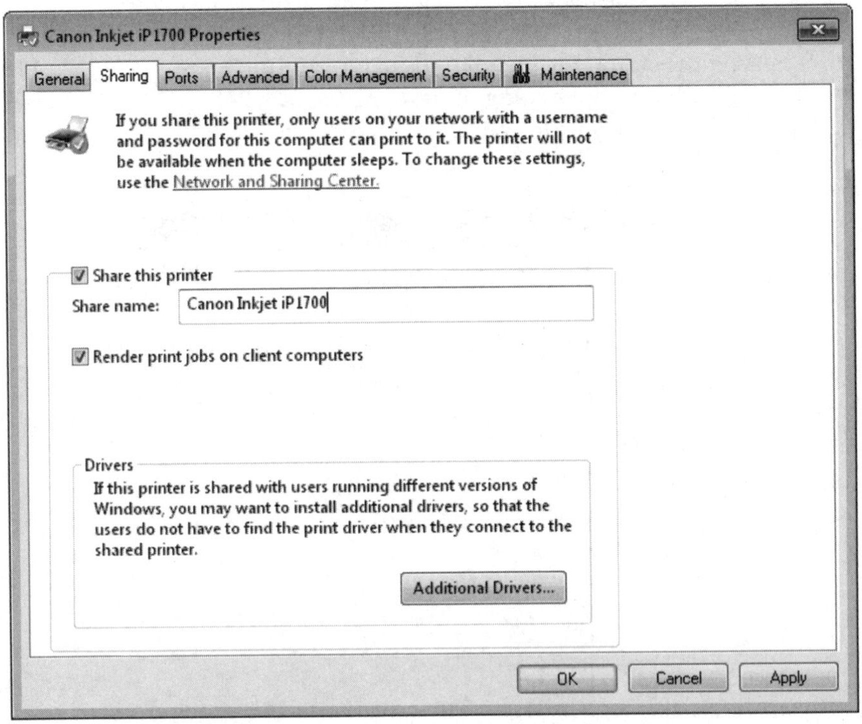

FIGURE A-6 Use the Sharing tab of the Properties dialog box to share a printer on Windows 7.

Share Other Hardware

You can share other peripherals as well, as long as they're smart enough to work on a network.

For example, if you're planning to buy a scanner and you will want to share it on the network, make sure you get a network-aware model. Sharing on the network is far easier than moving the scanner from one computer to another.

Go Green When Buying a New PC

If you're looking to green up when buying a new PC, keep these points in mind:

- A laptop PC typically uses much less power than a desktop PC. Being designed to run from their batteries much of the time, laptop PCs use various techniques to reduce power consumption. As a result, performance often suffers.

Why You Must Replace the Hard Drive If You Buy a Used PC

Computer prices have come down to historically low levels—but even so, buying a PC remains an investment. And even though computer manufacturers have reduced the size of most PCs so that they require less material and improved the efficiency of their manufacturing processes, building a PC still has a considerable environmental impact.

To keep down the cost and environmental impact of your computing, you may be tempted to buy a used PC.

Buying a used PC can be a good move—but there are three serious concerns you must address.

First, a used PC may not last long. Even if you check it out carefully, and perhaps enlist an expert to examine it for you, it's hard to be sure the hardware is in good shape. Unless you're buying the PC from someone you know well, you will likely have little idea about how vigorously the PC has been used or abused.

Second, the hard drive may fail. Hard drives typically last for several years, but beyond that, it's wise not to trust them. If the PC is two or three years old, you should probably replace the hard drive immediately to avoid problems down the line.

Third, the PC may have a virus or malware on it—and the seller may not know. Even if you load up a full-scale antivirus program, update it to the hilt, and then run it, you can't be certain that the PC doesn't have malware that the antivirus program is unable to detect.

The only way to be sure is to replace the hard drive with a new drive and install Windows from scratch. This takes time and effort, which is why most people don't do it—but it is essential if you are to use the PC with confidence.

- When upgrading your desktop PC, you may be able to keep many of its components. If you buy just a new CPU (central processing unit—the main box of a typical desktop PC), you can reuse your keyboard, mouse, monitor, and other components. This cuts down on your carbon footprint as well as the cost.
- Whether you choose a laptop PC or a desktop PC, you can cut down on its energy usage by configuring it to turn off the screen and hard drives as soon as is sensible. You can also set the PC to go to sleep after a short period of inactivity, thus saving more power.
- If you have a desktop PC or use an external monitor with your laptop PC, use an LCD monitor rather than a CRT monitor. (A CRT is a cathode ray tube, the old style of monitor—the type that's a foot or more from front to back because it's got a vacuum tube inside it.) LCDs use much less power than CRTs. They're also smaller and less ugly, although some manufacturers seem determined to neutralize the latter advantage.

Dispose of Your Old PC the Green Way

After you upgrade to a new PC, use one of these environmentally friendly ways of getting rid of your old PC:

- **Reuse parts of it** If your old PC is a desktop, and your new PC will be one too, see if you can use the monitor, keyboard, and mouse for your new PC. You don't need to buy new components if your old ones are still good.
- **Donate it to charity** Various charities accept old PCs that are pretty much worthless in resale terms, fix them up, and ship them out to developing countries. This is a great way of getting your old PC off your hands and doing some good at the same time.
- **Give it to a family member, friend, or local school** If you're getting rid of a PC that's still got some life in it, give it to someone who'll appreciate it.
- **Sell any viable components** If your PC has suffered an accident or a failure and will never run again, sell any viable components on eBay.
- **Recycle the rest** If you can't dispose of your PC in the four aforementioned ways, recycle it. Some PC companies will recycle your old PC when you buy a new PC from them, so investigate the recycling programs they offer. Otherwise, search for a computer-recycling company or organization in your neighborhood. Whatever you do, don't put your PC in the trash—it contains all kinds of vile substances that need professional disposal.

Index

J

L

Q

R

U

V

W